Ambivalence

M. Day. Kendall

To request permissions, contact the author at:
author.day.kendall@gmail.com

Paperback: 979-8-9898454-0-8

First paperback edition: January 2024

Edited by: Brian Hershey
Cover art by: Emily Hensley

Savannah, Georgia

Table of Contents

Chapter #1: Rewind 1

Chapter #2: Childhood Interrupted 3

Chapter #3: In the Eyes of the Father 30

Chapter #4: What is Love? 62

Chapter #5: Yesterday, Today and Tomorrow Maybe? 113

Chapter #6: There's Something About Laurel 148

Chapter #7: Seed 214

Chapter #8: The Bonds That Break 240

Chapter #9: Vampire 291

Chapter #10: Funky Town 352

Chapter #11: Tell Me Lies 435

Chapter #12: Balloon 479

Chapter #13: Anything for Love 533

About the Author

Loud Thunder by Cody Jinks
Drink Before the War by Sinead
O'Connor
Keep Me Hanging on by Kim Wilde
(Cover)
Keep Me High by Adaline
Tell Me Lies by Fleetwood Mac
Never Gonna Give You Up by Rick
Astley
Me and the Devil by Soap and Skin

Be A Good Girl...

The Good Girl

Revenge is an act of passion: vengeance of justice.
Injuries are revenged, crimes are avenged.
-Samuel Johnson

Mikey

Blistering heat engulfs me as I step out into the too bright light.
I almost want nothing more than to go back inside, but I have not seen the sun in days.
My time in its warm embrace, limited.
Soon darkness will be the preferred state of my being, the toasty rays of sunlight will no longer grace my nape.
The yellow dwarf, a giant in my eye.
Skin puckering to feel the warmth along my neck.
I allow it.
Embrace it even.

Why lose a chance to see the sky?
It could be my last.
Why lose a chance to speak?
To talk to the man who stands next to me.
His arms are crossed, defensive in fact.
No smile on his face.
I just want to see someone smile.
I need a reason to smile before I no longer have a reason.
The minutes tick down inching me closer to real freedom, death.

How I got here is no mystery, doesn't mean I want to accept what I've become.
Memories that threaten to fade fill my dreams, they don't play out as strong or as vivid as they once had.
Losing them now would be devastating.
Her face.
Her smile.
I can't forget them or how they plagued me for so long.
Death of the first-born son.

How did I get here?

Laurel

Everything feels cold, despite the wet warmth that seeps
puddling beneath me.
Undisturbed.
Peace washes over me in euphoric waves.
The world keeps moving around me.
Too fast.
I'm completely still, amidst chaos, and I can't seem to care.
Unbothered.
Numb, I can no longer feel and despite being so close to
ultimate freedom and knowing full well what had led up to
this moment, I can't help but question how I got here.

Laurel

I'm nine and I have never seen the ocean, well I have, in pictures, at least.
It would be asinine if I hadn't at least seen the mass of water in print.
My Dad used the word asinine this morning in his crossword puzzle, his dark eyes like darts aimed at the Sunday paper.
With a deep groan, he runs his hand through his thick, dark beard, it's something he's very proud of. My mom seems to like it too, it's a sharp contrast against her blonde waves.
I think I might use that word if someone upsets me, it'll probably be Mikey.
No, I have never seen the ocean, but I have a lot of time to get around to it.
I just need to get out of Indiana.

Mikey

Indiana.
It's a small town, not unlike the hundreds of characterless pit stops that spread from coast to coast.
Nothing special, and due to its complete lack of attraction and tourism, the townspeople cling to a fake veneer of dignified charm.
Outsiders are intruders and the insiders were unjustifiably territorial over their slice of the American dream.
It lacks character, a trait barely redeemed by the forced small-town feel.

Small mom-and-pop shops line the roads of downtown, tended to by old couples who had only hit their forty-year anniversaries thanks to the determined locals who would swear that they were the best at whatever they produced or sold, which was often more of a matter of opinion than a fact.

Red brick and big glass windowed shops littered with insignificant and useless trinkets and homemade jams with dust-gathered lids, open each morning, lit with pride, and manned by a scowling old woman.
Investments in the local "Culture" included the purchase of billboards and window signs that irritate the eye, pulsating red and hot like some type of infected wound.
An infection begging to ooze from a gaping hole that refuses to close, at night, the signs throb with fluorescent desperation.
Store owners hold their breath every time a pedestrian walks by the windows, knowing they are only moments away from losing their nest egg.
All that charm.
Forced.

The type of place where the unremarkable dwell undisturbed and unmotivated to better themselves.
Minimal comfort and lower middle-class aspirations are enough to satisfy, and those who are unsatisfied are viewed as either ungrateful or greedy.
There is no room for individuality or the peculiar and absolutely no room for growth.
Rather, there is comfort in the norm, people dying to preserve outdated gender roles and social etiquette a lot of the world has done away with.
Conservative Indiana.
Windy Indiana.

Here we do not like "Fags," as the town folk calls them, and we do not care for loose women unless, of course, they were servicing us in some way, then the looser the better.
Men, on the other hand, are allowed to run rampant, dicks swinging in the Indiana wind, humping everything they see with frenzied speed and carelessness.
Good old double standards.
The promiscuity of men is praised, the promiscuity of women is chastised.
While he becomes a modern-day Casanova, she is ridiculed and viewed as some cheap nymphomaniac, and opens the

door for a line of men to harass her, expecting the same treatment.
Guess women are not supposed to enjoy sex?
Given the choice of men, my guess is that most of them don't.
Sun-battered and beer-bellied slobs who stink after a day's work at the plant, or after working construction in the summer heat, are their options.
Unappealing to most.
The chastising of a sexual woman was never kept quiet.
It spreads almost as quickly as a case of the clap does around town, and a rumor moves even faster, making its way around as quickly as a loose ember could demolish a dry countryside leaving destruction in its wake, the blemish engraved on the unfortunate soul who is at the end of the talk.

Secrets of a large magnitude have a low chance of staying, so without the implication of a threat and smaller ones are seemingly impossible to keep.
Honestly, it's altogether surprising they ever make it to a place where the information could be classified as secretive.
My family manages alright in that department, not that we have much to hide.
Our laundry is clean, sparkling white, and almost wrinkle-free.
Love flows freely between my parents, and my sister and I are the epitome of perfection.

Despite the loose lips of the catty older women in town, you would rarely see them exchange an embrace, whether familial or romantic.
Mothers rarely coddle their young and partners keep an appropriate distance, except young lovers who seem to be in their world, lips locked, fried hair standing at attention, stiff, along with other bits of the human anatomy.
People would frown and glare, beady eyes focused and bulging.
The youth would sense it and separate instantly, the heat of judgment searing from the intense stares.

Fear that their parents would quickly hear of their indulgent and sinful behavior, is a quick motivator for action.

Town isn't all that bad. It has a certain air of pride that almost makes the lack of charm forgivable.
Friday night football games at the high school, Saturday night dances at the local bars, Sunday mornings at church where patrons who had been drunk the night prior come to judge and pray a night of inebriation away.
The patrons almost always stumble into their car after a dozen or so drinks.
However, if you were to ask them, it was always, "Just a drink with dinner."
The town's infrastructure is riddled with evidence that it's a bit more than that, from a fallen stop sign on Kensington to numerous maimed trees along the dirt roads leading to the old quarry, to the destroyed Ashburn house off old Mill Road.
The house had been hit by drunk teens returning from a night at the quarry last summer.
Luckily, no one had died.
Miraculously, they had all been at a church function.
Gone to a congregational Easter dinner.
Thank you, God, for giving us your one and only son.

Mr. McGill from five doors down paid the ultimate price with his prized red truck, its glossy glaze leering from his hilled driveway.
My father always coveted it, almost salivating as he drove by on our way to school.

It was demolished as it met the toad-infested pond down the street.
The same pond my sister and I had frog hunted in, along with the other neighborhood kids or perfectly warm nights in our younger years.
The truck was not the only loss as it flew into the stagnant waters.

His vehicle, along with a body, was found in the murky depths two days later after his worried wife reported him missing.
A couple of kids hunting for toads caught a glimpse of something in the water and told their worried mother, who passed it down the line.
My father caught wind at the station where he worked, and the experts were called in from the city to investigate.
I rode my bike down to the end of the street that evening to get a good look as the tow truck pulled the cherry red truck from the depths, my morbid curiosity getting the best of me.
I hoped so badly then to see him when he emerged. Just a peek.
The large pine was a perfect cover as I gazed on from behind it impatiently.
Sap stuck between my fingers as I clung on to the sturdy trunk for balance, only allowing my head to come through.
The body didn't look as grotesque as I had imagined.
Or maybe hoped?
I had certain expectations that were not met, although he looked like you would expect someone whose body had been submerged for a day to look.
Blue skin.
A bloat that was more than an extra serving of dessert.
Fish munching on his skin.
I had read somewhere that it took longer for a body to decompose under water.
Mr. McGill looked as if he had just days prior, fat and red-haired that was severely ungroomed, and wiry despite the time it had spent in the murky depth.
It should have bothered me.
I was shocked to learn that I had absolutely no reaction other than a dribble of satisfaction.

Over the next week, I sat in the library, immersing myself in everything related to drowning and decomposition.
Learned fun facts like how it could take anywhere from thirty seconds to five minutes to drown depending on who you are and in rare cases there are even people who can hold their

breath upwards of the double digits with training and
genetics.
I tried to imagine the panic of a longer drowning by feigning
being trapped underwater in the small bathtub, my arms
draped over the edges just in case I was to pass out, although I
am certain it would do no good.
Never made it far past a minute before my chest was
screaming for air just as panic kicked in.
The next night I would repeat the process, discarded soap
burning my eyes, a thin layer of suds lining the top layer of
warm liquid, then I would repeat until those bubbles turned
into an oily upper layer on the undisturbed water.
I imagined then that drowning would not hurt in the way
most people imagine the pain of dying.
It would be panic-inducing yes, but not painful, and somehow
that was far more terrifying.
That's when I decided that drowning would be a horrible way
to die.

Laurel

Beauty.
Left to wither.
Those poor Dollanganger Children.

Flowers, hidden away with the hope their growth would not
falter.
Instead, the children grew like weeds unseen and unheard.
Beautiful blossoms that slowly began to wilt from the lack of
sunlight and care, desperate to be seen and loved.
I could not relate.
While they were hidden in a small room away from the world,
just four simple flowers, I was displayed as a bouquet on the
mantle for all to see.
A prized possession my parents had worked so hard to have.
Beautiful, smart, and obedient.
My parents loved me.
Loved the potential I harbored.
Flaunted their reward for the world to see.

In my home, every flower was painted yellow.
Every meal was met with laughter.
Every hug with love.
My heart bloomed with hope.
Until.
Those words.

"Mom is sick."
It wasn't the first time.
We had gone through this before, but this time there was
something eerie about the way he spoke.
"It's serious."
Stuck.
Was she sick enough to die?

Death is inevitable, but was the timing completely out of our
hands?
Does God give us chances to prolong our time on earth, given
the right choices?
Three strikes in the game of life.
Nine lives.
"God will take me when it's my time," she often chants, hands
raised in the pews of the depressingly white church for all to
hear.
I could see the dirt clinging to the intricate wood carvings of
Jesus bearing the cross up front.
The exposed beams across the ceiling would at times attract a
stray bird or two that would need to be chased out before the
sermon, little bits of hay from where they had tried to build.
Today the Priest stares us down, silently, standing behind the
pulpit.
A non-secular throne dressed in a long purple cloth of
authority and royalty.
He requests another hymn, lifts up the prayers and the
church's grievances to the one who watches down from up
above.
Hands lay across my mother's shoulders as tears stream down
her full face.
"Lord, be with us!"

Church-wide repetition, a slew of hands caressing the air as if
God might be lingering between the wood beams and the tips
of their fingers.

I keep my arms folded and my distance from the orgy of
parishioners that crowds my mother.
Close enough to seem supportive, far enough to keep from the
unwanted touch of the church family.
My mother falls into the church.
Plummeting deep within scripture and hope, something far
more dangerous than illness itself.
The worn pages of her bible became her medicine.
My mother still shone brightly.
Not sick enough to lose her light, but there was certainly a
breeze causing it to falter.
She was still able to belt it out at choir practice, her ivory robes
tight around her middle.

"Can I get sick too?" I would ask, half out of curiosity, half out
of a sick need for attention, my green eyes hopeful for
affirmation.
The dinner table had been too quiet tonight, the white
tablecloth marred with remnants of tomato sauce from last
night.
"It's a different kind of sick Laurel," my father explained once
again.
I kissed his once clean-shaven face and excused myself from
the table with a skip, leaving those eyes lined with dark
circles.
Worry was written all over, but I am too young to truly grasp
the gravity of our situation.
Beneath the shadow of his jaw lay his badge, a badge of honor;
triangles sloping in before sharply jutting back out.
Seven points sitting over his left breast.
"It's molded that way to protect my most vulnerable asset," he
explained.
"What's that?" I chirp.
He chuckles a chuckle that is more of a growl as it catches the
ridges of his throat, "My heart, but in all honesty your

mamma keeps it pretty safe, mouse" he informs me, quick to throw in my nickname as a comfort measure.
"She will be just fine as long as she listens to her doctors and makes some changes."
"Is that why you made me eat broccoli?"
"Partially."
My nose scrunches up. "I hate it!"
"I know, but we need to help her out honey," he pauses his lecture and takes a drink, "Be supportive."
 I fidget with the faux gold encrusted pin, it held little to no value to me, but to Daddy, it means the world.
Being sheriff in a small town like this one held a lot of weight. Brought forth respect.
A vow to serve and protect his community.
Power and admiration, to my father, are needs.

Mikey

The all-American family.
Perfect, we were perfect, which is probably why it all unraveled so quickly.
We had never built up that tough skin, the callouses that protect you.
No grit, no grime, and no callouses to protect us from harm.
Our hands are blemish-free.
"We need to make some changes… we are all going to make some changes," Dad informs us in his authoritative voice, his inky eyes washing over us cooly.
The voice I imagine he uses with a suspect as they would drive.
to the small station; stern yet kind.
We all agree.

In sickness and in health.
They had vowed they would see it through.
To the bitter end.
Her sickness.
Left us all ill.
It bore consequences that ballooned out.

Explosive in nature.
The strain my mother felt, the pain my father dwelled in
as he watched his mate dwindle.
The strength my brother projected.
My inability to shut myself down.
To sleep this nightmare away.
I feel too much, and I'm not sure how much more of this I can
take.

The innocence my sister projects is something I had never
understood.
The vulnerability. Her sick need for love.
She has become malleable.
Softened by the loving warmth of our parents and now, while
it's time for her to harden her heart and take a page from
pharaoh's book, she softens further.
Meanwhile, my heart becomes like a stone.
Impenetrable.
The strength I used to shut myself down has built me up like a
fortress.
But even the strongest structures have a weak spot, and if I am
going to be honest, Laurel is mine.

Fate takes over.
We all turn to our unpredictable, uncontrollable coping
mechanisms just to get our minds off the sickness that was
now causing my mother to dull.
Uniquely designed to protect each one of us.

My mother is dying.
That much is clear.
She clings to hope, like a child does to its favorite blanket.
Hope can be such a dangerous gift.
My father could not bear to watch her fade.
He was not selfless, and I could see him beginning to crash.
Then there was the resentment.
He resents her for being sick.
Resents the thought of being left to raise us alone.
Resents her lack of control over a good meal.

"Watch those portions, dear," he would try to remind her
lovingly, but always with a hint of animosity.
The love is still there.
He loves her.
Loves her more than he has ever loved anyone.
With all the love comes hatred.
It makes me ill.
Seeing them pretend.
My anger would bubble over when I would take out the trash
and find the wrappers and half-eaten candy bars, she had
attempted to hide under food scraps and used paper towels.
This was an addiction.
No one would agree.

Laurel

We still have so much growing to do.
That's what adults always say as if we don't understand the
world around us. They're wrong, we understand more than
they know.
I have changed so much in a few short months, learned to
adapt, and in a way it's terrifying.
It was happening fast, and we clung to our childish ways,
desperate to slow the process of aging.
Mikey and I grasp on tightly.
We build, run and dance.
Hide.

Away in our forts, we found solace, wood forts, dirt forts,
blanket forts, and barriers from the outside world.
Little architects, with unsound foundations, we made them
out of old shingles of abandoned trailer houses, gaudy floral
blankets, and the fallen branches of the large trees that lined
our property, on the outskirts of the dense forest.
In the afternoons, the neighborhood kids would drop by with
sodas and lunch boxes, and we would all laugh and play.
We created an intricate bartering and trade system the
government would be proud of, tax-free of course.

Sandwiches in exchange for leftover pizza, fruit snacks for snack cakes, individual pudding packs for chips.
Unfortunately, that had dissipated by the end of summer when Daddy had set up a strict diet the whole family would abide by.
We were not alone as Kyle and his sister, who lived just one house over through the woods, had also been pushed into clean eating by their mother, who believed it would cure the "Sadness" that Kyle's father was feeling since he lost his job.
I later came to know this sadness as depression and clean eating were not going to cure it. Kyle's father could attest to that.

The long days of summer turned predictably to cool nights and sorbet sunsets.
Mikey and I would spread out in our forts waiting till the last acceptable second to return to the house (mom flipping the porch light on and off furiously to get our attention).
Abandoned would be snack wrappers and old matchbooks, comic strips, and cutouts of quizzes from teen magazines with pen marks lining the edges.
Since Mikey had learned how to strike his first match, he had been obsessed.
Rubber cement and fire made for hours of fun.
Intricate designs set ablaze with palm trees, smiley faces, bubbly flowers, and their long stems.
Fiery light.
Fireflies lead us back to the house in their own brilliant glowing green light.
At night the chirping of the crickets' songs would rock me to sleep and when we were lucky enough to spend the night in the woods, their songs became amplified in the dense.
Those forts were a safety blanket, a protection against the silence that lingered in the walls of our home.
Something we could call our own.

Mikey

Laurel snored softly next to me in our little fort. Another night worrying about our mother had left us looking for an escape, and it made sense with the warmth of an early fall night to hide out and camp out.
Outside the birds chirped softly, my mom gently calling out for us with promises of breakfast.
My stomach grumbled with hunger, yearning for a large stack of pancakes and some bacon.
Mom doesn't usually disappoint. The thought brings excitement rushing through me and hunger pangs to scrunch my belly tight.

"Laurel, wake up," I urged, shoving at her shoulder, a ravenous hunger attacking my belly with an angry rumble.
Laurel shifts to her side, rubbing her moss-colored eyes, that beautiful silky hair flowing like wings along her shoulders.
The bud of her lip quivers as she tries to cling to sleep.
Rubbing her eyes, she glares at me in awe, "I'm tired, Mikey!"
The words almost come out as a wail as she sits up, the light of day crossing through the crack in our fort wall, ringing around her head like a halo.
"Mom is calling for breakfast, and I'm starving Laurel... race you there."
With that, I dart out of the fort, almost slipping on loose leaves as I steadily pace to the house. The smell of damp leaves and sticky syrup luring my legs to pump vigorously.
Behind me, I can hear leaves slip and slosh, Laurel clearly set on making it there before me.
Working my legs harder, I can picture a pancake slathered in gooey syrup and melty butter awaiting me. Mom breaks her diet when Dad is out.
It drives me forward when suddenly I find myself writhing painfully among the fallen leaves, my thin pajamas growing wet.
A weight catches above me, followed by a giggle.

"Last one there's a rotten egg," she says before hopping off me and sprinting.

We fight and tumble among the carnage of fall, tossing and flipping until I have her pinned, my hands tight along her wrist. "I can smell you rotten egg!"
Squealing with delight, she struggles beneath me, our breath heavy, eyes hot against each other, moss swirling among the clear skies of my own.
Competitiveness is palpable, the need to prove myself against my sister's flaring motivation.
I was not going to let up, and she would certainly not get the best of me.
"Those pancakes are mine!"
Audibly and with the intention of making her mad, I laugh at her ferocity and taunt her, despite her clear disadvantage, my body starting to develop its male strength.
I am about to retort and torment her until I can get a good lead on her. "You're nothing but a – " the words catch a yelp from behind the cut wood near the shed.
I shoot up, hearing Ruby the neighbor's dog yelping from somewhere just beyond.
"Ruby!"
Laurel calls her name, her love for the mutt blinding her internal compass, steering her away from the house and breakfast.
I not only catch up but surpass her, halting and freezing when I find Ruby.
The mutt is there, standing and panting as if she is in pain.
Behind her, I catch sight of a large German Shepherd hovering above her, his tags jangling with each movement.
Mounting her.
I can't believe my eyes, don't understand what I am seeing, but it somehow inherently feels familiar.
Ruby yelps once more, the larger dog jerking himself, wrapping his paws around her reluctant hips.
"Stop it!" Laurel screams, her eyes almost bulging, fists curled.
"Laurel! Relax!"
She grips my hand as if it tethered her into place. "Mikey make it stop! Make him stop! Hurting her! Hurting Ruby!" she wails, snot bubbling, a shaky finger pointing expectantly.

Waiting, she grabs my hand tight, a tear falling down her unblemished cheek before she lets go of my hand, snatching a stick and swinging it furiously at the conjoined canines.
The whole time she was swinging furiously, attempting to split the dogs from one another, hoping not to hurt them but to separate them, all the while wailing as if it pained her too. Finally, the black dog lurches forward once more, Laurel's makeshift weapon hitting him square in the back.
With a yelp he takes off running, Ruby pacing and panting as if she can't breathe in enough air.
Frozen, I lingered, watching in admiration as my sister called for Ruby who was bound to her accepting Laurel's kind hands, "It's ok girl," my sister comforted, Ruby content in her embrace, "It's ok girl!"
With what I perceive to be soothing words, I catch my sister's hand and lure her back to me. "She's ok Laurel, let her go home.
My sister hesitates, the fur firm in her hands, the dog settling in her grip.
"Come on, before mom gets mad."
My sister's round eyes, full to the brim with tears, pleading with me to take her home.
Shakily, we make our way to the kitchen. My palms are weak and sweaty, my heart pattering against the bones of my chest, rattling them like a caged bear. "Mommy! Mommy!"

Laurel cries for her the moment we cross the threshold into the kitchen, and I stand still, shocked and dazed by what I had seen and yet still didn't understand.
Why was Ruby crying? Why was that dog on her?
"What is it, Honey?" My mother beckons to my sister, who is clinging around her waist, like a blood-hungry leech.
Mother bends down and smoothes Laurel's messy locks and grips her face. I watch on as she coos, repeating my sister's name like a mantra, her ivy-painted nails curling around her face, an apron around her waist, sticky with syrup.
I can smell breakfast, yet my appetite is gone.

"Sweetie, what's wrong?" She poses, concerned.

Laurel tells her in sobs and broken verbiage, "Th- then the big mean dog, he was on Ruby!"

My mother lets go of her and fixes us each a plate and suddenly what I had so yearned for only moments ago now had my stomach in a vice.

"Sit down," my mother motions, a still crying Laurel plopping down next to me swinging her legs, her hands balled into angry little fists." Mommy, I don't want that dog hurting Ruby. No more!"

"Sweetheart… he wasn't hurting her," my mother informs her, sipping on overly creamed coffee from a steaming cup, her face deepening into a cherry red as if she was afraid to tell us something.

Sighing, she sets it down and continues, "Laurel… take a breath," their hands join for a soothing moment that is short-lived.

Laurel huffs and puffs next to me, crossing her arms, "Don't like that big dog," grumbling as she shoots my mother an angry look, displeased that she hadn't already sided with her.

I watched on, catching a small smirk on the woman I called Mom's lips.

"I don't understand," I chime in, siding with my sister and her interest.

"You will someday, honey," she soothes.

Not good enough.

"No! I wanna know now!"

"Yeah! Me too!"

We berate my mother, demanding answers.

My sister almost snarls as she bangs her fist against the table, causing some orange juice to spill over her glass onto the yellow tablecloth.

"Enough you two! I will tell you now if you stop throwing a fit this instant!"

Her stern voice quickly loses steam, and her features soften those full cheeks, catching the hint of a smile.

Enthralled, we both focused, longing for each revealing word.

"What you saw was… well, they were making a baby… or at least trying to."

Baby?

"What do you mean? Mom! Is that how we were made?"

Her eyes grew wide, so round and similar to my sisters, "They were mating…. Or some people call it sex, and yes, that's how humans make their babies."

Laurel lets out a loud, "Yuck," shame and anger still in her glare, "That's gross! An- and Ruby was crying! Why did it hurt her mommy?"

Again, I could see my sister crumbling faster than an overcooked pie shell, relating to Ruby, fearing her future demise.

"Laurel, honey, you will understand more when you're older. Those sounds were probably not because she was hurt…she was probably making those sounds because it felt good. Humans make those too…. Like when I kiss Daddy and we giggle, or he sighs after a nice hug. They are little sounds of appreciation. Or…like when you fall and get hurt, you cry or scream…same idea."

Laurel doesn't look convinced, in fact, she looks beyond enraged.

"But we don't have any brothers or sisters, so that means you and Dad don't…" I trailed off, full of shame, my face feeling like a fire had spread across it.

"Oh honey, it isn't just to make babies. Making love is wonderful with the right person. With someone you love!"

We eyed her curiously as if she had ignited something, and she took notice.

"When the time is right," she hastily adds.

With that, she takes a long drink.

I think of what she had just said.

I loved Laurel. Would I someday do that with her?

To her? I couldn't imagine.

It seems unspeakable.

The thought of the sister that I adore writhing beneath me, mewling and whimpering like Ruby had, makes me feel sick. And for me to be such a dominating force? To hurt her? Unimaginable.

The thought leaves my stomach queasy, the smell of butter and salt causing my stomach to tighten.

"I love Laurel!"

I blurt it out, immediately feeling foolish for doing so.

My mom almost laughs, "Oh! Of course, and she loves you too, but sex is reserved for another kind of love. The romantic type that we fall into with someone outside of our family. You will understand someday, honey."

Far more confused now than I had been earlier, I tense, knuckles blanching, but I let it go, eager to rid myself of the uncomfortable pulsing that had filled my groin.

Something about this feels less than innocent, yet it feels right as if the act that I would commit someday was already hard-wired in me.

Out of place.

Laurel, however, now has a tight grip on her fork that she tightens and tosses onto the floor in fear-driven anger.

She flies up. "I don't want to do that. Not ever!"

With that, she flies up the stairs, slamming her door behind her, causing my mother to jolt.

My mother sighs in defeat, rubbing at her temples as if it pains her terribly to see Laurel upset.

Laurel

Sleep.

Sleep does not come as easily as it once had.

Sleep – is – my – enemy.

To sleep is to be vulnerable, and to be vulnerable is to dream.

Dreaming always leads to inevitable disappointment.

Mikey

Sleep.

Sleep would not come as easily as it once had.

Not how it used to be.

I could always hear her.

Hear her rustling to the bathroom every couple hours, walls adjoining.
I could hear her make her way down to the kitchen for a snack she believed she had earned.
Truth was that she hadn't.
"Carol and I made it three miles today," she would boast at the dinner table.
In part, she was trying to soothe my father and receive affirmation.
He would always smile and encourage her.
Little did he know it's an addiction.
Plain and simple.
Sugar, and as benign as it may sound, she really couldn't kick it.

Laurel

Daddy doesn't cope.
At least not effectively
He was a man of great emotional need.
That's not to say that he was weak.
The opposite was true.
My father was strong.
I had never once seen him shed a tear.
But he was a loving man.
Mad for my mother.
Desperately craving her affection, her kisses, her soft words that seemed to melt him.
Growing up, they spent every Saturday morning cooking up a big breakfast.
They would listen to all the felt good.
Neil Diamond, and Presley, all the while they would dance around, kissing and feeding each other bits of waffle or pancake.
Swaying to songs of love and blissful summer nights.
Change.
Not always good.

The songs now consisted of slow country ballads of lost lovers and whiskey-drenched evenings.

There was no more singing, and waffles were replaced with microwaved French toast sticks and bowls of cheap, colorful flakes.
The kind that caked the bowl and dyed the milk off-white.
The kind my mother should not consume. We hid the bowls if she was around and substituted for fruit and dry wheat toast.
Whiskey had replaced the splash of the Bailey in Daddy's Sunday morning coffee, and it was no longer just a splash.
The coffee was all but gone.
We were left with silence and the overwhelming feeling of eventuality.

Mikey

Worsening. Rot. Deteriorating.

My mother is frail now.
Susceptible to infections, her body could not fight.
Sugars too high. Sugars too low. Never just right.
My mother kept her strength to fight while doing none of the actual work.
She had lived with the illness for years, but something triggered it to affect her like it never had before.
It was too strong, overwhelming her.
She couldn't seem to shake it and it devoured her.
She caught the toe on her right foot on the dresser.
It never healed.
They had tried to save it, to no avail.
She almost didn't seem to mind when they took it as she made jokes.
I could tell it scared her because she started to change.
Kept an eye on her diet.
Lost some weight.
Was never unreasonably large, but enough so that her body did not agree.
Things were looking up for a moment.

Then came the back aches, followed by a follow-up.
Kidney failure, which led to dialysis.
Too late.
Back in the bright, unwelcoming hospital room.
At least this room had a view of the river.
The cellular function was failing.
Small life-giving structures take her closer to the inevitable.

The constant buzzing of home health providers was almost
welcoming.
The music of monitors beeping at her checks and the hushed
whispers of the readings that usually only were shared
between my parents and the nurses made the house feel
almost lively.
My father took a step back from the persistent need to reassure
my mother and worked hours on end.
He was now more or less promoted to chauffeur duties, to my
mother's many bouts of blood flushing.
Dialysis was a commitment.
Mom quit teaching.
I could tell it discouraged her, and to lose such a nurturing
position led her to smother us with as much affection as she
could muster.
Despite her critical state, I could tell the affection made her feel
better.
Always perked up after my dad would hold her.

Laurel

The smell of waffles and sticky syrup caused me to stir.
I had missed it.
Two months ago, I would never have expected to have a
normal family breakfast again.
I caught a whiff of coffee as I entered through the flowered
arc. That would soon be gone. Mom wanted more of an open
concept.
No whiskey.
For the first time in a long time, the brown sludge was void of
burning liquor.

My mom had spent the last week painting dainty daisies along
the kitchen window ledge.
It kept her mind off her diet.
It showed.
She was feeling well now.
She wore it well.
"Love you, " she whispered as she caressed my hand across
the kitchen table.

Mikey

She excused herself after our meal.
Tired, she told us.
Fair enough.
Her head was hurting, as it often did.
Recovery was tough, and no one expected her to bounce back
in such a short time.
She had had a rough couple of months, yet we couldn't help
but feel hopeful.
Things were looking up.
Mom was almost well now.
She had just needed to find her footing.
The rest of the day was spent out of the house, then to physical
therapy at the clinic on Delaware Avenue.
A meek street tucked away in the center of town. It boasted
little, the only attraction being a locally planned and sculpted
community garden.
I always begged to tag along so I could wander over to the
arcade.
Rot my mind for a couple of hours on meaningless violence,
the soft glow of the cubical screen reflecting in my eyes.
Then a scoop of black cherry from Duncans.
Always black cherry.
My little treat to myself.
Mom always caved and took me with her.
The best way to spend a Saturday.
Sunday was reserved for service.
So many kind words to my mother.

Beneath was nothing more than indifference.
But God was watching, as was Bishop Graham.

Laurel

Sunday best, my ugly ivory dress with its gaudy flowers, and
the gloves my father always insists I wear.
Service ran long and was as grim as always.
Luckily today I had a bird to distract me, a sparrow perched
on one of the beams, singing sweetly while below, from the
pulpit came a darker picture.
Fire and brimstone. Miracles and rewards. Heaven and hell.
Obey your elders or you may just feel the devil's hot breath
running down your back.
I had always hoped my parents would go to one of those non-
denominational churches.
The ones where you could wear your street clothes, and the
band plays guitars.
The type of place that seemed more focused on worship than
appearance.
My parents would never allow it.
It was always a dress or a suit topped with a dizzying pattern,
the type that made you anxious to stare at it for too long.
We had to look better than everyone else, but more
importantly, we had to be better.

Mikey

Coping.
Laurel his mechanism of choice.
Laurel is strong. They have a bond that most people would be
jealous of.
There is a mutual need there.
Someone to bring him joy.
To bring him hope.
Promises, ones she had never spoken or guaranteed.
He found that in Laurel.
He had made his promises too, of love and growth.

I can't say I am not a little jealous when I see them watching movies together, going on long bike rides, and sharing the Sunday paper.
On days when mom is feeling well, they all laugh and play board games, always inviting me, unconcerned with my lack of desire.
It's not that I don't want to join, it just seems too risky.
She isn't out of the woods yet and I'm scared to further attach to someone whose light is burning out.
I found her lost in the deepest bits of the woods a few nights later.

She passed in the master bathroom shower, making a mess of the peach tiles with thick crimson blood. A trail of something yellow pooling.
A brain aneurysm, or so we are told, and the sunny puddle, urine from losing control of her bladder when she passed.
My dad had found her first which must have killed him.
I was watching TV in the living room, not truly paying attention.
A heavy thud, dull and sinister made me jolt my eyes pulling from the game just as the ball fumbled.
I saw my father run downstairs, his shirt soaked through, strong forearms bulging as he reached to grab the phone from the hook, the long rope tangling itself around him like a hungry boa.
He gave out our address, his breathing choppy.
"Mikey, I need to move the truck, the ambulance is coming," he explained the words breaking apart as they left his mouth, his eyes wide and full of fear.
Somehow, I understood.
Then I did something I should have never done, and I crept up the stairs.
I knew it was wrong.
But something deep inside me made it impossible to stop myself.
I had to see it.
Had to know for certain.

I opened the door to the bathroom, its usual squeaking
drowned out by the falling water in the shower and the feeling
of a drum that hammered violently in my chest.
The room was filled with steam, the mirror ghostly, denying
my reflection.
There she sat, naked, wet, eyes glossy like a glazed donut, her
skin pale.
Her clothing was draped along the floor to be used as a floor
mat before disposing of them in the washer post-shower.
It was a habit I also mirrored after seeing her do it in my
younger years when we would all shower together.
The fabric served its purpose, absorbing the water from her.

Laurel

"I miss her," he whispers sadly, his fingers running through
my hair.
"You know how sad it makes you that mommy is gone? I feel
it too, honey. Do you understand, mouse?"
I nodded yes, and I meant it.
I felt it, deeply.
Jim was heavy on his breath, stinging like a bee's attack.
Heavy on his limbs.
Mouse.
I loved it when he called me that.
Attributed to my ability to move as quietly as a mouse.
A trait I had picked up playing with Mikey.
Whenever he referred to me as such it made my stomach do
somersaults and gave me a strange sense of pride.
Daddy had sunk onto my bed like a sack of potatoes.
Not red-skinned; dainty and light.
More like Russet; Heavy, and mediocre.
 He sprawled across the cherry sheets, work uniform long
gone and replaced by an old shirt,
arms open, signaling his desire to hold me.
"Let me hold you," he would say "just for tonight."
I obliged, wanting so desperately to be held and soothed.
What little girl didn't want her father's love and attention?
Most of the other dads didn't make time.

I was the luckiest girl in the world.

Mikey

We lay her to rest on a Sunday in her Sunday best, a white
satin dress with a dipping V-neck.
Icy flakes settled across the uneven pavement as we made our
way to the funeral home.
Laurel cried that cold December day, Christmas only a week
away, frost eating away at the last of the leaves from a long
fall.
Her tears fell like rain, her skin cold as ice.
I'm still not sure why she cried so hard.
Didn't she know it was inevitable?
Did she not recognize the impermanence of life?

Laurel

"Sorry for your loss."
Are you?
"She is in a better place."
Is she?
"It's better this way."
Was it?
"It was a beautiful ceremony."
We aim to please.
"Great turnout."
Is this a concert?
Since when did we start quantifying the value of a life, by the
number of cars parked outside a funeral?
Is that how people attributed worth?
And if so, what did it matter if you were dead?
It was all surreal. All too real.
I clung to Daddy's hand and watched wet trails fall.
Fall off his jawline. Fall to his knees.

Mikey

The months pass at a painful speed, each day just blending with the next.
The pictures of her are fading from my memory, memories of her touch long gone.
Her scent fades as we wash away any trace of her.
You never notice a person's scent, but somehow notice the absence.
My emotions faded along with it.
Her name was taboo.
Her memory, nothing more. Gone.

Sit

Stay

Listen

Laurel

I had opened the door.
Daddy held the key. The master key,
Only he has access to every room.
No permission needed,
No, access denied.
"Why did she leave us?"
I always ask, knowing full well she didn't have a choice in the matter.
"I don't feel right, Laurel," he would whisper, "I wish she had fought harder. I just… I don't know how to move without her around."
I want to help.
Was I the cure to Daddy's sadness?
Was it really sad?
Or was it something far more complex?
More fragile and intricate than words could ever describe.
If it wasn't despair, then how else could you describe the return to the bottle?
The total lack of control.
Why did his presence make me feel so alone?
Why should he suffer alone?
Face the pain.
Alone
A lone
Lone
One
"It's us now Laurel… One. You and me."
It sounded so good, yet I couldn't help but feel for Mikey, discarded and thrust to the side.
But I needed Daddy.
I needed him almost as much as he needed me, and if that meant experiencing his hurt, then I would.
Why suffer alone?
When we would spiral as two.

If misery loves company
then this was a classic case
of folie a deux.
And together we spun.
Spinning. Spinning. Spinning.
Like water down the drain.

Mikey

Strange, out of sorts.
Shut off to the world around me.
It was like everything was moving while I remained still.
The eye of the storm.
The lack is thick as a fall fog, wrapping itself around me and
pulling me into a conflicting embrace.
I could not see through it, and if I desired to escape and I'm
not always sure I do, it would take something big.
Something to excite all senses.
So when the time came to leave the safety of my dulled state, I
chose my first victim.
It started small, cluster flies.
Pleading for entrance. Changing of the seasons and all.
So I would invite them in.
Wait like a cat, till one rested just long enough and made
himself just vulnerable enough.
Then I would strike, fast as a flash of lighting.
Dead.
A life snuffed like a flame.
It always starts small.

Laurel

It started small.
A kiss.
A father's love.
Something that had always been.
Kisses that fall gently across my cheek.
Pedaling.
Tender on the silky skin of my forehead.

Lips that travel slowly. Cautiously.
Testing the waters to make sure they are just right.
The waters of my soul. Steady, he always finds them steady.
First to the lobe of my ear.
Eventually to the petal of my lip.
Bubbling in anticipation.
Daddy tells me that a kiss is a picture of love.
A thousand words.
A thousand words that would fall from his lips.
And from mine.
Silence.
But inside it had formed.
Two powerful letters. One word. Zero voices. One word.
One that I could not bring myself to utter.
A word that formed a full sentence.
Syllable vowel.
No. No.
And yet I always hear myself say yes.
The puppet to the master ventriloquist.
"I love you, little mouse," he would whisper as his lips would
leave mine.
The taste of tobacco.
Long cut, never straight.
Daddy was set in his ways.
The raspiness of his bristles.
Bumps rising from the cold.
"Let me stay here, with you."
Begging for something he could take.
Yearning for comfort.
On those nights, I would always nod yes.
"I love you, Daddy."
"Love you, Laurel."
I didn't doubt it in those moments that he loved me.
It always starts small.

Mikey

School was a bore, much too easy.
It was like nothing challenged me.

The words of famous poets.
The discoveries of brave men, and in the background, silenced women.
Equations and formulas.
The suffering of the silent.
None of it elicits any response.
Merely actions: sit, listen, regurgitate, wait for the bell, repeat.
Prove your worth by filling out the bubbles on this little sheet.
But I had found something.
Something sick.
Something that made my heart race.
Made my palms sweat.

Cluster flies.
The smashing of their gooey bodies had lost their appeal.
But a new opportunity had presented itself.
Its name; Amaurobius Ferox.
Commonly known as the black lace weaver.
An elegant, sleek, arachnid.
Soon, she will find a mate.
Spring will send the males hunting.
What a sight she was!
A beautiful matriphagious spider with sprawling legs.

First, she lays her eggs.
Act one.
Later, a second set.
Act two. Intermission.
As her offspring hatches, they devour the remaining eggs.
Brother! Sister! Carnage!
Their very first meal, an act of cannibalism.
Then the mother will encourage and allow her young to consume her.

She is the Joan of Arc of arachnids.
The ultimate martyr.
There she was, in the back corner of the garage.
The damp darkness gives her life.
The game was different now.

There was no more smashing.
No viewing of innards evacuating the body.
My movements are delicate.
I would grip the poor soul between my fingers.
Flies, ants, and sometimes even other small spiders.
 I would gently place them on her trap.
A silk prison that signals the end.
How they struggle against the residue.
Some would pull so hard that bits of their frames would tear right off.
I had never tilled and then seen a fear so great.
In that fear blossomed my excitement.

Laurel

It doesn't feel right.
His hands move to the crook of my neck, petting lightly, my heart thrumming nervous vibrations.
"Relax" he half orders, half encourages, his voice rough, his hands gentle.
Voice like a watery cream, smooth, yet carrying a hint of authority.
Half and half.
He didn't even need to raise his voice, and I melted like butter in his hands as his nimble fingers moved to the flesh of my uncovered thigh.
I sizzle.

Fourteen.
I'm fourteen and my mom is gone, and she has been that way for far too long.
Forgotten.
I am fourteen and daddy is broken, the light that used to shine in his eye is snuffed out.
Shattered.
Fourteen and I am certain he cannot be fixed.
But maybe if I try.

He is glass split beyond repair.

Still, I try to pick up every piece, the glimmer too promising to
leave behind, too appealing to discard.
Knowing what this vessel once held.
It doesn't matter if it makes me bleed.
There is some comfort in that.
I am fourteen and only I have the power to heal such a broken
man,
or so he believes.
I am fourteen and Daddy's kisses now travel past my lips.
That much I am capable of handling.
I am powerful,
Fruitful. Strong.
I am fourteen, and as my body grows, so does his.
Harder. Longer. Stronger.

His finger is still adorned with the band of their love, circling
the digit like the Rings of Saturn.
It had once been tightly bound, now loss had robbed him of
his appetite.
I watch as it orbits.
Cool gold running over me, twisting, spinning as it finds the
pert flesh of my chest.
Titan.
My tallest peaks retreat as if they had once occupied too much
space.
I gleam down.
Titan is gone. Black hole. Hot, wet.
Pulling me in like a vortex.
To his touch, I eclipse.
That night, gold would be found in foreign territory.
A region ready to plunder.
Rich to the touch.
The Amazon. Warm. Wet. Deadly.
Virgin land that had been void of human presence.
Undiscovered, now claimed.
Untouched, now looted.
Once free, now conquered.
And when I should be like the Mojave,
I find myself a slave to my anatomy.

It's not right,
And yet I'm told, through a slew of vowels and syllables that
it is his right, that I am his right.
It feels wrong.
I feel the illness spreading.
Most common symptom: inability to speak.
The one-word sentence forming on my lips.
Yet never do I dare.
Speak.

I am not dense, I fully comprehend.
Hollowed. Weak.
It's intrusive, and yet when it is over, his fingers bear my
shame.
 Proof of his entitlement.
I am fourteen and it feels so right.
It feels right.

"Laur."
 I hear it, my name being called out.
A shortened version that I only ever heard one person use.
"Laur."
Being called at a low octave, laced with enthusiasm.
I spin around and he is there.
He is safe and chivalrous, as always.
His smile is crooked, sandy hair clings to his ears.
Kyle, the boy next door.
Strong shoulders adorned with a heavy bag.
Smile revealing his charm, slightly crooked teeth, and words
of affirmation.
I hear the rumbling of cars as they pass by, the bus stop is
crowded.
Budget cuts are causing us to have to trek further distances to
stops to reduce gas usage.
I didn't see that smile as often as I would like.
Not since his dad.

That had been the talk of the town for weeks.

It wasn't every day that the high school gym teacher and
football coach takes a noose to his neck and jumps.
He had left a note for his mother.
Salt on the wound.
Accused her of being a cold, adulterous waste of space.
He had written nothing about his two children.
Something he had once said hurt him more than the actual
death.

Kyle is fifteen
Older than me. Too old for me?
Probably.
For a moment, one could say we are the same age.
Those short summer weeks between the end of June and the
middle of it.
To Kyle, I was the neighborhood girl.
Sweet, innocent.
Like a little sister. A friend even.
But that's not what I want, I want more.

As kids, we spent hours hunting down frogs and playing in
forts.
We laughed, and all played tag.
Jumped from house to house.
A welcome light in all my dark.
And when it rained, we all danced, trudging mud through our
homes much to our mother's dismay.
My friend, and yet lately it feels like something more.
He is good. I know this, I can see it in his deep blue pools.
He is humble, all the girls fawn over him, and yet he doesn't
seem to notice.
He never seemed to notice, and if he did, he didn't pay it any
attention.
He notices me, but I'm not alone.
Tracy Mason drooling all over him, long red fingernails
running up and down his arm inciting goosebumps,
interrupting what could have been a conversation.
Despite his complete lack of acknowledgment, she clung to
him tight.

"Are you ready for the pep rally?"
Her voice seems to lighten with each high-pitched word.
"Yeah, I could use some pep," he replies, pulling himself from her grasp.
He was hoping she wouldn't notice, but she did, quickly closing the gap between them.
"What are you doing Saturday?"
Kyle shrugs, eyes on the incoming bus that creaks its way up the road.
 "Not sure yet, might go to the lake, get some fishing anyhow," he informs her, pulling away once more, bending to grab his raggedy book bag from the dusty ground.
 "You should come to my end-of-the-year bash," she giggles as her feminine curves smash into him. "My brother has a fake ID."

We move towards the opened doors.
"And there's going to be plenty of booze."
"Yeah, maybe I can swing by," Kyle smiles, hands stiff around the straps of his empty bag as if to keep them off her.
Trying to keep a distance.
Or maybe that's what I'm hoping to see.
It's what I want, ever since last year when Kyle had his first girlfriend and I found myself feeling hurt, unrightfully so.
"Eat it, Tracy" I whisper under my breath as I climb into the belly of the yellow beast, taking a spot towards the rear.
The tin can on wheels stinks of an overabundance of body spray and hormone-induced sweat.

Mikey had already abandoned me for his pack of future felon friends.
Today's activities seemed to include tearing into the leather of the seats.
Dad would blow a gasket if he found out.
As I settle in, I can see Kyle walk towards my seat, ready to plop down next to me before being pulled in by Tracy once more swiftly.
"I'm sorry," he mouths back to me as the rumble of the yellow beast begins to shake the cab.

All I could do was smile before I retreated into my flimsy headphones.

Mikey

I have a voice.
I'm not mute.
Yet, when it came to my father, it faded.
I could remember how warm he had once been.
Bike rides by the roaring river, cherry Gracia ice cream to follow.
He used to sit on the porch with my mother and they would talk for hours about nothing.
For a long time, I felt like we were invincible,
like things could never go anywhere but up.
There is nothing more dangerous than hope.
No pain sharper than hope lost.
Hope is a dangerous vessel.
Beautiful, comforting, disastrous.
So, I disarm.
I think that's when it all changed.

Did I have emotions? Did I feel?
Joy. Fear. Anticipation.
The sun on my skin.
The cold bite of winter.
Did I feel?
Anything.
I guess it just depends on the day.
Some days I feel everything.
Rage. Jealousy. Loneliness. Fear.
A crazy thirst that I could not quench.
Lust.
Not created by choice
This was not my choice.

Laurel

School this week passes in a blur, history was a snooze, and
math left my head spinning.
Surprisingly, it all comes to a head today.
The last day of school usually drags on and on, but with
Natasha there, everything seems light.
My friend since diaper hood.
Beautiful Natasha with her long legs and dusky skin.
Lips that always seem to pout and eyes that pierce.
We laugh.
We migrate from classroom to classroom.
Parties in each room boasting a variety of sweets and treats.
People celebrating the start of summer leave.
But for me, it signals something different.
While their lights flash green, mine vibrates yellow.
Warning.
Slow down.

The start of summer for most was like a release from a stint in
prison.
For me, it was a return to my own, with no daily yard time.
I don't want to leave.
Don't want to be home.
A home no longer filled with love.
A home that is cold and silent except for the rustling that
periodically alerts me outside my door.
Daylight held just as many dangers as nightfall once had.
Yet, when my class begins its party, I slap on a smile.
I devour the saccharine desserts. I fill myself to the brim.
Glucose, fructose, all the dyes.
Brilliant reds and frosty blues, yellows that harden against the
top of a sugar cookie, and pizza.
Loads of pizza.
Out of control. Indulgent.
A distraction, I need a distraction.
Another cookie, a plate of fries. Mindlessly I devour it all, and
by the end, there is no longer any flavor.
No sweet, no savory, nothing sour, and yet I continue till I feel
like I might burst.

Natasha's eyes me, almost as if to ask what I was doing, but wisely decides against it.
Instead, I watch her strap long manicured nails wrap around Dean's strong arms, a soda in his large fist.
She had told me she liked him.
In reality, I think she liked the idea of Dean more than Dean himself.
They would be a fierce power couple.
Cheerleader meet football player.
Cliché.
Who am I to judge?
It's a cliché for a reason.
"You want to go grab something to drink after this?" I hear a voice whisper behind me, hot breath along my ear.
I jerk to face the voice.
It's handsome, has dimples, and cool gentle eyes.
I want to drown in them, who needs air anyway?

"How about it?" Kyle asks, delicate and vulnerable, frozen by my lack of response.
"I probably shouldn't have snuck up on you like that."
My stomach's contents threaten to vacate, newfound nerves pushing the food into my throat.
I wish so badly that these feelings would go away.
It had been so much simpler before.
Playing without a care.
Touching without fear.
Teasing without implication.
Simplicity. Childhood.
Before death had complicated our lives.
Pool parties, block parties, birthday parties, and any other reason the adults needed to get hammered, uncomplicated.

But when mom died, we stopped showing up to the get-togethers, and then Kyle's father less than a year later and they also stopped showing up outside of each other's funerals.
I no longer saw Kyle outside of school after that.
Kyle looked at me intensely, waiting.
Wake up, idiot!

"Umm, yeah" I stammered, my cheeks flooding with heat,
partially humiliated by my newfound shyness and partially
humiliated by my sudden inability to form a sentence.
"You don't have to say yes if you don't want to."
I forced a smile. My face must have concerned him.
I looked down at my feet.
"I would love to."
The words fly out before I can even consider what this means.
Dad wouldn't like this.
Dad would be upset.
Dad might get jealous.
Dad wouldn't want me to share my love.
Love?
Was I serious?
It was a drink, not an invitation to sleep with him.
I wouldn't dare.
If he ever found out, he very well might banish me to the
house for the summer.

The man had a way of finding things out, a bird's nest, three
hundred sixty-degree view, and a slew of ammo just waiting.
The town was his playground. He had power and a badge.
He smiled, dimples suck in, fading into his smile.
They always got to me, and I knew he hated them.
"Girls have dimples," he would complain.
"So do boys, unless…" I would eye him playfully.
"I am too a boy!"
We would eventually burst into fits of laughter.
Warm childish afternoons.

I don't care if he considered the craters feminine in nature.
It was the only thing remotely close to womanly about him.
It gave him balance.
Gave him an air of safety.
"I could swing you back by your place after."
I shook my head not fast.
Maybe too fast.
His eyes narrow in on mine.
Definitely too fast.

I need to be suave.
"I'll just walk."
"That's crazy. You live like one house down," he argues.
"It's *really* ok," I reply a bit defensively.

Pictures of the repercussions flow freely.
Motivating me to hold my ground.
He doesn't argue and takes me by the hand, walking me out of the building.
It was something I loved about him and missed that assertiveness.
He was never pushy, knew when to let things go, and always knew when to take charge.
"We still have the pep rally," I complained.
"Chicken."
"I am not… I just don't want to get in trouble is all," my head ticks defensively.
He leads me gently and I follow till we are in his truck. A flimsy air freshener that should have been tossed months ago sways at our entrance.
"Don't you ever get tired of following the rules, Laurel?"
"I don't follow all the rules," I shoot, annoyed for a moment that he thought me a square.
Snickering, "I bet you even brush your teeth for the full recommended three minutes," he teases.
"I take my oral hygiene very seriously, Kyle!"
He was right, though.
"Don't you?"

Kyle turns over the ignition, tires propelling loose stones back into the open parking spaces.
"I do. But sometimes I want to rebel a little and I only brush my teeth for two and a half minutes instead of the dentist's recommended three."
I had never felt a thrill like this before.
And yet I was only leaving an hour early on the last day of school.
He was right.
I am a chicken shit. Laurel the square.

Mikey

When mom died, I watched the tears pour from their eyes.
Yet, I never felt the sting of my own.

In fact, at times I didn't even know if I could.
Cry. Hurt. Feel love.
Feel anything other than this void.
I had grown accustomed to keeping my every feeling in for so
long that they left me.
They could only take so much neglect.
Packed their oversized bags and walked out that door.
And now I have to plaster a smile on my face.
Just so no one knows the truth.
That inside my soul is not a void or a darkness, but rather my
soul is a desert.
An emotional drought.
So I continue to play through the day.
I frown when I should.
Laugh when I should.
Smile as much as I can.
And when I should feel pain
I can slant my eyes just right to mimic dejection and shame.
I blend like a chameleon.
A social chameleon.
I do feel though.
The thrill is something I live for.

It started out so simply, when the caterpillars used to fall from
their little nests up in the trees and lined the sidewalk, I would
crush them.
Little oval pill bodies bursting with yellow goop, lining the
concrete sidewalks of the town park.
It had been accidental at first.
Then I sought them out, the crawling buggers trying so badly
to get away from the rubber of my tires as if they could feel
the ill intent I harbor, but it has nothing to do with them.
They are simply convenient.

A tribute.
A safe and easy release.
Much like the person who vexed me most, they would never cocoon and spring forth beautiful awe-inspiring wings that sat as fragile as silk, and even if they did blossom… someone would find a way to crush them.

Laurel

When we arrive, I can't help but scan the room.
A million scenarios popping into my mind, my breathing hastening.
My paranoia sometimes gets the best of me.

I had made Kyle take the small back roads," If my dad sees me out of class, he'll kill me."
Kyle didn't argue. He simply followed my instructions with a chuckle and looped around, settling on the small cafe on the edge of town.
Littered with truckers and passersby, and very few locals, it was a fairly safe place for us to enjoy a moment.
Watery coffee and old slices of pie were stale, and somehow the business was successful.
"A root beer, no ice please, and some fries," I hear Kyle tell the overweight server who shoots him a big smile.

We had sat in the back corner, out of view of the entrance, tucked away, just as I requested.
It was cozy.
I ordered a Coke, my stomach protesting from the full state I had forced it into at the end-of-the-year party.

"Worried your dad is going to catch you skipping?" Kyle teases, a small strand of his hair falling over his eyes.
I desperately wanted to reach and push it out of his eyes, but my sensibility kept my urges at bay.
"Maybe."
"Come on, it's the last day of school anyway…Scared of getting grounded?" he teases.

"Something like that."
I tuck myself into the corner of the booth, pulling my knees to my chest.
"Must suck having our dad patrolling the town all the time."
He has no idea.

I don't want to think about him though, not when mentions of him make my stomach twitch uncomfortably.
Not when I'm with Kyle.
Especially when he does things to me that I sometimes imagine Kyle doing.
"Things are different now…since my mom," I confided in him, hoping this train of talk would cover all the sad bases so we could move on.
"Yeah, I understand," Kyle drawls, pulling his beanie down to cover his ears, his longish hair almost fully covered.
He does.
The wound was still fresh for him too.
"My mom blames herself."
I remain silent wanting to give him a chance to elaborate.
"It wasn't her fault; he had a long history of depression…but she still blames herself."

Reaching across the table and without so much as a second thought I grabbed his hand and held on tight, "It must be hard for her not to feel guilty considering the note… and the-" I stop myself too afraid to say the words that might follow.
I had heard my father talking about the scene down to the smallest and most painful details.
How Kyle's father had used his last moments to demolish the woman he had claimed to love, using the tie his sons had bought him on Father's Day a few years back to hang himself.
The wicked note that was focused on demolishing his mother for years to come, in his pocket.
"He spent his last moments trying to tear her down. That wasn't fair of him."
A confused frown came across his face, the corner of his mouth teasing downwards as if he felt a pang of guilt.
"Do you ever blame yourself for what happened to him?"

Bold, too bold.
Why do I always go from zero to a hundred?
Maybe it's because I want to hear him say yes.
"Should I?"
With a weak smile, I assure him that he shouldn't, azure
sweeping over me quizzically.
He smiles back, his slightly crooked teeth flashing, before his
mouth purses tightly into a slit, "do you blame yourself?"
"For what?" I ask automatically.
"For your mom?" He questions with a confused look on his
brow.
My stomach churns angrily, hoping my drink will come soon.
"Oh, uh no, I don't."
Saved by the waitress.

The drinks arrive, small, carbonated bubbles flowing through
the cold cups.
I look as the waitress sets down the steamy fries, and suddenly
I feel hungry again.
Get a grip.
Daddy wouldn't like you eating like this.
He wouldn't like you fat.
He wants his daughter, not an overweight slob.
Kyle takes a long drink, ice clinging on his teeth audibly.
"There's ice in your drink," I point out.
"Not the end of the world."
I love that about him, "I like that about you" I blurted as he
sucked the amber liquid up through a straw this time.
He half chokes and pulls away from his drink "Oh yeah, you
like things about me."
This line of teasing instantly turns me into an awkward little
girl, and my hide grows hot with embarrassment.
"Enlighten me Laurel… tell me what else you like," my friend
insists, pretending to flex his biceps, "Is it my bulging
muscles?"
"I'm sorry, I didn't mean it like that."

I must be beet red now, my eyes drawn to the muscle of his
arm.

Pretending to gloat he kisses at a bulge before putting his arms down.
Daring to glance up, I find there a teasing grin perched on his lips, "Should I flex again?"
"What?" I questioned half defensively.

Kyle picked up a fry and dipped it in a cup of ketchup
"Nothing" he continued, knowing just which buttons to push.
My breath was shaky, and I desperately wanted to shove a handful into his mouth to shut him up.
This was the last time we would go out.
Go out?
That's not what this is…or is it?
"Tell me what else you like about me."
He has such confidence, his charm alluring, almost enough to get me talking, almost.

I smile, deciding that the only way out is to play his game, "Nothing."
He dabs another fry, the red sauce catching on his finger, licking it off before grabbing the fry between his teeth.
"Come on. Stroke my ego."
"I'm sure you hear these things all the time," I tease.
Everyone loves him, especially the girls.
"Please," he asks, his face serious now, drawing me to make a list.
The look on his face grows darker with more need with each passing moment.
"Well," I cleared my throat knowing I needed to pace myself, "You're always kind. You don't look down on people, and that's saying a lot seeing as how almost everyone else lives and breathes gossip in this town."
I stopped and snagged a fry mischievously, making him smile.
Kyle grimaced and pretended to smack my hand away.
"But not you. You're not like them, you don't need to talk poorly about other people."

The waitress comes over, her feet seemingly heavy as she drags herself to us, her presence giving me a moment to

gather up my thoughts and prevent them from coming out too desperate.
"Refill?"
I nod, a light wave falling over my eyes.
Taking my glass she pours more bubbly into my glass, the melted cubes mixing in and returning to their suspended state, the straw rising with the carbonation, threatening to vacate the dark blurry plastic cup.
Kyle tells her that he is set, and she vacates.
"You're not like them either" I hear him say before he swallows down the rest of his drink, the waitress out of earshot.
He isn't wrong.
But it's not because I am nice, or because I care.
It's only because I am so wrapped up in my thoughts to find time to gossip lately.
"You also have the worst laugh."
Embarrassment fills me, my hand falling over my mouth.
"I like it though! It's contagious," he adds, noticing how flustered I had become.
His words are like a warm blanket.
They made me feel again.
Secure.
Tingly, like I might float through the ceiling if he doesn't pull me back in.
I feel my glow return, and I'm far from the only one to notice.
"You're beautiful Laurel."

I say nothing.
Instead, I look down, stir my drink with my straw, plugging the top to gather some in the flimsy tube with no reason other than to diffuse the networks firing in my head.
It wasn't unusual at my age to have these thoughts.
The pictures of Kyle are rapidly firing, making me blush.

Kyle kissing me.
Kyle's hands on my naked waist.
Fingers in my hair.
His mouth falling over my rosy nipples.

My chest rising to his tantalizing touch, aching for more, then falling against his weight.
I can feel it forming. The ache below.
The pressure between my crossed legs.
Unbearable, yet undeniably sweet.
The tingle that runs a sprint from the tip of my nose to my welcoming femininity.
I wish it would go away.
Want it to stay so desperately.
I had only felt this a few times before.
After Daddy would venture down below, relentlessly bringing me to the edge, dangling haphazardly before letting me fall.
The tingle begins to fade.
Tainted. Poisoned by thoughts of him.
Kissing me. Hands on my naked waist.
Fingers in my hair.
Mouth falling over unwelcome bits of flesh.
Causing them to reconsider.
I can feel it forming.
Disgust, guilt.
The ache in my stomach.
Unbearable and undeniably bitter.
The tightness that threatens to strangle the air from my lungs.
My face must have been a dead giveaway.
"Are you alright?"
I snap back to reality jumping from my train of thought, the tracks tough beneath my feet.
"I'm fine...I just gotta get going."

Kyle looks down at his watch then back at me.
"School just got out."
I gulped down the watery soda, sad bubbles trying to float to the top, "Yeah my dad will be home at four so I should really go" I informed him reaching into my pocket for a five that I had earned doing extra chores.
"I got this," Kyle interrupts pushing the bill back to me.
I don't resist, allowing him to prove his male worth in whatever way he sees fit.

"It's the first night of summer break, are you sure you have to go?"
I badly want to stay.
Tell him no.
I clearly have a problem using that word.

"My dad wouldn't be ok with me being out without his permission.
Kyle looks me up and down an air of concern in his gaze.
"He worries is all" I deflect seeing the worry, my hand exposed.
Kyle nods, "Right… but at least let me drive you home."
I shake my head no.
"It doesn't have to be all the way but let me get you to the end of the block."
I consider, nervous thoughts clouding my mind meshing and winding with excited thoughts of spending more time with
"Just to the end of the road" he pleads once more with authority this time, throwing his book bag back over his shoulder.

Kyle was true to his word as we pulled up to the corner of Elm and Ridgeway.
The Cooper home, a large rambler with the most beautiful wrap-around porch that somehow seemed to have flowers sprouting in glorious blooms, almost year-round beams at me.
I began to gather my belongings, quick to exit when I felt his hand on mine.
The touch is electrifying.
"Thanks for talking to me. I know it sounds stupid, but I needed it."
His face is serious, glimmering eyes full of authenticity, and appreciation.
"I like talking to you too, Kyle."
If only he knew just how much.

Car idling, spewing pollution, something hangs in the air
between us, but I can't explain what, and for some reason, I
am certain he feels lit too, hopeful in fact.
"You know you can talk to me Laurel," he confides.
I can't, but that wasn't his fault.
"Thanks."
"About anything," he adds with emphasis, his hand skipping
to mine.
A tingle fills me at his touch.
Again I lie with, "Yes."
Will there ever be a time for honesty?

Sleep evades me that night, but I am forced to feign little
sleepy moans and the periodic fluttering of my eyes.
If he suspected I wasn't truly asleep, he might pounce given
his state.
The TV is off now, the room is smoky with crushing silence
outside of the feeble sounds of sleep I offer.

He had lured me in with promises of a movie night to
celebrate the end of the school year and asked me if I would
like to watch it in his room and on his bed.
I couldn't say anything but yes.
Dad had pointed to the cover of an R-rated movie and gauged
my reaction and excitement at the notion of watching
something slightly forbidden.
"I'm not sure you're old enough," he had taunted.
At that moment I hadn't realized I was like a dog being led to
its cage with a trail of carelessly dropped treats and it
infuriated me that he still didn't see me for the woman I was
becoming.
"I can handle it!"
I'm not a little girl anymore.
Chuckling, the battle was won with four words, and his trap
was set.
 We sat, the sun setting behind his window, the movie taking
all my focus.
The movie had several more explicit scenes, sexual in nature,
each time I could feel his gaze fixate on me as if he was trying

to read me, and he must've liked what he saw because, by the end of it, he asks me if I liked it and If I was ready for something a little more grown-up.

That's when he put in another movie, one I had never seen before.
My father had warmed me up enough as I hadn't protested when I realized what it was.
I had heard about all of this in class, but I had never really seen it being acted out aside from our neighbor's dog being mounted by a stray.
Ruby.
The grotesque way the man drove his almost too large member into the frantic, almost hysterical woman beneath who kept begging for more had me tingling the way I did when Daddy and I explored.
He watched like a hawk reading its prey, waiting to go in for the kill.
Blessedly, he couldn't read my mind, so I tried desperately to look away, burrowing myself into the ivy comforter.
A stray feather from the goose down pierces through the cotton, grazing me, and shooting my eyes back up.

At first, I felt humiliation, slanting my eyes down to avert them from the copulating couple, nervous to have him catch me viewing it, let alone enjoying it.
Something so forbidden.
Thoughts of the day I had seen Ruby and the stray mating flitted like old footage, morphing with the panting couple glowing on the screen.
The way I had felt that night flooded back.
The gall and abstinence I had had that day, yelling out that I would never do such a thing when my poor mother tried to explain.
The day I had seen Ruby mating, fear had warped my brain, the cries Ruby had emitted haunted me, and tightened my throat.
Not anymore.
It feels so different now.

No fear taints the actions portrayed, only curiosity and the heavy shame that threatened to expose me.
What might happen if he noticed me enjoying the footage?
Fathers shouldn't know that their little girls have less than childish interests, no matter their age, let alone be sharing them with her.
It's special.
He wouldn't lie to me.
What we have is so special.

Eventually, I had enjoyed myself, desperate to soak in each moment, each moan and writhing of the submissive woman whom they disguised as strong.
I couldn't pull my eyes away.
Felt myself grow hot below.
Felt the urge to stifle the pressure.
I was enchanted by it all; the way she cried, the way her body twitched with release, how it only took one thrust of his hips to cut her down to nothing.
Only minutes earlier she had been a warrior, clad in metal and honor, only to be unarmored, and made to lay still beneath a man, unraveling as if she had not an ounce of control, as if his penis drugged her upon contact.
She had lost all sensibility, the man pulling her strings.
How easily she lay down and accepted the male who would put out her flame only to ignite his own.
The act was appalling!!
Tantalizing!
Riveting!
It left me feeling uncomfortable in places I wasn't sure had so much sensation.
Made parts of my body flood.
Made my eyes sting with tears.
Made the beating of my heart catch in the valve of my chest.
Made my breath fall choppy.

Out of sheer fear of being seen enjoying the second movie which no longer had a story, I lay down and clenched my eyes

shut, eventually pretending to be asleep, my father's hands wrapping tight around my waist, his hands strangely and thankfully shy.
His mouth was alive though, full of sickening, damning words that he lulled me off to sleep with.
Oh, if only God could see!
If only he could hear!
If only he were there in that excessively large bed, space unutilized!

Hours later I woke up, his arms still around me tensely. He is still awake, despite the darkness that had swarmed overhead. Silence gave me away, the room too still, my breathing too quick now.
"I know you're not a sleeping baby, and there's nothing to be afraid of Laurel… it felt as good for her as it did for him. What they did in that movie is a wonderful gift! To be able to please each other… two people who love each other."
"Is that what two people in love do?" I asked, rubbing my eyes, hoping he might offer another movie up, although I'm not sure why.
I couldn't help but ask, Mother had already told me it was, but I wanted to hear it from him.
"Yes, Laurel… it is," pausing he takes in a deep breath, my shampoo igniting something within him, his ache apparent against the curve of my ass, his pointer twinning in my hair, dragging it to his inhaling nostrils, "It's how they show their love."
"It looks scary, the way she lost herself… under him."

My father kisses the back of my neck gathering up my hair, "It's nothing to be afraid of, that's just the way women look and sound when they feel good… when two people love each other they share their bodies and become one, and their bodies respond accordingly… didn't you see that she liked it?"
I flipped to face him, my face burrowing along his strong chest, "Yes… I guess she did."
Even through my thick locks, I could feel the grazing of his beard on my scalp as he held me, and something hot and

desperate hovered between our bodies, something that we knew we couldn't explore yet.
"Laurel?"
"Yes, Dad?"
With a swift flick of his finger, the top of my gown fell, and his lips pressed gently against my lips, that so easily fell open.

Still waiting for a response he kisses me with fervor as if he might resolve some unspoken conundrum by exploring my face, his hands cupping beneath my chin, elongating the embrace.
Chewing tobacco, buttery popcorn, and desire swim along my tongue, battling against the riptide of disgust that comes naturally.
The same hot mouth draws away from mine and dips to catch a sensitive nipple before giving it a soft suck that I retreated from, blood rushing to my face.
Why did that feel so good? Why did it feel so bad?

His words came out breathy, heated as if they hurt,
"Remember when I say this Laurel, what you saw on that screen tonight is something you share with the man that you love… it's not something to be trifled with."
I shook my head obediently, my nipples skimming along his own, his hand tight around my growing hips, my head tucked beneath his chin.
"Now, let's get some sleep. Want me to sing you the song?"
"Yes…please."
He was about to taint it for me, but I don't want to hurt him, never.
The song. Our song.
The one he had made up in my childhood and always sang to me when I was sick or afraid.
Sometimes we would play hide and seek, and I could hear him singing it as I hid in a painfully obvious spot, increasing the volume until he found me.
By then I was usually reduced to giggles that had him laughing too.
Tonight he would use it to lull me to sleep.

"Oh there she is my little mouse," he begins, a deep bass, his
voice at a melodic whisper, "hiding in such a big house."
He continues for a while.
The words vibrate in my head, fill me with a sense of dread
rather than comfort.
I force my eyes shut and will myself to fade.
"I love you, Laurel." He ends the tune just as he senses me
dozing.
I understood. Completely.
Summer break starts with a bang, although it was something I
should have been expecting by now.
Womanhood.

A bright crimson scream freeing itself from my body, clinging
humidity to my inner thighs.
Waves of pain course through my abdomen, only to be dulled
with a couple of painkillers that I pull from the cabinet.
The bottle rattles almost empty.
It couldn't have come at a more inconvenient time.

A trip to the movies with a group of friends, Kyle included,
just not on the list of attendees I had given my father.
Curfew is set for nine, giving me another two hours of
freedom.
The fear that daddy was somehow watching is a burden on
what should be a fun evening.
I excuse myself from the movie about halfway through,
needing a moment to compose myself after Kyle's hand grazes
my thigh probably accidentally, but wishfully purposely.
I wasn't watching the movie, anyway.
Too focused on every slight movement that transpires
between us.
It was strange, Natasha had easily settled into Dean's grasp.
They held each other tight, lips rarely parting, the sound of
their passion echoing in groans in the mostly empty room,
leaving Kyle and I to be third wheels.
Third and fourth wheels maybe?
Was that a thing?

I was probably the downer of the bunch, the wrinkling grape
on the vine.
Training wheels.

I leave the bathroom after frantically checking myself in the
mirror, the idea of anyone knowing I was menstruating would
mortify me and I wasn't sure exactly how to handle the flow
yet.
That morning I had propped myself up on the toilet and tried
a tampon I found in my mother's old drawer, the one dad had
not emptied yet and the angles were all wrong.
I had tried calling Tasha to help me figure it out, but she
hadn't answered and the best information I had was from the
"talk," just the year prior in health class.
An awkward hour of stifled giggles and rosy cheeks.
Feigning disinterest.
My mind had been completely fascinated by the intricate
functions of my future body.
I am less than impressed now.

When I determine it is finally safe to emerge from the stuffy
room.
I fork left back to my theater.
There he stands, almost as if he had been waiting for me to
reappear.
In front of the auditorium doors, he starts to come towards
me.
My hair is messy, beanie thrown over it making it appear
longer.
"Tired of the movie already?"
His head shakes no, the red tapestry moving with his head as
he leans against the wall.
His voice is low and throaty, more serious than I had ever
heard before.
"Just distracted," Kyle looks me up and down, "and tired of
watching the amateur porn show that Tasha is putting on."
I laugh, face hot, his laugh mingling with mine, "They really
are going at it aren't they?"

Kyle puckers his lips imitating them causing me to burst out laughing.
Maybe a little too loud I realize as a passerby glares in my direction, their hands too full, popcorn falling over its buttery tub.
Kyle playfully grimaces at another onlooker, a less than impressed elderly man, hobbling his way to the theater.
"Old stick in the mud" he whispers almost too quiet for me to hear as he walks to close the gap between us, hands interlocking with mine.

He has a way of making me smile, and tonight is no different.
Kyle, always teasing me, funny, yet never cruel, honest yet never crass.
"You know what it is? "
My head shakes a firm no.
"He is just jealous that I get to stand out here and talk to the prettiest woman in the place."
I know he is full of shit, yet I blush, the old man now entering his movie, no longer staring us down.
"So what are you doing out here, anyway?" I recoil.
"Figured hanging out with you would be more entertaining."

We didn't need a screen or poorly written dialogue at that moment, so I offer him an eye roll, "Doubt it."
We had a dialogue of our own going, a tangible conversation, and with his next, he showed me how much more exciting he finds me than the movie.
His fingers part mine, palms caressing and falling flat against each other's, I can feel his heart racing.
Our touch is deafening, unspoken feelings ruminating between us.
"Let's get out of here…go grab a coke or something."
I can feel his whisper now, his face close to my ear and yet I hadn't witnessed him fastening that gap.
He is close, so close I can feel his words.
The lack of space is tantalizing, yet nerve-wracking.
A pestering feeling that was not welcome joins in.
What if someone sees?

Sees and tells.
What would he do?
Why is he always on my mind?
Interrupting these priceless moments?
Complicating what should come naturally.
The moment when Kyle pulls me tight against his chest.
The moment when I feel Kyle's lips brush mine, only the
bottom of our pouts contacting.
I can't help but picture his anger. And it rises with my own in
this act of defiance.

Parting my lips I accept his kiss, and although this first kiss
should be simple, I find it's anything but, further becoming
complex when he pulls his fingers around my waist, pulling
me into his touch.
Never urgent, never forceful, but certainly powerful.
I fall into the kiss; I live in the kiss.

Tonight, I will dream of our first kiss and for many nights
after.
Our cherry coke-flavored kiss.
My normal state of trepidation is gone and now it's only Kyle
and me.

Mikey

Laurel seems renewed, happy even.
Fresh and bounding. Lightweight.
Blissful.
It will not last longer than the week I'm certain but it's
refreshing.
He has a way of ruining our happiness and I'm sure this will
be no different.

Take last week for example.
Drunk, again.
His friends had been watching the game.
Eyes full of predation despite the house full of guests.

It's the little blessings that count and the numbers keep him at arm's length.
With their absence comes the burdensome presence of silence that washes over the house.
I tiptoe to the fridge, pull out a pop, and down the carbonation too quickly, making me want to gag.
He eyes me, tossing an empty beer bottle with a clunk into the newly emptied bin, and asks me to clean the kitchen up despite the time.
"It's late."
He does not give a damn.
"What did I say, son? It's a mess, and you have been prancing out all day," the man slurs, the beer heavy in his stomach, sloshing as he stumbles off the bed. His state encourages hasty work.
Plus, there's a look I had never seen before. An anger is bubbling within him, one I fear I might come face to face with soon enough.
When I'm done, the clock reads just past midnight.
"Love ya, son," I hear him call out as I pass his bedroom door.

   Not as much as he loves Laurel.

Laurel

A week had passed since I had seen Kyle.
Thoughts of his kiss burned strong against my own, even days later.
Everything that surrounded me was now frivolous, and not in the usual manner.
No, this is not the gloom filled with disdain I usually carry, not that this disdain is fueled by something beautiful.
Nothing could compare to it.
Nothing shone as brightly.
Next to it, nothing seems to matter.
Food has lost its taste. My dreams are less vivid.
I was sleeping through the night, thoughts of the neighbor boy lulling me to sleep.
For the first time since my mother passed, I can say that I feel happy.

The rasping of skin against oak draws my eyes up.
Mind ripped away from the fantasy I had happily wandered into.
Again a knocking.
More of a formality than a show of respect for my privacy.
If I could say no, I would.
But I know that he will enter.
Response or not.

I don't turn as he sways through the doorway, limbs heavy with drink, but sadly not enough to knock him out, or to turn his brain to a buzz.
Just enough to let him lose his sense of rationality.
My eyes match him in the mirror, the mass of his body honing in like an incoming meteor.
I know it's coming, flying at a catastrophic speed, but the impact hurts no less.
I sit, incapacitated.

Like a deer, banking on complete stillness to shield it from the predator.
A hunter.
On a mission.
An arrow waiting to pierce the heart.

My hand grips the brush, long hair falling over my nightgown, clad shoulders, dressed in embarrassment, the white fabric gliding over my frame.
My blanched skin is ready to be stained.
It fit snugly against my new found body.
"Let me help," the man I know as my father encourages as he reaches for the brush.
His hand meets mine.
Clammy, riddled with anxiety and intent.
Nail beds were greasy from an afternoon of work.

"You look so much like mom when you wear your hair down," he comments as he begins to work the brush through each strand.
I do.
We share the same eyes, ones that sit round and wide, mossy tones with dirty blonde hair that falls so elegantly with just the right amount of volume.
He works with a feigned delicacy for the keratin structure, stroke after stroke, grooming me in silence, despite my already groomed state.
He had done that.
Slowly.
My walls were knocked down.
Jericho.
Patiently marching me down. Calculated. Patient.
"You know you can tell me anything Laurel," he implies, setting another strand of hair carefully to the side, its gloss shining off the bulbs of the mirror.
I noticeably shudder at the thought of telling him anything, but I toss him a bone now and then to keep him from snooping.
"Yes," was all my tongue could muster.

Teaching for a band on the vanity, he begins to braid my hair
the way mom had taught.
"Tarzan swings from one vine to the other" he recites my
mother's instructions still in our hearts and minds.

As he finishes the first one, he wraps the small black band
around the brittle ends that need trimming to catch up with
the rest of my locks.
"Then why didn't you tell me?"
Tell him what? Is this about Kyle?
Does he know about my date at the movies?
Does he know I had left with him?
That he had had his hands on my body?
The thoughts devour me, leaving my mouth dry, a weight like
an anchor in my belly, and still, that anchor doubles in heft
when he reveals what he means.
"You're a woman now," he whispers, interrupting my flighty
thoughts.
Anxiety is instantly replaced with disgust.

With the second braid complete, he allows his hand to stroke
my lips, gently parting them from behind, the reflection
showing the tender way his hand moves as the slick, gritty
chemicals of a day's work cling to my lips.
I want to jerk away, but I stay still, allowing his finger to dip
in, kissing against the top of my tongue.
There is foreshadowing in his touch.
"Growing up so fast," he groans, retreating his hand and
reaching into his garment to retrieve something.
Green Monday panties show in the reflection.
My panties.
Hadn't even worn them on the right day of the week, which
seemed somehow more humiliating now than the fact that my
father held them.
The bulbs adorning the sepia vanity catch the maroon stain the
washer had failed to completely wash out.
I sting a burning scarlet.
My shame burns, almost as hot and as red as my introduction
to womanhood.

How had he found the garment?
I had tried to hide them, blended them with the daily loads to
not draw attention after I had spent the evening scrubbing
them in the sink to no avail.

"It's ok, it's only natural, and I know it's not fair that your
mom isn't here to explain it to you, but you got me."
An offer.
One that should be seemingly normal.
But not him! Not from him!
I was aware it was normal.
What wasn't normal was his glee.
His fascination with the garment.
His excitement at the thought of my menstruation.
"Thanks," I shrug, wishing the moment would pass.
Mortified.
Daddy lays his hand reassuringly on my shoulder, building a
bond.
Building up courage.
"Are you clean now?"

Does womanhood make me dirty?
I had never thought of it that way… but now?
Am I untouchable?
Unlovable?
No longer his girl?
A slave to the womanly wiles of my own body?
Further captive?
I am suddenly filled with shame.
My body betrays the portrait of an unblemished girl I so want
to portray.
"Laurel?"
All I can do is shake my head yes.

Tonight, the turkey clings to his words. It stings my nostrils as
he kisses my cheeks from behind, hands maneuvering my
gaze back to him, gazing back.

I can smell it on him, not enough to obliterate his senses but just enough to blur the lines, although he did that well without the alcohol.
I pull from his touch, gazing down at my lap, my fists tight.
"I'm going to show you how to be a woman… now that the time is right."

His words cause me to turn and face the monster.
His lips were no longer soft,
A touch that was no longer gentle.
The reflection captures the metamorphosis.
"But I am a woman," I state naively.
I had been told as much.
He chuckles. Whatever he found humorous caught in his throat, and I can't help but hope he might choke on it.
"Almost Laurel."
It's clear.
Crystal clear.
Transparent as the waters of Great Exuma.

I shake my head in hopes that feigning innocence will drive him out and bring him to his senses.
Naivety indicating that I'm not ready.
That despite what flowed from my body, my mind was still that of a girl.
"Is that something you want?"
Less of a question, more of an instruction.
"Yes, dad," I reply with an automatic nod and smile, not meaning a word of it.
There is no other answer.
"Good," he says, kissing my forehead wet, tilting my head up and back.

Freedom is only a dream.
I yearn for it at this moment.
The freedom to say no.
Freedom is not real.
A myth and reality were staring me in the face.
Duty.

Obligation.
To fulfill.
To spread love is to spread myself.
Thin.
I am the vessel.

A catalyst to his search for freedom.
The viscous spittle pulls from his lips.
Cakes my neck in sticky streams.
Dehydrated.
Sick. Toxic. Lips.

"I'm going to show you something, Laurel."
I nod, knowing what something is.
"Something to show you how much I really love you… like in
that movie we watched. Do you remember that, Laurel?"
"Yes."
I remember the way the woman lost her power and squirmed
beneath the weight of the man, and now it was going to be my
turn.
I'm certain of it.

My body flutters with the need to escape, goosebumps
erupting over me.
"Is that ok, Laurel?"
I nod.
I don't rebel against his word.
Refuse to shrink away from his touch. Maybe part of me wants
him.
I had grown used to this flavor of abuse.
It feels like home.

Content with my response he takes the reins.
Reigns over me.
Leading bit in my mouth.
I am ready.
Ready to be led.
The final step of my indoctrination.
Giddy up.

It begins with a rerun of past violations. My frame lay gently
on the queen-sized bedding.
A field of cotton, an ocean of waves to be ridden.
A kiss on the forehead. A kiss on my lips. His hands on me.
Groping, tweaking, moving me to greener pasture.
His touch is desperate.
Impatient.

Ivory straps fall gathering along my biceps, and I lay,
humiliated by my developing body; hips that were widening,
breasts that were budding in little pyramids, the fullness still
some time off.
My body prepares, constantly releasing signals, the flower of
my sex begging for pollination.
My small breasts embarrass me as I watch him beam, rolling
the pebbled flesh between his fingers.
They make me feel like a little girl, less than womanly, trapped
somewhere in the middle.
It isn't just a feeling.

"You like that, don't you?" he coos, gently sucking an erect
nipple into the vortex of his mouth.
The rosy bud darkens as the flow of blood pulls to the surface
against his lips.
Eggshell nightgown falls beneath the curve, plumping at the
pull.
It continues to fall, his mouth retreating, tumbling until it's
gone.
Although he is moving quickly, his touch is delicate, wary not
to disturb my flawlessly arranged locks.
Careful not to tarnish his doll.
His plaything.
His lips meet me again, explore my waist,
Ribs. Hips.
Spaces no father should kiss as if it was uncharted territory
that he could lay claim.
Each slope and mound were a new discovery.
Then the most sacred, my lips.

My response alleviates his guilt.
"I asked you a question. I want this to feel good for you too,"
he grumbles, moving up his face pressed to mine.
A red flush emerges beneath the beginnings of my summer
tan.
I feel him, hard against my inner thigh, the belt of the robe
digging a little further up.
Cheek to cheek.
Music is absent and we don't dance.

"Yes," coldly I utter.
Those three letters are enough to make the guilt rise up like
bile.
This began because of me.
It's my fault he keeps doing it.
I learned about this type of thing in health class.
About your private body, and consent.
Yet, I had never been taught how to say no, and so I never
did.
If you don't say no, it doesn't count, does it?
If you don't tell anyone, then nothing really happened.
Right?
I knew the answer, and yet reminded myself that at times his
lust is also mine.
Sometimes Daddy made me feel so good.
Sensations that were strong enough to coax groans from my
lips.
Maybe that's why I don't say no.
My fault.
It's my fault he wants me the way he wanted my mother.
It's my fault my honey tresses and round moss eyes remind
him of hers.
It's my fault that I am soft-spoken, spineless, and weak.
Not like Mikey.

"That's good," he whispers his face below now, tongue
plundering forbidden loot, pulling me away from self-
deprecating thoughts, and into deprecating acts.

He had jumped forward quickly.
I try to focus on the ceiling.
Play connect the dots.
Styrofoam popcorn ceilings, a perfect platform for such
entertainment.
Tilt my eyes to the left and I can see a cat.
Tilt my eyes up and I imagine an airplane waiting to take me
away.
Where would I go?
France?
Japan?
No, I would never run, would never fly from my cage, even if
it was left wide open.

I feel his mouth leave me.
Watch him remove his robe.
Appendage springing as fabric meets the floor.
I had never looked at it much before, always shut my eyes
tight when he made me touch it.
Even tighter when I could taste it, yet now, knowing what he
intends to do with it, I can't help but stare at the springing
appendage and wonder, how?
No. Please.

He senses this, "It's ok Laurel. I'll take good care of you," he
drunkenly smiles before burying his face beneath me once
more, wrapping his arms beneath my bottom and holding me
close, bringing forth the ultimate pain, Pleasure.
She hurts me more than anything.
He is relentless, every move aimed to coax further
complacency from me. "Does it feel good for you too? I want
you to enjoy this."
I won't grace him with a reply, because simply put he doesn't
want one.
The forbidden thrum of pleasure has me surrendering.
The tingle, the pressure, the probing becomes all too much.
The patterns fade from the ceiling, brain fuzzy. I can't ignore
this much longer. I'm too new to this.

Small grunts of encouragement, hand moving up to my
delicate breasts, reaching.
Another touch, strong hands spreading me further apart,
leaving me exposed.
Forcing me to open up for him.
Better access to the space that brings me so much.
Shame.
Guilt.
Pleasure.
And as I fall over the edge, I try my best to hide it.
I tumble.
Fall from grace with a stifled whimper.
God can't help me now.

My body gently sways with convulsions that I try desperately
to diminish.
But he knows.
He always knows.
He knows my body.
Owns my body.
Destroys my body.
And somehow brings an indescribable sensation to it.
No matter how good it felt.
The warmth, the pulsations, that moment right before it hit, it
was never anything less than sick.
It was all lacking.
It lacked.
Love, desire, basic morality.
But since I allowed it to happen, he weaponized the act.
Digs himself in deeper,
And I am.
Complacent.
The sad reality is this, he is just as much a slave to me as I am
to him.

It happened.
I am what society would call a "woman" now.
At least by the world's standards.

Men are the path to the definition of what we are and who we become at their hands.
Man's twisted claim to creation.
Man's way of controlling women once more makes us dependent on them to claim our womanhood.

I didn't cry, nor did I profess my undying love.
Instead, I shut my eyes tight as he lovingly kissed from my forehead to my lips, gently cupping at my chin as he used his free hand to notch himself against the barrier he had no right to breach.
The barrier between childhood and adulthood.
Not for him, and yet my thighs fell with ease, his chest heavy on mine.
I pretended.
Imagined it was another man who was buried inside, invading my space and eternally linking me to him.
Prince Charming.
A man.
One I loved.
Cherished.
A man who was kind, gentle, patient even.
A true man.
He would lay me down on the bed mid-embrace.
Rose petals strewn about, adorning my alabaster tone.
Like the movies, he would tell me how much he loved me, how he would never hurt me.
I would trust him, instinctively.
Then, when the moment was just right, he would ask me if I was ready, already aware of the answer yet never assuming.

I zoned in on Prince Charming, and it abates my need to scream out.
Tried to envision his crooked smile, the smell of his breath as I ran my fingers through his locks.
Not my father.
Not breath coated with stale liquor.
Not this horrible ache that had formed between my thighs as he pushed himself in, his bulbous head tearing away my last

bit of dignity, and while he had moved gently, it hadn't made it any better.
No claim to my own body.
With a flick of the hips, he claimed me as his.
Disregard for the straggled whimper that left my throat when he did so.
Already I hoped it would end.

"It'll get better, "he whispered, easing out with painful precision, resting just outside of me.
 I could feel the heat radiating. I didn't dare look down as he carefully examined what he had just done.
Stinging pain settles, localizing where we had just interacted.
"See, baby, it wasn't so bad, " he informed me, clueless as to what I actually felt.
Baby, that word.
I was a baby…his baby!

His face was cherry red as if it pained him to stifle and keep the movements of his hips slow and leisurely.
Testing his patience, his mouth moving to choke down a groan.
That kiss was a vow of his lust for me and suddenly he shows me his "love," but there's nothing loving about the way his hips snap into mine sending a sting radiating through my veins, or the way his teeth gnash along my lips.
He was wrong. My body was in spasms, a psychosomatic symptom of the intrusion.
My mind knew how wrong his touch was and my body was paying the ultimate price.
"Not so bad," I whispered through breaths as jagged as a serrated knife, as if admitting the excruciating sting might somehow disappoint him.
Anything to appease him.
Anything to get him to leave.
"That's my girl," he responded before pushing himself in again.

This stroke, unlike the first, wasn't as gentle. His care seeped out of him as he took me. Heavy.
Strong.
Greedy.
His body told a story of a ravenous hunger he had caged up, gaining traction, his pleasure mounting as I felt his hips slam hard against my inner thigh.
Bone on bone.

I wrapped my arms around his neck then, and pulled myself to him, afraid he might see the look in my eye and as much as I didn't want to touch him, I needed someone to anchor onto at that moment.
Forced to make him my lifeline.
His prickly hair scraped at my skin like a branch against the window on a breezy night.
Small cries erupted from my throat.
I wanted to make him feel better.
To take away all his pain.
I truly did, but my body was screaming for resolution.
Did that make me selfish?

"Turn over," he coaxed as he gently guided me onto my knees and out of myself, leaving me in a submissive state.
It screamed, " Have me".
The only way out was through the pain.
My shaking thighs were pushed apart, bared for him, served up like a Sunday lunch.
I remained silent, didn't even dare breathe too loud.
There I knelt like a bitch.
Sit, stay, repeat.
Don't speak.
Never disobey.
"You look so beautiful under me."

Dad didn't stop till he was satisfied, the salty plunge leaving him waterlogged.
Each thrust the length of a lifetime, as he tore apart both mind and body.

Bitch. I was just a bitch.
Primal sounds began to build behind me. They made me feel ill.
Then there are the vile words.
"Your body is so fucking perfect baby… so tight, like my body was meant to fill yours."
A warm spurt of fluid filled me, wet heat against my womb.
My master returned to his human form.
No longer beast, never fully man.
The cycle is complete.
And the afterglow, like clockwork, ended with a kiss.

Kissing me so gently, as if tenderness would excuse the darkness he had just released.
Kiss it all better.
Please make it better.
Fix this Daddy. Fix me.
Take it back. Make it stop hurting.
Please.
You said it would get better, but it hurts so much worse now that it's over.

"I love you so much, Laurel."
Words of affirmation followed by tears.
Not my tears.
Although I had every right, he had plucked me before I had even bloomed.
He waits for me to wilt.
His tears water me.
Falling like the rain of a tapering monsoon.
Tears that should have been falling from my own eyes.

Mikey

I knew what had happened that night.
I could hear her through the walls, as I had many times before.
This was how I had been introduced to the world of sex.
Not by websites.

Not by magazines.
Not by the whispers of men in dirty, water-addled bathroom
stalls.
Nor by the chatter of little boys whose bodies had outgrown
their brains.
Although I did partake in all the above, especially the talk.

Chrissy let me touch her tits!
Mandy is a slut.
Did you hear what Matt and Liz did at the party last
weekend?
I hear that Toby is still a virgin. That's so pathetic.
Did you know that Kyle and Bri hooked up at David
Fergusons' party?
Talk, talk, talk.
It was all supplemental.

My sexual education was much different.
I saw it when my father's ache grew unbearable.
When the booze dulled inhibition.
You would think a man with a badge would never fall so far.
Would never dull himself with alcohol to the point of
predation.
Most people would think wrong.
It is a particularly interesting fact that men of the badge have a
higher prevalence of domestic violence than others.
Not that my father had ever laid a hand on Laurel out of
anger, or my mother, for that matter.
That was part of the problem.

At first, all I could hear was a small whimper.
Or a whisper in the night.
Like Laurel, I didn't understand, not at first.
If he was hurting her, she would say something.
If he was hurting her, she wouldn't hold him close.
Or so my limited mind thought when it first started.
Curiosity took over.
I had to know.
Had to see.

To understand.

But what I saw was inexplicable.
His head was buried between Laurel's thighs, and she made
sounds that almost sounded painful, her hands tight along the
sheets, her chest heaving towards heaven, and yet not a prayer
was muttered, and she certainly wasn't on her knees.
Couldn't understand what it meant, or why I felt funny.
So I allowed curiosity to lead me to ask all the right questions.
I learned. Learned what it meant.
Learned how to touch myself and relieve the pain.
Bring myself to the brink without falling over, prolonging the
moment.
Learned to revel in the ability to get off.

Laurel

It's over. For now.
I am anything but dumb.
He will be back.
There was always more to take.

I lay there, my skin vibrating, the buzzing growing in my
head, swarming like a million cicadas.
The pain beneath dissipates with each rise and fall of my
chest, lungs ballooning with undeserved air.
Traces of Daddy vacate me, pooling on my lilac sheets,
gathering and smudging along the inner bends of my legs.
I lay where I found womanhood, frozen in a state of girl-like
confusion.
My mind struggled to work through the events of the night.

My one and only desire is to bury the memory deep.
I would only need to follow simple instructions.
First, locate a shovel.
Second, mark the best spot to dig.
Third, proceed to dig a hole at least six feet deep.
Fourth, lower myself into it.

I imagined it all knowing full well that there is no shovel big enough.
No pit deep enough.
No dirt is dense enough to keep it buried.
So instead, I would smile, pretend I was strong, pure, whole.
I would pretend I was someone.
Or I would fade into no one.
How could anyone desire me now?
Damaged goods.
Not even desirable at a reasonable discount.

Girls like me.
Girls whose daddies touched more than the heart.
Damaged girls.
Girls.
Still just a girl, despite his claims that I was all woman now.

It wasn't too late.
Daddy could make it right.
If he loves me as much as he claims, he will never do that to me again.
Let me move on, but I know he won't.
The internal battle was reaching critical levels.
My stomach tightens, nausea sweeps over me like a wave over a ship.
Completely burying me beneath it.

I run to the bathroom, in search of comfort once I am certain he has lulled himself to sleep, the heat tingling in the back of my throat.
My stomach was tight as if a belt had been looped around it and tugged by two opposing forces.
Head in the toilet bowl, my arms cling tightly around,
I wait for the contents of my body to expel.
A release that never comes.
Swept out to sea with the waves of nausea.
I find no comfort.
No release.

The room is like ice, yet the thought of returning to my bed is
mortifying.
Instead, I pick myself up.
Reflection catches in the mirror as I sink into the porcelain.
I am different.
The glow that had once adorned my round face, gone.
Snuffed out like a flame.
How could fire burn without oxygen?
How could I glow when I had been blown out?

I lay there in the empty tub, the small womb-like space
making me feel safe, the feet digging into the tile, just as his
nails had dug into the meat of my thigh.
A continuous loop of my night flashing as if I might make
sense of it all.
As if the repetition would reveal some profound truth.
My mind yearns for knowledge.
Understanding.

Despite it all, I can't cry and that confuses me more than
anything until I realize that I am too afraid to cry. The tears
might bring closure, and I know this is far from over.
Worse yet, I don't want him to see me cry and feel any
responsibility for my state.
I just try to remind myself that he cares.
Daddy loves me.
Daddy needs me.
Daddy *really* loves me, and all he wanted to do was show me
as much.
Why can't I be happy with that?

Mikey

At twelve, my mind had kicked into overdrive.
Testosterone flooded me.
Now, at almost fifteen the desire is suffocating.
I resort to foolish activity to stifle my urges.
I listen.
Listening leads to imagining.

Imagining leads to the ache.
The ache to the touch.
The touch to release.
How could something that feels so good be so wrong?
Why do I feel numb after each encounter?
Why do I inherently keep it secret?
Still, I imagine.

I imagine Laurel and what our father sees in her when there is
a world of gorgeous available women out there.
Her body would be fine.
Less developed, less refined than that of the women adorning
the paper covers.
My first true exposure to a woman's body was handed to me
in the stalls after class.
Sex created not from the flesh of palpable skin, but rather
made tangible by the mixing of ink and the click of a camera.

No, Laurel wouldn't be touched up, made up like the girls on
the covers.
Playboy, Penthouse, Hustler.
Dozens of crusted pages full of lust.
Much like the models she would be directed, and eager to
please.
Smile. Lay still.
Raise those hips. Just like that.
Unlike the women in the magazines, there was still life in her
eyes.
A gleam of innocence.
A smile symbolizing that she was not yet beat down by the
ways of man, up until recently.

Suddenly I am overwhelmed with emotions I rarely feel, at the
thought of my sister being turned into some sexual being.
 I love her.
She loves me.
For her, I desire a life of happiness, void of pain.
Yet, I allow him to hurt her.
But maybe I can do something.

Find the courage somewhere deep.
Do I dare look the beast in the eye?
Dare I confront my demons?
Expose him?
No. Not yet.
But I am there for her.
Whenever she is scared. Exposed. Alone.
I am there.
My ear firmly pressed to the forest-colored wall.
Hands balled up into fists.
I am there for her, and maybe someday she will know it.

Laurel

It wasn't till I woke up to the unwelcome light of day that I
found my bearings.
A small pool of water had gathered at my feet from the
weeping tub faucet that my father has yet to fix, the uneven
incline bringing a cold sting to my toes.

Sleep had allowed me to forget.
But only for a moment.
I reached down between my thighs, hoping it had all been a
bad dream.
Would the ache be gone?
The heaviness returns like an anchor as I felt it.
The throb.
All I want to do is forget, escape within the realm of sleep.
An alternate reality.

Dream.
I want to dream again fearing that if I refuse to do so,
repercussions will ensue.
I sit up deciding that I am all right. I just need to crawl in bed
and rest a while longer.
You are making a big deal out of nothing.
Just shut up and go to sleep.
If ignorance is bliss, then denial is nirvana.
I slept until nine.

We had French toast and fruit for breakfast, but outside of that everything was devastatingly normal.

Mikey

When two frantic sperm cells met two eggs Laurel and I came into existence.
Since that fateful orgasm, Laurel and I had always been together.
We had shared a womb, separated by thin tissues, and had fed on the same nutrients.
We had grown strong together, developed fully, and when we were ripped from the safety of the womb, (my body emerged first to make sure the coast was clear) and held under harsh lights for our weary mother to see us we were inseparable.

Together, we slept.
Together, we cried.
Together, we learned.
Together, we competed.
Laurel always won.
Smarter. Kinder.

But I took pride in my strength and became her comforter.
When she fell, I picked her up.
When she skinned her knee, I felt her pain and made sure that she was bandaged up,
and when mom died, she wept into my arms so easily.
She never questioned why she never felt a tear fall from my own eyes.
Yet, when our father began paying special attention to her, we faded, drifting in different currents.
There was only distance now.
No room for two men on her plate.
Somewhere deep down he knows.
Knows how to break us, knows how much the distance hurts.
Isolation.
It's unnatural.

With all their secrets Laurel doesn't come to me anymore.
Can't trust me while equally loving him.
Her cold calloused rejection only leaves me needing her more.
It was almost as if she sensed my need and she could not bear
to please yet another person, because simply put Laurel
doesn't have much left to give.
At capacity.
It makes me so angry; I hate to admit it even to myself.
I wished she would pay me the attention she gave him, but I
understand, although I wish I didn't.

Laurel

I trek slowly to the school for open gym.
Dad had signed up for a biweekly session, to keep me out of
trouble this summer, according to Rachel and him.
Oh, yeah, Rachel.
New to the picture.

Dad's girlfriend as of early spring, only revealed to us at the
end of the school year.
Already keen to give me instructions.
Mikey had been told to get a summer job and make good on
getting to wrestling practice.
He starts next week at the small western-themed amusement
park that sits on the edge of town.
The employees all dressed as cowboys or natives, which was
uncomfortable, and operated rides that operated with all lever
and pulley systems.
The largest attraction is a ratty wooden coaster named the
Rattlesnake.
It creaked and shook, which always scared me.

Somehow no one had died there yet, and not just from the
rides.
The food itself is often old and undercooked.
The only food worth munching on is large ears of corn
seasoned and served in foil, that much I know is fresh.

Mikey informs me before I make my way to the gym that he can share his discount with me if I want to go ride some rides this summer.
I nod.
My mind elsewhere.

Mikey

Work and summer don't mix but if working at the Ol' Texan keeps my father from badgering me all summer, I will gladly welcome it.
Plus, I can use the cash.
Soon I would need a ride.
Soon I would be the one picking up Gale.
My girlfriend.
Feels strange to say, but it's official, I have a girlfriend although we had been fooling around since New Year's.

She made it clear this morning that I also needed to drive her around as she sped to the most eastern end of town and dropped me off in the large dirt lot, the flying dust giving it a real Texan vibe.
"I don't mind driving you but you're going to need to pitch for gas or something," she bitches screeching to a halt, already we were past the honeymoon phase.
I tip my hat to her, 'Will do m'lady, and may I request a ride home at four? I can make it worth your while," I flick my tongue at her unamused face.
"I'm not off till five, so you're going to have to wait."
She peels off without another word, my lunch still in the back seat.
Corn dog it is.

Laurel

Open gym is the last place I want to be.
Miss Grayson runs the class along with her big fake hair extensions, and a shrill whistle.

I see Miss Anderson peek her head around the corner as we sit on the bleachers taking a water break after stretches.
Rumor has it they are lesbians, or "dykes" as my dad likes to call them.
I don't see it as an issue, but apparently, I should.
My father calls it unnatural.
What he means to say is that it is unnatural that a man should feel threatened or that some women don't worship the ground he trudges upon.
Then again, I am fairly certain it's only unnatural to him in a natural setting, pornography doesn't count.

Tasha sits next to me, nudging as she catches the copper-haired woman peek in, "You think it's true?" she asks me, her nails gripping my arm, eyes glancing into the dark corridor just beyond the edge of the gym.
I crane my neck as if it would make the wall disappear.
Christy Morgan interrupts with her obnoxious perm throbbing as if it had its own beat bumping into my arm to chime in.
Her head sits between us, she smells like cotton and spearmint, teeth grinding down on a stick of mushed-up gum, "I hear she is a rug muncher," her lips smack, a bubble forming and popping.
"I don't know," I shrug, gently easing from her touch, chin now resting against my upper arm.
It bothered me.
"It's a fact, Joel Hoover told Tanya that he saw them making out in the teacher's lounge at the start of summer school," she smacks again.
Tasha eats it up her nails clicking against the wooden bench, "Joel talks a lot, that being said… I totally buy that; I mean come on just look at her shorts."

I try to recall what she had been wearing that would scream "lesbian."
"Exactly, my point," Christy's hair chimes in with an obnoxious ding.
They both laugh as if I had been robbed of the ability to laugh.

"You should be more worried about trying to get a good
workout in with those claws on Tasha,' I tease, trying to keep
her from noticing my noticeably foul mood.
Moving her hand to her face she rubs her bottom lip with the
long brown nail, a daisy-toned faux garnet sitting smack dab
in the middle of a white swirl.
It looks good.

A vote follows and more than half the girls insist on a game of
basketball which I may have enjoyed but today I feel awkward
and uncoordinated.
As if my body doesn't want to obey, and that's because she
knows she no longer belongs to me.
I am no longer the master of my flesh.
 In addition to the mental, the physical is also in a state of
pain, despite the fact that it had been almost two days I was
still aching.
It hurts, where it shouldn't and I don't want anyone to notice,
so I half-ass my dribbles, fail to make passes until I get called
out.

Fifteen to eight.
I take a break.
Bathroom, panties puddling around my ankles, a dull throb
seemingly burrowing into the bones of my pelvis as I sit in the
little stall, staring at the four corners of the teal box.
I relax my bottom to urinate.
Like fire.
Did sex always hurt like this after?
Wasn't a question I could ask anyone, so I decided that it must
be and returned with a forced smile and clumsy dribbling.

Mikey

Gale is true to her words.
Her bitchy words.
Shows up at a quarter past five, clearly annoyed that she had
to come get me.
I'll make it better if she lets me.

That all changes when I dump a corn dog into her expecting lap.
We both stink of grease and sweat.
Tired from working in cheap fast-food kitchens dealing with angry old women who have nothing better to do than complain to teenagers making minimum wage who couldn't care less even if they tried.

"Where to?"
I am not sure.
"There are always people up at the quarry. Let's go see if we can get anyone to buy us a bottle."
She nods, her makeup smudging along the corner, lipstick still inexplicably perfect around those voluptuous lips.
I can't wait to feel them, maybe tonight will be the night.

Laurel

Tasha and I walked back to my place per her request.
"I didn't want to say anything in there, but my dad got busted last night."
I don't know how to react, but now understand why she insisted on coming over, almost pleading to stay the night.
Her poker face is good.
I should be keen to share my encounter with my father, to find some release but no one is safe, and I'm humiliated and what's worse I would hate myself if he got into trouble.
"What did he do?"
Already I knew full well it was probably another drunk driving incident I still ask.
We stop at the edge of the school property, her eyes running over me, "You seem different," she comments, tugging her backpack tightly on her shoulders, slow to answer my question.
I chose to ignore her comment and pull the attention back to her and off myself, guess we're both good at deflecting.
"Driving drunk again…and all that, ya know?"

I did.

This was the second time this year, and it was only June, chances are there were numerous incidents of impaired driving he hadn't been busted for.

Tasha's dad was a nice man, but he loved his rum and a good night of dancing, often playing DJ for local events and weddings, and there was always a drink in hand no matter the occasion; barbecue, school dance, birthday, A relaxing evening after a day of coaching the basketball or track team.

The last time I had stayed the night he had downed a six-pack to himself before the movie we had rented was through and went out for more.

That next morning, he made us grits and bacon, and for himself a rum-laced pineapple drink.

I didn't like grits or bacon, but he seemed so pleased with himself that I downed it anyway as he sang loudly and happily, his big burly frame making the pan look miniature by comparison.

Tasha just kept rolling her eyes every time he flipped the bacon and loudly cried out about the bacon grease getting him.

"I'll have to check with my dad if you're staying the night."
I know she would be home alone if she didn't come over, her dad getting busted on a Friday night meant no court appearance until Monday.

"Only if you want me to," her big smile hopeful that he would allow it, I'm sure my father won't tell me no.

"How could I ever tell you no?" I tease, batting my eyes at her, my mascara winging.

I welcome Tasha's company.
With Tasha around he wouldn't dare come my way and I needed time to recuperate.

Allow the confusion and desire to fade.
Is it sick that I want to see him?
That I want him to hold me and kiss me?
Tell me how special I am.
No one ever made me feel that special, and I had grown accustomed to the praise and the love he gives me.

Tasha and I spent the afternoon goofing around in the woods, and staring up at the heavy flint sky, thunder rumbling in the distance, and teasing rain, that's when we decided to head out of the forest and back to the roads.
Eventually, we decide to grab the bikes that are sitting stagnant by the rusting shed and make our way to the road, and into town.
I take it slow trying to hop onto the bike, trying not to wince.

"Let's go to the video store and get some snacks and movies."
"Girl's night?"
She nods, taking the lead, "I'm thinking horror, a comedy, and of course a rom com to end the night."
She is already biking circles down the long driveway at the corner of the county road and mine by the time I lift my leg over the skeletal red frame and pedal.
The sun begins to fade in the sky as we finally turn down my road.
On our way back a car pulls up before slowing to a creep.
I pull off into the grassy embankment and drop off the bike.
Not a car.
A truck.
"Hey gorgeous, need a ride?"
I pretend to look around, "Who me?"
The voice is music to my ears, bringing a smile crawling along my face.

Kyle smiles from behind the wheel of his Dad's old, beat-up, gray Chevy, windows wide open as he slows to a stop. The driver's door rattles when he stops, a darker shade of gray, it had to be replaced last year after his sister dented it with her boyfriend's car.
Dad says Chevys are for fags and he would never be caught driving anything that wasn't a Ford.
Just another reason for him to dislike Kyle.
Kyle's hair is running free, the usual beanie gone in the heat, his smile is directed at me, Tasha a dozen yards ahead, glances back at me with a quizzical look on her face.

We share a smile.
"I just got off work, thought maybe you could use a ride."
I look at Tasha, her eyes encouraging me to say yes.
"Want a ride?" I called out to her.
She signals for me to come to her, so I do. "I'll ride back and
wait," she offers winking.
I don't want to ditch her, and I tell her as much.
"It isn't ditching," she argues, "it's just a quick ride up the
road and a chance to smooch."

I don't fight it any further because more than anything I want
to get in that truck, and maybe steal another kiss or two.
 Tasha takes off, the vibrating of the old engine warming my
already hot body, beads of sweat falling between my breasts,
clinging along the metal of my bra.
No AC.
I toss my bike in the back, knowing I still have an hour before
he gets home.
"Sorry, the AC is on the fritz."
I act like I don't care but my body protests, and the closer I get
to him, the more I feel the heat.
He nods in agreement and begins to make the short drive.
We stop, right at the mailbox.
"I haven't seen you since the movie and I want to... maybe we
can go up to the lake or something?"
My mouth freezes, suddenly the pain that I had been feeling
all day turns to a gnawing pang of need.

That cherry-flavored Coke kiss floats back into my memory.
"Yeah. When?" I pose quickly.
 I try to be as nonchalant as possible, which is hard to do when
my heart threatens to escape the bones of my breasts.
He gives me a basic idea; tells me he will call.
I ask him to call me tomorrow, around four when I know Dad
will be out.

We sit in agreement, wrapped back up into silence, my mind
trying to find a story for my father so I could sneak away.

Kyle's fingers no longer run against the steering wheel and instead move under my chin, tilting my face to look at him.
I see his lips.
Gentle, sleek, and longing to taste me.
I don't want to be presumptuous, so I allow him to take control.
"I don't want this to be too forward but," he stops, almost chuckling, cheeks flurried with red.
"But what?"
I want to hear him say it.
Want to be wanted.
Kyle sucks in a deep breath, flustered.
This was not the smooth-talking boy next door I spent summers playing tag with, this was Kyle the almost man, awkward despite his seemingly suave facade.
"I just want to know if I can kiss you, I haven't stopped thinking about the movies, and – "
I stop him there, gently place my hand on his collar, and inch him to me, "I haven't either."

He kisses me, and easily I accept his mouth.
Sweet and simple, but over too quickly.
I want more. So much more.

Tasha grills me for information all evening, the movies completely ignored in the background as we lay on my bubble gum pink sleeping bag. Candy wrappers are strewn along the rickety wood floors, a can of soda dripping the last drops of its carbonation across the hem of my pillow.
Right around bedtime, I work up the courage to ask her.
"Can I ask you something?"
She rises a little beside me, the sheets tangled between us, the glow of the TV lighting up her heart-shaped face.
"Does it hurt after?"
"After what?"
Her mouth clucks coyly, and she's combating a smile.

She knows what I am asking, but she wants to hear it, "After what?"

With a serious tone, she repeats the question, smirking, a blunt contrast to my serious stare.
"After you do it for the first time…and for the record I know you know what I was asking."
I try to push thoughts of him out of my mind as she describes in great detail her first time with Dean.
It was nothing like mine.
"He is just really big, and it was scary, but Dean was a perfect gentleman, and honestly, Eric was such a bore, I was happy I didn't sleep with him." she refers to her ex.
Mr. No personality.
"Did you...you know?"
"Come?" She interrupts, sitting upright, leaning against the leg of my bed.

For a moment I'm hopeful that she would say yes, but everyone I know says their first time wasn't great and that most men aren't great or attentive in bed.
Instead, she laughs, speaking in brutal honesty, "Not at all, but that gets better. After my first time it hurt like hell the next day, but every time after, got easier," her hands split to demonstrate, "I just wish he would actually go down on me." The thought makes me nervous as I imagine Kyle venturing beneath.

Mikey

I do not get lucky at the quarry, but my hands do bring Gale to a swift orgasm in the back of her beat-up car, or so she says.
She did not return the favor despite the clear bulge that had grown uncomfortable in my pants.
Better luck next time.
Hello, blue balls.
I guess it was not a total loss.
I got to bum a few beers off a group of seniors and caught a pretty decent buzz and a possible saliva-borne virus off the communal joint.
An almost perfect summer night.

Laurel

"Laurel" I hear my name, the one me. Mother had blessed me
with the day she found out she was having a boy and a girl.
They had been to the arboretum and the bay trees had spoken
to her.
She always told me I would grow to be as beautiful, and as
abundant as those trees, sprouting and spreading love.

"Laurel," he calls again before he comes, an unusual knock
followed by the turning of the knob.
He only knocks when he wants something, the observation
makes me nervous.
I'm not ready to truly face him.
A few days had gone by, Tasha was now back home with her
dad.
I had tried to get her to stay longer, enjoying the safety she
brought, but she was keen to see Dean.
Dad was distant.
Worked long hours and spent the rest of his time with Rachel.
He avoids me at all costs.
I can tell he feels sickened by his actions, even though he
cannot stop, and for that, I can only love him.

I feel the vibration on the floor as he walks to me, my body
contracting with anticipation of his hands on me.
The life in my chest flutters, my breathing quickens, fast as
light.
Unintentional.
"Yes," waiting for him to continue, I slump my shoulders,
actively trying to soothe myself, releasing the tension.
"How would you feel about painting your room this
weekend?"
My father moves his hands to the walls of my prison, off-
white that had covered the original lead paint.
He was quick to cover it when we were born.

The consumption of lead can cause the following: irritability,
loss of appetite, weight loss, fatigue, abdominal pain, and so
on.
Maybe the fresh coat hadn't kept me safe after all,
I half-joked to myself, realizing how defensive my body was
being, my belly aching.
It's what psychologists would call a psychosomatic symptom
of my stress.
Maybe I shouldn't paint the walls, instead, I could pick away
at the coat of satin and expose the original grimy, chrome
yellow that had been favored just decades prior.
Perhaps, I would pick off a few slivers, let them sit on my
tongue.
Maybe they would dissolve like sugar, and I would swallow
the poison.
I can only hope that it would be enough to at least scramble
the networks of my mind, leaving me unable to interpret the
fast-moving world around me.
The thought brings a smile to my face that he interprets as a
"yes".
I return to reality as I watch Daddy smile back, it warms me,
making him happy despite my feelings towards being
currently subarctic.
Once again, he is victorious.

Mikey

My way of apologizing to Gale without even saying a word is
to take her out to breakfast.
Cheap diner at the edge of town with soggy waffles and burnt
bacon, but the price is right.
I am not sure what I am sorry for, but Gale was not happy
when I called her this morning despite a nice date just the
night prior at the movies.

It only takes a few minutes for her to dump her problems on
my unsuspecting lap.
Turns out, she was not mad at me, which is a great relief.
Her mother was the source.

"She is always judging me, and trying to get me to her stupid mass, saying my soul needs cleansing or whatever," her eyes roll, pastel eyeshadow, layered on much too thick, fanning at me.
I listened intently waiting for her to spew the words of denial.
"I don't even believe in God or any God for that matter, I just can't understand why she won't just let it go, like sorry I don't want to be wasting my time at church Sundays, Wednesdays, or any day!"
Tossing an inappropriate amount of salt on my runny eggs, before spooning a mouthful, the white undercooked, almost making me gag, my eyes lurch up.

Stifling it down with a thick gulp, my stomach clamps working hard not to eject the slimy bite, making a mess of our moment.
"She just wants to save your immortal soul," I joke.
Maybe only partially, I'm not sure what I believe.
I am not sure what was out there more than any other individual.
Who's to say the Buddhists are not the ones with true enlightenment, or the Catholics for that matter?
Well, let's hope it's not the Catholics.
I guess what I am trying to say is I do believe in a higher power, I just have no idea which one is watching over me.
"Plus is it so bad? Having a mother who cares?"
Feline-like eyes prowl over me as if she is trying to read me.
I push it, anyway, not caring if it upsets her.
"I mean she just wants you to go to mass with her."
Eyes rolling, "Your point being?"
"Just go occasionally and she will leave you alone. It's a win-win really."
The meal is silent after that bit.
I can tell Gale is thinking, maybe even considering my suggestion.
With a handful of crumpled bills, I cover our bill.
This is my way of apologizing, without ever uttering those three words, for not fully siding with her.

Laurel

This is his way of apologizing without ever uttering those three words.
Similar to what men do after a fight with their wives.
A trip to the store to pick up some flowers, as if the blooms might inspire forgiveness in a heart that is much more closed off.
Then before the flowers have a chance to wither another fight would ensue and they would be replaced with a new ornate bouquet.
Perhaps if they hadn't reserved the loving gesture as a tool for apology they would be more at peace in the home.

My father was always a gentleman, good to my mother and never bringing flowers to heal the wounds of a fight, but rather to fan the flames of their passion.
My father isn't much into flowers anymore, although he had brought me home a beautiful rose the first night, he dared breach the hem of my gown.
It reminded me of Beauty and the Beast.
The beautiful secret the beast kept captured in the vase.
I am the vase.

Daddy's secrets would become too big for the simplicity of a rose, and I am nothing but the thin glass that keeps our secret contained.
If I part my lips, he will wither, and I will crack.
I am a delicate glass.
Sharp and dangerous when I finally shatter.
Cutting to the core.
Those cracks are more apparent now.
My gift to him is my silence.
His gifts are far more tangible.
I have a pendant; white gold with shiny alexandrite, matinee style, two bands of yellow gold that he tells me cost him a fair amount of money.
"Your birthstone," he told me as he gently clipped it around my neck, a gentle kiss where the clasp lay, and my hair ended.

The frontier.
Between right and wrong.
I had been reluctant to take it off since the clasp shut, not
daring to do anything to show him how much I detest the
shackles disguised as jewelry.
It didn't suit me.
My hair is too light and yet somehow too dark for the gaudy
stone.
My neck is too delicate for anything larger than a single band,
but he didn't notice.
Then there was the new bed frame.
 A wicker style that I had wanted for Christmas years ago.
The first time my father dared have a taste of what I had to
offer he went straight out, then stayed up past midnight just to
assemble it.
The camera, well that was a gift to himself.
The gift of memory.
I wonder if he ever watches the videos we make, not that he
uses it often.

Daddy knows how to buy my silence, knows how to make
himself feel guiltless.
He always makes me the guilty party.
Does that make me a whore?
Isn't this what prostitutes do?
I wonder what he will get me next time, and what price I will
have to pay.

"What about this color?" Mikey points out a cool gray.
Daddy doesn't acknowledge Mikey as he glances at the pinks
and purples with determination.
A wall of assigned femininity.
Nothing too dark for his little girl, nothing too adult.
"What about this?" he asks, pulling a small pink palette:
carnation, flamingo, lemonade.
Pink. Pink Puke. Barf.

My eyes glaze over the blues, something to remind me of the
sky.

My fingers grasp at a powder blue, and a darker sapphire,
extremely different in their tone, each still soothing.
My father sees this.
Understands my longing but, knowing I would not oppose
him, pulls out a lilac instead and suggests it.
Withholding me of what I want, almost reminding me that
this might be a gift for my silence, but he is still in charge.
It reminds me of the type of purple you might see your
grandmother in on her way to mass.
Well, some grandmothers at least.
My grandmother on my father's side is still too young in the
soul to resort to women's suits and short hair.
"It's nice, isn't it?"
I can tell that he thinks it's perfect for his little wallflower, but
I can't stand it.
It's too dainty, too perfect, and those are things I no longer feel
about myself.
A thought crosses my mind.
Risky.
Alluring.
Why not play my hand while the ball is in my court?
"I know you like the blue Laurel… but don't you think it's a
little boyish?" He questions, my gaze still tight on the blue
section, the color samples still in my hand.

I watch him squirm for a moment, palming the square of
paper that I place in his, my eyes wide and hopeful.
My eyes dart and hold focus longingly at the liberating blue
that sits between us.
"Laurel, honey," he starts to argue, shutting me right up.
I don't dare argue further.
Chicken.
"It doesn't have to be this color, we can even do a yellow," he
says pointing to the rainbow of colors that line the walls, as I
glance down both angry and disappointed.
An employee excuses himself as he carts a large flat platform
down the aisle, momentarily splitting us as we move to
opposing walls, Mikey's shoulder pressed to mine.

At this point, Mikey understands that he is a third wheel.
An undesired presence, that had to be there for the sake of
appearance.
"That's fine," I tell him, stepping back next to him.

My courage is gone, his long fingers curl around my waist as
our eyes scan the yellows.
I grab quickly at a bright yellow, whatever is within reach, his
touch making me want to crawl out of my skin.
The yellow is too bright, assaulting my vision.
I just want him to stop touching me.
"You sure?" he questions unfazed.
My brother steps in, extending his hand to reach between my
father and me pretending to reach for some more color
samples.
Welcome space.
The intercom goes off, calling for cleanup.
"You like this one?" Mikey asks with a smirk curling across
his upper lip.
Of course, my twin would pick out the perfect shade; a light
blue that had intertwined with the softest of violet.
Harmony. Calamity.
Everything I yearn for.
To the outside, it would seem like a normal interaction.
I know better.
Can see the tension rising like steam between them, yet our
father doesn't interject.
Testosterone clouds the space between them.
Neither speaks, instead they look back at me, the girlish
purple and bright yellow in my father's hand, the almost blue
in Mikey's with questions in their stare as if choosing a color
would ultimately assign my love for one of them.
It's a decision that will seal my fate.
The type of decision that will leave one vexed and the other
determined to make me pay.

My heart thunders.
I know what I want.

Swallow hard.
I know what I should say.
"This one," I say with the smallest sliver of confidence,
grabbing the paper from my brother's grip.
Hesitation fades and I feel so strong.
Powerful. Vindicated.
Simultaneously guilty.
I almost feel bad for Dad on the quiet drive home.
An unspoken war had just commenced, and Dad had been
knocked down a notch.
How the mighty would fall, dragging me down with them.

Mikey

I didn't mean to size him up.
Ok, maybe a little.
But he interpreted it as such.
In Laurel's eyes, I spotted a small glimmer of something new
today.
Was it hope? Pride maybe?

All I knew was that the distance had been bridged.
The minute we got home she and I were inseparable again.
I could tell it upset him and his face says it all.
Resentment?
Anger?
Or even jealousy?
I had dared question him.
I had dared,
And for a few moments, I felt a tingle in my chest.
A fluttering in the deepest pits of my acid-filled stomach.
Happiness. Had I forgotten what happiness felt like?

Laurel

I had conquered.
No credit to myself.
It shone on the walls,
Cool. Relaxing. Soothing. Blue.

A new start. A haven.

"What do you think, Laurel" Dad asks, poised against the
beams of the doorframe, the veins of his forearms bulging, his
face screwed up with desire.
Badly, he wants me to praise him.
His shoulder rests against taped borders.
Lifting the bottom of his shirt, revealing the pricky pine trail
that curves down, he wipes his brow, capturing a shimmering
bead of sweat.
He seems worn out from a day of painting and shuffling
furniture.
Had those bags that lay just beneath his piercing eyes always
been there?
"It looks great."
I smile big.
A look of satisfaction broadcasts across his face as he dips the
brush back into the bluebonnet liquid.

He resembles a modern-day Picasso with a limited color
palette, paint strewn about an old shirt, beard stained with
little flecks of pigment.
Daddy is no artist though.
Didn't have a creative bone in his body.
Unless of course, one considered mastery of manipulation a
form of art.
In which case, he was a master sculptor, like Michelangelo, the
Renoir of Impressionism, the Mozart of composition.
A master of his craft.
My eyes scan the room.
Meeting him.
Moss swimming in deep blues.
The paint smells strong. Floods my senses.
Beauty is pain.
The amount of chemicals we are willing to inhale for the sake
of aesthetics.
Pain is beauty, beauty is pain.
I inhale. I smile.
He smiles back.

Maybe he will sleep well tonight.

Newton's first law of motion.
An object in motion will stay in motion.
I am in motion.
I was moving at the speed of light.
At least my mind was.
The pain was still there, but I had silenced it.
Speeding past the stages of grief.

I fill my time with activity over the next two weeks.
Constantly on the go, exploring the forest, riding my bike with
Tasha, burning brain cells of bad romances, meeting with Kyle
and Dean whenever we get the chance to sneak away, just
living summer the way it was meant to be experienced.
In motion.
A state that was heading towards a predicted halt.
What I forgot to mention was the second part of Newton's
law.
An object in motion will stay in motion unless the object is
acted upon by an outside force.
Damn physics.
Damn science.
Damn, the laws of nature.
I was like a rock rolling down a very steep hill, heading right
for a brick wall I hadn't known was there.
Moving towards destruction, smashing and crumbling into a
million pieces.
And when it finally stopped, I was stuck, immobile at the
lowest possible place, unable to stand.
I thought I had been doing better.
Memories of his violation became less of a blur and more of a
fragmented video.

A hot dew clung to me whenever I lay in my bed waiting to
hear his footsteps, half expecting them to linger as he quivered
behind the door.
Something was changing, and it left me teetering on the edge.

Discolored, yet vibrant, emotional yet somehow emotionless,
and it sat on my mind constantly.
I had let my minute victory blind me.
I had believed the battle to be the war.
Had believed my enemy conquered when in reality he lay in
wait.
A Venus fly trap, patiently holding back giving its meal a
chance to perch.
I fell into the trap.
Fell into a state of conquest.
His unquenchable thirst is at the root of my complacency.
Carnal in nature.
A quench no whiskey could satisfy.

Heavy steps, full of intent fill my head.
I can hear them.
Outside my door, they are real now.
I am paralyzed by the initial bite.
His paralyzing agent injected into that burning touch.
Venom.
It doesn't hurt as much this time.
I am nauseated by the whispers of her name.
"Renee."
His body inside of my body.
Mommy.
"Renee."
Mom, I don't understand.

Two become one as nature had always intended.
Just not like this.
Tonight, Daddy lacks motivation.
I became confused by his apathy.
His thrusts grow less full until I am empty of him.
Daddy is rocked to sleep by the malted grain mash.
Incomplete.
And even though I have never felt relief such as this one, I
wonder if I am enough.
Mom, I understand now.
Oh, Ruby.

It isn't until I hear the soft snores that I pull away.
Repulsed. Relieved. Rejected.
In the morning, he would find himself in a compromising position.
The guilt would creep in.
The alcohol would take over once more.
Guilt pacified by anger.
Anger only quenched by love.
Love fixated on the wrong being.
The cycle on repeat.

Mikey

Laurel follows me to the depths of the forest, to a small fort we had once played in.
It had been weeks since we had ventured there together, and the first time this summer.
Our birthday is only a week away, stirring excitement in me.
Although there is no party planned, I know I can use the day as an excuse to stay out for the night and systematically obliterate my senses one by one.

I will find healing in some of the same ways my father does, a year closer to freedom.
Dad is busy with his girlfriend and their honeymoon phase, he won't notice, anyway.
Rachel.

I had never met a Rachel who was not beautiful, and she was no exception.
Rachel.
Willowy.
Long flowing deep red locks.
Pale and blemish-free skin.
Big lips that always formed a smile, and beneath sit perfectly white teeth.
She is truly beautiful; I hope that's enough to distract him.

They had met at the courthouse months ago, and yet we are now just getting to know her.

She was the courtroom interpreter for a man my father had ticketed for speeding feloniously.

Spanish was her biggest clientele, but she also spoke a little Mandarin, and German.

Smart, employed, and beautiful.

How had a man like Daddy prevailed?

We all first met and had dinner last week.

Barbecue and uncomfortable talk, that had morphed into more personal questioning.

I'm not sure If I like her and I let Laurel know.

"It's just that she prances around the house like she lives there," I say, hitting the fort with a thick branch, the sound of anger crackles in the crisp evening air.

It isn't an unfair assessment, since dinner she walked in and out as she pleased.

Laurel

I pick up my branch and examine its elegant curve and dark hickory color.

"Well, she has stayed over every other night since dinner."

He slammed the tin of the fort hard now, causing me to jolt.

"I just can't believe they are having a baby."

What a surprise that had been.

Rachel and Dad had announced it at dinner, which was probably why they rushed for us all to sit down together, and although I was excited to have a baby around the house, I can't help but have reservations.

It happened so fast, too fast; I also quickly came to the realization that It had happened simultaneously to our encounter.

I hope we have a brother.

"Well, if that Dale prick moves in, I'm going to have a field day, "My brother responds ripping me away from the thought.

Mikey was referring to Rachel's brother who had lived with her.
We had met at dinner, he was almost eighteen, homophobic, and pugnacious with bad breath.
Any reason to bring up the topic and he would, dinner had only lasted a little over an hour.
Secretly, I believed he is gay himself, self-loathing at its finest.
"You know what I think?" I ask a sheepish smile spread along my lips.
"What's that?" He smiles back.
"I think Dale is probably gay."
Mikey laughs at that.
"No really."
He takes another branch and breaks it over his knee this time.
"Come on, Laurel," he says half encouraging me to continue.
"You ever notice how he always finds a way to bring up Tony and Carl?" I say referring to our neighbor's three houses down.
An openly gay couple everyone loved to hate.
Sometimes I just thought people were jealous of their flawlessly manicured lawn.
Mikey laughs, "Well he better stay away from my goods," cupping the air in front of his nether regions he starts to laugh, his face burning red.
"Ok… well I'm sure your balls are safe, he stays with his dad in Chicago, so don't panic yet. Plus, it's more action than you can dream of!"

We both burst out laughing at this point, my stick falling to the ground, into a pile of wood.
 I hadn't felt this way in a long time.
A dark cloud had entered, the rain never came.
It hadn't been living, hadn't been dreaming.
"It's good to see you laugh."
It feels good.

My first official solo date with Kyle had arrived, and I had no one to tell other than Tasha who was my cover.
What a day it had been.

I lay in my bed worn from swimming.
Bubbly.
My belly tingles as I think back to it.
All I yearned for was perfection, and Kyle delivered.

He picked me up at the end of the road where I stashed my
bike in some underbrush, making sure it was well hidden.
I told my father, who would be at work for the day that I was
going to Tasha's and we had some plans around town, maybe
catching a movie.
She was also going up to the lake with Dean, so in the worst-
case scenario if he found out I was at the lake she would be my
alibi.
I could tell that he found it odd when I threw the bike in the
shrubbery and checked it twice, but I didn't care to explain,
and Kyle didn't pry.
"You look beautiful," he had stated boldly as he set the car in
drive at the top of the hill that overlooks the lake, a murky
puddle of mud water.
The man had little reservation, and a world of confidence as
he looked over at me, taking me all in.

I had certainly tried to look my best, shaved every inch of my
body, and even spritzed extra perfume.
"Like stunning Laurel," he adds.
The strongest part was how authentic his awe of me was.
He truly found me gorgeous, and I knew that.
The lake was packed, a popular hangout spot for youth and
adults alike, today was no different.
Groups of teens littered the less than picturesque sand line of
the man-made beaches.
It had been an old junkyard at one point.
Owned by an even older man.

When he passed, the city had bought the land from the family,
dumped the litter in another junkyard, filled it with water, and
began charging five bucks a car per day. To cover the cost of
maintaining the land and shorelines.

The scenery hadn't changed much as far as the trash went and the fee paid certainly didn't seem to be going towards waste management.
The sand was overcome with it.
Grains of crushed rock littered with cans and bottles of low-alcohol beer that everyone seemed to be nursing and old candy bar wrappers.
The red and blue labels were like a badge of honor, or dishonor depending on how many one may guzzle throughout the day.
No one tried to hide it.
Not the booze, nor the cigarettes that had been swiped from the purses of unsuspecting parents, here in the summer months everyone felt free to do as they pleased, and I felt it too, knowing that it was unlikely any cops would venture this way given the road conditions.
I couldn't help but smirk at a group of bottle blondes all smoking in a circle, not one of them seemingly confident in their ability to handle the red-hot phalluses.
Rather, they were just holding it in their mouths momentarily then making a show of seductively blowing it into the air to impress the guys.
None reached their lungs.
Smoking was not going to cause cancer in their case.

The boys didn't seem to mind and were drawn to the flock, their feathers ruffled like a pack of male peacocks waiting to mate.
Scratch the reproduction goal, they want all the fun and hopefully none of the consequences.
We had pulled up to a small hill far away from the group of partiers.
Trees had surrounded us on every side except the one that held the dark waters of the lake that Tasha and Dean were probably already making out in.
"Is this spot alright?" Kyle questioned, his hair falling over his eyes, arms clad with towels and bags.

We had set up three large towels across the small patch of sand right beyond the grassy hill, a couple of books thrown across them.
It was perfect.

A hot day, good conversation followed by a good book, and Kyle's arms wrapped around me.
Eventually, I dozed off in them and dreamt of Kyle.
His kiss, his touch, his hands clasped along my waist as he pulled me to him, and when I awoke, I was in that dream.
The almost man was holding onto me tightly, my ear pressed to his chest, his hands moving through my hair, combing out the knots gently, only returning from the end of the strands to massage my scalp.
I had laid there for a long while enjoying the music of his life, as it rhythmically played.
Then the song was gone, and he hovered above me, his lips lazily kissing a trail to my collar starting right at my navel.
Still unsure of whether I was truly awake, I wrapped my arms around his neck and brought his mouth to mine unabashed.
Then and only then did I know it was real as his mouth yielded to mine, opening and sharing.
I shudder at the memory.
He is lilac; a first love.
He fills me and yet leaves me weightless.
I pull the memory back; recall how I had pulled him close and allowed myself a moment of freedom.
The freedom to take it all in.
Tactile.
Warm air. Rough sands sticking to newly exposed flesh.
Hands coarse. Guiding me. Guiding me to holy parts.
I had not resisted.
My cheeks remained pale. No room for coy.
Gathering wetness filling and seeping from my core, his knee pressed and twisting gently, spreading it beneath the flimsy bottom of my suit.
All fear was swept away like a wave gathering debris and pushing it out to sea.

We spent the rest of the afternoon soaking our feet from the
dock, a comfortable silence sat between us, both of us
comfortable and relieved of any stress we had come with.
We didn't need words.
Not when we had a view.
Not when we have tension and matching energy.
We had lingered in momentary perfection.

Mikey

What I saw at the lake that day would have my father burning
red as coal.
Perhaps she wasn't as innocent as she seemed.
No one ever is.
Especially not Laurel.
I had put her on a pedestal.
Had not realized how little self-respect she truly had.

His mouth was on hers, hands creeping beneath her swimsuit
top, and slowly untying it, until her breasts were free.
Fingers toying with the material that covered her most private
parts next, dipping and seeking.
Slowly at first, then gently picking up speed.
I had to turn in shame and head back to the spot we had
established for ourselves.

Meanwhile, Corey would spend the rest of the day teasing me
about Laurel being easy after he also caught a glimpse.
I wanted to deck him in that big mouth, but I was too busy
trying to impress Gale while simultaneously ignoring my
sister who had no idea I was also at the lake.
With any luck, she would stay oblivious to what I had seen.
I'm not sure I want to embarrass her even though I would love
to embarrass him I can't, and I couldn't stop sneaking peeks.
Their acts bother me, even now.
So public. So brazen. I just wanted it to stop.
Wanted his hands off her.
I would get my wish, but not without a price.
Satisfaction, trembling satisfaction.

Just when I think it's over her hands meet him and help him find his own relief.
It was only natural, they were doing exactly what I did with Gale, but I hate knowing my sister wants that, wants sex.

Laurel

The ride home is freeing, windows down, summer heat pouring in. The pines zoomed past the windows, the smell of fire from barbecues, and fire pits galore in the air.
We talk about everything and nothing all at once.
That was the beauty of being with Kyle.
The simplicity. The easy conversation. The happy silence.
I feel at ease with him.
Being with him is simple, the only complicating factor being my father, whose feelings for me were murky at best, and I was lost in the silt and muck.

Mikey

Church.
Rachel and my father cling to every word, applaud when they must, and give generously to the clinking plastic buckets that are passed around.
Hebrews 4:16 is the lesson of the day.
Pray and you will receive.
With a twist.
"The answer to our prayers isn't always what we expect. It doesn't always come in a neat little bow," the assistant pastor preaches in jeans as if to try to make the house of God more casual.
"Praying for a million dollars isn't going to work," he jokes.
"Or perhaps it will, but God will grant you what you ask for through hard work and dedication. The point is God doesn't just give because we ask. He makes us work and toil. We also must consider that sometimes God hears us, but our timing isn't right."
I zone out for a while glancing over at Laurel who seems uncomfortable, smashed between my father and me.

"Sometimes we feel like we can't hear God, or that he can't hear us, let me assure you he can hear you just fine, but your sin is standing in the way of your relationship with God!"

Laurel

My sin had stained me crimson red.
If there is a God, then what my father and I do must truly interrupt the air between us.
It clogs up the line.
A busy tone on his end.
Sin. Sin.
I am tarnished by it.

But how do I ask God to save me from my sin, and fix me when it stands in the way, a boulder on a narrow path, and he sits on the other side?
I don't see a way through.
Am I damned?
A damaged woman who would spend all eternity dancing among coals, chained to a pit whilst demons use me and mock me?
Would I be made to lie in a lake of fire?
Might I roast on a spit like a stuffed boar?
Or would my punishment be a great nothingness, a numb so deep and overwhelming that it consumes itself with agony?
Is this how Eve felt when she ate the apple?

Cheapened

Deceived

Mikey

The air is tense in the house.
He had seemed so happy until Rachel seemingly let him down.
Canceled a big event she was supposed to go to with him.
Work came first.
It killed him to know she was seemingly abandoning him, and what was clear was that the man could not take any more abandonment.
Not after Mom.
Not after the way she left him.

All morning he grumbled around the house, fixing things that didn't really need fixing.
A buzzing coming from the fridge.
It had been there for years.
A creaky floorboard that he could not fix without dismantling the entire room.
The wobbly washer.
I wish he was at work.
Was sick of hearing the restless pacing of a man who had nothing.
I want to shake him.
Tell him to quit brooding like some petulant, tantrum-ridden child.
I would never.
I had to become a ghost.
I make a few calls and disappear.

Laurel

Daddy was drunk.
The kind that makes you stumble around the house aimlessly.
The kind that makes you wallow in self-pity.

They had been arguing all morning.
But Rachel had put her foot down.
She had to go. This was work.
Big case two counties over.
A man accused of beating his wife into a coma.
The accused didn't speak a lick of English.
Cue Rachel.
Cue Daddy's insecurities.
Cue a last-minute cancellation.

His brain was probably full of questions.
Was he enough?
Was she *really* coming back?
How could he heal the pain he felt?
Didn't she care?
Didn't she know how important this was?
Sheriff of the Year.
My father.

If only they could see him now, stumbling around, knocking
frames off the wall.
Grumbling nonsense.
Mikey is out and I am alone.
I had tried to make my escape to no avail.
Natasha was out of town visiting her aunt in Chicago. She had
left just after our trip to the lake. Kyle was on a hunting trip
with Dean and his father, and Fiona who was a good backup
takes turns between her divorced parents.
I don't have many friends to choose from.
I am so vulnerable.
Still exhausted from my Friday at the lake.
Sunburnt.
Mind in a haze.
My brain is still stuck on one station.
Plus, my back hurts, deep cramps piercing along my kidneys,
and I feel bloated, my breasts aching and heavy.
I know what is coming again. I'm not sure I can tolerate this
every month.

I was alone, shipwrecked, with predators circling beneath.
There was blood in the water.
Then comes the literal blood.
My period, making its entrance in full force.
She had seemed to me like a punishment the first time, or at least the idea that I bled because of Eve had been drilled into my head.
Today, I welcome her. She represents safety.
Every gut-wrenching cramp, every crimson drop, every pain tells me that he hadn't irreparably damaged me.

Last night he had been on edge and tonight he was fuming.
I can read him like a poorly written book.
He had pulled an extra shift, cruising for any action he could find; kids tagging buildings, jaywalkers, parties to break up, basically any excuse to project his irritability outwards.
Tonight, his feelings are murky, clear eyes with a sandy bottom that swirls violently with the copious amount of drink.
The Crux of whether to act or not is the only thing we share tonight.
He has descended and embraced his darkness now because no one will stop him.

I see the flicker of anger in his eye at dinner, the way he stabbed his fork into the roast he had instructed me to put on, the way he curled his sneer over the carrots that had not been cooked thoroughly.
I sit across from him, clothed in silence, trying to keep his attention off me.
My fork remains busy, shifting my food from one end to another, stress robbing me of my appetite.
"Mikey still at Corey's?" He grunts, taking a swig from his Glencairn crystal glass.
He had once explained that the shape of the glass was ideal for someone learning to swirl their whiskey.
That was back when he only drank with friends.
"What does swirling do?" I had asked back then, sweet and curious, drawn to anything my father did.

"Releases the aroma."
I remember him allowing me to inhale from his glass.
How did something that looked so sweet sting so harshly?
It reminded me of the forest, deep woods, and pines, the
heaviness of a fading campfire, and something sweet that I
can't seem to pinpoint with a simple sniff.
As if he can read my mind, he does just that, a drop spilling
over the rim onto the table, before downing the rest of the
glass, his third tonight.
Treading in dangerous waters.
"I don't know," I muttered, wishing I had a better answer for
him, as if it would calm him.
He scoffs, clearly annoyed at the lack of conversation. I just
don't know what to say.
I make an effort with the meal, pressing a carrot to my lips and
slowly nibbling the sweet end, fighting the urge to gag as I hit
the crunchy core.
"Can I be excused?" I ask meekly, already knowing the
answer, yet hoping that the submissiveness in my voice may
motivate him to let me go up to bed and far away from him.
Dad drops his fork with a clink and sneers, ignoring my
words.
I don't dare move.
Won't give the predator a chance to pounce.

Dad gets up, chair scratching against the wooden floors, and
pours himself another glass from a half-empty bottle.
No ice this time.
Neat.
That's what the pour is called.
"You know why we are having dinner alone, Laurel?" he asks,
plopping back into his chair.
"No."
I can sense that this is a trap, one he easily leads me to.
He drains the glass with lightning speed this time.
Up again.
This time he doesn't return to his spot, opting to stand next to
my chair, arm settling along the spine.

"It's because Rachel doesn't seem to understand how important tomorrow is to me. But you don't?"
His fingers grip the back of my chair hard now.
"I do."
Every muscle in my body contracts with nervousness.
"I have worked so hard for this Laurel."

I reach for my glass, inhale the warm water, trying to stifle the desert growing in the back of my throat, the ringing in my ears. I'm not afraid, I feel bad for him and it's making me ill.
"I know dad, and I am proud of you."
A long moment of silence, his hand now running through my hair.
I become like a sculpture.
He bends his head down. I can feel the bristles of his chin against my ear.
Inhaling deeply, my scent enters him and fills him with something animalistic.
There is greed in his tone. Pheromones tearing him apart.
"Well then, you will have to be a good daughter. Cheer me on like Rachel would."
I nod yes, his breath tickling the hair behind my neck, hand moving down to my collarbone.
"I will dad," I promise.
He releases his grip, moves his hands from my chair, and takes a long swig from his glass, our eyes meeting, his rimmed red and bloodshot from the continuous flow of poison, mine uneasy.
"You know I love you?"
"I love you too, Dad," I reply without a hint of dishonesty because I do.
"Go get some sleep, Laurel," he chants picking at a loose carrot.
The words surprised me. Maybe he knows he is treading in dangerous waters.

He didn't have to tell me twice.
I shut my door, and then my eyes.
Not bothering to change.

In my childish mind, my bed will keep me safe, but my
primitive mind knows better.
Pile enough blankets to hide under and you're bulletproof
proof my inner child argues.
I chose to believe in my inner child.

Mikey

I get the hell out of that house and not a moment too soon.
I could see the flashes of intent in his eyes.
Booze that seeped from his pores before dinner even started.
Sire, I could've taken Laurel with me, but I doubt he would
have allowed it.
Packing a bag and heading straight to Corey's was on the
agenda.

Immediately, we cracked open warm beers that my dad kept
boxed in the garage. I had transported in my backpack, their
tops clinking the entire way down.

He wasn't going to notice given his preference of whiskey to
beer.
We probably won't end our sipping with beer.
Corey's dad is an alcoholic.
Lucky for us.
A functional one.
Lucky for Corey.

A politician that DC had chewed up and spit out.
Too high speed, they said. Burnt out, he accepted a local
position.
The city manager. Coordinating programs, and planning local
events. On the side he was fucking his secretary.

That part wasn't in his job description, but it didn't deter him.
That is not even the best part.
Corey found out that he was also sleeping with a coworker.
A cop...*he.*

Corey had come home from school sick, and his dad was bent over their kitchen table.

"My dad's a faggot I guess," he had informed me on our way to school in a hushed tone one morning, "Or at least half a faggot seeing as how he is also doing it with his secretary."

"Doesn't that make him bi?"

His dad had bought him a TV for his bedroom that night and asked him to keep things quiet.

So far, so good.

Corey's mother was none the wiser, and between her volunteer work at the hospital , and her career, she was too busy to notice her husband's nervous ticks and devious deviations.

Corey's dad says she's a frigid woman as if that somehow made the cheating ok.

"Men need to get off. It keeps our heads clear. That's what he told me. Can you believe that?"

I do.

Fluid.

Evolving, changing, and for most men it never fully fades.

It's always in the back of our minds, and often in the front.

Sex. Sex. Sex.

It's on my mind now.

I want to go see Gale and I tell Corey as much.

"I'll tell her to invite Charlotte."

That coaxes him off his sofa chair.

If he sits in it any longer, he might melt into the ugly patterned chaise. I for one will not sit around all night and watch it happen.

"Charlotte's a bitch."

He calls her a couple of other names while quickly getting himself ready to leave as if he had a chance with her.

"Yeah, but Gale says that Charlotte mentioned that she thinks you're hot, or some shit."

That perks him up, a too-thin smile crawling across his face.

Guess he doesn't hate her.

A quick shower later, he emerges patting his acid-washed jeans. They scream desperate. Worse is the ring forming in his pocket. "Just in case."

Eager.
Maybe too eager.

Laurel

I try desperately to sleep.
Tossing, I set my clock radio to my favorite station before slamming my lids shut.
Every creaking of the floor causes my eyelids to flutter with worried anticipation.
Below, glass shatters.
A broken man with his broken objects sitting alone in his kitchen.
Turning to face the light blue wall that I had found freedom in, I do something I had not done in years.
I pray. I pray, not because I'm afraid, I am not.
Praying for safety, for strength to tell him no. More than anything I pray that the blue of my wall will feel as freeing after he comes to me, as they do now.

He doesn't want to hurt me, he only wants to love me, and I want to let him, anything to make him better.
But he drains me, and I feel like I'm running on empty, with no pump in range. I'm not sure who I am calling out to.
I don't know if anyone can hear me.
I pray into the silence.
Cry out into the dark and unknown.
All unanswered.
Or maybe I just don't like the answer that God provides.

Mikey

Gale arrives before us.
Allegedly she pulled in at a quarter past eight, and is deeply annoyed that we're "late."

The hills are quiet tonight, except for the chirping crickets.
Annoyed as always at our tardiness, she half grunts a hello
toward Corey.
"Wishes he could fuck, needed to shower," I inform her
pointing to Corey whose cheeks have flushed to a deep red,
his elbow slamming into my ribs.
It takes my breath.

I finger the spot he had hit, the sting still radiating through
me.
Charlotte glares from behind Gale, her overly large breasts
and square waist flaunted by the checkerboard patterned
spandex dress.
"You didn't tell me he was coming," she bites through her
ruby lips, lined and filled to perfection.
Corey tells her to piss off.
This was off to a great start.
"Let's all just calm down and take a hit or something,"
nodding at Gale who I assume is holding and on board to get
these two quiet. I try to defuse the situation.
Nodding, she digs into her overly sized purse, retrieving a
pre-rolled joint, white with a puckered tip, quickly wrapped
around her puckered lips.
Everything is going to get better soon.

Laurel

I must have fallen asleep, although I can't pinpoint exactly
when.
Funny how it can be such a struggle to get to the edge, but the
fall is quickly forgotten until one's alarm screams out in the
morning.
A bright light fills the room, interrupting the safety of the
darkness I had worked so hard to hide in.
I don't jump.
Don't rub my eyes.
I look straight ahead, eyes on the wall at my side.

There is no confusion. I am focused.

I know what this is, and I know what I have to do.
I don't dare turn.
He is here and judging by his breathing he is angry and
seeking the ultimate comfort.
The way he kisses my neck reveals a ravenous appetite, one I
hadn't witnessed till now.
I continue to feign sleep.

Shallow breaths drizzle slowly from my lips, attempting to
convince him of my state.
He pulls away, anchored to the valley on my bed, causing it to
dip under his weight.
Contemplating a replay of our last interaction.
Or is it something more?
Plotting?
Working up the courage to commit such a heinous act?
I can hear his breath, raspy from the drink.
Can feel his arms turn me onto my back.
I can no longer pretend.
Sleep will have to wait.

His attack is quick.
Cyndi Lauper plays from my radio that he has dialed to full
volume in a half-assed attempt to cover any sounds that may
be produced.
The clock reads just past ten, teasing me that I would end my
day in such a wicked position.
I listen to the girlish voice, trying to ignore the way he moves
me.
I focus on her words.
Take them in.
Oh Daddy dear, you know you're still number one.
He is my number one.
"But girls, they wanna have fun," I mouth the words, praying
this would be the only song I would have to endure.

The ironic lyrics don't faze him. His brain is much too
muddled with a drink to even notice, his hands roughly

groping beneath my gown, curling around my pad-lined panties.
I tried to hide it, jumping to life for the first time since he entered, my hands pressed firmly on his.
He doesn't seem to mind and slurs as much, "A lil blood… nothing."
In one swift motion, he pulls the panties along with the pad out of his way, the wet top pressing against my inner thigh, hot and repulsive.
Humiliated, I shut my eyes tight.
Allow his body to command, and my own to obey.
"Look at me, Laurel."
Slurred commands that are barely coherent bleed from his covetous mouth.
Glossy eyes meet.
Small flecks of dark adorned in the deep emptiness.

I watch his every disgusting pleasure-filled grimace.
Heed his every desire.
All in hopes it will end.
But he had drunk too much, and keeps needing encouragement, and before long I am aching.
His hips bite into mine, clasping tightly like the mouth of a python, twisting and taking the air from my lungs.
A sick, feverish sweat falls over my frigid hide.
There were many songs.

My beacon of light.
My lighthouse in the storm had a faulty bulb.
Darkness.
Darkness I hadn't seen till tonight.
Or maybe I had just chosen not to see it.
I want his love.
No matter what form it takes.
Even when it leaves me bitter and hurt.
Shattered.

Mikey

Shattered.
That's how I feel right now.
I had expected it to be so much more.
Now, I am not saying that I was expecting movie-quality sex,
but I had expected some passion.
Maybe I was the only one who hadn't felt the passion.
Maybe I can't.
But I do feel something.
A deep break somewhere within me.

Gale and I fucked in her car.
Fast. Furious. Disappointing.
The climax was nothing to rave about, but it was there.
Then it isn't.
I didn't tell her it was my first time.
She would have overanalyzed my every move, or even worse
she would have rejected me.
When it's over, I toss the condom I had bummed off Corey
into a bush and sit by the small fire we had built.
I tell Corey I feel sick.
Too much beer, not enough weed.
He tells me that we can't go back to his place as drunk as we
are.
I know it's all bull, but I do not argue.
I was not about to interfere with the unmistakable chemistry
that had grown between Corey and Charlotte.

 Gale can't let me come back to hers in our state, either.
Her overly strict bible-thumping mom was most likely waiting
up, fingers frantically grazing her large rosary.
The woman practically lived in the church and brought it
home.
Saint Lucy.
I don't know much about the Catholics and their saints, but
my understanding is that she was some woman from Syracuse
who lost her life during the persecution of the Christians.
Then her name got spread around Rome or something.
Gale's mom had told us once when Gale was driving her to
church, and I was bumming a ride to work.

Laurel

I can sleep now.
Be vulnerable now.
The clock flashes after midnight.
Happy birthday.

I am fifteen now and feel less of a woman than I did at
fourteen.

Mikey

It started as a whimper.
The shuffling of steps upstairs.
Similar to that of a small puppy.
A sound I had heard many times before.
When Jelly had her pups beneath the porch.
She had been so anxious to greet them.
The proud new mom.
Experience ripped from her teat as the rat-like babes suckled.
Warmth had been all they knew until they were tossed into
the cold depths.
Murky waters that lay in the forest.
Just a short walk behind our bungalow.
It was the darkness that dwelled beneath.
My release.

Laurel had seen.
Not long after Mom died.
All she could do was weep and yell at me to stop.
Beneath the deciduous tree, our eyes met in shared shame.
She knew, yes, she knew even then.
Saw my darkness.
A darkness we shared, but one she had not familiarized
herself with.
Not yet.

Such ravenous carnage would allow the darkness to seep.
Tonight, my darkness returns.
Shame-driven darkness.
Disappointment granted to me from an unrealistic expectation
of what sex was going to be like.
Unannounced, I make my way home and up the stairs, where
Jelly lays quietly.
The squeaking of the bed frame, although subtle, is present.
The absence of her voice is unsurprising.
What voice?
Behind the door was just what I had expected.
The acts were no longer elementary.
No more gentle kisses.
No more lapping of the tongue.
No more direction.
Just need. His need.

My eyes fixate on the interaction between the two bodies.
Her breasts are bare and riddled with evidence of predation.
Red marks forming, waiting to erupt in various older pools of
purples and blues.
Her body opened around him, engulfing.
One act.
Two bodies. Two states.

Hers conquered his plundering.
His body; rough and beaten by the sun and the teasing of age.
Hers lies below, soft and beaten down by the hands of a man.
She is hairless except for the golden silk that womanhood had
sprung abundantly.
Silk is all but lost in the thick forest of prickly pine.
The smell of iron and rye mash tangles in the air, clinging in
the humidity, a damp Venetian red tints their interaction.
What I witnessed should have horrified me.
Made my stomach churn.
But it does nothing.
I feel strangely little.
Maybe because I knew.
Knew it would come to this.

Why fret over something I cannot fix?
My eye pulls away from cracking the door before either
notices.

Laurel

It doesn't hurt anymore. At least not physically.
That is a woman's burden.

Mikey

Sex is confusing.
I had expected so much more.
I have had better orgasms masturbating.
Thought I was going to have a hard time holding out.
None of that happened.
No fireworks.
No passionate post-coitus kissing.
No proclamations of love.

Laurel

Sex is confusing.
What he does makes him sick. But he still wants it.
Like a dog returning to its own vomit.

The drive was long and silent.
I spent the trip feigning sleep.
Daddy spent it guzzling coffee and popping pain pills.
The night's excursions had left his head beating as if he had
placed it between two large gold-plated cymbals.
His obvious discomfort brought me some satisfaction.

Was I sick?
My own pain was not on his mind.
Was he sick?

...

The big day.

The day Daddy finally got the recognition he so deserved, or
so he thought.
He plays it up.

We arrive a half hour early, the room abuzz in a sea of
uniformed officers.
Dark blues and beige.
Daddy shaking everyone's hand, fake booming laugh filling
the room.
His charisma and charm demonstrate obvious worth.
I stood among the crowd, watched the room move, the small
crowd conversing.
My body is at a standstill.
My mind is at war.
My soul caught some between dutiful silence and a rebellion.
A blood-curdling scream.
A moment of unadulterated rage
I teeter.

I try hard to smile, but my body won't let me.
My father's stone face watches on as our eyes meet, changing
quickly as he accepts his award.
A flip switch.
His speech begins. It's all talk.
Muffled. Blurred. I hear none of it.
Deep eyes fixate on the lack of a smile on my face as he
speaks.
"My beautiful daughter."
All eyes on me.
Still, I couldn't smile.
He would scold me after.
Pull me into a back room.

"This is a big day for me, and I need your support. I don't
want to see anything but a smile on your lips for the rest of the
day," squeezing me into a strange hug, he commands my
participation.
Tightly enough that I could feel the warmth return when he
released a smile on his face.

"I just need my best girl there for me."
Smiling, "I'm right here."
I smiled. Didn't stop.
Wouldn't want anyone to think something was wrong.
I smiled all the way to dinner.

There I gorged myself with an abundance of food.
Mashed potatoes, fried chicken, peach cobbler.
Southern buffet.
I didn't even like green beans.
I consumed like an animal; Daddy was too busy to see.
The food was tasteless, but somehow richer than anything I
had ever consumed.
Rich. Filling.
Filling the void.
Baseball-sized organ stretching to accommodate my pain.
Stretching to comfort the shame in my head, to silence that
sickening inner dialogue.
I smiled all the way home.

We stopped and had ice cream for my birthday.
Kissed him good night and told him I was proud and for a
moment when his eyes lit up, I almost felt bad for him.
I smiled.
I displayed happiness when there was no such thing in me.
My parted lips were a mirage. I'm nothing more than an
illusion.

Mikey

He hung his award up by the fireplace for all to see.
A man of the badge displaying yet another badge of honor.
Rachel came in glowing, her belly seemingly growing rounder
by the day.
She kissed him hard.
A kiss full of longing and hurt over their spat.
Never knowing where his mouth had been just the night
before, tight on my lips.

"I'm sorry I couldn't be there," she apologized, his hand
traveling to touch my future brother or sister.
"I missed you, babe. Both of you."
His hand was firm on their child.

I watched my sister look on.
I watched her smile.
Fake.
No pleasure in the stare.
Perhaps we were more alike than I ever imagined.
The major difference was she blended in to hide her true
emotions, anger, jealousy, and confusion.
I blended in to hide the absence.
Two complementary pieces to a puzzle.
Yin and yang.
Guanine and cytosine; strong and complimentary.

Laurel

AP math.
Second period.
Blue jeans and a white virginal blouse buttoned to the top.
Hair worn down and pushed back behind my ears.
Daddy's choice for my English report that afternoon.
Next to me sat Mikey, looking just as quaffed.
Not a hair out of place.
Not a sign that something was amiss.

I am the sheriff's daughter.
Dutiful. Obedient. Intelligent.
I will behave. Bring home straight A's.
I should not talk to boys. I will make curfew.
I am not to drink, curse, or smoke.
I am not to disobey.

Mikey

While Laurel was being burdened with a rule book of restrictions, I was free to move freely, so long as I stayed out of any noticeable trouble.

The only trouble I could sense was the trouble that brewed within.

Laurel wouldn't look at me.
Wouldn't linger alone with me.
She was growing distant, and I tried to gap the bridge consistently, but she pushed as I pulled.
I filled the lack of her with a new object of desire.
Well, at least an aesthetic desire.
Gale.
Gale with her honey-colored hair, finally void of box color, and fiercely moss-toned eyes.
Maybe I had been drawn to her because she looks a bit like my mother.
Like Laurel.
A poor dye job takes away from the resemblance.
Her ratty hair was almost red now.
What a shock that was when I saw her this morning.
It turns me off, but I need to get off.

Tonight, at the party I want to make up for my first time and pretend this was it, so I flaunt my worth.
Say all the words I know she wants to hear.
It proves easy. Maybe too simple.
Not the hunt I had hoped for.
How I craved that hunt.
How I wish I could have waited for the desire to pressurize to the point of eruption instead of going flat.

It doesn't take long to get Gale out of her costume.
Angel wings peeled to reveal supple breasts and a more sinister side.
Yet, the halo remains.
Sacrilegious.
The devil coursing through my cock.

Four beers in and she is straddling me on an old worn-out
loveseat hidden behind a cluster of trees.

The party is being held just yards away, the sounds of girls
squealing at failed attempts to flirt and the football team
encouraging the consumption of an unholy amount of liquor,
bustling in the background.
But that's a different world.
This is my world.
Gale's kisses are full of want rather than need.
Cotton candy puckered lips toy with mine, tasting cheap.
Acting cheap.
Those lips that drip with desire, "Let's fuck," she slurs.
Not graceful. Not a turn-on, but I will take it.
Her hands begin searching for more as she struggles with my
belt buckle.
No interest in any false professions of love.
No need to say those three words.
She yearns for control, and I allow her as much on the filthy
loveseat.
Not much love to go around.
Is this what normal sex was supposed to be like?
I didn't feel the excitement I had always heard about.
Didn't feel the rush.
Felt myself lose blood quickly.
Too young for such betrayal.

"Are you alright," she whispers, my body soft inside of hers,
skirt pushed up to her navel.
I hadn't even noticed myself entering.
I was so distracted.
So much for foreplay.
We lock eyes.
I stared deep into the moss, trying to force an attraction.
Those moss eyes. So similar.
So much like Laurel's.

Laurel, she makes my blood flow, thoughts of her heal me,
they help me feel safe, accepted.

Wanting to keep her safe made me feel strong.
"I'm fine just needed a second," I said wishing she would shut up and let nature take its course.
Her voice was only serving to disrupt my thoughts.
I hear the words come from my mouth and can sense how phony they sound.
She doesn't seem to notice though; her lips are far too concerned with the nape of my neck.
My name is on her lips as they travel to my jaw.
I sigh and she meets my pleasure with an equally lustful gaze.

I am ready now, she knows it, can feel me grow into her darkest caverns, like a column of stalagmite.
I don't dare pull away from her gaze as she begins to ride me vigorously, her thighs clenched around me.
Flashing, burning memories of what I had seen.
Scent, flowers, and iron, heavy in the room, small whimpers of hurt.
Gales's tongue is playing a record of pleasure, low groans followed by my name.
I erupt like a shield volcano, silently.
I hear Gale almost scream her own eruption.
Rhyolite calderas, loud, explosive, uncommon, at least at her young age.
This sensation was new for her, perhaps I had judged too quickly.
Maybe she really wants me.
Would it be so bad to be wanted?

I feel her pull away. Slump.
"That was nice", she half states and half questions.
So uncertain and young. Girlish.
I'm equally dumb.
I don't reply, trying to remain in the moment.
"Right?"
I nod, "The best."
Liar.

Laurel

Liar.
Imprisoned in a state of lying.
Not lying! Withholding.
Were they really that different?
Liar. Lying for him.
Physically and mentally.
I lose a little piece of me every time he enters my body, not
that I had much of an identity to begin with.
I had no idea who I was unless it was dictated by another.

So I continue down my path of dishonesty.
Allow myself to wear the mask.
To my teachers I am a good student; quiet and dutiful.
To my brother, a friend and sometimes rival.
To Daddy, I am his false sense of control.
Malleable.
Something he can lord over.

But if you ask me who I thought I was I simply regurgitate like
a well-trained cockatoo.
Laurel Catherine Wyatt.
Born in June, the youngest of her twin pairing.
A picture of a fairly pretty girl.
A big smile.
You would think she was so happy.
After all, it's what everyone says she is.
Happy.
I am happy.
So when people ask, I lie.
The question that has only one appropriate answer?

Even with Kyle, I have to hide, and I hate myself for it.
My mask is paper thin, yet somehow, he is the only one who
sees past the veneer.
Still, I lie.
It hurts so much to lie.
I want to scream.
Tell the world. Expose the truth.

But that would force honesty.
To tell the world that I am in fact not happy.
That I feel like I am in hell.
I'm not in hell, not in his domain, but while hell may be the devil's domain Earth is his playground.

Mikey

I guess I had felt something.
Although, it truly was not the right thing to feel.
It was a start. It was something.

Laurel

I am totally his.
He is the moon, and I am the sun.
Get too close and I will burn you up.
Suck you dry.
I am needy.
A desperate thirst to quench.
I am the sea.
He is my moon, always shifting my tides.
In control of me.
Never of himself.
Waxing. Waning.
Cycling exhaustion.
Eclipsing into someone new.
Hot. Cold.
Stormy. Brewing.

Tonight I find the storm momentarily pacified.
I allow substances that drive my father's darkness to touch my lips.
I let it find its way to my stomach.
Filter through my liver.
I am poisoning my body.
Who knew poison would make me feel this good?
Tonight, I want to disappear.
I don't want to be Laurel, at least not the sweet one.

Tonight, I want to find my darkness.
Dad wouldn't approve.
Wouldn't approve of my lies.
"Natasha's house," I had told him as I planted a dutiful kiss
on his stubbly cheek.
Rachel had smiled at what she perceived to be daughterly
love.
Natasha's sister Ray, who was back from college for a visit,
promised to cover for us.
"I remember when I used to party up there. Good times," she
had slurred, popping the top off another beer.
Like father, like daughter.
"Just don't do anything dumb, I'll come pick ya up if ya
need," she offers downing the frothy alcohol.
I nodded, knowing full well that she was not driving
anywhere, and we wouldn't call her for a ride.
"Thanks," I smiled at her, eyes asking for a taste.
She popped a top and handed me an icy beer, "Just don't get
too crazy."
Tasha stepped out, not a hair out of place.
A little rebellion, a taste of chaos was on the menu.
A false sense of confidence was found in the bottle or maybe it
was a sense of power I was experiencing.
Like father, like daughter.
The woods are moving now and my coordination fades with
each drop.
"Cheers," Natasha offers, Dean's arms around her shoulders,
long pianist fingers lingering dangerously close to her pushed-
up cleavage.
She giggles and turns to face him, lips meeting without
hesitation.
Their tongues dart and fight like opposing jousters.
Kyle is on my right nursing a beer, a black hat thrown over his
hair, his fingers nervously meeting mine in the warmth of my
pocket.
They dance.
The type of dance that two nervous middle schoolers dance.
Yearning for closeness, yet not daring to take it.
Complete lack of coordination.

I watch as Dean lights something, the red glow catching my eye.
Excitement fills me and I put a stop to our dance, gripping Kyle's fingers between mine.
My inner child bounded with excitement at the thought of taking part in such devious acts.
"Give me a toke", she demands pulling at the base of the joint, her smooth ebony skin in beautiful contrast with the ivory paper.
Nails long and manicured.
Stiletto styled, with a black and purple crackled design.
She takes a long drag as if it were nothing.
Clearly used to this.
The smoke is so sweet, so thick, clouding the space between us.
Natasha blows it out seductively and it falls all milky into the night.
Cream swirling into a dark roast cutting through the bitter bite.
I can barely contain my desire to experiment anymore.
"Can I?"
My friend looks at me with her feline eyes for a moment only to find herself distracted by the sudden introduction of music to the party.
Someone had turned their radio on, a soft classic rock ballad traveling through the air.
"Little goody two shoes wants a hit?"
Dean teases me, taking his hit.
I blushed, unsure of how to answer, embarrassed that he was putting me on the spot, pointing out my virgin state.
"Just let her try," Kyle chimes, extending his hand.
He wraps his lips around the joint and takes a long drag, "like this."
I watch him hold it in for a long while, I am surprised the sheer thickness of the smoke hasn't caused him to choke.
Slowly he releases it along with a small cough, then reaches his lungs. "Make sure to hold it a little and cough, it helps you get higher," he instructs as I take hold of the joint, careful not to burn myself on the red-hot cherry.

I am suddenly nervous, but I don't dare let anyone know and I boldly take a deep drag, perhaps too deep and I immediately cough it all out.
It doesn't hinder the effect and quickly I feel it fill me.
Weightless and warm.
I want more.
"Slow down," Natasha cautions me as she takes another drag of her own like it's nothing.
"Hypocrite."
"Cocky much," she teases," I'm just trying to be a good friend and here you are going all Tommy Chong on me."
"You made me this way," I shoot back, a little spark of excitement coming through.
I want more, I need more.
"You want some more?"
Kyle's voice tickles my ear, his breath is intoxicating, his touch almost unbearable as if he reads my mind.
His touch is new.
There is heaviness and implication in the way his hand runs circles in my hair.
Or maybe I'm just high.
"Laurel?"
I nod.
I'm not in my right mind, and maybe that's how I'm meant to be.
Everything is so effortless.
Everything has its place.
My place is here, in the cold woods, with his lips pressing against mine.
I had wanted more; he hadn't disappointed me as the slow trickling of smoke flows from his mouth to mine.
I didn't cough this time.
I accept.
I inhale him.
Inhale comfort.
Smoke.
And where there is smoke there is fire.
He had set it, and I was consumed by the licking flames.
I am tingling all over.

A warm buzz runs from my nose to my toes.
Blood is coursing below, pooling in the space between my wobbling thighs.
The alcohol was winning.
I want someone to touch me.
Do things to me that should make me feel ashamed.
Flesh on flesh.
Tonight, I want Kyle.
His body inside of mine.
I need him to repeat what we did on the beach, but this time I don't want it to stop, not until we find the place where I end.
I am fueled by a deadly concoction of grass, booze, hormones, and teenage angst.
Recipe for disaster. Recipe for freedom.
Freeing. So freeing.
Kyle walks me to his car and buckles me in, my neck sways as he pulls out of the crammed spot between a black Jeep and a cherry red Hyundai Excel.
The little tree wobbles around his mirror, the scent completely drained.
"Ya know you're not supposed to pull the tree all the way out," I slur. "the package."
"I didn't know that actually," he giggles, pulling off the withered faux tree.
"It says so…the packaging."
My knees stick to my chest childishly, the car spinning to leave.

"Got to get you home," he mutters as he fumbles with the dials on the radio, finally he settles on Soft Cell.
Tainted love.
"No, can't," I groan knowing full well even in my current state of stupidity and inebriation that home is not an option.
"You're wasted Laurel, you need to get some rest…sober up."
He turns off the dirt road onto the pavement, the sudden smoothness of the road bringing me a strange sense of pleasure.
For a moment I forgot what was going on, only to be reminded by his husky voice.

"Laur, you got to go sleep it off somewhere."
"Please, not my house," I beg suddenly, feeling tears well up in my eyes.
I don't know if it's the booze, or the fear, or a combination of both.
My stomach churns painfully.
Kyle stops at a light, a candy apple glow shining across his dimples.
Dimples that only appear when he smiles.
Why is he smiling?
"Have you ever been drunk before?"
I shake my head no, the weight pulling it forward.
Did my hair get heavier?
Did my head get heavier?
Granny Smith replaces the red.
"It's alright, the first time I got drunk I puked all over the back of Nick Grooven's son's car. He had to make up some bullshit excuse about what happened and with a raging hangover I had to clean it all up the next morning."
He catches me smiling at this.
"I almost threw up again."
He drives forward slowly and pulls into a gas station parking it in front of pump two.
"When I get back, I need an answer, Laurel," he states, allowing the door to meet the clasp.
I stare at the neon lights that reflect in the store windows.
They scream "Tops" in flashing green.
The local strip club.
Tops and bottoms.
Not very creative, but who needs creativity when you have sex?
Momentarily distracted, my mind flips back to panic mode.
I know where I should go and know where I couldn't go.
Worse yet, I know where I want to go.
"Where do you want me to take you?" Kyle asks, plopping back down on the driver's side, a bag of sour straw candy in his lap.
He peels the package open and hands me a raspberry stick, grinding the tip with my front tooth.

I know the answer, maybe he does too.
I think he wants to hear me say it.
He would be alone, his mom working night shifts.
I become nervous suddenly, my feet tingling, my ears ringing.
It robs me of my voice.
Did I dare be so brazen?
"I will take you wherever you need me to," Kyle says, running his fingers through his hair.
If only he knew how far I wanted him to take me.
"I can't be home."
"Can't go home?"
I nod and try to swallow.
My mouth is dry, booze and old mint gum battling between my teeth.
The raspberry candy conquers.
"You could uh… you could come to mine," he offers his hand gently lowering the radio before letting it touch me.
His hand is on mine now, he holds it tight.
"Just till you're sober, then I'll take you to Natasha's unless you want me to take you to hers now."
I know I should go to Natasha's; I know it's the safest option.
To crawl into her bed and sleep until she returned in the morning.
Her hair would be frazzled, earth-toned skin glowing from a night of teenage passion.
I don't respond right away.
I am torn, suddenly filled with anxiety, yet simultaneously overwhelmed by desire.
Then I say it, I dare agree.
Kyle puts the car into drive and heads down main.
While daddy slept tonight, he would never know I was just at the other end of the block.
Kyle's room is just as I had imagined it in its more grown-up state.
Clean, uncommon for a guy his age.
The comforters are dark and blemish-free. There is no clutter.
A minimalist where it counts.
The last time I was here we were kids; the room was far more cluttered then.

The wall had been painted green.
A strip of wallpaper had tracked the room, race cars darting across the sheet.
It's all so different now.
In the corner is a keyboard.
The walls are bare except for two expensively framed posters, hung with a nail.
Not a thumbtack in sight.
He would cringe to see the torn corners that had been repeatedly re-pinned on my walls.
Pink Floyd and The Offspring.
The curtains are drawn, the light dimmed, almost as if he was eternally hosting.
A small picture of his dad hangs on the wall across from his bed.
He smiles, holding a young Kyle on his shoulders.
Two smiles. Two sets of dimples.
I stand nervously despite the drink, feet aching in the shoes I had unwisely settled on.
"l can get you some water" he offers, standing just as nervously, shoulders tense.
Was I just imagining the tension?
There was a certain implication, being in his room and all.
What have I gotten myself into?
"I have some shirts and stuff that you can change into if you want," he points weakly to a gray three-door dresser.
There is definite tension in his gaze, but there is also hunger.
We both understand we shouldn't be here.
I reach in and grab a large shirt and flannel bottoms.
Plop them on the dresser not knowing if it's appropriate to strip down in his room.
He senses this and steps out to give me privacy, trying to play it cool.
What am I doing?
The reality is sinking in.
If dad finds out it would be over.
He would never let me go out again outside of school.
I suddenly feel the urge to run, but my lust is paralyzing.
Kyle comes back in, a water bottle in his left hand.

The water shifts slightly in the container as he steps up to me.
Is he trembling?
"I forgot a towel," muttering slowly, his words seem full.
I look at him, he looks at me.
I feel something and I am sure that he feels it too.
Not the kind that paralyzes.
Not the kind I feel when Daddy takes me.
No, it's the kind of lust I feel when I crave him.
When he truly feels me.
The kind that makes me sick.
I fear pleasure, fear desire.
My mind is racing. Rushing.
The uncontrolled waters of a raging river.
Quickly, I twist the cap of the bottle and drink greedily, setting
the crunching plastic on the dresser.
There is nothing left to distract us, and I surprise myself by
kissing him, causing a small jolt as my lips crash into his
without another moment's hesitation.
My body is pushing into his, feverishly, hungrily.
Impatiently, I wrap my hands around his head and traverse
the room to the bed, using what little weight I have to take
control.
Control.
Something I had never felt before.
Why does it feel so good?
Why am I finding such pleasure in his helplessness?
Swiftly and without much thought I hook my fingers under
his shirt and lift it over his head, his skin speckled with
evidence of the cold.
A small brown birthmark sits at the top of his chest, flat,
similar to a paint spatter.
I destroy all evidence of the harsh cold with a litany of
uncoordinated kisses, none planned, all needy.
I feel his fingers mimic mine, the buttons of my shirt slowly
opening, circular pieces of plastic escaping from the cotton
grasp.
Each twist of his finger allowed chilly air to bite into my
flushed skin, a reddish glow running along my cheeks.

I won't stop kissing him, I don't want his lips anywhere but tending to mine.

I am out of control, filled with a warmth I have never felt before, my beast making its appearance.

My shirt is on the floor now, my bra unclasped, cups slowly peeled away, and I don't know if it's the booze or the grass, but my body has become like the Amazon.

A pheromone-ridden dew glistens; it reflects off my blushing nipples.

It becomes intertwined with Kyle's spittle.

I reach down in a rush and run my hands between us and onto his thigh, I can feel his erection digging against the fabric of his jeans.

Leg twitches as I stroke it with my longest nail.

Then I feel his grip, his hand holding mine firmly.

It changes. He changes.

His kisses are not as eager, they are solemn and sporadic.

His lips no longer danced along mine.

Suddenly, I am absent from his warm hold.

His nose nuzzling against the crook of my neck, fingers wrapped around my waist.

They hook beneath my thighs, and he holds tightly "Laurel, I know I'm going to hate myself in the morning for saying this, but maybe we should wait," he whispers between shaky breaths.

He is still holding on to me, still hard, still filled with wild teenage lust.

Despite his lustful state, he says it again, words like a searing knife, "Wait. Laurel, wait."

Reasonable.

My mind was unaware of the loving place his rejection was coming from.

Wasn't I enough?

Suddenly I am overwhelmed, a tear falls down my face.

Had I done something wrong?

"Please Kyle, touch me," I plead, kissing him once more, the saltiness of my confusion mixing into the kiss.

He resists pulling away, placing his hands between us now almost as if to shield himself.

"Laurel we can't do this," he whispers, eyes shut as if staring at me might turn him to stone.

"Why not?"

His shoulders tense, hand on mine, "For starters you're drunk. I shouldn't have let it get this far, and I am so sorry for that," he tries to continue but I unreasonably cut him off, humiliated.

"And what?"

I want to cry.

Could he not feel how much I needed him?

Had I not done enough?

In an effort to show him, I move his hand to my breasts, his resistance beginning to melt away, as I hold it there firmly, I need this. I kiss him again, "We can do whatever you want, Kyle."

His hands V, nipples protruding between his pointer and middle.

"Anything," I remind him, using the only weapon I hold, his weakness, the lust of man.

We sit, heavily breathing as one for a long while.

I had conquered, his hands massaging the space above my soul.

His soul is in a torn state, lust over decency.

Decency.

From a decent man.

He jerks away as if I made fire from me, latching onto my legs and rolling me off.

Death roll.

When our eyes meet all, I see is a look of absolute bewilderment spread across his brow.

"Laurel, no," he groans, hovering just above me.

"It's not just that you're drunk, Laurel."

I sit up, lean against his wall, arms crossed as if I was being punished, like a petulant little child.

"I want you so badly Laurel, I do… Please trust that I'm being honest."

Throwing my hands up I protest, "I'm right here Kyle!"

He was trying to comfort me despite everything, his hand on my cheek, "Not like this, that's not who I am. That I would take advantage of you. I don't want it to be like this, no matter how much I want you… and I do want you."
Right again.
He deserves so much more, that much is painfully clear right now.
"I need this," I repeat as if it may sway him.
I'm sobbing now, but I can't stop. I want to feel good.
There's a terrifying need, and want him for him driving me, lacing my voice.
He kisses my forehead, "I can sleep on the couch, and you can sleep it off here, we can talk in the morning, and I will drive you to Tasha's early."
I didn't want him to go, know what I need, and what I need is to know.
To know what sex could be.

I shake my head and wipe away a tear I had not given permission to fall.
He brushes it away with his thumb.
"I think I'm going to go."
The tantamount need for him to both tug me back and let me go leaves me chaotic.
I don't know what I want.
Crawling off the bed, the soft mattress makes it difficult, causing me to fumble, adding to my humiliation.
Stupidly, I had been vulnerable, and he had rejected me, and I had never been rejected before.
Had never wanted something so much.
Before he can complain my shirt is over my head, being pulled down to cover me, nipples sensitively grazing along the fabric.
"Laurel come on, let's lay down."
"No," I snapped, jumping out of his bed.

I see the pain in his eyes, see the strength, the restraint, and yet I don't care, I want out.
Don't care that he was doing the right thing.
Don't care that I am hurting him.

That he was being a man.
Like a tantrum-ridden child, I storm off into the night.

Mikey

All I had ever wanted was to be wanted.
Gale wanted me tonight.
It is not enough. It is never enough.
It must be on my terms. My terms.
I am not sure exactly what they are.

Laurel

All I had ever wanted was to be unwanted.
I prayed. Wished on a shooting star.
To be rejected. To be untouched.
Guess wishes do come true, just not on our schedule.
I feel the storm brewing, or maybe it has never left.
Tonight, I had become caught up in the winds.
Or maybe I had been there the whole time.
Deceived by the eye.
False calamity.

...

After I stormed off, I grew more and more disoriented, a mix
of my emotions and the chemicals mingling.
I stumbled around unsure where to go, or what to do.
Why had I been so stupid?
What I knew for certain was home was not an option.
The only choice I had was to make my way the three miles
back to Natasha's.
I stumble, and my head begins to ache.
Maybe I had acted childishly.
It wasn't a maybe.
Kyle was right, he was always right.
Right for me. Right about me.
I am untouchable. Undeserving
He hadn't said those things and yet, I felt it.

The tears pour from the sky.
Then from my eyes.
They nurture the earth.
Cracked earth nurtured only by the violence of a storm.
When I wake up, I hear birds chirping.
Dew has fallen across the grass.
It's settled across my cold skin.
I am like ice, feet throbbing, hands bright red.
I sit up and stare straight into Natasha's basement window.
So close.
I sigh as a piercing throb enters my being.
Temples pounding at the beat of a drum.
Welcome to my first hangover.
Welcome to my stupidity.
Where do I go from here?

Mikey

I see her stumble in.
Hair was a mess, something I perceived to be a twig caught in
the honey mass.
"Dad here?" She grumbles, making her way around the dining
room, avoiding any real eye contact with me.
Our eyes had not truly met in ages.
Not since Dad's award ceremony.
I am almost convinced that I may turn to stone if she allowed
our eyes to meet.
"Still asleep," I tell her, forcing eye contact.
I cannot read her.
There is nothing to read.
An empty book.
Blank slate.
She was void. Empty.
Numbed by the confusingly soothing effects of a poison we
call alcohol.
What I see next is the effect.
Remnants of last night's meal splattered along the sides of the
kitchen trash bin, her back curled angrily like that of a
threatened feline.

Deep gagging sounds falling from her open mouth.
There I am.
A comfort.
My hands moved to her hair to hold it back as the heaving
became dry.
Her body had given everything it could and yet it still heaved.
A true testament to who Laurel is.
"Let's get you cleaned up," I offer, allowing her hair to fall
loose once more, the strong acidic smell of stomach bile
flowing from the top of the drawstring.
She nods and her fingers begin to twist the bag shut.
"I got this," I say, almost scolding her.
Again, she nods and proceeds to make her way to the steps,
taking them one at a time, painstakingly, as if each step might
be her last.
It very well could be if she awoke the sleeping beast that was
our father.

Laurel

A scalding shower.
Heavy head, pushing into soft pillows on my terms for once.
A soft rain outside my window.
I did not stir till dinner.

Mikey

One last night of freedom before the weekend is up.
Then it's back to school, regurgitation, and drama.
Rumors spreading like a spark in a drought.
Eating up anyone who stood in its path.
I aim to participate in the spreading of information.
Oil on fire.
I have no intention of being that spark, however.

Laurel

I spent the rest of the weekend between Tasha's house and my
room frantically scribbling in my journal.

If anyone ever found it…well the thought scares the shit out of me.
They would lock me up, take him away, and still I wonder if anyone would truly, wholeheartedly believe my words.
Dad was back to ignoring me.
Next weekend, I would start picking up as many babysitting gigs as I can and keep myself occupied.
Driving lessons with my father begin.
It almost seems to annoy him.
I miss the way he makes me feel special.
Wish it was that simple.
I wish he believed I was special.
Wish he would stop vomiting lies to keep me complacent when the time was right for him.
There is nothing special about me.
Plain.
Pale.
Moss colored hair.
Average height.
Average body.
There was no undiscovered talent hiding beneath the surface.
No special warmth within me.
The reality is the opposite.
Cold; it's what I've become.
My blood ceases to flow.
If he refuses to love me, then I won't love him either.
I can keep him at arm's length.
Hurt him just as much as he hurts me.

…

I keep no one further than Kyle.
We had barely spoken since the incident.
I am both humiliated and seriously pissed at myself.
The truth is that anger is not a solitary emotion.
My anger is also humiliation.
Brokenness.
His rejection really stung.
Hurt was becoming a consistent state.

A hurt no one can see.
When I am home, I am irritable and often take to my room.
Truth be told I am horribly depressed.
Is it possible for someone my age to feel depressed?
Can teenagers harbor emotions so deep?
Can the chemicals in my head already be so jumbled?
Distorted?
I took all the hurt and try to walk it off this evening, my
homework done, my dad and Rachel nauseating me in the
living room.
The warm evening is still brightly illuminated by the early fall
sun.
The forest's warm, rough bark against my hands, bare feet
stepping over moist leaves from last night's drizzle.
For a moment, I can breathe.
Above the birds sing.
Momentary peace.
I can breathe.

Interrupted by the shuffling of a bush in the distance.
Tense.
A coyote? Bear?
I tense, hoping to avoid a mauling, unsure of what I would do
if the beast dares come to me.
The shuffling ceases.
I look up and see an even more frightening sight.
Kyle.
He jumps up, just as startled to see me as I am him.
Uncomfortable silence fills the space between us.
Guilt on my end.
Kindness on his.
The two don't mesh.
Oil on water.
Just pray there's no spark.
He had tried to call. I ignored him.
He smiled on the bus. I refused to make eye contact.

"I didn't know anyone else was here."
Based on his startled look I believe him.

His hair is disheveled, only partially tamed by the gray beanie he wears despite the sticky heat.

"It's ok."

I begin to turn to leave, but he moves, drawing my eyes to him.

He takes a step towards me, hands tucked into his jean pocket, "You can stay, I was just passing through," hands motion back to the fallen log as if to offer me a spot.

"I need to get home, you stay," I inform him, beginning to stalk off, eyes to the ground as I push past a tense and thick maple toward my house.

"Wait!"

My face pointed towards my route home.

"Laurel, look at me."

I don't want to. I already feel myself on the verge of tears.

"Can you sit for a minute? I just want to talk and I'm sure you do too."

His eyes are so innocent, so kind, blue like a sapphire, glistening previously.

A large black bird flutters its wings a few branches up, shaking the dying foliage that crunches so happily beneath my boots.

"I didn't mean to make you feel bad or anything the other night. I was just trying to avoid making a mistake, taking advantage of your state."

Mistake?

Anger begins to brew, hands growing hot.

"I didn't mean it like that," his mouth sputters clearly hearing how it came out. "I meant mistake in a less than negative way."

I knew he didn't mean it like that, but it would be easier to stay mad if he meant it negatively.

"It's ok, Kyle. It was for the best and I should thank you for not crossing that line. It would have been a mistake after all," I bite immediately, regretting the venomous tone at the end.

"That's not what I meant Laurel. I don't think being with you would have been a mistake… under the right circumstances."

At a loss for words, my lips thin to silence.

I have no idea what I can say from here to ameliorate the situation.
He had said all the right things and all I could do is simply turn and walk off.
Kyle doesn't try to stop me as I hike into the sorbet sunset.

...

The months pass at a painstakingly slow speed.
Rachel is growing bigger every day and as it turns out I am having a sister come December.
Kyle had tried to reach out, and I had spent every ounce of my energy pushing him away.
I was humiliated, hurt, by the perceived rejection and despite our interaction in the woods I still can't swallow my pride and face him.
Or maybe I realize I shouldn't waste his time, that I am not worth it.
Yet, as time passes, I realize Kyle really was just trying to protect me.
He had seen something in me that I wish he hadn't, and I don't have the words to explain it to him.
Addled.
Although the gray skies of late fall have settled and remained stagnant, my own horizons morph daily.
Some days I would see Kyle in the halls with his new girlfriend and a sense of relief would wash over.
I am happy he isn't alone.
Sometimes that relief turns dangerous, into a winding ivy jealousy.
I wanted to be the one he walked to her locker.
I wished it was his hand in mine.
That I would be sharing his bed.
Rumor was that Kyle and Shelby had gotten frisky at a homecoming after party.
With little regard for my complaints Tasha had dragged me along, and I saw the lovers.
They had definitely been cozy.

I had tried to be happy for him as I caught a glimpse of them slowly kissing on the kindred family couch, his hands softly grasping along her jaw with precise delicacy.
It was a kiss I was familiar with.
One I longed to feel once more.
That night had ended with me and Tasha passing out drunk in her basement, myself crying bitter jealous tears that Tasha couldn't hear.
Other times I would feel an uncontrollable rage take over.
This was always followed by the inevitable lustful fantasy; one where his new girlfriend would be caught sucking off some random guy.
Kyle would be heartbroken and run to me.
I would comfort him in any way he desired.
I would be powerful, a source of ultimate comfort.
The connection would feel amazing for both of us, and we would lie in his sheets, tangled in cloth and arms.
Sadly, all my fantasies lately had involved his initial downfall and hurt with me there to pick up the pieces, and the more I imagined his pain the more my pleasure mounted.
Fantasy culminates in the unsettling new habit of masturbation.
Actions and pictures that brought nothing but shame in my post orgasmic bliss.
My fingers would reach beneath the sheets of my bed, past the elastic of my panties, and I would meet my inner hedonist.
My very own beast resembles daddies in all the worst ways, torn between the monster I nurture and the angelic voice of reason that I shun.
What is worse is the imagery; if it isn't Kyle that brought me to the edge, it's a series of violent videos that I had encountered after I dared ruffle through my father's collection of VHSs.
Women tied in various knots, breasts screaming in a confusing mix of pain and pleasure.
Azure bruises, battered flesh, a man taking her from behind mercilessly.
Pain and pleasure drifting uncomfortably close.
Non-linear.

A woman being forced to choke on a hooded figure's cock till spittle ran down her chin.
Small black streaks of mascara covering her breasts.
No, not breasts, tits.
That's what the men call them as they covered the peaks in their orgasmic fluids.
She would kneel, grateful for his pleasure, the streaks of black now running dry from the elongated degradation.

You love it, you whore.
Say thank you daddy.
Thank you! Thank you!
She would shriek, then the abuse would resume just as he caught his second wind.
Of course, daddy wasn't a complete sadist, he had vanilla pornography too; missionary lovemaking, a nurse tending to a patient's wounded cock and ego, gentle lovemaking sessions on rugged sand at sunset.
It didn't catch my attention, though. I was all about the dark, gritty, brutal pornography he also seemed to favor.
It was all in violence, degradation, and humiliation.
There I found myself panting and repeatedly releasing the TV volume down low, my eyes constantly flipping to the driveway to make sure no one was coming home.
It was sick. I was sick.
When it was all said and done, I would rewind the tape back to the spot I had found it in.
No one could know. Especially not dad.
My dad. I can't stop thinking about him.
I hate his touch.
Can't understand why he won't come to me.
What had I done wrong?
I am so fucking sick.

Mikey

A closeness had returned between Laurel and me.
I had cared for her.

Tended her hangover that day, helped her rinse chunks of vomit from her hair.
Watched them slowly spin down the drain of the kitchen sink.
I watched closely as she ascended the stairs, each one seemingly taller than the next.
 "Get some sleep," I had called out.
"I'll run up some dinner later," I added in need of her approval.
She nodded, seemingly indifferent.
Couldn't she see?
Couldn't she see what it was doing to me?
That I was also his victim.
That I don't know how to help her without betraying her trust.
I am so fucking sick.

…

Gale and I were going strong despite a lack of definition of what or who we are.
She didn't seem to care, and if she didn't question it, neither would I. After all, it wasn't everyday you met a woman who was so fully content in just being present without all the frills, unless you counted the sex of course.
There was plenty of that to go around, and she never said no.
I love her compliance.
Don't love her.
Love the sweet spittle that runs from her voluptuous lips.
Didn't love the words that follow.
Despite our developing relationship, I still always shut my eyes tight when we fuck.
Replay my sexual introduction.
It made my heart race, and in that moment right before I would release it controlled me.
That amazing moment where your head is light, and the energy around you bursts in tangible spurts.
It's so intense because it's the only thing I feel.
I can breathe again.

Fall fades from red and begins to hit the dull browns of the latter parts of autumn. Winter is right around the corner.
Another hoorah in the woods.
Laurel and I trekked deep this time. Our fingers and noses were cold from the biting air.
We watch as the leaves begin to lose the last of the rich chlorophyll.
Our conversation is rich in color, however.
The bridge we had closed would crumble until next summer.
We will rebuild once more.
For now, this is enough.

Laurel

She is finally here.
December third, eight pounds even with a swirl of Rachel's fall colored hair.
Her eyes are our fathers, though.
I had gone to meet her in the hospital.
Rachel's hair pulled up in a messy bun, eyes bursting with exhaustion, red and dazed.
"Her name is Ava," Rachel tells me, handing me the stiff bundle with a wince.

Ava, a variation of Eve.
The first woman.
Created perfectly, just like my sister.
She is perfect.

Mikey

Rachel limps as if a boulder sits between her thighs, carrying a crying bundle that is my sister into the living room.
I am still apprehensive.
Not sure if I want to cuddle her or toss her back to Rachel or my dad when she starts to scream at the top of her tiny lungs.
It's intense.
A signal of her disdain for her current state of hunger or exhaustion that all will hear.

I wish I was still allowed to scream.
To express my needs.

My apprehension fades when I notice how truly adorable, she
is swaddled in her thick pink blankets.
"She's perfect, isn't she?"
My dad interrupts my staring.
"Yeah, she is," I tell Ava as I tighten my grip on her.
He reaches down to take her from me. "You are so lucky to
have such a good big brother," he whispers, rubbing his cold
red nose against her bulb like snout, little hands jutting out
from the loosened swaddle to bat at him.

*He had once held us, kissed us like he was doing to Ava, and now,
well I do not even want to think about it.*

Not anymore.
"You are going to protect her with everything you got,
Mikey," he notified me.
I can do nothing but agree.
Can't help but wonder.
Wonder if he will change his mind when she reaches the right
age for him, and he becomes the source of danger.
Wonder if he will repeat his crimes.
Wonder if I will have to protect her from him.

I doubt that I could.
I could not even protect Laurel.
History may repeat itself and I can do nothing to stop it.

Laurel

I had built a wall around myself.
Brick by brick and I hadn't even realized it until I had become
walled in.
Parent-teacher conferences roll around and my inattention has
become apparent.
My grades had dropped.
Nothing drastic, but A's had become B's.

Rachel tags along, Ava fast asleep in a tightly wrapped carrier, huddled at the sacred breasts.
She is really trying to embrace a motherly position.
"Laurel's grades are still good, but this is certainly not the level of work I would expect from her. She and Mikey are both exceptional students, and I would hate to see this pattern persist," Mrs. Goulding drawls.
Her southern accent struck me as so foreign in the old Indiana school.
She had situated herself on a student's desk. Feet where the bottom should be an attempt to seem down to earth.
She was trying too hard, and it wasn't just the dialogue, or the way she held herself, it was her clothing.
Dressed about ten years too young in a brightly colored pencil skirt and tight shirt. Perhaps it was a mid-life crisis.
Do women have those?
"Well, I can assure you that we will work on it ma'am," my father tells her reassuringly, a dip tucked deep in his lip, a lustful gaze dominating their interaction.
 Miss Goulding half grimaces when the word "Ma'am" hits the air.
"We have tutoring available on Wednesdays during free period," she begins. "…and also it's Harris now," she adds, her eyes widening almost excitedly.
"I apologize," my father mumbles uncomfortably.
His hand was on Rachel's, a smile on her face despite the conversation.
She was just happy to be allowed into this family matter.

I didn't mind.
I can tell that it makes her happy and, in a way, she is family now.
"Laurel seems detached lately. Now I am aware of her mother's passing, and although it was almost four years ago," my dad cringes at the mention of my mother, "That doesn't make it any easier, I'm sure. However, this shift seems to be more recent. Are there any new stressors in your home that could be contributing to her dropping grades?"

Nothing.
That is the only appropriate answer.
It's not what I want to say.
What I want to do is scream.
Cry out.
Tell her what is happening between my father and me, but in this room, there is no ally.
There are only repercussions, plus I don't want to hurt him.
There is nothing to say, so I say nothing.
Instead, I stare at a peeling patch of striped wallpaper next to the chalkboard.
I want to pick at it, expose what lies beneath, but I resist.

My hands moved, tucked up into my sleeves, and began to clench my fist, long nails digging into my palms.
I almost like the sensation, it's soothing.
My father looks at Rachel, lifting his shoulders in a disingenuous shrug.
His gaze returns to Miss Goulding, "I can assure you that we will work on it. There's just a lot going on in our home lately, between the new baby and their mother's passing. Things don't just heal overnight."
Rachel grabs my father's hand as if to comfort him.

A bolt of lightning-hot anger swells in me.
Jealousy? Jealous that she is comforting him?
I swallow hard, burying the emotion and avoiding their touch with my eyes.
A twinkle of jealousy also sits in Miss Goulding's' eye as she looks longingly at Ava.
No children on her end, but the desire is there.
"That is a big change! Congratulations," Miss Goulding…well now Harris says softly, her lip trembling to a pout.
Stilling.
It almost sounds fake, her eyes lost on Ava, filling with longing, "But it mustn't get in the way of her studies. Your children are bright Mr. and Mrs. Wyatt. We need to harbor that natural intelligence."

She knows that they aren't married. Clearly, she is upset with
them, but can't say so.
"It's not Wyatt," Rachel informs her.
My teacher apologizes, knowing full well.

There was a long moment of silence.
The air is heavy with unspoken annoyance and jealousy, and I
now can't wait to be home.
"We can assure you we will support her and help get her back
on track," Rachel interjects.
"You can count on us," my father says, chipper, shifting along
his seat.
I remain silent, my stare floating to the dusty chalkboard, an
almost erased plus sign sitting on the right corner.

Apathy has swallowed me like the whale did Jonah.
My attempt to push emotion out had pulled me further out to
sea than I had intended.
"I'll work on it," I say, smiling wide, my teeth primal, a
symbol of my weakness rather than dominance before
retreating back into the box.
A box too small to break out of, the walls too close.
I want to escape.
But I am afraid.
Maybe I had built the walls for a reason.

Mikey

Winter lost its battle against the rising temperatures and the
snow began to dissipate as it always did.
It would leave behind a brown sludge that would get tracked
under the shoes of all who dared venture out.
I hate these intermittent seasons.
 Moments in the year where there should be another season,
yet no name was ever given to such a short period.
It wasn't all bad though, it leaves behind nurturing
components and moisture for the soil.
The days begin to grow longer, less time left to be spent in the
safety of darkness.

...

Prom rolls around.
Juniors and seniors only unless otherwise invited.
Gale, being a year older and a grade ahead invites me.
It's mostly a guise for us to go get high and party in a cheap hotel we had no business renting.
We only spent an hour at the prom despite the suit and her dress.
The punch had not been spiked.
The music had been too slow, and I desperately wanted to get high and lay in that order.
Gale wears a short, puffy, hot pink dress with only one shoulder.
It was bulky and ugly.
That's about all I could say about it other than it's ugly and I want it off her.
She wore her hair in a tight bun, still colored.

Gale whined about wanting to go back to the dance, but after a liter of burning vodka between the three of us, Corey acting as a squeaky third wheel, we were all belligerent and drunk.
The tv is on full blast, pillows fly as we bounce from bed to bed, tumbling and drunkenly laughing on the bristly ruby carpets.
An ugly painting of a fox stares from the space right above the tv.
"Truth or dare?'
Corey wants to play.
I know it's trouble, but I welcome it anyway.
It would be so much easier to just inform each other of our perversions, but we were basically still children and children love to play games.

It starts off light enough and almost dwindles after several unsurprising truths from Gale.
I gave in and chose to take on a dare.

A prank knock on the neighboring room's door which
happens to be empty leaves me stumbling along the hotel
halls.
Corey takes on the next dare, a prank call to the front desk.
It is innocent until I push it; daring Gale to kiss Corey.
Surprisingly, she does so with no hesitation.
It turns me on.
The winds change from there.
Sinister.
That's when we dare Gale to call Charlotte and invite her to
our room.
At this point she does anything we ask, nice and drunk.

Laurel

Prom night.
No invite. No plans.
Tasha is dancing the night away with Junior Dean despite
only being a sophomore herself.
I listen to the soft spring shower.
Shut my eyes tight and imagine slow dancing with Kyle under
the lights of a cheap disco ball.
I can almost hear the music and it helps me sleep.

Mikey

School is over.
Freedom soon to come.
Sixteen is only five weeks away and soon I will start my junior
year.
There are endless possibilities.
The world is open to my interpretation.
Or is it?
The path seems clear.
Apathy washes over me. The future doesn't excite me the way
it excites other people.
College is a must in my father's eyes.
A career? Perhaps a wife who loves me. Kids?
I could have it all, well almost.

I would never have the true passion that most people seem to inherently cling to.
I wish I could feel it.
Love. Like. Passion.
People may think there is beauty in this lack.
The void.
But if you knew you would change your mind, because with a lack of emotion and pain also comes a lack of pleasure.

Food is bland.
Colors dull.
Words are meaningless.
Touch is numbing when it isn't followed by sex.
To feel the better things in life, one must also feel the worst, and in those moments that are few and far between where I do feel I become overwhelmed, as if my heart may beat from my chest.
My cardiovascular system is pumping like a tambourine.
I reserve those moments of sheer terror and glee for Laurel.

With her, I feel.
She is the only person I truly care about.
That care is an all-consuming force.
A force that leaves me wanting her to reciprocate.
The flame I carry for her burns bright and sturdy. I will always love her.
My father is flickering, his love waxing and waning as quickly as the moon does.

Laurel

Summer is just about to peek its head out like the groundhog looking for his shadow.
Nature was returning from a cold slumber; cardinal flowers sprouting along the edges of the property; elegant and tall, they had pushed through the harsh cold, ready to show their colors; shades of ruby and scarlet bursting along the dark backdrop of the woods.

Rachel's garden is fenced.
We spent the last weekend together with Ava trying to crawl around creating and lining the spaces we are going to plant.
Watermelons, pumpkins, and tomatoes are on the list, along with sunflowers per my father's request.
"I'm not sure any of this will grow, but we are bound to at least learn something," Rachel chirps happily. As we stab the ground with our labeling sticks.

I brought my grades up in time for summer to roll around.
Dad had scolded me.
As he should.
I was failing and to fail was to fail him.
In more ways than one, I had become problematic.
I had put on a few pounds. My hips were wider, stomach rounder, as was my face.
My breasts are more bountiful.
I look like a woman.
My body's final and ultimate betrayal.

Dad is disgusted by my body.
I can tell.
Distant. Disinterested.
He won't touch me, and hardly acknowledges me unless it's checking to make sure I am still following close in the line of his shadow.
I wonder if this is the same hurt that Mikey feels at his indifference.
All his love is aimed at Ava and Rachel.
I don't want to be jealous.
This is out of her control.
But I can't say that I am not a teensy-bit green.
Whenever I look him in the eye or try to touch him, I am met with a vacancy that matches my own.

I wish he would touch me, no matter the form it takes.
There's a deep-seated need to know he still loves me, even if he does so in the most hateful ways.

At least then I would know that he still feels something for me still.
I try to make myself known by helping with my sister, and by getting along with Rachel.

Ava, sweet little Ava, so beautiful and sweet, with her auburn locks and round eyes that are always full of wonder and curiosity.
She is so calm, rarely crying, while I feel tears well in my eyes on a daily basis.
Rachel appreciates all the help.
I am not doing it for her though and that in itself is wrong, and although I am getting along well with Rachel beneath lies jealousy, and I fight against it daily.
I won't let her see it.
Can't let her know how much it hurts that he loves her more than he loves me.
Loves everyone and everything more than he loves me.
It hurts.
More than anything it hurts, and I am so tired of being in pain.
I decided that if Daddy does come back to me, I won't give him a reason to stray because his distance is far more excruciating than his touch.

…

I will try.
I even allowed myself to regress and asked him to take me out for ice cream like we did when I was young.
My body is weak with anxiety, hands dug deep in my pocket, the seams pulled tight as I try to keep myself upright.
We used to ride bikes along the river, Daddy on his big bike and me trailing yards behind, knees buckling with each turn of the wheels as I tried to keep up.
I was desperate not to be left behind.
So little has changed.
I ordered vanilla despite not caring for ice cream anymore and even kissed his cheek at the end of the night.

He didn't care, seemed preoccupied and bored with the simple conversation.
I went home and devoured a tub of vanilla yogurt.
Don't stop till the spoon hits the bottom, the scraping sound speaking to me.
Telling me I had gone too far, and still I felt void.
So I don't stop there.
Move on to the potato chips, a leftover burger from dinner the night before, a few slices of bread, heavy on artificial butter, drizzles of amber honey soaking through the starch, and eating away at the cheap paper plate beneath.
I eat and eat until my body deceives my mind and I am momentarily filled.
Full.
Fuller than I had ever been before.

I sat against my bedroom door, stomach aching, about to burst, bile rising in my throat, but that was nothing compared to the guilt I felt when I realized what I had just done.
How gluttonous I had become.
My floor was littered with dirty plates and almost empty containers, and no excuse as to where it had all gone.
Calories and numbers swirl in my head, a veritable tornado of gluttonous shame.
Anxiety.
Rhythmic pounding accelerating like the hooves of spooked wild horses.
Somehow, I can feel the food coursing through me and settling in all the most unflattering locations; my hips spilling over my jeans, my stomach bulging through the seams of my shirt.
All in my head. All in my head.
Or is it?
The mirror doesn't lie, and what the mirror shows is untouchable.
I picked myself up physically whilst mentally beating myself down to a pulp.

Stumbling to the bathroom the thoughts fly like a violent tornado, flattening everything in its path.

Overwhelmed.
A thought stirs as I turn the knob.
Shame oozing with each twitch of muscle.
The floorboards creak beneath my weight, the same cry the
hallway boards make when he lingers.
My feet land heavily as I pass the bathroom mirror.
I become like a statue, eyes refusing to meet the reflection,
brain telling myself that I should.
That the exposure would help me work up the courage to
become empty again.
After all, who would it hurt?
I wouldn't even hurt me.
Not really, and this needs fixing.

With tears heavy in the rims of my eyes my body collapses,
knees meeting the clamminess of the light tile, awareness of
what the hell I am about to do thrums through my chest.
I kneel as If I am praying but instead of God being my
comfort, I find it in the strangest place.
My toothbrush jammed deep into my throat, a tickle as the
long sleek handle scraped against the flesh.
I pray to the porcelain God.
Tears fall from one rim to another.

They say the first time is the hardest.
Whoever "they" is knows a thing or two.
But I am determined, this is the one thing I have to do right,
the one way I can make my body obey, and if I can't do this,
then there is no strength in me, not an ounce of courage.
I push down deeper holding it still, ignoring the urge to stifle
the reflex and trekking past it.
Stunned at the sound of liquid flooding the bowl, I am filled
with a sense of power.
Again.
Another splash. A sense of euphoria takes over, fills me.
It is warm and tingly like an orgasm, stretching from the tip of
my nose to the deepest pit of my stomach, and much like an
orgasm the shame is soon to follow as closely as a summer
shadow.

Lost. Lost and I have no desire to be found.
Lost in the bliss of the putrid tawny discard that swirls in the
bowl.
Adrenaline. Strength.
I had done that. Had chosen.
This is control.
My belly quakes gleefully, the walls churning to find only
emptiness.
This is what I have been missing.

I brush my teeth, still avoiding the mirror and return to my
room, high, starting to wear thin, tingle fading.
Shame putting me back in its chokehold.
Invisible hands.
I close my eyes and vow that I will never give in to such
destructive behavior again.
Lying down on my bed. Lying to myself.
Again, I am hungry.

Mikey

I had developed a bad habit of watching.
Watching the surrounding people.
Watching the hands tick by on a clock, each minute wasted on
an uncaring mind.
Indifference.
He lingers like an unwelcome guest, hanging around and
taking up space.
Beautiful in some ways.
He is strong.

Safety from the harsh words of my father, and Rachel's
judgmental eyes.
She can see that something is wrong with me, and yet never
seems to catch onto her own lover's darkness.
The man she sleeps with, the man she is raising a child with
and whom she loves is a monster.
The enemy is entangled in her sheets.

The tension that remained widely unspoken in the house has bubbled over into other areas. Rachel doesn't want me alone with Ava, not that she would ever admit it, but I can tell.
Her body reveals what her tongue won't.
Always tense, crossing her arms when I give Ava any attention.
I want to tell her that I am not the monster she thinks I am.
There's no ill intention towards Ava or Rachel for that matter.
That restraint doesn't extend to others.
There are people I would love to hurt and at the end of the day, insects and neighborhood strays have lost their appeal.

Laurel

Summer heat. Unbearably hot and stuffy.
Tasha and I make our way to the reservoir, Dean in tow complaining about the quality of the water.
He wasn't wrong.
Corey's dad always told us to steer clear.
Carved earth that had been abandoned and over time filled with water.
No one listened to the warnings.
No one cared. Not with so little to do around town.

We set ourselves up near the edge, a good twenty-foot drop, old towels with holes scattered on the prickly dirt.
Mom never let me take the nice towels out of the house and I still don't.
"Use the beach towels," she always badgered me when I would ask to go for a swim.
By beach towels she didn't mean long fluffy towels with summer patterns, she meant the old, rejected bath towels whose seams had split over the years.
I am apprehensive to take off my sundress.
I don't want anyone to see my new figure.

I feel like the third wheel, and it doesn't take long for me to try to escape.

Tasha and Deans constant kissing is irritating me, but also leaving me needy.
I am jealous.
I want someone to kiss. Someone to love.
Although I am not sure what love feels like, I am sure that it has a lot in common with lust.
I try to cool off, standing on the edge of the aggregate rock face.
A cheap mixture of recycled concrete and crushed stone.
They had abandoned it years ago.
The cost of transporting materials is growing economically burdensome.
Instead, they settled on creating a new quarry on the east side of town, closer to the suburbs.
That quarry was dry.

My feet dangle over the edge.
A plain between two worlds.
Apprehension. Fear.
I want to jump.
Want to feel the freedom of the fall even if it was only momentary.
Weightless. Nothingness.
So I stand.
Suck in a deep breath, Dean calling me a chicken and flapping his arms, my head turning to view the eccentric movements.
I am honestly surprised that he and Tasha split mouths long enough to see me linger.
Behind us I see a couple cars pulling up, stirring the dirt into a flimsy tan curtain.
Probably another group of bored teenagers.
Sucking in a deep breath I balance a leg off the edge.
"Jump ya chicken!"
Annoyingly, my friend joins in, taunting me, "Go on Laurel! Don't be chicken shit!"

I am a chicken. I am afraid.
Afraid to speak. Afraid to tell the world how I feel.
Afraid to rebel. Afraid to feel. Afraid of normalcy.

Terrified to be loved while horribly wanting to be loved.
Scared.
Of.
Everything.
I step.
Falling.
Off the edge.
Momentary bliss. Freedom. Weightlessness.

I inhale before I enter the crisp waters.
Darkness swallows me.
No air.
Surrounded by peace.
The abyss.
I wish it would swallow me.
Keep me under and journey me to a momentary panic that
would subside into permanent bliss.

Dean is right, I am a wuss.
Chicken. Afraid.
Typical.
Extrication.
Free of the clammy grip of old rainwater and runoff.
Silence interrupted.
Peace is gone.

Above someone has turned on a portable radio.
Music blaring, people laughing.
I lie on my back.
Floating.
Allow my ears to sink beneath the surface.
The music is growing fuzzy.
Muffled notes.
Eyes closed.
I breathe in and for a long while I remain there.
Trying to think of nothing.
Trying to remind myself that these are the moments worth
sticking around for.

I am interrupted by a crash to my left.
Jolting.
Water circling white, rippling out towards me.
Head bobbing before bursting through for breath.
Then I see him.
A big smile, bobbing head, his wet hair bundling around his
eyes.
Those eyes that discreetly wash over my plain face, before
clasping.
"You look beautiful."
That's all he says before he breathes slightly and disappears
under the water.
The moment steals my breath, I was going to have to write
about this in my journal tonight.

Mikey

Wednesdays are saved for Gale, and me.
Her mother is always at evening mass teaching the preteen
group.
While she praises her God, I praise a different entity.
Dry forest bundles, with fuzzy red hairs.
Long red hairs that fall across Gales's breasts from another dye
job, smoke thick in the air, her own forest budding beneath.

I take a hike.
We both end up on our knees.
She had been ravenous since prom when Charlotte had shown
up, clad in a small plaid skirt and long-sleeved white shirt.
She stunk of bud, glossy eyes, and a ravenous hunger.
"We were playing truth or dare, it would've been more fun
with you here," Gale led.
Was she thinking what I was dreaming?
"We can always pick back up," Charlotte had informed her by
downing the bottom of the bottle of vodka with a wince.
"Truth or dare?"
"Dare," Charlotte had replied, voice husky.
Had they planned this?
"Kiss Gale."

Charlotte sauntered over to Gale without a second thought.
Gale smiles, runs her hands through her long hair, holding her
face.
They didn't kiss.

...

Driving lessons take up my Tuesday afternoons, and I work
Friday through Sunday.
I'm getting pretty good at shifting, and rarely stalled at
startup.

We drive his rusty truck.
Back roads and summer air.
I can even downshift now
Soon enough I'll be out on my own.
Open road. Freedom.
We never talk.
Not about anything important at least.
"Ease off the gas," he often instructs, eyes narrowing straight
ahead, hands tight as if he might jump at any minor infraction.
This is a matter of life and death after all.

I stall out suddenly.
Backtracking.
He doesn't react and I start the truck back up, fully aware of
his frustration despite his lack of voice.

We pull back into the driveway right before dinner.
Laurel is ready.
Patiently awaiting, fingers twisting nervously through her
loose locks of hair.
The pink of her nailbed peeks through the smoky ash of her
hair.
I assume our driving lessons are very different.

Laurel

Attention.
Regarding someone or something as important.
Cite whatever dictionary is lying around.

Attention.
My heart's greatest desire.
The stress of fatherhood had proven difficult on my dad, and
when it all finally grew to be too much, he slipped right back
into my wet embrace.
He had reached over to help me shift.
Accidentally grazed my uncovered thigh.
Fingers gliding over silky-smooth skin.
Sun kissed.

We pull into an abandoned wooded lot.
He claims this is the perfect spot to teach me to park.
A busy parking lot would have made more sense.
One of the most important lessons in driving.
It morphs into a different kind of lesson.
Steering almond-toasted flesh along his blanched torso.
Attention.

My father morphs quickly back to his icy state.
He gets like this a lot lately, Rachel claims it's depression, that
he went and started on medication to help.

I am left completely perplexed.
He is like a pendulum always swinging so drastically in one
direction or another, never stilling long enough for my eyes to
focus.
It's driving me mad.
Each extreme is as bad as the other.

He refuses to touch me.
Refuses to look at me.
Then suddenly he covers me like a second skin.

Tuesday rolls around and he doesn't take me driving.
Ignores me when I ask when we are heading out.
Mikey shrugs me off, not wanting to rock an already leaking
boat.
He grumbles about taking me next week.

With great anticipation, I wait.

Tuesday morphs to Wednesday, then by Friday I am
constantly on the verge of tears.
I feel so unloved.
Pouting I sit on the porch, eyeing the fading day, hoping he
might give me a morsel when I need a full bowl just to sustain
me.

"Laurel, get in the truck."
My feet about to take off on their own, my toe slipping from
my sandal, skimming over the old wood.
Time with my father.
The man I love.
I avoid a splinter, controlling myself.
Don't come off as too eager.

We get on the road before he tells me to park, and I just about
stall out, downshifting too quickly.
Tilting my head, I turn to try to read him.
His eyes are somber, lips tight as a zipper.
"Dad…" I trail off stopping myself, having no idea what I
could say to get him to look at me.
Instead, I allow my hand to talk, moving it to rest on his thigh,
and let it tickle its way up.
He snatches my hand, asks me what I'm doing, a heat that
burns me to my core rushing to my face.
"I just thought – "
He pipes in, bewilderment lacing his tongue, "Thought what
Laurel?"
I'm not actually sure, and that makes me cry uncontrollably
which is humiliating.
"Get out, I'm driving home. You're clearly too emotional to be
behind the wheel."

He holds all the cards.
That night he and Rachel had me watch Ava.
I pop in a movie and watch her babble and soak her teething
plush with her drool while I veg out.

Quickly, it becomes apparent why they asked me to watch her
as the slapping of a headboard against the wall fills my ear
and almost threatens to shift the picture frame that is poorly
mounted above the TV.
I am seething.
Mad that they are doing exactly what they should be doing as
a married couple.

That night he does his own seething, comes to my room, tosses
something on my bed, colorful papers.
Women. Men. Fucking.
"Why do you have these?"
I can't help but blush as he holds up the cover; a colorful
photo of a woman clad in only thigh-high white boots, getting
fucked like some animal.
Part of me thinks he wants me to be a hundred percent honest.
Give him something to think about.
The other part of me blanches at the thought of telling him
what I was obviously using it for.

Truth be told, I use them to find release.
Truth be told, Tasha and I had been skimming through them
as kids our age often did.
Curious minds. Idle hands. The devil and whatnot.

Tasha had pointed to some contorted position and assured me
that it was the best position to achieve orgasms in.
I felt ashamed to see it, and even sicker knowing full well that
that exact position only brought me pain.
"You are going to love it when you start having sex," she
informed me, pointing out the act of oral sex printed on
paper.
On her knees.
Power in her eyes, his hand right on frazzled hair.
She had no idea that I had been having sex.

I couldn't bring myself to answer and only blush with feigned
virgin-like innocence.

He tears into me telling me this is wrong, that I shouldn't be consuming this type of material.

"I'm sorry, I thought it was ok since we watched those movies together," I tell him, face blank, his hands red around the now curled paper.

He twists, his hypocrisy making him writhe on the inside no doubt.

"You read them too," I add.

Eyes snap back to me, "That is different Laurel, I am an adult. I am your father. I thought you could handle what I showed you without going overboard!"

I am your child.

I hold my tongue.

He paces, trying to keep my anger in check, pausing to turn the page, moving it up for me to see.

This one is even sicker, gag falling in strings from her mouth, her eyes bloodshot.

"Never again Laurel…not without me. Is that clear?"

I shake my head yes.

"I will take care of you. I love you, Laurel. Do you understand?"

Nodding, I tell him I understand while not comprehending a damn thing.

Mikey

Laurel seems desperate for our father's attention.

She spends her day cleaning and waiting for him to arrive at home.

Rachel has taken notice of Laurel's reluctance to stray.

Jealousy brews in Laurel's heart.

No creamy buffer.

Rachel eyes an anxious Laurel who finishes scrubbing last night's dishes, "Why don't you get out a bit."

She hesitates.

I step in, offering to take her to work with me.

She moseys around, till about four when I tell her we can go ride till close.

She agrees and we have a blast, laughing, spinning, and running until our stomachs are about to burst from a mix of excitement and nausea.

"One more!"

"Fine but it has to be the rattlesnake," I tell her pointing to the empty line.

It seems that the thundering clouds above had moved the crowds out.

"Sounds like a plan," my sister agrees before frolicking toward the makeshift shelter outside of the ride's entrance.

Together we strap into the front, climbing the hill.

Reaching that peak.

Anticipation.

Falling.

Roaring wood and metal.

Laurel laughs beside me.

Finally, authentic happiness.

I love seeing her like that.

Gale drives Laurel who had hung out at the park all day, and me to her place after closing.

We all share a soda and Gale almost begs me to stay.

Which means Laurel would have to walk the last two miles alone in the dark.

I'm not sure if I want her to do that, so I decline and promise her that I'll see her in the morning.

Anger crosses her face, a hint of jealousy twinkling in her gaze before squaring her shoulders and storming off.

"You could drop Laurel off," I hint.

She was already too annoyed to catch on let alone get over her anger which is typical of the fiery woman. I wave her off, kissing her a quick goodnight.

I could deal with Gale in the morning.

We walk, crickets and lightning bugs all around us jumping in the too-tall grass that should have been cut at least twice already this season.

The night rings warm, the wood line ominous as the sun drains behind the dark skeletons of the ancient trees.

I want to have a real discussion, and more than anything I need her to know that I am here for her.

"Laurel," I break the silence, kicking a rock up the smooth pavement.

Her head turns, long locks flowing as if some destructive current flowed behind her.

"You know you don't have to try to get dad to like you."

"What do you mean?"

I sigh, pace ahead of her, not sure I could meet her glare as she already seems angry.

My foot catches the rock again, this time it travels into the embankment off the road.

"Just seems like you're pining."

Eyes turn cold, "I'm not pining, I'm just trying to be helpful, and it wouldn't kill you to help more."

"It could, so I try not to risk it."

Her eyes flit my way dangerously, and she stops in the middle of the road to glare.

Maybe not the right time for a joke.

This was supposed to be an important conversation, and I had already ruined it.

"Let's keep going," she mutters leaving me behind.

The rest of the walk is uncomfortable.

I keep stopping myself from speaking, the words never forming perfectly in my head.

We pace to the porch, I can't keep silent, grab her hand, and turn her to face me.

Her body reacts poorly, tense, as if it's upset to be touched.

"Laurel, you do not have to say anything, but I want you to listen."

I feel her relax against my hold, softening into my suggestion, "OK."

"I just want you to know that I am here for you, ok? You don't
have to protect him."
Pulling from me her eyes burn like fire, "I have no idea what
you are talking about," biting words rush from between her
teeth.
She looks like she might cry but stops herself, balling her fists
in her pocket as I rummage for the key.
If I had not seen the truth for myself, I might have believed
her.

Laurel

Swirling thoughts.
Milky in the dark brew of my mind.
I question what life would have been like if my mother had
exerted some control.
If she was still here, would things be different?
The delicate side of me wants to believe that life would have
progressed the way it had been.
Not a bump in sight.

I would have maybe become a cheerleader or maybe class vice
president maybe graduated high school with honors.
Mikey would be happy; he would sport a letterman's jacket
and make it to state for wrestling.
We would spend Friday nights catching his games and end up
at home with a good movie and a supreme pizza, greasy on
the coffee table, and half a gallon of soda, sticky and sweet.
Daddy would have a beer or two, mom a glass of wine, a
cheap chilled rosé, her favorite.
She was never a snob.

My logical brain knows better.
Knows that there was always something sinister.
An unwelcome kiss, a hug that lingered for too long, or
accidentally entering a room at the wrong time, which left us
both in an uncomfortable silence.
 Death may have opened the door, but he had always been
there behind it lingering.

He had always had demons to fight off.
Maybe it was destiny.
 I was always meant to be his, but he would never be mine.
So I still lie.
Consumed by the theories and possibilities.

Victim.
I had gone right to the source of the pain and tried to carve it out only to find that it is too deeply ingrained.
Too intricately sculpted.
To kill the pain would mean to kill my being.
To morph myself into someone new, but right now I am too weak, and tomorrow I will be too small for such a massive task.
For now, there is only temporary relief.
Someday soon I hope to find permanence.

Mikey

There is only temporary relief.
I know that as a fact.
But just because it's temporary does not mean it is not worth seeking out.
Sex was growing burdensome.
The thrill is not what I had hoped it might be.
So, I revert to my old ways.

Laurel

Forgiveness.
Saying sorry isn't the end all.
Words don't mean sit when they sit stagnant.
Forgiveness requires action.
In action I find forgiveness.
He acts.
A movie. Quality time.
A recompense in the form of a glowing screen and a shared laugh.

"I'm taking Laurel out to the movies, get a little daughter time in," he tells Rachel who fawns over what a great father she is perceiving him to be.
I can see her own daughter's future flash before her eyes.
Movies. Bike rides. Father and daughter dances.
Time alone.

I hop in his truck and make small talk not trying to let on to how excited I really am.
School is the main topic.
Normalcy.
He smiles, "I think you are going to enjoy what I have planned."
My smile appears, "What are we going to see?"
No answer.

Mikey

Relief takes many forms.
A swift, hard encounter in the back of an old car, a long swig from the flask I stole from my dad.
Drifting in Dad's truck that he had been allowing me to drive around town.
Warned me not to get pulled over with only my provisional.
Relief.
It's the scraping of fingernails on my back, the hard biting of my collarbone when we kiss, the way she whimpers my name when I want another drink.
But still, sometimes those external outlets are not enough.
Those beautiful moments when I watch Laurel.
When I can see her brushing her hair, the brush harmoniously pulls each strand into place.
Those mornings when she carefully applied her makeup; never too dark, never too heavy.
Simple and virginal, her desperate attempt at gaining some approval from a man who does not care about her.
Those moments where she would sprawl across her comforter and remove her pants, hips pressed up high so she could easily slip them off.

The tension would drive me to the brink.

If I was really lucky, she would unbutton her blouse, or peel off her shirt, always folding it before depositing it into the hamper despite their state.
I love her quirks.
Sometimes it was almost as if she somehow knew I was watching, almost putting on a show; the way she would peel away the cups of her bra from her breasts, her blushing nipples hard, breasts swaying gently as she would strut around her room on a quest for her nightgown.

A voyeur.
She likes being watched.
I can tell by the way she dipped and moved her hands along her body.
How I wish I was that bra, those panties, anything that pressed up against her taut body.
That thrill.
I am careful to cover my tracks, to tape over the small hole I had created so light would never enter one room or escape another.
If anyone ever found out, the thought excites me.
The worst part is it's not even sexual, not really, it's all about love.

The view was not always angelic, but it was always breathtaking.
God, she was beautiful, even amid her self-destruction; when tears were rolling down her cheeks silently, when she would stare in her mirror, always seemingly disgusted.
I hate those moments.
The moments when food became emotionally nourishing rather than serving its physical purpose.
The times I could hear that same food being disposed of with the flushing of a toilet.
She always seemed lighter afterward.

Laurel

Alone, despite the cream puffs clouding next to me.
In a stinking bed that is not mine.
I have my thoughts, I have myself to lean on, but there's so
little of me left now.
I'm not sure how much longer I can find comfort in that
thought.
Utterly disappointed.
In him. In myself. In us.

There had been no movie.
He had told me as we drove past the cinema and up into the
hills that he had something else in mind.
I put on a brave face.
We turn off into a small trailer home.
Dad rattles the keys between his fingers.
"Nate is out of town; I have to feed the cats."
I entered the small trailer house.
Suspended by large bricks, critters littering beneath.
Escaping the heat.

It smells of cat urine masked with cheap apple cinnamon
candles.
Old beer cans littered the counters, and week-old dishes sat
accumulating water in the sink from a rusted faucet.
Dad feeds the cats, a large orange male and his companion,
both mewing and begging for attention, a third cat darts
across the living room before utilizing the worn armchair as a
scratching post.
I pet one, "We're going to be late Dad," I inform him, the clock
above the stove reading a quarter to seven.
The movie starts at seven.
I always enjoyed the trailers and taking my time to settle into
an oversized chair.
"I think maybe we can skip the movie."
I continue to pet the cat, his hand stroking mine.
"Come sit down, we can have a beer, I won't tell anyone."
Patting his lap he lured me.

There was no saying no, his hands had begun to travel over me, tweaking my nipple above my cotton shirt, other hand skimming the button of my jeans.
Taking what is his.

I had wanted to cry at an opportunity lost when the clasp released its bite of the material.
A belief that he wanted to love me and spend real time with me.
To know me.
But I hadn't.
I reminded myself instead of how badly I craved him.
So I allowed it, and we made love that was more similar to fucking.
Not a loving touch. A groan.
Details I shouldn't recognize. Stretched out arms.
I sat there, completely naked.
Incomplete.
Relieved he hadn't made me feel good, disgusted that it's what I had wanted.
"You ok, Laurel?" he had asked, placing a cigarette from the nightstand to his lips.
I lied.
He hadn't bought it, took my hand, and ran it over his barrel of a chest.
I wanted to bury my nails in him.
Draw blood.
Reclaim the blood he had drawn from me.

...

Rachel had taken the day off to plan our upcoming birthday, just a month away.
Sixteen.
She had gone with yellow. Light and neutral.
A smaller guest list to save some money.
Just some family, Dad's coworkers, and a couple of friends.
Grandma, who Rachel surprised him with, is staying at the small motel at the edge of town.

Mostly it was an excuse for a barbecue.
An excuse to suck some beers down.
The real fun would come after the party.
Rachel was taking my grandma back to the city to catch a
flight after the festivities were over or at least that's what she
planned, as a surprise for Dad.
Honestly, I'm in awe that she is staying a full day.
She never stayed long.
Not even after mom passed as if she had her own life to live,
or that's what she had said.

Kyle had caught word of a bonfire.
There would be cheap beer, weed, and Kyle.
The cover of night would allow us to explore the wild depths
of our hearts.
It would be my chance.
I had made up my mind.
Kyle had broken up with Katie, and we had been growing
closer.
It wasn't serious, but we were back to normal, and he had
made his intentions clear.
The quarry had forced us together.
Diving. Jumping.
We had not talked much that day, just enjoyed each other's
company, and while everyone had proceeded to get drunk off
stolen beers we had watched, sitting across from one another,
his face drawing shy smiles from my lips.
I had chosen to stay sober.
Felt the high and the rush of the jump, a rush that warmed me
for a long while in the freezing waters until I was shaking
cold.

When the heat left me, I had tucked myself up in a warm spot
under the ledge where the water had receded, and the dirt had
softened, the sun shining brightly in my nook.
Goosebumps, blue, shaking lips, and hot sun kisses.
He joined me.
Goosebumps grew, reaching for the warm light.

Cold-tinted lips had grazed against mine, his nose gently nuzzling my own.
He had been so coy, tender hands wrapped around my waist.
It ended with his fingers caressing beneath my chin before he sank back into the cool liquid.
Disappearing and leaving me hopeful.

There was silence after that.
Days of want. Days of desire.
I wanted so badly to hear his voice.
It hadn't been his voice that I had heard but a familiar rumbling of an old truck.
A long conversation had morphed into rides home from the open gym and phone calls any chance I could get.
He would drop me off at the end of the road.
Still, he hasn't kissed me.
Then the other day he put his hand on my thigh, and I could barely breathe.
The opposing hand gently tucked the other under my chin as we sat under the large oak outside of the school.
The sun beamed down, catching between the tree's thick leaves, dispersing in linear strands of gold.
Disorganized rays across his face.
Then I felt it.
His lips, hesitant against mine.

I was in no mood for coy anymore, my hands had reached and pulled him to me.
That was it, one kiss.
One perfect kiss, and a genuine smile.
"You taste fruity," he had commented, cheeks flushed, on account of the hard candy I had just consumed, cherry.
We laughed.
Intoxicated by the chemistry our bodies had released.
It was all so simple.
Perfectly simple.

What was not simple was the atmosphere back home.

Dad hasn't touched me, let alone looked at me since Nate's house.
Those sick moments post bliss that he had tried to force.
"No one would understand Laurel, that's why we need to keep this quiet," he reminded me.
I didn't know how to respond.
He already knew he had my silence, and I couldn't understand why he would need to repeat himself.
"I love you, Laurel. What we have is special."
His attitude had shifted on the drive home after he had checked the names of the movies playing that night.
Alibi.
Our special bond had begun to fill him with dread and had left him crying on our drive home.

We had to sit at the end of the road, under a menacing oak that swayed above us in the breeze for a good while just to allow for the swelling in his eyes to diminish.
The next day he brought home a set of Asscher cut diamond stud earrings and a chain to match.
I wear them with pride if only to make him smile, understanding that they are chains.

...

My depression begins to dribble over.
Jealousy.
Rachel is always clinging on to him.
Daddy is always holding Ava.
He had told me I was special.
That our relationship is special.
I don't feel special. I feel cheap. Used.
Completely confused.

I don't know who I am without him, and sometimes I think that he knows that.
He is toying with me.
I hate him.
I never want him to touch me again.

But there is always a *but*.
I also desperately want him to love me no matter what that means.

Mikey

Physicals.
Scheduled by Rachel.
I hate answering all their stupid questions.
As if anyone was ever going to be honest!
I wished there was a way for them to detect bullshit, so I did not have to lie.
I don't have to lie.
Yes, I do.

Surprisingly, people who are educated are so blind to the signs of abuse.
Clueless to the safety one feels when they have sunk so deeply into it.
Hiding it at all costs.
They do not even catch on to Laurel's hurt.
It seems so obvious, but maybe she had progressed in her ability to lie.
They do not notice her weight loss.
Slowly wearing enamel.
The sadness that follows her like a shadow as if it had become one with her, appearing heavily on the brightest of days.
My own shadow overshadows me.

Laurel

I lied.
Through my teeth.
For some reason, I feel proud.
I was keeping him safe, keeping us safe.
He was hurting. Needed to be fixed. I could help.

I was due for my first pap.

The Doctor asked me all the questions she had to ask before having me strip to a paper-thin gown and I hid my panties beneath my jeans on the chair.
Lied.
Told her I was a virgin when she had inquired about my partner count, my legs spread wide open, feet sitting in the cold stirrups.
I feel like an idiot lying now.
"Move down until your bottom is hanging off the bed."
I did so, reiterating that I hadn't had sex yet as if repeating myself might fool her.
She didn't seem to believe me after she pushed the speculum in with little care, the click of its spreading making me suck in a breath to silence the pain that wanted to be vocalized, my entire body nervously clamping down around the spreading plastic bit.
So impersonal.
"Relax, Miss Wyatt. It'll make this easier."
She almost hisses it as if annoyed at my body's response to the intrusion.

The light shines into me and she hums, below her ministrations last longer than I would like.
I was told that I should be honest, that it was important.
She would not tell anyone, in fact, she couldn't.
I admit that I had been having sex.
"There's a little scarring, nothing too pertinent, but there's also some discharge that has me concerned. When did you start having sex?"
I think back, remembering that it had been right before my fifteenth birthday, so I lie and say fifteen.
Fourteen just sounds much worse.

"I'm going to run some tests because from my experience this looks like an STD… one we can easily treat," she swabs my insides with a long q tip, focused on the task at hand, "I'll call when I get the results. I'll only disclose them to you so tell your guardians that you are expecting your pap results. That being said, you need to be careful not to let this happen again,

we have condoms free of charge in the lobby. It's not good for your body."
She doesn't have to tell me how she feels, I can feel the judgment leak like a faulty pipe from her tongue with each word.
I, however, don't say a damn word, my face hot, sweat dripping down my paper gown.
Anxious and humiliated at being talked down to in such a vulnerable position, my legs in the air, my young body in full view, and for something that wasn't my fault.
I want to scream but I abate the urge.
It pretty much ends with a cold, "You can get dressed now," and a question of what I wanted to do for birth control.
I decline knowing that Rachel and Dad might see it on their insurance charges.
I want to throw up, I need to get this dirty feeling off my skin before I lose it.

A small part of me wished someone would pry a little harder not that it would have helped as I still would have kept silent. But I could have used a little hope and the ability to dream.

...

I'm ill, as it turns out.
I now have to take oral antibiotics for the next two weeks as do my father and Rachel.
He made me sick, and I had to tell him, which was utterly humiliating, but it moved him to get himself tested too.
I feel so fucking dirty, tainted even, but what am I supposed to do other than swallow the horse pills.
It was a devastatingly bitter pill that I had to choke down.

He was thrilled to hear that my pregnancy test was negative though, beaming as if he had done a good job at protecting us, having done absolutely nothing.
I assume the three of us are on the same course of antibiotics, dad told me to hide mine in my room so that Rachel wouldn't see.

Wonder how he explained it away to Rachel, or if he tried to blame her.
Allegedly, we'll all be thoroughly STD-free quickly.
Not something I was hoping for with just three weeks to my sixteenth birthday.
Gonorrhea!
He gave me fucking gonorrhea and I could have gotten Kyle sick had he not turned me down.
Dad apologizes but I can't seem to accept it, despite telling him that it's ok and hugging him tight.

Accept it.

He says we need to be more careful.
The proverbial *we*.
I'm not sleeping around, getting people sick, he is, and I have no say in our encounters.
Not really.
Not even allowed to be mad because I am afraid to hurt him.
Since we are both already sick, he decides he can still fuck me.
No harm there.
As if I have a choice.
It's uncomfortable though, the antibiotics make me feel sick and leave me itchy.
Still, he doesn't wear a condom, and he doesn't give a shit about my body as long as he can still use it.

...

Food has become comfortable.
I take after my mother.
The only difference is that I have guts.
Easily disposed of the evidence of a good binge with a flush.
Maybe a little too good.
I stopped menstruating recently.
The curse now my longing.
I had become too thin for her, my body desperate for safety.
She has shut herself down.
I miss her. Miss the reassurance.

Meanwhile, Daddy and I fight after we don't agree on curfew.
He had had me a few times since and had had enough.
No one is aware. It's silent.
A push.
His pull is always overpowering my resistance.
He is a lure, hooking into my flesh, pulling me to him.
I struggle, knowing full well that breaching the surface could very well kill me.
No avail.
Hook. Line.
Tossing me back when he is done admiring his catch, saving me for later.
Writhing in pain, giving in with defeated stillness.
Still, I take that bait.

Oh, daddy.
You are unlike other men.
Preferring small slopes over a bra-busting bulge.
Brushed pink lips over a womanly red.
No eyeshadow on my lids.
Blush only given by your touch.
Sweet dresses over curve-hugging fabrics.
You are unlike other men.
Only when the haze finally lifts can I see that you are weak.
You are not a man at all.
You will always prefer your little girl over the woman I am struggling to become.

Mikey

Laurel is like an overly ripened plum, oozing but never bursting.
Dark.
All it would take is a bite, something to truly tug away at that skin, and finally, she would reveal the juicy truth.
People would talk.
They always do.
But she would be free. I would be free. He would be free.

I have seen it.
The way he looks at her.
I have seen him cry.
I see many things.
That's what happens when you're forgotten.
When your father turns his need to possess into a weak target.

Invisible. Until I mess up.
Negative attention is still attention.
One minor infraction.
Gale and me.
Broad daylight.
The school parking lot.
I want Dad to know that I need him too.
That I am still here, and I need guidance.

I – Am – Here – Too.

I tell him as much as he shoves me into the car after picking
me up from his place of work.
His coworkers were laughing and joking at the predicament.
"He and his girlfriend were – " the stern officer who had
picked me up hollers before mouthing at my father, "making
out."
The stern look spreads along my feathers curled lip.
A tense drive home.
Silence until we burst through the front door.

Rachel is there, as is Laurel.
He screams, spittle flying along my face.
Rachel cries out, the fire of her hair fanning about as she
frantically moves to dodge the mug he throws.
Onyx ceramic shatters into a million pieces, losing itself
amongst the dirt on the floor.
He tosses another, this one full of curdled cream from a
morning coffee, it shatters against a frame, coffee streaming
down the walls, contorting in all directions like streamers
forgotten after a juvenile birthday party. Speaking of birthday

parties, ours is only a week away, the bag of decorations slumped by the front door.
Rachel shouts at my father, more upset about the mess he had made than his actions.
Laurel stares, arms crossed as if she is shutting down, her lip wobbly, a weak tear glistening down her delicate cheek.
"I was just hanging out with Gale!"

In a sick way, I am loving this attention.
"He was with that – " he pauses, angry spit foaming at the dry creases of his mouth, gathering the words for a hard blow, only coming up with, "that little whore, making out in broad daylight! What has gotten into you?"
He knows exactly why I'm acting out.
I want to shout it from the rooftops.
I need you to care! I need you to be normal!
I am more subtle.
"The same thing that is wrong with you! Fucking women I shouldn't be!"
Rachel assumes I mean her, or maybe some random woman; she has no idea just how bad it is.

My father knows better, he knows exactly what I am saying, and he grabs me by the shoulder and shakes me almost as if he could shake his secret back in.
"Dad, stop!" The voice is my twin's, her strength returning, our DNA beckoning her to action.
Laurel has her hands on him trying to pry him off me, pleading with him to stop.
I had not expected Laurel to step up.

It's all a blur after that.
Dad moves Laurel off easily by almost gently placing her on the couch as if she was some doll he didn't want to disturb.
It's an act that goes unnoticed by Rachel but speaks volumes.
Once she's safe he hears up to face me once more, lunging at me with a crazed look on his face. His eyes are wide, his arms bulging, hands wound tight to come at me.

Tensing I step back with avoidance, my gaze winding, a large hit to my chest takes my air. It feels like a brick has hit me in the chest, the deep pain radiates from the pit of my stomach, flowing down my arms.
Blinded my other senses perk up, I hear crashing.
The feeling of impenetrable hardness against my back that leaves me gasping for life.
Rachel cries. Ava shakes from sleep with a scream, the red locks of her hair shaking with fear.

Laurel

Dad had lost it.
Slammed Mikey down onto the coffee table, the legs giving beneath the weight of my body.
The tabletop is still fully intact.
Strong wood.
Rachel had to pull Dad off Mikey before he had the chance to really hurt Mikey.

They had both sat there, catching their breath, knees tucked to their chests, glowering.
This was not over.
Not by a long shot; Dad knows it, so he storms off before taking it any further.
Red in the face.
Seething.
Rachel scolds Mikey for the way he had acted with Gale, her face scrunched in disapproval.
"He is just trying to do what's best for you!"
He brushes her off and walks past, a wealth of profanity spewing from him.
Disregard and fury drive him, his hand curling around the oak banister of our stairs.
He limps up them, wheezing, his lip coated in a natural red lipstick from his busted lip.
When he reaches the platform before the curve he shoots me a wink, disappearing down the hall.
I have no idea what it means and I'm not sure I want to.

...

Dad comes back home at midnight, piss-ass drunk and hyper-
emotional.
I hear him stumbling up the stairs, Rachel's hushed
commands, "Get to bed, sleep it off, Edmund."
I crack my door open, watch Rachel walk him to Ava's room
before exiting with the sleeping bundle of a sister to their
room where Ava will likely suckle away all night.
I feel bad for him.
This is not what he wanted; to hurt his son.

He sobbed as Rachel put him down and it twisted at my better
senses.
"I messed up bad Rach!'
She had hushed him, enabling him by reassuring him that it
was going to blow over and that we would all do better
tomorrow.
That is not what he needs though.
She is clueless.
He cannot be left alone.
Not yet.
He needs it. Needs to be held. Needs to be loved.
Reassured.
I can provide that.

I know he will be here soon.

Seeking out comfort.
He needs it like a man needs water.
I shut my eyes tight and wait for him to find me.

The clock flashes after two.
In the guise of night, he stumbles to my bed somehow
unheard and uninvited, and pulls me into an entitled embrace.
Tightly held, soft breathing emitting the smell of strong
whiskey and cinnamon that stings the senses.

How can the slight anatomical difference that makes him
stronger than I make him fumble and falter in pertinence to his
basic human drive?
Hailing at the altar of my youth.
How can the staff that he lords with and drives into me with
such strength and entitlement leave him so weak?
Why does something as seemingly insignificant as a difference
in testosterone leaves him salivating and growing at the site of
my sex, reverting to his teenage self?
Less than a man.
Never a man. He's my father!
I had never imagined I would think of him as a man with a
drive, urges, and violent human need but that had changed.

"I don't feel too well," he drunkenly coaxes me into a guilt
trip, destination well-known.
If only they could see him now.
No one would believe their eyes if they saw the man clad in
justice squirming on his daughter's small bed.
They would gasp at the way he would claw and suckle at the
hillocks of my young breasts, drinking greedily my milky
power from me, only to pummel to the furthest depths of my
body with little thought at the fact that he hits rock bottom
with each thrust.
"Just let me hold you."
I won't say no. Can't say no.
I don't want to say no.

The minutes rotate red to the single digits on my nightstand
and although I should fear getting caught, I can't seem to care,
I want to take care of him.
"I'm sorry," I tell him, tucking myself into him, my curve
digging into his pelvis.
I take his hand, run it under my satin shirt, my eyes focusing
on the bit of slanting light that peers from beneath the door.
It's deceiving, illuminating a photo of my mother holding me,
perched along the wall. She smiles, her blonde brow cocked,
green eyes staring me down, almost haunting me.

If only she could see what her little girl was going through,
what she was doing to cope, to survive, she would be so
disappointed. Not in him, but in me.
He hiccups behind me, "Laurel no. That's not what I – " he
stops giving in easily as he makes contact with my still
forming mounds.

"I shouldn't be here, this is wrong, Laurel."
I know and yet, it doesn't keep me from curling into him.
It had never stopped him before.
Am I not good enough? Not young enough? Not sweet
enough?
This was his fault after all.
He had created a monster and now she wants to ravage
something.
Giving him what he is going to take.
Dulling the hurt through pleasure.
Tonight, I am the one who will open the door.

I take his hand and let him cup my hot skin, move his other
hand down between my rotund thighs pulling my name from
his lips.
"It's ok, Daddy, I need you to feel me, let me make you feel
better."
He sighs a drunken yes, his eyes hooded in a cocktail of lust
and drunkenness.
I take charge.
Run myself against his hand, hips rocking slowly until I
inevitably come with a small whimper.
"Thank you," that really means I'm sorry.
He kisses along the hairline, "Do you feel better now Dad?"
He sighs a yes.

I lay still until his breathing becomes rhythmic and sleep finds
him before taking my leave.
Ava's room.
Ava's cherry oak crib lies empty next to me, the guest bed
pushed against it, and I bawl like a baby on a mattress made
for big girls.

The tears come tears of uncertainty. Tears of shame at my actions.
I don't understand how he can make me feel so good and so sick all at once. So heartless.
Not even Rachel could make him feel the way I do and that made me proud.
It also makes my stomach churn.
Causes me to drift further away from normalcy.

I recall the long sermons.
Teachings that God is always there.
Listening. Healing. Giving guidance.
So again I pray.
I need guidance, and I was told the ethereal, omnipresent, being above would provide it.
God.
The one I had been conditioned to believe was up there.
The one they promised me would answer my prayers.
But I am met with silence.
Only Silence. Silence.
Silence as deafening as a roaring river.
Maybe there is no God.
Maybe he can't bear to love what I had become.

God, please.
Please.
If you're there, I beg you; save me, if not from him, then from myself.

Mikey

My back is sore, bruised, long gashes streaking down my skin, from our one-sided fight.
Good luck trying to explain this away come wrestling training.
Only a day away.
No hope that this would fade by then.

Dad apologized the next morning.
Hungover, with Rachel's tense chatter all through breakfast.

Laurel looks like shit too.
Wonder what kind of despicable acts she had committed last night.
Rachel is still clueless, which means she is either an idiot or complicit.
I hope it is the first.
"I apologize for losing my temper, son. I think we need to talk about you and Gale though."
So we do.

During the driving lesson.
Dad asks me to pull over for fresh air.
I can tell he is about to blow chunks.
He returns to the car seemingly happier.
"Look, I behaved poorly yesterday, and I know that you and Gale are having sex, but I want you to be careful and discreet. We have a name and appearances to uphold."
"I know and I'm sorry," I lie, eyes fixed on the road.
I'm not sorry.
I am beside myself with something warm and tingly.
Joy. *He cares.*
"You need help though."
My father shoots me a dark look that has me taking pause, his deep, sad eyes guiding my words. The knowledge I have is not unbeknownst to him. That kind of pisses me off because it means he has power, one that he is well aware of.
Silence, he owns it.
"With?" He asks, the upper corner of his peach lips hitching.
"With the drinking," I add.
He remains calm despite my rude and blatant suggestion.
"I will do what it takes son. AA before work, more time in the church. That can all be arranged," the promises that tumble from his lip sound like a business deal.
I want to tell him that's not what I'm talking about but why ruin a good thing?
"Sounds good Dad, and as for Gale and me, we are being safe so don't worry," the clear lie comes from my mouth, the words sounding as if they exited with the right emotion behind them.

His deep eyes focus on the upcoming dead end, "Guess it's
time to head back."
We had reached a dead end.
Road and conversation.

Laurel

June heat wraps me into it.
Today Kyle and I take advantage of Mikey's second summer
working at the Ol' Texan.
A deep discount and a day of fun on rides that may as well
have been built of twigs rather turn steel and wood.

Dean drives his dad's cherry sports car, the Italian leather
interior leaving me half afraid to sit.
Tasha steers the roach that is making its way around the small
car.
What could it hurt?
We turn into the hills, the glow of the rides, and the screams of
children leaking into the car through the cracked window.
This was going to be fun; lord knows I need it.

Mikey

I work the morning shift, big asphalt is hot today and burning
through my cheap sandals, but it's well worth it to ride till
close with Laurel and her friends.
They all stink of weed and devour funnel cakes before they
even make it on to one ride.
Munchies.

I'm ok with it, especially when they hand me a burning roach.
All I was doing was checking wristbands for another fifteen
minutes, so what could it hurt?
So I bum a hit off Tasha who eyes me with an animalistic
hunger.
I hear her whisper to Laurel that she thinks I'm cute at some
point before we ride the Ferris wheel, the lights gleaming all
around us.

We had known each other for years and she had never expressed the slightest interest, so I have no clue what's going on tonight.
Maybe it was the bud talking.
Dean hears it too and quickly sours on me, his brown eyes searing into me, gray flecks throbbing. He spends the next ten minutes acting as a physical barrier between his girl and me.
"Thanks for the discount," Kyle offers as we make our way to our Ferris wheel box.
Limit of three.

I chose to ride with Kyle and Laurel, but Tasha insists that it should be guys and girls and with those big bouncing breasts, and tight curls I can't say no. Damn, my animal brain.
Who am I to deny the woman?
Here I am uncomfortably sat between the guy who wants my sister and the guy whose girlfriend I want.
Let's just say it's a quiet ride compared to the constant laughter of Tasha and my sister just beneath.

Laurel

Dean and Kyle go ride the rattlesnake one last time, my stomach is empty, the funnel cake from the afternoon gone from my stomach, the hollow ready for something to eat, and then some.
I am feeling tired, so I chose to sit on the sidelines.
My stomach churns and I catch my friend shamelessly flirting with my twin. In a way, she may as well have been flirting with me, and I let her know with a glint of disapproval in my stare.
 My friend ignores me, and I can't say I'm pleased but, I'm not sure exactly how to feel.
Best friend and my kin, I am not sure how I would feel about her filling me in on how my brother is in the sack.
I hope it doesn't come to that.

Mikey

Tasha stays the night.
Laurel makes sure to inform our father who is out with
Rachel.
Wouldn't want him sneaking into her room with a friend
there.
Might raise some questions. The lengths my sister has to go
through to protect that monster are pretty impressive.

Problem is I want nothing more than to sneak into Laurel's
room myself and have a talk with Tasha.
She is so beautiful, free-spirited, and her smile is sumptuous,
melting me.
Laughing and teasing, always, her thick hair bounces and her
slightly crooked teeth are always on display, her smile
crinkling a beauty mark right above her lip. It's very Monroe
of her.
Gale is cold and demanding. Some might call her a bitch.
But she had her advantages.
Easy to get naked, and her lips are phenomenal granted, it
takes ages to get her to shut up and part her lips to kiss.
It's a breath of fresh air, the woman is free-spirited, mind
uncaged and I cannot help but wonder if that extends to her
body.
Temptation tells me to test the waters, followed quickly by
trepidation.

As it turns out her waters are warm and inviting.
The house is quiet, it's a warm summer night, but it's not
overbearing. The fans go off all over, giving the perfect cozy
temperature.
Laurel is asleep on the couch, wrapped in a thick mauve
blanket, snuggled up soundly with Ava whose red curls fan as
the breeze overhead falls over them.
Tasha and I sit together at the kitchen table, sharing a beer, her
cat-like eyes like two garnet stones flashing across my face,
lips tightly wrapping around the head of the bottle.
Slowly she sucks down the wheat mush, pink heat flushing
her cheeks.
I imagine her lips elsewhere.

Laurel

Kyle was such a gentleman.
A sweet kiss under the lit arch at the entrance of the park
while Dean made out with Tasha behind the corn dog booth.
My brother was long gone, off with an angry-looking Gale, his
face tense with resentment.
The arches' lights flashed methodically as if to warn us that
our stay was ending, and the park would soon be closing.
Lips like two petals, silky, and iridescent from cherry
Chapstick slowly stroke mine once more beneath the heavy
flicker.
Hands wrapped around my waist as we parted, "I want to say
something."
I wanted to listen.
"I don't ever want you to think I didn't want you that night."
The memories flooded me with embarrassment at my petulant
attitude. "I just wanted you the right way…still do."
A smile creeps along his lush lips, curling all serpent-like. It
matches my own.

What does the right way look like?
Despite having had plenty of sex, I can't say I know anything
of intimacy.
Can't help but wonder what the line between right and wrong
is.
"I want you to really want this. I want this to be for us, not just
me."
I understood.
It was my turn to kiss him, and I did so gladly, parting
reluctantly after a long moment, one that had butterflies
fighting in the lower panes of my belly.
"I know what I want Kyle."
We parted, the intercom telling us it was time to go.
Tonight he is heavy in my heart, my pen scrawling every
moment down in my journal.
Still, I hide it, taped beneath my mattress.

Mikey

Wow.
That's all I can say.
There are no words to describe Tasha.
Well, I guess there is one…unavailable.

After a couple of beers, the bottle seemingly becomes more
phallic in the way that she had gripped and stroked it with
shimmering lips.
"Tasha."
She had set the beer back on the table, a wet ring sucking the
cold bottom to it.
"Micah."
Damn.
I had not had anyone call me by my real name in ages.
It had hit deep.
"Natasha," I teased right back.
Grimacing, the gorgeous woman shows me just how much she
hates that, only adding on with a simple, "I hate that," her
eyes had warned seriousness.
I knew she did that's why I did it, not keen on flirting too hard
in case she was to reject me.
"What's going on here?" I had asked, my hand wrapping
around my beer, as I took a long drink, terrified that I might
be imagining it all, the way her eyes had honed in on mine, the
way her lips wrapped so tightly around the head of the bottle.

"I have no idea, but it's fun… and honestly," momentarily she
takes a well-timed pause, provocatively sucking her finger,
"it's a turn-on…the danger of this."
Winking as if it was a game, she made good of the rest of her
beer, the amber liquid sliding deep into her ungainly throat.
"We could make it more fun," I had suggested.
Her hand moved to my knee, "Half the fun is the buildup, it
makes the climax so much better."
I almost lost it right there like some virgin.

Laurel

I saw something I had never expected to see.
My brother and Tasha's tongues, stabbing each other in the kitchen.
It didn't bother me, but it certainly wasn't right given that they both had less than significant others.
I simply shut my eyes tight and held Ava until they scurried upstairs to do exactly what I imagined they would do.

Mikey

Amazingly enough, she was softer and sexier than I ever imagined.
Her ebony skin reminded me of silk, it glistened in the hot glow of the incoming hall light.
We held each other, enthralled, easily reaching the promised land without a prolonged trip in the desert.
Kissing her had been fulfilling to my surprise.
Fuck gale. Fuck Dean.
Fuck the headlights that had flickered up the driveway, cutting our moment short.
We swear to keep it a secret.
I wish I could tell the world.

…

Practice for our meet against Lakeside High next week.
Was hoping we would just train cardio today, the rain leaving my mood sour.
Run. Do sit-ups.
First practice of the summer and the coach already has us trying on gear and picking numbers.
No need for tryouts. Not enough participants to make cuts anyhow.

I try to avoid trying on the ugly rust-colored leotard, worried that my back looked bad.
Stallions.

The school mascot, blown up all over the gym walls, a stud running wild through the desert, kicking up dust.
A poorly sculpted horse in the front of the school that had on several occasions been stolen as part of a senior prank.
Wincing as I pull my shirt off, I model it in the single bathroom, coach requests we all come out to see if any adjustments may be needed and I know I won't be an exception.
I hesitate, eyeing the blue that has stretched across the place where my wings should be, and poke it.
White tips, fading back to blue.
I must hit the table hard, although the pain didn't register then.
I need a story.
Nothing comes to mind.
Look who is protecting him now.
Who am I to judge Laurel for keeping her mouth shut anymore?

I rack my brain.
I need a good excuse.
Then it hits me.
We went four-wheeling a few days ago.
Gale and I went up to the ridge.
A romantic view, with a less-than-romantic ending.
Of course, we would find something to fight about.
I could just say I flipped my four-wheeler.
Just in case anyone asked.
I slap on my off-white headgear that is much too tight around my ears, it reeks of bleach and sweat from last year's season.

Practice goes on.
So far so good.
I see people eyeing me, a wealth of laser-focused stares.
Ignore. Ignore. Ignore.
What I really want is to deck their stupid wide eyes till they swell shut.
Then they won't have anything to look at.
Just ignore them.

Final drill.
Single-leg takedown.
Up against Hoffman and his bearlike chest.
I gag at the thought of my fingers slipping through those
springy curls that reflect with sweat, I swear I can see myself
in one of those beads.
Sweat beads at the base of his outfit floating comically towards
me, the smell rocketing upward and out.

A bomb of testosterone and a hint of onions.
I stare across the red mat, the white circle seemingly playful.
Hand on his shoulder, a quick sweep behind on his part and I
go straight down.
Once, twice. Whistle blows.
Time to switch.
Hoffman does not hold back; in fact, I think he relishes the
thought of taking my ass down.
It was not as if we had had a positive relationship.
He had spent my elementary school years attempting to bully
me with little care on my end, and my middle school years
attempting to humiliate me to no avail, usually, he ended up
humiliating himself with his limited vocabulary and lack of
hygiene.

Physically he would not go down easily.
Flattened.
My paternally inflicted wound takes most of the hit.
"Fuck!"
Hoffman throws his hand down and pulls me up, "Sorry,
man," he grins, clearly proud of his handy work and not sorry.
Coach takes notice.
Drawing attention to myself was not wise, but it had
happened.
"Whatever man," I tell him, straightening out my headgear
and avoiding his eye.

Again.
I brace for the fall this time, the impact softened despite the
tension in my back.

Closing whistle, sweaty ball sacks stinking up the gym make haste for the showers before the cheer squad pops up for tryouts.
I watch as the separator comes down, safeguarding the girls from the hungry prowling gazes of horny boys.

We all make haste towards the locker room, night plans requiring prep work.
There were girls to call.
Balls to shave.
Pullouts to find for a sip of booze.
Loitering in front of gas stations and begging adults to buy was getting old.
I get stuck in the bottleneck, anxious to feel the hot water.
I would have to wait.

Coach stops me, waving me to his office.
I recited my story on the short walk.
Practice makes perfect.
Just as I suspected, he wants to know if everything was ok at home.
I play dumb.
"Of course."
Glancing up and down I watch him calculate his next move.
"How did you hurt your back Micah?"
Eyes may give me away, so I force them to focus on his desktop, cheaply decorated with ugly figurines and photos of his too young wife.
Or should I say, second wife.
"Fell off my four-wheeler."
I add a small chuckle in for good measure.
Coach doesn't buy it.
Instead, he sets a small bit of paper with his number on it and pushes it across the metal top, "Just in case."
I smile and thank him, assuring him once again that there is nothing to worry about and that it had just been an accident.

The slip of paper is buried quickly in the locker room trash along with old paper towels and cans full of dip and spit, the smell of wintergreen nauseating me.
Maybe he had rattled me after all.
The paper was useless anyway.
What had happened between my father, and I would never happen again.
After all, he had promised.

Laurel

Dad wakes me from a deep sleep. "I have a surprise for you. Get dressed."
A surprise?
He had mentioned nothing of the sort.
"It's a special day mouse."
I'm not sure what he means until I glance at the digital clock, the day flashing a reminder, causing my stomach to lurch with disgust.

One year.
One year since he had first truly made me his.
I try to blink away the shame, dusk still looming along the wooded depths of our yard.
"Why did you wake me?" My weak mouth stammers, the comfort of my bed calling me back to it.
"I want to take you out and do something special. I feel like everything's been so tense lately."
His eyes are sweet, innocent even, and behind them, I see no ill intent, but I also know this is subject to change, and telling him no was a surefire way of doing that.

He lets me drive his truck with the four-wheel drive turned on low through the mud pits, the car frantically sliding through the mud, forcing me to laugh even though I had been somber just moments ago.
I had been so quiet at first, nervous even, but now I feel…
Well, I feel almost happy.
Free despite the invisible chains that bind me to the man in the car.
I'm relieved to be spending time with him, laughing as I hit a big wet pothole, the mud splashing over the windshield, obstructing my view.

Quick to regain control I hit the windshield fluid and wipers, spreading a brown rainbow over the top of the windshield, catching sight of a big boulder coming our way, or rather we were coming its way.
Slamming my foot on the brake, I feel the truck spin, my dad hollering, "Laurel, take it easy," before we come to a harsh halt, the truck threatening to topple as we slide, the back end slanting away from the front, fully skewed.
I hit the accelerator, shifting to first gear, the truck's back tires spin out, almost digging into the dirt but I quickly readjust turning us the other way before we come to a screeching halt.

"Damn, you hit that good, baby girl!"
Beaming I eye him, joy apparent on my face, spreading from the corners of his upturned lips, and deeply present in his eyes, the way he looks at me with pride, swells pride in myself in my own heart.
We breathe heavily. His finger comes up, moving a strand of hair from my eyes gazing at me as if he had never seen a woman as beautiful.
Air hitches in my lungs, I try to turn my face away and slap my hands back on the wheel, ready to get back to it and get his hands off me, and yet I won't press the gas until he tells me to. With hands that grow tight and clammy over the leather-bound ring, I set my foot back on the gas, revving it as an indication that I am ready to go again.
"Laurel, stop."
His voice commands it, and I am powerless to disobey his rule.
"Dad – " I find myself starting to protest.

Turning me to face him, he doesn't hesitate, because he knows he can take, and I will always give. He will take right then and there, starting with his hands, climbing them on top of me before he twists his fingers in my hair.
"Laurel, I just want you to know that I love you and that today means a lot to me. Getting to share such an important moment with you was… well it was the best bonding experience we could have had and I'm grateful that you allowed me to be the

man to take care of you," he almost squeaks, his cheeks red as if he means every word, and I believe he does believe that he has given me some beautiful moments.

We remember it differently, but I won't tell him otherwise, I don't want to hurt him.

"Thank you. It meant a lot," my pitiful voice agrees, and it wasn't a lie. It had meant everything, in all the most confusing ways.

You are so fucking weak.

All I can do is thank him again and allow his lips to part mine, his face scruffy against my chin, the stubble making my body tight with anxiety and ailing hurt.

Curling fingers pull around my waist and grip tight, threatening to pull me onto his lap, but my frozen statue of a body quickly deters him.

Pulling away, I take in some air, my hand tight along his scuffed knuckles, his aftershave bitter on my tongue, seeping along my taste buds.

"Dad, I...I'm...well you know?"

His head shakes. "No...I don't."

Violent red hits me, not because I am embarrassed but because I'm lying, and seeing him so lost in our loving moment makes me feel culpable of not just my current sin of lying, but all of our shared sins, past, present, and future.

"I'm... on my period," I followed through with my fib, already knowing it was not a deterrent to him, at least not when he was drinking.

"That's ok, Laurel," he assures, although I'm not sure if he means that it's ok because it doesn't bother him, or he means that he won't explore this any further.

"Let's get lost in those puddles over there," he points out to my relief, dropping his hands back to his side.

I take him up on the offer and hit them full speed ahead.

We have the type of day most girls wish they could have with their father, right up to a picnic, a blanket laid out, the cheesy checkerboard pattern in a gorgeous clearing in the woods, making it a picturesque scene.

The trees are bountiful, the leaves a beautiful array of deep ivy tones and brilliant yellows.

"Have some more."

The bottle clinks against the amber glass, then my teeth as he coaxes me to drink, and I find myself lost in the first phase of inebriation, knowing full well he's doing this to ease any fight I might give.

My words from earlier had kept him away, momentarily, but he either doesn't believe them, or he doesn't care, so I down the other glass, nausea filling me, the trees above me spinning as I fall to lie back onto the checkerboard blanket, disappearing in tightly sewn squares.

Hot all over, a silky dew covers the uppermost layer of my skin, and despite the heat, goosebumps crawl slowly.

The trees continue to spin as my hips fall as far as they can.

The outside of my thighs pushed into the fleece.

I cling to him, looping my arms beneath the pits of his arms as he falls over and over.

I hold him because I love him.

I hold him because I know it makes him feel loved and I want him to feel loved by me.

I hold him because If I let go, he will see how wet my cheeks are.

Just how much I have cried.

I hold him until the stream dries and he floods me.

"I love you Laurel, and I never want to forget this day," my father kisses along my neck enticing my skin to blossom, keeping me complacent beneath him.

"I love you too," I say with full honesty because I do.

I love him.

It ends like any date would, a generous kiss and proclamations of love.

...

Sixteen
Two years of freedom, unless of course, I get the early
acceptance, which to be honest, I am hoping for.
Ava is sleeping wrapped up and stuffed into a carrier that sat
across Rachel's back, her brow randomly furrowing as she
threw tablecloths and cups down.
Her locks are turmeric and slightly curled at the ends.
Some mornings it stood rigid on the sides, and she would pull
on as if it was some type of intrusive tumor.
It always ended in her pulling too hard and crying.
Babies are not the brightest.

Dean and Tasha were running late, but Mikey's brood of
troublemakers had somehow shown up bright and early.
My dad and his friends circle the barbecue like wolves getting
ready to make a kill.
The only time men would cook without it emasculating them.
I watch on, nervously awaiting my chance to snag my dad's
truck keys.
Mikey and his friends stood out at the furthest corner of our
property, tossing rocks out into the thick woods.
Corey hung back behind Mikey as if he was perpetually
awaiting instruction.
Follower.
Or perhaps he was avoiding the sunlight, his fair skin and red
hair making him an easy target.

I never cared for him, he was an entitled brat and always
stunk of cheap beer and sweat.
He once tried to touch my thigh during a movie, it made my
skin crawl.
I had vacated the premises of our living room like my life
depended on it.
Still couldn't tell you how the movie ended,
William, on the other hand, beamed over Mikey.

He had at least a foot on him. His hands were tan and rough from a summer of working with his uncle. Despite his stature, it always seemed like my brother was the ringleader, and he always had the final word.
William was a wimp.
Too dumb to realize that he could easily overpower Mikey.
They were all over too often and were always too loud.
I, on the other hand, rarely had anyone over.
The disgusting thought of my dad making a move on one of my friends made it easy for me to suggest anywhere but home, and if anyone did come, I made sure to let Rachel and Dad know.

Gale had arrived too.
She leaned against a large oak, her eggplant skirt jutting up as she pressed harder.
It revealed a lacy set of panties.
Red. Crass.
It suits her.
Then there was her face, caked in makeup with her usual dim expression.
Scowling.
I could tell by the way that her lips shook that she was jonesing for a cigarette and Mikey had probably told her to wait till after the party, or at least till no one was around, their little excursion in the parking lot still souring the air between them despite a heart to heart.
My father would have a lot to say if he saw her smoking, despite his habit of chewing tobacco.

We had never said more than a couple of words to each other, and it was more than enough.
I could tell that my dad didn't like her, guess we had that in common.
Sometimes I wondered if Mikey had picked her just to get some of Dad's attention.
He certainly was brazen when she was around.
They weren't shy with their physical attraction.

I look over at Rachel, her shoulders look like they ache, "I think little Miss is ready to eat," she comments as Ava begins to fuss, grabbing Rachel's locks and tugging.
I smile, something warm filling me as I look into my sister's eyes.
Cobalt orbs so expressive you could never mistake her desires.
"I can finish this up," I offered, grabbing some napkins from the bin.
Rachel nods a big smile. "I am lucky to have you," she tells me.
I don't reply.

Rachel and I had been getting along lately.
We had even gone out shopping the other day.
We made our way out with three bags full of baby clothes.
The conversation was always superficial, but there was no way I could ever confide in her.
She would never believe me. Could never accept the facts.
That the man she loves is a *lost man*.
That her baby could be his next target.
But I know.
I believe it's inevitable.
My stomach churns at the thought.
I grab another pile of paper napkins, the textured design brushing against a paper cut.
A sting pulsing up the nerves of my hand.
I peel away at them and begin to set them next to each plate.
Plates that don't match the decorations.
A warm breeze passes through the decorated yard, wind chimes wishing me a happy birthday.

My eyes scan the yard once again.
Mikey and Gale are gone.
Brazen.
The men are gathered around the grill, talking dirty, not realizing how loud they are, smoke swarming around their faces like an angry swarm of flies.
Teasing.

Teasing my father's coworker about his new, young, post-divorce girlfriend.
"Ain't she a little young for you?" A coworker I don't recognize asks, jealousy clear in his glare.
"She's legal alright? If it bleeds it breeds, right boys?"
They all laugh as if the monthly torment is some sort of trap our bodies lay out, so they finally have permission to take us without guilt.
I'm even more disgusted when my dad chimes in, flipping the burger patty, specks of blood jolting away from the undercooked meat and back into the black cloud of the grill,
"If she ain't bare, it's fair."
Strange, considering he likes me lacking any womanly hair.
That one gets all the men hollering, leaving my stomach tight, and acid rising in my throat.
It took every ounce of strength I have, which isn't much not to vomit all over them and display my disgust.

Mikey

Gale basically begs for it.
"Take me to the house."
She wants to rub my lantern.
Her wish is my command.
I let that genie out of the bottle, and Pandora out of that little box.

Laurel

"Hey there," I hear a silky voice run into my ears.
The feel of another body against mine makes me jump.
I spin around the voice, causing a sudden surge of energy to fly through me.
Grandma.

Grandma Jean, Dad didn't take after his mother at all, and I had never met his father, but I assume he resembles his sons.
There she stood, as hip as always, refusing to grow old.
Earring dangling frantically along with her excited state.

"How are you doing honey?"
She wraps her arms around my waist and pulls me close. "I'm great, I didn't know you were coming," I whisper as she holds me, lying. I knew.
For some reason, her touch makes me uncomfortable, and I weasel my way out of her bedazzled clutch, her hold too possessive.
I sprint my eyes over her in awe, hoping she won't see.
Despite being in her mid-sixties, she could've been mistaken for a much younger woman.
Hair always styled, dyed copper, her real color closer to a bland ash.
I liked that she dyed her hair, the true color washed her out. It didn't compliment her large honey eyes.
Brought too much attention to her upturned nose and pointy chin.
She never let her age stop her from living, whether it was her flashy jewelry and bright over-the-top outfits, or her taste in modern music.
She was a force to be reckoned with.
All five feet four inches and one hundred ten pounds of her.
"You need to get some meat on you dear" she criticizes, looking me up and down, like honey dripping along my frame, "That's absolutely beautiful, hon," she adds her thoughts scattered.
I blush, forgetting his gift.
"You know the boys like a lil' stuffin' on their women. I mean you are, after all, a woman now dear," my grandma states tenderly, taking my hand and caressing it.
I didn't need to be reminded just how much.
Physical affection was her way of showing love.
I couldn't say it was mine.

She is just happy to see me, I have to remind myself, allowing her to hold my hand.
"I'm not too worried about boys right now Grandma," I fib, my thoughts all racing back to Kyle.
Was this whole conversation going to be composed of lies?
They often are.

"Don't put ideas in her head Mom" a voice interrupts, evoking
goosebumps.
"Son," I hear Grandma Jean exclaim, her frame quickly
turning to meet him.
I watch them hug, their straight noses tipped with a slight
upturn and their wide foreheads revealing their lineage. It
trickles down to my face.
Grandma's large hoops jangle as she pulls away with a
motherly smile.
"It's good to see you ma! How long are you staying for?"
"Surprised?" she asks.
My dad nods yes, eyes brimming with happy tears.
"Well, Rachel and I planned it. It's been a while, and I thought
it would be nice to make a pit stop before I head out to Carol's
house," my grandma says, each word more excited than the
next.
The two separated, my dad beaming, "Carols, huh?"
Grandma nods
"Took a cab over. It cost me an arm and a leg, but your dear
Rachel offered to drive me back to the city tonight. Even
offered me a room at her sister's place."
My dad stiffens.
"So, you're heading to New York, then?"
"The big apple."

They share a smile, but all I see is disappointment in his eyes.
Her eyes.
I see him there.
A lonely child who needs his mother.
Grandma hadn't been around much.
Not when it mattered at least, and my grandpa died when dad
was only eleven.
She spent a lot of time partying and dating, leaving him home
with a string of babysitters.
Neither of his parents had been ready to have kids, but they
were blessed with two boys, regardless.
Neither really wanted kids.
Then came my mother, and in her he discovered that want.

To make a family.
One that was slowly crumbling.

"That's great ma," he interrupts her before the train wreck that
he was surely feeling at being left once again could crash and
burn.
I felt as if I was stuck in the unsaid that lingered between the
two. "Now, what kind of ideas are you putting in Laurel's
head?"
I could sense a bit of anger in his tone. This went unnoticed by
her.
"I mean look at her. I blink and here she's gone off and
become a fine young woman."
I blush, wishing I could run away from the interaction.
I, for one, didn't see what she saw, and my father doesn't need
a reminder.
"I bet you have to beat the boys off with a bat!"
She howls at that.
Dad does not.
"Well, you know she's growing fast, they all are," the
uncomfortable words muddle out of his mouth before looking
me up and down, feigning paternal innocence.
A hyena watches his prey, waiting for the right moment to
pounce but not daring to reveal its intention with the rest of
the herd looking on.
Why share a meal when you can have a feast?
"Of course they are! Speaking of growing, I need to get my
hands on my new granddaughter. Where is my little Ava?"
They haven't met yet. She has been too busy living and
finding herself and visiting friends.
A wide proud smile crosses his mouth, 'I'll take you up to the
house. Rachel just took her up to feed her."
I could see the joy on my grandmother's face as if she was
about to unwrap a Christmas gift.
I watched them start to turn and decide that I should seize the
opportunity with my dad.
He was, after all, vulnerable.

That vulnerability could go both ways, but I doubt he would
lash out given the context.
"Can I take the car for a little?"
Head jerks back to face me with a half-smile on his face.
To the outside world, it would seem like a sweet interaction,
but they would be wrong.
"What do you need the car for?"
Should I lie?
Tell him I was running to the store and ran into Kyle there.
I choose honesty, knowing full well I would get my share of
lies tonight.
"I told Kyle I would pick him up." 'I paused, gazing down at
the sparse grass.
I could sense both sets of eyes on me as my grandma lingered
just feet away, waiting impatiently, her toe clicking.
"Kyle lives right down the road. Why would he need a ride?
Boy can walk."
Disdain.
"His sister is visiting and has the truck. I just need to get him
at work."
The tone changes, yet his smile spreads further to compensate.
I was starting to grow warm, thoughts scattered.
Maybe I had tried to push my luck too far.

Dad destroys the space between us and places the set of keys
in my hands, a small jangle escaping as it leaves his.
Before I can celebrate, his hand wraps around my waist
pulling me in for a hug, beard scruffy against my cheek.
He is hot, literally and figuratively.
 "Make it fast, Laurel."
"Dad," I began to protest.
No chance. He pulls me in a tight, hoarse voice, spews honest
words.
His words sting and bury themselves deep. I can feel my skin
crawl and he kisses my forehead gently.
"Even after I'm long gone, you will always be my little girl," I
tear my eyes back and meet his lustful stare, "Happy

birthday," he added in a whisper, his minty breath cooling the skin of my cheek.
He had never spoken to me like that before.
It may have seemed innocent to some.
I know better.

Mikey

Sweet frosting sits on my tongue.
Lingering, stabbing at the pleasure centers of my brain that scream for more.
Her hand is on my stomach, slowly inching down, the kitchen island hiding my eagerness.
Before I could stop her, her hands had made their way down past my buckle.
Rock hard.
That was all it took.

"Babe," I groan.
"Take me to your room," Gale orders, leading me by the cock.
I resist.
She pulls in another direction, my belt buckle clinking against the floor.
If anyone walked in, I would have no way to explain this away.
Major turn on.
I grab her hand tight, feel her nails dig in, gasping. I pull her lips to mine.
"Not here," I pant, sinking my teeth into the crook of her neck, inhaling cotton candy and sweat, "My bedroom," my voice orders with a growl.
I tried to come across as masculine, and dominating, but it sounds so foreign.
Recently, I learned that the way to her heart was to demean her.
Gale grins; shark teeth, predatory almost.
Apex predator.
She likes it. Is ready for blood.
I move my hand to her hair and push her against me.

Not much effort.
No resistance.
Crimson lips wrap tightly along mine.

I entertain her for a long while, hands eagerly gripping the base of her head as we kiss.
My fingers twist into her hair, her pale scalp now snow white, and yet I twist harder, a knot building between my digits.
She doesn't mind as she sucks down on my tongue.
I close my eyes, feel myself about to break.
"Fuck Mikey," I hear her complain as she jerks away, my tight grip pulling her hair free.
Long fake berry strands. Damn.
"Mikey!"
I snap out of it, knuckles like pearls.
"Don't stop," I order as if I owned her.
She falls to her knees, eyes lustfully looking up at me, spit running down her chin, a hint of fury behind her large pupils.
"Take me up to your room and I promise I won't," her serpent-like tongue flicks out delicately.
She is keen on rising back to her heel-clad feet, hands massaging my bicep from one end to the other.
I pull her by the chin, the adrenaline is making me feel sick, lightheaded almost.
"Take me to your room then," she orders as she cups my chin squeezing.
I pull back from her ironclad grip.
The strain on skin that shouldn't stretch is apparent, and my chin wobbles.
Not a moment too soon.
I see Rachel heading up to the deck.
"Better hurry, babe," I tease.
Gale shoots up before Rachel can see with a delighted squeal.
I follow close behind leaving the risk downstairs, chasing that little death two steps at a time.

Laurel

I didn't dare disobey.

Drove faster than I intended.
Kyle was waiting, as promised.
"Didn't expect you to be my ride," he says, getting in the truck, an old soda can crunching beneath his feet as he takes a seat.
He set his bag in the empty seat between us, dimples already sinking deep as he analyzed me.
Not for long.
Nimble fingers pull through my locks as he pulls me into his embrace.
Quick. Simple. Minty. Prepared.
"I feel like I haven't seen you in ages," he comments, pouting his bottom lip pouting.

His sweats are a cloudy gray. He lifts me to meet gray skies.
The type of gray you see right before a tornado hits.
A shade that evokes a stillness.
Heavy, low-toned static fills the space between the Earth and the sky.
"Are you trying to make me feel bad?"
He shakes his head no, then yes, as his hand sneaks to mine.
I did feel bad.
"Maybe a little."
"Get it all out now," I ordered, before sneaking another kiss.
I tried to make it quick, a sense of dread filling me, knowing I was going back home.
The heaviness dwindles along his lips.
A new kiss.
This one isn't as simple.
It lingers, building before threatening to explode.
His mouth works against mine, knocking.
I allow my lips to part, tongues slowly caressing.
Calloused hands on my waist pulling me in close.
Ash meets the glaucous cool of my dress.

The beauty of a three-seater.

Mikey

I see her, from the streaky patio window, Gale helping pour
ice into the bucket, our little romp complete, at least mine was.
It had been quick, rough, and exactly what I had needed.
He is with her in the yard.
My sister. Kyle.
His hand gently moves to hers, caressing her palm as if he's
worried someone might see.
She smiles wide, taking advantage of the moment and
snatching his hold, her smile directed at him as if it's a little
secret they share.
Perceived privacy.

We had never been friends, Kyle and me.
We used to bicker; always competing over whose bike was
faster, or who could run further.
Childish.
Now he is here.
We are no longer children.
A feeling of annoyance flows from the pit of my stomach.
Lingering. Burdensome.
There is something complex there.
Something that needed to be talked out.
Therapy? A good old lock-up?
I had seen one. A therapist, that is.
After my mother's passing.
It did absolutely nothing.
My father had not pressed me to continue.
For all he knew, I was fine.
Still am.

"What are you staring at?" Gale hisses into my ear, bringing
me down.
I ignore her and tear the seal of another twelve packs of fizzy
crap and dump it into the bucket.
The metal cans clink as they succumb to the cool cubes.
"Hurry the hell up," an adenoidal voice whines behind me.

Corey.

His nose is always whistling.
Allergies he claims.
Will follows close behind, his oaf-like build towering over
Corey's scrawny build.
"Well, if the two of you would stop messing around this
wouldn't take so damn long," I half joke.
They both laugh, almost as if I had ordered them to do so.
There was nothing funny about what I had just said.
"Speaking of messing around," Corey shoots Gale a look.
I could tell he had a thing for her since prom night.
Hell, for all I knew they were messing around.
Not that I cared.
If it came down to it, I could muster up the energy to play the
role of a defensive jealous boyfriend.
Would probably break something and storm off, secretly not
giving two shits about what had transpired, not with Natasha
on my mind.
I could imagine them.
Corey bumbling like an idiot trying to get Gale there,
wheezing from his lack of activity.
Gale bitched the whole time about what was taking him so
long.
Clearly bored.
The thought caused me to crack a smile.
"What's so funny?" he asks, a smile appearing across his face
as if he knew without knowing at all.
I shrug, "Nothing."
It really was not funny because Gale was bound to cheat
eventually and although I don't care that she might leave me,
or find someone else, I certainly don't need the humiliation
and the "I told you so," my father might offer.
"What's the plan tonight?" I change the subject quickly, not
asking anyone in particular but fully expecting a response,
peering to see Laurel leaning against the rotting wood of what
used to be a white picket fence that outlined the properties of
full mass.
Gale's brow furrowed. "I thought you were taking me to the
movies," whining her fingers, twisting her fingers with unease
as if I might bail on those plans.

I break the seam of a twelve-pack box, it collapses on itself, the army print folding in.

"I never said I wasn't taking you. My dad's out working late. We have plenty of time."
Gale grins and takes my hand. "You got time for me then," she teases.
The girl is insatiable.
"You guys are nasty. Didn't you get it all out earlier?" Will complained.
His voice suddenly rang through, distracting me from my spying.
I shot a disappointed look, "You wouldn't be upset if you were getting any."
He could not dispute the fact that he was jealous.
Will had never kissed a girl, and he had never slept with one. Sometimes I wonder if he might be gay.
He never seemed interested when Corey used to bring his old man's stash of nude magazines.
"My mom will kill me if she catches me looking at this," he would complain, diverting his eyes from the ink-splattered covers.
"The worst thing your mom's going to do is take you to the church and make you sit in that confession booth," I would tease.
Corey would always follow my lead, "The only thing that fat fuck is going to do is make you say twenty Hail Marys," he pauses "And maybe recite the lord's prayer out loud," he would add.
Corey had a very strong opinion of the church, as did Will.
I could always see the struggle in his eyes when we would bash his faith, not that he truly practiced.
His mom, however, lived and breathed Mother Mary in all her pure, untouched divinity.
The eternal virgin, despite the flock of kids she is alleged to have.
Now, I was raised in church weekly when my mother was around, and then on the holidays, or when it was important to make an appearance, but this was another level.

I can't blame people for believing in a higher power. I just chose not to.
Hated when people would try to debunk the existence of a higher power by pointing out the wrong in the world.
War. Starvation. Murder. Theft. Abuse.
The list drags on.
That argument was an easy way out.
If they thought about it, the evils in the world do not disprove a God.
God gives free will.
If you believe in a higher power.
Free will leads to the monumental wrongs we commit.
It did not disprove God, but it also did not prove the existence.
I always wanted to ask Mrs. Ruiz what it was that had convinced her but never did, her chocolate eyes too kind. I couldn't bring myself to argue with her.
It would sound like I was mocking her.
Which would be my intention.
She attends confession weekly, her gold rosary always in her pocket, red lathered Catholic Bible front and center in their living room, the binding worn.
It sat on a podium.

One unfortunate night I had gotten up for some water and had seen her rest her hands on it, her beige lips moving furiously in complete silence.
Will had even once dragged me to service after I had spent the night.
My dad was no help when I called for a ride. "It wouldn't hurt you," he preached as if he enjoyed the Catholic church.
It definitely would not hurt him, and I would much rather go to our church.
I was bored to tears by a priest in long robes whose voice sprung out as flat as a plateau. I vowed then and there to no longer stay over on a Saturday night.

"Anyway, about tonight," I pipe up, tousling my hair, "The movie should be out before ten."
Gale shoots me a look that tells me to shut up.
I ignore her.
"How about we go to the quarry?" Corey suggests.
The quarry was always a good time, as it was always littered with bored youth and a litany of possible pull-outs to buy us drinks if you offered some incentive.
It was never hard to convince still pimply boys in their mid-twenties to buy you beer.
They clung on to youth for too long and desperately wanted friendship or a good lay.
A stroke along the arm, a whisper in the ear, and sir struggling to find a zipper were suddenly motivated to at least get a chance to try.
"Maureen and Reese said they would be there, and they already have someone getting them booze," he adds.
No one needs any more convincing.
"Maureen?" Gale questions, eyes as large as dinner plates.
Corey stares at her, popping a tortilla chip into his mouth, catching it with a loud crack.
He chews fast, waiting for her to continue.
"What's your point?" I snap, the wait irritating me.
Gale grins, obviously excited by the gossip she is about to unleash.
"I just heard that she was knocked up."
Will's grip tightens around his can of soda.
He had had a crush on Maureen since the second grade, and she had never so much as looked at him.
"No- "Corey started, taking a quick guzzle from his can
"That's all-bullshit Gale."
Gale taps a long fingernail on the counter, "How the hell would you know?"
He plops down off his chair and tosses the empty can into the overflowing bin. It hits the edge with a clink before falling to the sticky floor.
"Because Reese told me that she wasn't."

She looks at me disappointed, the attention in her story
already draining.
"Dodged a bullet," I called out into the open.
Corey adds a jovial howl.
I don't dare look up at Gale who I assume is pissed off.
"And that-" I begin before popping the top off a water bottle
with a crack," is why I always wrap my tool."
That was not always true, but what would they know?
I take a long drink, the water disappointingly warm, sloshing
in my belly.
Thirst left unquenched.
I make my way to the red cooler.
The so-called adult cooler.
There were two coolers floating around today, which made for
easy swiping, the beers sunk beneath the eternally melting ice.
Unabashed, I lift the lid and grab the coldest beer I can find,
gripping each bottle in my palm and gauging its temperature
before settling on one.
Truth is the beer I had selected was probably not any cooler
than the other, but I like to believe it is.
I twist the top, droplets of water weakening my grip.
The maroon lid pops, amber liquid flowing down my throat,
and I drink deeply till it's empty, then reach for another,
glancing up to gauge my friend's reaction.

Will looks uncomfortable. Gale, irritated that I did not get her
a beer sneers Guess I'm in trouble.
Corey follows my lead.
The reactions I had hoped for.
Followers.
Dying to fit in.
"Don't get wasted," Gale whines as she attempts to snatch the
bottle from my grip.
As if two beers were going to mess me up.
The glass clinks against my teeth as she tugs, a stinging pain
running from the roots to my head.
I try to play it cool, but I feel as if I could slap her.
Again, she snags at my grip, this time pulling the beer to her
lips.

Gale proceeds to sip the beer, clearly not enjoying it, "I'll stop after this one," snatching it back after a few moments, "Get your own," I add.
Corey downs his beer and tosses the cap against the wall.
 It clinks and bounces off, ending its journey on the kitchen floor.
I can feel the warmth climb, my muscles loosening.
Relaxed.
"Speaking of wrapping your tool," Corey sings as he tosses Will a beer.
By pure luck Will catches it, clearly startled.
Apprehensive.
He twists the top while taking a drink with a grimace.
So much for looking like a man.
Will was a sloppy and emotional drunk, and a rare one, thankfully.
The last time we had convinced him to have a couple he sobbed the entire drive home, his neck seemingly boneless, swaying at every bump and turn in an exaggerated manner.
Corey thought it was funny and deliberately hit every pothole he could.
Will responded by vomiting wine coolers and hot dogs all over the side of the car.

"Don't be a fool," Will interrupts.
Corey glares before helping himself to another beer.
I am through my second and am starting to feel a warmth rush through me.
"He isn't wrong," I add in support of Will's statement.
Corey rolls his eyes "Well let's hope Kyle isn't a fool,".
My head snaps.
What was he getting at?

"What?"
Corey loves to get a rise out of me, my birthday is no exception.
"Kyle is totally going to bone your sister tonight, and there is no way she can say no."

I mull over the thought for a moment, cautious in what I would say next, offering a cool gaze.
"Why would she not say no?"
Gale scoffs. "Have you not seen him?" she interjects with a little giggle," I mean you have known him for years; you have to admit…Kyle is smoking hot."
A twitch of anger hits then dissipates.
She was not wrong, Kyle was handsome, effortlessly so, and that damned beanie he always wore gave him a cool air of mystery.
"If she says no Kyle would just move on anyway… all the girls at school are always throwing themselves at him."
Gale nods in agreement, her hair bouncing, along with my wavering patience.
I roll my eyes.
"That is if he makes it out of here alive," Will buzzes before he stuffs a marshmallow deep into his mouth.
I shrug, the action pointed directly at him.
"I think what Will means is that your dad is probably going to kill him before the party is through."
Her voice was irritating, her words were not far off.
"What's with him anyway?" he inquires, a string of white goop dribbling down his chin before he hurriedly sucks it back up.
"Who?" I play dumb.
"Don't deflect, you know damn right who we are talking about," Corey interjects, crazed and hyper-focused eyes drilling me.
I take a deep breath, "My dad hates Kyle. Plain and simple."
I can tell they want me to tell them why.
"There's an old adage."
Gale's eyes roll, "Please enlighten us, Mikey."
"You don't put your dick where another man has already been."
Will chokes momentarily, the sound of wheezing resonates around me.
Corey scrunched over laughing, Gale silent, the joke going right over her head, which seems impossible given that her head was full of air, floating far above her shoulders.

"Geez that's a fucking good one," Corey wheezes, his hands pushing into his side.
"Wooo-" he continued to laugh, "You got me dying over here."
I can't help but join in.
It's infectious.
Viral.
Instead of aches and boils, the affliction is laughter.
Loud.
Echoing.
Laughter.

My cackle is cut short, abruptly I click my jaw shut when I catch sight of him.
Wiping a tear from my eye, I feel regret-like bile in my throat.
I had messed up.
Royally.
Kyle.
Kyle who had been walking to the guest bathroom.
No smile.
Not amused by the dark truth that I played off as a farce.
We connect. Pupil to pupil.
He knows. He can read me.

"It's a fucking joke," I inform him defensively.
There is no convincing him it is.
"Time to blow out your candles," is all he states, ice in his eyes.

...

A little while later, Laurel and I share spittle, blowing it from our mouths onto the shared marble sheet cake.
Vanilla for Laurel, chocolate for me.
At least we could agree on the frosting; buttercream, green dye, our names written out in black ink.
Then come the gifts, Uncle Cal lurks in the background, his daughter munching on a piece of cake a quizzical look on her face as if she can't discern what she is tasting.

Cal offers me a shaving kit, men's blades, and aftershave.
I wonder if I'll ever grow enough hair to utilize it.
Cal and my father both got five O'clock shadows around two
every day, while I still had silken peach fuzz that settled along
my upper lip like a newly sprung caterpillar.
I thank him, moving to the next gift, a set of cassette tapes for
my radio, one that's just rain sounds, something I would
certainly enjoy come night if my insomnia creeps in.

Tearing into a new box I am filled with contentment when I
see a couple of shirts that would fit perfectly, across from me
Laurel doesn't seem quite as happy when my father presents
her with a gift, he and Rachel had purchased for her; a
domesticated gray finch, with beautiful red puffed cheeks and
a sleek sharp orange beak.
It chirps a magnificent magnetic call, his eyes solemn against
the metal bars of the curved cage.
"What do you think Laurel?" My father asks, his arm around
her shoulders, her eyes low, peering through the bars.
"Why isn't he flying?"
The bird's head twists sporadically, twitching and emitting
little chirps.
"What type of bird is that?" My grandma asks, her fingers
rubbing the bar, her body close to Laurels, teeth bared with
excitement.
My sister peers up, my father's arms leaving her shoulder,
"Why isn't he flying?" I hear her ask again, her voice filtering
through to me despite the commotion of chatty partygoers.
"Don't you like her?
Laurel stamps a smile onto her face and caresses the slate bars,
her nail scratching the metal, before beaming her eyes up at
our father and telling him she loves it.
"Dad?"
 He sighs, seemingly annoyed at her line of questioning, "We
had her wings clipped Laurel, and we'll have to do it every six
to eighteen months or so, that way she can't fly away."
"What if I want her to fly?"
My mousy sister squeaks.
"She won't want to hon, she's used to her cage now."

It's all Rachel has to offer.
Laurel beams, trying to make him feel good, but behind that grin, there is nothing but rage.

Laurel

Fire.
I am like fire.
A small flame, a spark, all so innocent erupting into something
else.
Something destructive, and detrimental to all.
Tonight I am that flame.

Something has sparked in me.
My silence turned into a deafening roar.
No one ever talks about how loud the fire can be.
No one expects the roaring ferocity.
I don't hold back.
I laugh. I feel free.
Weightless.
I can feel it.
It isn't tangible, and that somehow makes it more authentic.
It is absolute. It's mine.

Drinks are pouring all around, filling the air with the scent of
burning alcohol.
Mostly cheap beer, bubbles ballooning to the top of clear
plastic cups.
Most end up spilled, mixing into the dirt, the reminiscence of
old beers destroying the home of thousands of ants below.
Little blobs spotted the khaki soil.
I treat myself to a drink.
One drink only.
I won't mess up my chances with Kyle again, and it has to be
tonight.
Maybe it's fueled out of anger.
Anger fueled by my father's words.
My desire to pull away from his control.
To share my body the way it was meant to be shared.

Here and now, I have a choice and I want to discover him, and in the end, find us.
The thought of the bitter beer doesn't sit right with me.
Instead, I settle for a swig of straight vodka from the lustrous flask.
It stings going down from my tongue down to the pit of my belly.
Kyle looks at me, a sheepish grin causing his dimples to wrinkle, "Just one," I promise.
I hand the flask and drop it back into Emma's open hand.
She quickly takes a drink of her own.

Kyle's sister, two years older and dating a college sophomore on a sports scholarship.
Football.
Lineman.
Emma made every game despite the long drive, and next year she would join him at university.
Kyle and Emma don't look anything alike.
She took after their mother.
Her eyes were dark like chocolate, her hair a shade away from platinum, with perfectly sculpted dark eyebrows that arched beautifully about two-thirds of the way through.
Natural.
She was truly beautiful with her long body, a small curve right at her belly that made her look like a real woman.
Then there were her legs, long, and always perfectly shaven showing off bronzed skin.
The only unnatural part of her.
She loved the tanning bed.
The only true tell that they were related was those dimples that concave with every smile.
Just like their father.

Emma tosses the flask across the pit to her boyfriend, it zooms like a bullet, flickering in the flame.
Anthony and she had been together since her freshman year despite all odds.

People always stared, questioning what she could be doing with a man like him.

A black man.

It was still taboo among the uneducated and this town is full of people stuck a few decades in the past.

Old habits die hard, and old racists don't seem to die at all.

Inherited hate keeps them alive well past their prime to spread their gospel.

Their love was strong.

They didn't seem to mind the stares of the elderly or the slurs the especially bold few would toss their way.

"My lady, maybe you should be the one playing football," he shouts, barely catching the drink.

She sticks her tongue out at him, "Does that mean I get your full ride," she shoots back.

I watch him try to think up something clever, eyes like ochre focusing on the flames.

"Stick to football baby," she teases, the words curling slowly, booze softening the edges.

Without a moment's hesitation, Darrell runs around the pit, bumping into an already drunk junior, almost knocking him down before grabbing Emma and throwing her over his shoulder.

She doesn't stand a chance against the brawny, six-foot-three hulk of a man.

Despite the force he exhibits picking her up, he puts her back down as if she were a precious Fabergé egg, his chiseled face meeting hers.

No hesitation.

They were so simple. Perfection.

"What's on your mind?" Kyle questions, trying to ignore the flirtatious vibes the couple was emitting.

The two giggle simultaneously. Adorable.

Kyle would disagree.

"Just thinking about how adorable your sister and Darrell are," I tease, my voice jumping an octave.

"Gross," Kyle asserts, conveying his distaste for anything that related to Emma, Darrell, and their love life by putting his finger into his mouth and pretending to gag.

''Jealous?''
My hand creeps meeting the base of the beer he had been nursing all night.
He turns his head, Darrell and Emma now engaged in a deep embrace.
''Not at all. I just have a zero-interest policy when it comes to my sister's love life.''
He finishes his beer and tosses the can in the roaring fire, a spark escapes and lands on his foot with a crackle.
I watch him quickly shake it off. "Once was enough."
What does that mean?
I stare at him, perplexed, waiting for him to elaborate.
With a distressed look, he recounts walking in on Emma and Daryl the summer prior with great emotion.
''They were just there on the couch going at it," he exclaimed. "The living room couch!"
I could picture the sharp contrast between their conflicting tones, and the described position, the two of them lost in their moment.
Night and day. Snow and earth.
Mixing in harmonious bliss.
''Let's just say there was a heavy lack of clothing and tan lines on my sister's end. I got out of there as fast as I could and proceeded to burn my eyes out.''
I can't help but laugh, and he shoots me a look that I can't describe; longing mixed with a hint of something mischievous, the shot of vodka that was coursing through me made the smile all the more intriguing.

Staring across the coral blaze I see Natasha, dangling all over Dean, his arms tight around the loops of her jeans, squeezing happily at the denim.
Dean was no lucky charm, and his charm was wearing off until Tasha was drunk and high that is and now, she is happy to let him paw at her.
I had seen the truth of how she felt about Dean.
Mikey. Tasha.
They had gone off upstairs, I wasn't dumb.

I was not going to bring it up, as far as she knows I am clueless and she and my brother can keep tiptoeing, playing their secret game.

"I think I might dump Dean tonight," she had stated boldly earlier this evening as she slowly and intricately applied a peach-colored gloss to her abundant pout, trying to coax it along my lips.
"Here," she said, stroking the sweet substance along the bottom arch for flavor.
I watch her sift through her box and pull out a long black tube, "Try this on," she orders.
I don't fight her and apply the mascara.
"What's your endgame?" I questioned twisting the cap off, "also won't this look weird with the gloss?"
The deep red almost mocks me, cardinal. It's bold, and it's so unlike me.
"No end game," her lips pucker, "and the gloss is clear and for flavoring and the red won't be too much. I promise."
Lies.
I twisted the red stick back into its enclosure and handed it back to her unused.
"Come on Laurel, this would look great on you," she had pleaded looking into the mirror, dabbing the corners of her lips.
She was so beautiful with her sun-kissed skin and rounded, groomed brows.
"Fine. So Dean," I coaxed, trying to distract her from my inability to apply makeup correctly.
She takes her turn shrugging.
"No makeup, no talk of Dean, that's the deal."
Deflection.
"Plus I know you want to look good for Kyle.".
"I want to look good for myself," I replied, eyes meeting my reflection, it was not necessarily dishonest.
 She smirked.
"Fine, just do it."
Defeated, I twist the lid off a dark red, "This better be worth it."

"Laurel, when you're getting plowed in the back of Kyle's truck, racking those nails down his back it will be so worth it."
My face flushes crimson, "Tasha!"
She nudges me and grants me a sheepish grin, happy to get a reaction out of me.
She had not told me why she wanted to break up with Dean, but I was certain the reason lived in my house.

Mikey

The party is lame, but the fire burns bright, hot, and fiercely, and everyone is already wasted when we pull up and that's enough to convince me to stay.
I am sure it will perk up once I'm good and buzzed.
Will seems apprehensive and I tell him to lighten up as we step out of Gale's cramped car.
"It's a party, just chill."
He wraps his arms around himself, a protective embrace, 'My mom would freak if she found out I was here. What if she calls your house to check on me?"
I shrug, "I'm not sure man. No one's home."
The answer does not comfort him.
"Corey, can you help him out," I motioned.
Corey's eyes scan searching for Charlotte.
She stands next to Maureen.
Allegedly pregnant Maureen.
The girls make their way over clad in short dresses and frazzled hair.
"So is it true?"
His head spins to face Charlotte, "Is what true?'
The girls giggle stupidly hand in hand.
"Well, a little birdie mentioned that you might have a little Zen."
The bird was Gale.
"Is that true?"
Corey laughs nervously, pulling a small baggy, "about twelve hits."
My eyes wander to the clear baggie.

Acid. Mellow yellow. Tabs.
Lucy in the Sky, made popular by the Beatles of course.
Rumor is they used to dabble, and they were famous!
Met the Queen of England.
Rich!
What could a hit hurt?
John Lennon did acid.
Then again rumor has it he was also a heroin addict.
That could hurt.
But a little acid was not going to ruin my life, not in small
doses at least.
"So you have how many hits?"
Corey looks at the bag, "Twelve hits and there's," I count for
him, "Six of us unless you are not partaking Maureen."
Rolling eyes, "Why wouldn't I be?"
Charlotte nudges her.
"What?" She snaps, her off-colored green hair swaying.
"Rumor has it that you're pregnant," I say, pacing to fill the
space between us.
Her eyes roll for an obnoxiously long time, "as if."
That was enough to convince me, but not Will.
"I am not doing that!"
 Of course, he would bitch.
"Just one hit man, it can't be that bad."
"It can be that bad! I heard about some guy that tripped so
hard he thought he could fly and jumped off the roof of his
house!"
There's a band of sweat dripping down his face now as if he
had just hiked a mountain.
I laugh, noticing his stressed state, my confidence pushing
through, "I'm not an idiot Will!"
Or am I?
I mean people do die.

LSD.
Lysergic acid diethylamide.
Shit.
It even has the word die in it.
I mean so do loads of other words.

Diet. Obedient. Etc.
Anyway, acid is a synthetic chemical made from something found in ergot.
Ergot is a fungus that infects rye grain.
Does that make it a mushroom?
Rye grain is a member of the wheat tribe.
Commonly used to make bread.
Cold winter.
Wet Spring and all the town folk of Salem freaked the hell out and began accusing many women of witchcraft.
Or at least that is one theory.
The even sicker theory being that either religion or pure greed and hatred was driving the madness.
Also, why do we associate the Salem witches with burnings?
Our minds always jump to it when the reality is that not one was burned and almost all were hanged with the exception of Giles Corey who was crushed to death.
Madness.
Then there was Joseph Smith.
Farm boy who saw angels on the October day in New York.
Maybe the farm boy was just tripping balls.
He had not seen anything after his original vision.
LDS. LSD.
Same letters…. Suspicious.
That is enough to really convince me.
If some unremarkable man from decades ago can found an entire bullshit religion off a possible trip, then it might be fun.
William on the other hand does not seem as convinced.
He paces nervously, "Seriously though I don't wanna guys!"
The only option now is berating.
Emasculate.
"Ok," I pause to raise my tone, "Pussy."
I can tell it pisses him off as does the rest of the group as they begin to badger him until he breaks down with a nervous groan.
Tongues out, square bits, patterned black and white.
Yin Yang. Cancer.
Feminine and masculine energy balanced and harmonized, much like my brain was about to become.

That or it might scramble itself into a mush.
Either way.
"Bon voyage!"
In unison.

The trip is just that.
A trip. Long.
Exhausting. Enlightening.
Simultaneously darkening.
Will is out of control, yelling, flailing, giggling till he pisses his
pants near the quarry's edge.
Close. Too close.
 "Don't be stupid!"
He ignores me, foot dangling.
His loss.
Charlotte and Gale lay side by side on a large blanket,
caressing each other's hair, giggling.
I hope that might progress.
Meanwhile, Maureen is curled in a ball at the foot of the
blanket looking guilty.
I plop down next to her, her long locks flowing in the light
breeze, Charlotte's painted toes kneading into my back.
Waves.
Snakes of pleasure slithering up my spine.
Medusa.
They turn my heart to stone.
Maureen, however, seems much more malleable.
"Oh God help. I fucked up bad, Mikey."
I had drug myself into this conversation I want nothing to do
with.
"What if I am? "
"What?"
Her voice begins to slow dropping an octave, it's really
kicking in now, "What if I am pregnant?"
Geez.
"You said you weren't though?"
 This is not the energy I need.
Good vibes.

Good vibes.
Corey is attempting to measure the moon on the horizon with his fingers, "Does the moon look big to you, Micah?"
Those are the vibes I want.
I eye it, the little cratered holes throbbing, light beaming into my eyes, "So bright."
I watch Gale.
An angel.
A bright halo throbbing around her face.
My toes curl into the dirt.
I cannot recall removing my shoes.
Pebbles.
Little stones, a particularly smooth one rolled between my fingers.
William runs to me, falling to the ground, his frame sending mine across the coarse ground.
 I can feel blood running down my elbow, little bits of sand dug inside, gritty and scrubbing my skin.
Will laughs uncontrollably, words that are incoherent, babbling, and nudging me, "Get it?"
 I have no idea what he is saying.
A sting radiates down to my feet, "Why would you do that?"
Warmth trickles from my torn skin.
The stars are a swirl above, shining over the thick merlot that has slowed.
Distracted.
Little twinkling lights.
Connection. Meteors.
The swirling, creamy milky way.
I wish upon the blinking ones.
I wish to understand the world.
A wish that comes true momentarily.
I see it all. I know everything and nothing.

The connection intensifies, the layers of sky morphing into a veritable ocean of glittering dots, each one only a stone's throw away.
Gale plops next to me abandoning the warmth of the blanket watching on as I reach yearning for connection.

"It's almost as if I can touch the sky," my words ooze slowly.
"That's because you can Mikey. You can do anything."
Slurs.
Gale stands up, strips down to nothing but her panties, Corey and Will are too distracted to notice, and I am too enthralled in the night sky to give a damn.
She can do what she wants.
Feminism and all that stuff.
I want to touch her, regardless.
I stand up grazing my hand over the free sway of her breasts.
I want to take a swim.
I need to feel my own sway.
"Let's go swim!"
No hesitation on her end.
I strip and before I know it, I am in the water with Gale and Scarlett.
Both girls on their backs, lips trembling from the cold.
Along the ledge, I spot a cigarette light up.
Fucking vagrant bums always getting in the way of our fun.
Bum.
There was a whole town to loiter.
This is our spot.
My confused eyes can see a green blanket haphazardly propped up by a few sticks.
The man yells something I can't understand.
A splash mere inches away from me.
Again, he yells, pelting a rock this time, a disgruntled, "Get the fuck out of here!"
"Fuck off!"
"Yeah, fuck off bum," Charlotte echoes.
We exit the water quickly after that but not before I exact my revenge, a handful of rocks angled down and tossed beneath the ledge.
The bum cries out.
Something about his face.
Like I give a shit.
Guess I had hit him, served him right.

"Throw another one," Charlotte urges, her fingers tangled in Gales, the two twirling in the bright moonlight.
Witches.
Dancing, freely moving in the moonlight, casting their spells.
Will joins in.
 I join Corey who is still eyeing the moon.
Maureen is still pacing and sobbing.

…

I awaken, my elbow throbbing along with my head.
Passed out, face caked with dirt, a stream of drool breaking my fresh skin free from the dust bed.
"Gale is a few feet away, wrapped tight in a dusty sleeping bag, Charlotte to her left still shirtless, Will drooling on his stomach to her right.
I have no idea where Maureen and Corey are.

Laurel

Dean was plastered, but so was Natasha.
A match made in hell, oozing sexual repression mixed with a complete lack of intimate knowledge, despite how often they fucked, they could barely stand, neither a steady hold for the other.
They hadn't stopped touching each other since we arrived, neither wanting to give in to the other. Little teasing gestures, none too overtly sexual.
They were toeing the line.

I watch on as Tasha hits a joint, Dean's American blue Letterman draped over her shoulders.
Maybe Dean wasn't so bad after all.
It becomes crystal clear that she was probably not going to dump Dean after all, Natasha does not handle being alone well.
I watch on, Dean spits into the fire, a large glob of tobacco-filled dip, spindly little brown fibers sticking between off-white teeth.

I grimace, olfactory memories seeping in.
"Dean is wasted," Kyle whispers, his breath like a feather
tickling along the shell of my ear, taking my pace and owning
it.
Peering over at Dean I stare hungrily as he takes a sip off the
top of a newly opened beer.
"Should we get a drink or something?"
I was not about to let liquor sit between me and my goal, and
the one shot had been enough.
"Sounds nice, but I have something else in mind."

Instant regret.
I can't believe I am so forward.
"What would that be?"
He laughs, eyes vast, hungry, scanning mine as if he was
searching for something, waiting for my loose lips to reveal
more.
They stay tight.
Sealing my desires in their tomb.
"Laurel?"
I can sense the hesitation in his voice, and I don't want to lose
the tension.
My fingers latch in his pulling his touch to my waist.
It's not enough.
He wants to hear it, a nervous smile beaming into mine.
Ice cream scoop cheeks.

Gradually, I run my painted lips up from the night till they are
at his ear, his entire body tenses as the heat dribbles, "Take me
back to your truck a bit later, and find out?"
With those words I gently ran my glossed lips from his ear to
his neck, goosebumps rising as my hot breath greets
unsuspecting flesh.
Kyle's hand tightens around my waist, my lips stopping just
short of his.
"Are you sure?"
I respond by pushing my lips to his, allowing them to part.
Can taste him, our tongues dancing, an intricate waltz, no left
feet.

He pulls in a breath of night air, "It's later now," he murmurs,
our heads pressed together, body taut and needy with desire.
I want him to want it and judging by the way his teeth catch
my bottom lip as I try to pull away, he is almost there.
One more long kiss before my body meanders out of his
grasp.
Ninety percent.
"Not yet," I purr, a long feline-esque nail running up the
exposed biceps.

I need this to be perfect.
My first time.
For real.
"This is a new side of you birthday girl," his voice draws me
back in.
I push him away playfully now and take his soda bottle from
his hand, the beer he had been nursing gone, pressing it to my
lips, the tip easing its way past the pouty red stain before
amber sugar disappears down my throat.
"Now you're just messin' with me," the words leave his lips,
eyes glossy, words slow.
 "Not yet," I mouth before finishing the rest of his soda.

We spend what feels like an unbearable amount of time
socializing around the fire pit, watching everyone grow
progressively more inebriated.
Drinking themselves to oblivion, others place small sheets on
their tongues in hopes of seeing the world in a new light,
although some might argue that all one needs to do to break is
make it to Sunday mass.
No one here was going to be in shape for that come morning.
Natasha and Dean pass a square back and forth, the sheet
dissolving quickly in their saliva, the journey becoming a
shared one.
Joints pass around the pit, the scent filling the air.
Heavy and skunky.
Cheap.
Despite the high-pitched chatter, the night air that surrounds
is cloaked in heavy silence.

My hands sit against my hips.
Thrumming.
Squeezing.
I see smoke, the cherry butt in Dean's hand.
I guess the acid wasn't going to cut it.
"Give her a hit," Natasha commands, pulling the joint out of
Dean's hand.

She won't remember a thing tomorrow at this pace, which I
guess is the point.
Kyle eyes me, "Just one hit, I'm a bit nervous," I admit.
"You didn't seem nervous earlier," he retorts, eyes darting
between the smoke and my lips, watching the red of my lips
wrap around the white paper.
"Let me have one," he instructs, his voice dominating, "For
my nerves."
My eyes focus on his, "As if you have anything to be nervous
about."
His lip bites into his, "I wish that were true," his voice says, a
little shaky.
A sudden burst of flames makes me jump.
"Don't pour that shit into the fire!"
Masculine voices all around bickering over the flammable
liquids being dumped into the pit.
Another gushing flame pours out.
This was getting risky.
"Seriously, cut that shit out," Dean yells, his hair bobbing as
he jumps back pulling Tasha by the hand.
"Fuck off!"
They all quickly turn on Dean.
Tasha paws at his biceps, head swaying, she was probably
starting to feel pretty good.
Her eyes focus on the tree line, their tops swaying gently in
the light breeze.
I make my way to her.
It's time.

"I'll be back in a bit," I whisper.
She smiles wide, "Dirty."

Slurring.
"Just don't wander off," I warn her, the weed bringing a warm buzz to my body.
I float over to Kyle who is taking his own hit before passing the joint to his left.
I eye him, wondering if he feels as good as I do.
"Feeling good?"
He chuckles.
It's raspy.
"Nervous."
Never thought he could be nervous.
He had done this before. Sex.

I mean I had to, just not like this, and as far as Kyle knows not at all.
Maybe we are putting too much pressure on tonight, forcing this unspoken arrangement, so desperate to meet my end.
"You expect me not to be nervous? I mean look at you!"
My face is on fire now, the gentle buzz now vibrating through me with comfortable waves.
Hearing the genuine infatuation made my toes tingle.
"You think I didn't notice the makeup and the hair?"
Was I being too transparent?
"The minute you got in my truck I-" he stops.
"What?"
Shakes his head, "Nothing, it's stupid."
I want nothing more than to know, "Tell me," I add a pouty.
"Please," for good measure.
"Alright, it's just that I noticed you always use that body wash."
Vanilla and sandalwood.
The same wash my mother had used.
He always buys it for me.

Anxiously I drag my hands into my hair, slightly embarrassed he had noticed how much effort I had put into tonight.
It screams desperation.
"Is it a bad thing?" I ask.

Closer, he pulls me in, nose nuzzling into my neck, I can smell his aftershave, can feel him breathe me in, "God no. It's amazing. Reminds me of summer. "

Suddenly my need is unbearable, but it's not motivated by carnal desires, rather it's fully dictated by some instinctive emotional need.

The need to feel free.

Only found in him.

His touch.

His love.

It all makes sense.

Too much sense.

I face him, guide his hands up my shirt, the skin of my waist meeting his shaky touch.

Why?

Nervous tremble.

I'm nervous for numerous reasons, all of which are reasonable. There's that voice in my head, the nagging one that's afraid of finding pleasure with Kyle when sometimes pleasure hurts so badly.

...

The first time Dad made me finish during sex I tried to hide it, evading his lingering stare, aware of his intent.

To be honest, at first, I tried to keep it from happening, shoving my lip between my teeth and gnawing with brutal strength which for a reason I couldn't understand actually made the pleasure mount.

There was a quiet battle, one he wasn't keen to lose.

He never lost.

I was humbled, my resistance proved impossible as he had learned to read my body and adjust himself in whatever manner needed to make it happen, partially to alleviate his guilt and partially to make me complacent.

The slope of my clit was under the flat pad of his thumb, and he perfectly circled it, causing a dark shudder to permeate my tongue.

I hated him for it but also loved him in the same breath.
Mostly I loathed my body and its sorrowful yearning for that touch.
Hated how it made me feel, disgusting yet astoundingly free.

I stifled the sounds, but I was on top of him in a position that should've felt powerful but only left me exposed and he could see it all, my body ratting me out, rattling like burning wood.
By then he knew what his girl looked like in the throes of orgasm even when I hid it.
He spoke words that made my toes curl and my brow furrow in defeated rage, my heart depleted, a staccato stroke of air flaming in my lungs.
"That's so pretty baby… coming for me…so wet for me."

He loved the word "me," was always heavy on it, implying that I was his, but he was never mine.
Me. Mine. His.
Property.
Afterward, he told me to never hide my release from him, that he wants to hear it, and it makes him feel good.
I was so embarrassed it caused a sob to ripple through my throat.
"It's not embarrassing honey, it's natural to feel good."
He held me and did it again, repeatedly.
I almost believed him then, but I know better now.

That night I cried and ran my hands to that spot almost afraid to touch it as if it might ignite something in me.
The last thing I could bear to feel was that wet spark and what followed.
Firmly, I clenched at the deceiving flesh that had allowed me to feel so good yet so fucking sick.
My grip sat tight, nails digging in until I felt the skin break with a subtle pop, crescent-like wounds printed on my mound from the nail's edge, a trickle of blood soaking along the bed sheets.
I wished it was gone.
Prayed I was gone.

I wished then I couldn't feel it.
Prayed he could never make me feel good again.
I stopped touching myself for a while after that, refusing to
reacquaint myself with my body and its free wonders.
The pain didn't make me cry, not the physical at least, it was
the theft that had me empty.
As if each time he made me come he was stealing from the
men who should be.
Betraying the future men who should set my body aflame.

Then there was the guilt, I am sickened by how normal it feels
to be with him despite how abnormal the interactions are.
Now, I'm here and I want to feel that with Kyle, but I'm
petrified, a stoic redwood, unable to move, lost in indecision.
I place my hand on his and inch it up fighting to abate the
need to run or just lie down and take what he wants to give
me, his nails skimming the curve of my uncaged breasts, skin
bursting with tangible excitement, but my mind is not there.
Speckling skin mounds yearning for friction.
My nipples harden, painfully, scraping against the cotton of
my top.
His hand stops just short of cupping my breasts before
retracing its steps, "Not here," he groans, leg digging up
between my splayed thighs.

I swallow hard in the desert that is my throat and hesitate.
You want this.
You can do this.
Just be normal.
Am I ready?
My body says yes, but my mind is still hesitant.
Heart, body, brain, shoot.
Mind beats heart, heart beats a needy body valuing love over
lust, and body beats brain because her desire to be touched
and fucked will always obliterate common sense, plus I think
the cerebral cortex will always side with bodily urges.
Body comes out the conqueror.
"I don't want to be here anymore Kyle. "

Kyle kisses me slowly, he smells like smoke and citrus, tastes
like weed "Get me out of here," I plead.

He ignores my request and instead takes my hands into his,
his voice is low and sultry, his grip strong, "You sure you
want to leave all this?"
Motioning to a large fire and the swaying frame of tomorrow's
doctors, teachers, and leaders.
It doesn't feel promising.
My father would have a blast busting up this party.
Just like that, he has taken over again.
Dad.
I am ready.
To be free of him. To replace him.
Kyle was just the vessel.

"It's later now," I whisper leaning into Kyle's touch, words
slithering up his jawline and into his ear.
An eager response that leaves no doubt of our intentions.
Straightforward, my body floating, thoughts racing, body
relaxed.
Limber.
Two opposing forces dictate my body, and two voices dictate
my heart.

Before I know it, I'm pressed up against his truck, his mouth is
on mine, hands strongly gripping along my thighs.
I barely recall trudging up the rocky road to where he had
parked his truck.
My feet leave the ground, my only response is to wrap myself
around his bulk.

I am the roar of the fire, and he is the delicate silence of the
flame.
Warm kisses envelop me, his tongue gently caressing mine.
A heat forms between our bodies, tangible in the slowly
cooling air.

I groan, lips leaving mine, seemingly disastrous until I feel them trailing cautiously down my neck, abruptly stopping along the hem of my dress, lips static at my thighs.
 His face is buttery as it caresses my silky skin.
A kiss is planted, wet against me, and there's a low thrumming in my lower belly, that threatens to coil into something more given the right touch.
Those nimble digits slowly trace my outer thighs beneath my dress, coyly, a hint of hesitation.
My heart in my throat, beating excitedly as pulls his fingers through the elastic of my panties, a slow tugging leaving them at my ankles, an unshifted dress still clothing me above.
He is controlled, never too eager yet fully motivated.

Instinctively I reveal myself, unaware my thighs have begun to part.
Early flowering.
In bloom.
A slow, painful progression.
Labor.

I expose only a little more with every change of his expression, centimeter by agonizing centimeter.
Mid.
I can tell he is turned on, eyes are glazed over, hyper-focused yet completely oblivious to his surroundings.
I know the look well.
He bites his lip, my body fully bloomed, nectaries pulsing a sweet flow of invite.
Late.
The peak of my beauty.

Kyle can't help but touch me, strong fingers slowly tracing, making their way to the source of life-giving heat, but before he dares meet the sweet dew my body has created for him, he moves up and presses his lips to mine.
It makes the moment all the more intense as he barely makes contact, tracing lightly.
The hunt. The wait.

Anticipation.
A trickle of nectar escapes me, it moves down my thigh,
running a short course before my skin consumes.
A doe startled.
Intrigued.

"I want you," he whispers as our lips part with complete
honesty, a trembling breath filling his lungs.
As the words fall from his lips, I feel the exploration begin,
slowly dipping into the wet valleys, never daring to breach the
unspoken barrier.
Not wanting to break something he does not know has been
gone for a long time.
My mouth clicks shut with an audible dentin clack.
I am overcome with a carnal desire, my heart threatening to
beat out of my chest as he reaches the promised land, but
instead of forty years and a desert I had sixteen years and a
desert heart.
God, the desert had been worth trekking despite the heat. A
small wisp of a finger and my head falls into the nape of his
neck as easily as the Israelites fell for their false idols.
I can't control myself, the air leaving my diaphragm in broken
chatters "What about now?"
I'm not even asking, I'm begging.
Had never felt a touch like his.
Not even my own.
It feels like want.
Has me; Aching, Mad.

Briskly, I pull away from him waiting for a response that
never leaves his lips.
If a picture paints a thousand words, then an action is worth a
million, and he is a man of action.
Hand eases away and up to my waist helping me towards the
covered cab.
The door opens with the creaking of old rusty metal.
An old Beryl sleeping bag is laid out evenly, hiding away the
hard slats.
Worn, a small hole at the foot of the bag.

Coincidence?

Kyle spent countless nights out hunting during the summer.
This was nothing.
But then I felt a big pillow press into my neck, my touch
releasing the scent of lavender.
Was that also just a coincidence?
Pillows?
A makeshift bed?
The sheets that sat beneath the sleeping bag.
He doesn't expect anything I remind myself, despite the proof
that he had assumed we would end up here.

"I thought it would be nice if I tidied up," he commented as he
teetered above me, aware that I noticed the makeshift bed he
had set up, "and I didn't do it for this…"
My elbows ache from the hard metal beneath the bag.
I let out a small laugh, completely out of my control.
"Sorry," I wave it off, pulsing up to capture his forehead with
a swift kiss.
Nerves.
I try to choke it down with a little luck and it spreads like a
blazing fire on a dry eve.
Contagious, and suddenly we were lying next to each other in
various stages of breathlessness.
Not the type I had expected.
Joy. Pure joy.
I miss her.
"I'm sorry, I'm sorry," I say, trying to catch some air.
He does the same.
"I didn't mean to ruin the moment, Kyle," I state half
apologetically, half relieved that I hadn't upset him.
"You didn't ruin anything Laur, and as much as I love what
was just happening this is nice too."
Silence.

I take his hand and squeeze it.

"I'm sorry if it seems like I was trying too hard. I just wanted you to be comfortable, and I had no idea how else to do that other than to literally make you comfortable."
I turn to my side, our eyes locking.
Hips like hills, gentle slopes meeting valleys.
I place a carefully coordinated kiss on his cheek.
It lands with delicacy.
I hold it for a moment just to take him all in before retreating.
"I'm comfortable, Kyle. You didn't have to do anything to make that happen, other than be here with me."
My nails run up the slopes of his arms, cold daggers raising his flesh.
Maroon pyramids on a summer tan.

"I did."
Lackadaisical. Honest.
I question why.
"Can't explain it without sounding crazy Laurel."
"You don't have to hide your crazy from me, I'm well aware that you're certifiable…plus, I won't judge you," I confess, interrupting the chirping of the crickets, their song adding to the tangible ambiance.
He sucks in a deep breath, chasing his grin away.
"I think that people get too comfortable with the idea of tomorrow.

We were about to go down a rabbit hole, and I'm prepared, waiting for him to continue, "We live with blinders on, and we only see what's directly in front of us, until something changes that."
His dad. My dad.
"It throws you off balance," he pauses, reaching to the side for something and retrieving a bottle of water, the clear liquid sloshing around the plastic.
I watch him force it open with a pop.
"There is no definitive tomorrow and that can be freeing."
He takes a long swig, the water catching behind his prominent Adam's apple, his dimples caving in with each stroke of his tongue.

I watch as he wipes his mouth with his sleeve before
continuing "It's also overwhelming, and uncomfortable. I
think we both know the feeling of being pushed out of our
safe space."
I certainly do.
"I just thought maybe I could give you some sort of comfort,
no matter how trivial it is."
It would be so freeing if I could just tell him.
True comfort.
But how? Where would I even start?
Would I leave out my involvement?
Do I disclose how I have been conditioned with desire?
My tongue wants to unleash the sickness while my brain
simultaneously locks it away.
The brain controls the tongue and conquers.
Unless anger takes hold.
But secrets, those the brain is good at guarding.
"You're right, it's been a long time since- well since I have felt
comfortable."
That's all I can say, and I hate myself for it.

I fall silent with his hand tucked under my chin, the fabric of
the sleeping bag purring as I tilt my face so that I am looking
deep into his cool eyes, "I don't expect anything more than for
you to trust me enough to tell me what you need and what
you don't. That's it."
Not an inkling of deceit, rather there's a wealth of honesty.
I kiss him with abundance, my fingers running through his
hair, stopping along his jaw.
Those dimples.
His cheeks, deep pails, a sunny disposition in his eyes.
I shake my head yes, "I have exactly what I need right here,"
slowly, kissing his neck with a shudder before my lips.
My fingers hook beneath his shirt, and I gently pull it over his
head, losing it in the padded flooring.
 Not rushed, not hyper-sexualized, or desperate like our last
encounter.

I am controlled, calculated, and ravenous, "Touch me," I whisper, taking his hand and leading it to the strap of my dress.
The straps fall, lost in the darkness. Unabashed, the spires of my body topple freely.
It doesn't take much persuading before his lips are firmly pressed against the buds, the humidity of his breath swirling over the rose peaks, his touch causing them to harden with anticipation.
Causing him to harden.
I am aware of my need.
My need for more.
My need for all of him, and for him to want all of me.

Trying to slow myself, I gently tug on his hair as he caresses me.
He obliges, leaving the night air to caress me "Can I," he questions eyeing my body with ravenous intent, his hands remaining as a gentleman's would, not daring to cross any unspoken line.
I'm not sure what he is asking, but it doesn't matter.
The answer is yes.
Always yes.
I quickly discovered what I had agreed to, my silky dress hiked up, our mouths marry.
God, his mouth!
Keep it together.
Don't be too eager.

Hard at work the man explores.
Theres no map in hand, just a heart yearning for discovery, traveling along the edges of my wanton body.
My back arches unintentionally, and I whimper out his name.
That leaves him smiling, and inherently guides him on.

It's as if he already knows my body.
Never makes me ask.
Reads me without issue.

My lower belly clenches, heat mounting as desire swells.
I'm dependent on him for my every need, and he's growing
drunk on it, but it doesn't fuel him to crass behaviors.
Is touch is languid, patience guiding his every move.

Pausing at the barrier between sweet and serious, he halts,
training his gaze to me, seeking permission.
Not until I allow it.
I don't just allow it; I desperately crave it.
"Please."
Winking, he takes my blessing and progresses.

Quickly, and ferociously, it all comes together, my chest, my
pelvis, even my mind.
I find the world around me still, my mind quiet.
My body sits on another plane, very much alive.
It's short lived.
Beaming down, at my crude frame, I freeze.
Guilt hits me.

Shame.
Shame for allowing myself to enjoy this. Shame for allowing
any of this to happen.
It all slips away and suddenly my breathing quickens for
another reason.
I am overwhelmed.
Enraged.
On the edge of potential.
I try to chase it out, my fingers tightening around his locks,
and I drive myself up pressing hard against his wet
appendage in an effort to lose myself.
I want him to be rougher. Want it harder. I want it to hurt.
I don't know why, but I need the pain.
In pain, I find the pleasure intensified.
The contrast.
A light in a dark room. Warmth in the volatile cold.
"Hold on!"

Kyle jerks up, relinquishing my power back to me.

I run my hand against his chest, full palm, scraggly hairs.
Sparse.
Only my touch notices them, grounding me.

"Lie back Kyle, let me take care of you," I command, refusing
to allow myself a simple pleasure.
Not yet.
I'm not ready.

Disconnecting, I focus my energy on him instead.
He complies, his back firmly pressed against the navy warmth
of the sleeping bag, his chest rising and falling with desire.
I want more and so does he, my fingers on his belt buckle, the
metal bit falling with a light thud.
The teeth of the zipper part quickly under my touch and he
doesn't say a word to stop me.
Once white cotton now onyx, the flap leaves space for me to
gently ease him out of the suffocating restraints.

Hovering in a half straddle I kiss at his neck, then collarbone.
Guiding my hand down, I follow a trail of masculine bristles.
A proverbial Yellow Brick Road, taking me to the emerald city.
I find a superior jewel, freedom.

Pine, salt, sweat. I care for him the way he had tenderly done
for me, taking it a step further.
Thoughts of my father consistently creep in, perturbing me
despite my close proximity to Kyle.
What if Dad finds out? This isn't fair to him.
No. Fuck.
Get the fuck out!

I drive him away and focus on Kyle instead.
Reactions.
Low grunts.
Moans that some men would shy away from.

Reaching an unspoken limit, he coils his fingers through my
proud locks.

Our eyes lock and his head tilts into a nod.
 I understand, aware of what he wants.
It's exactly what I want.
"I want you Laurel… all of you."

Kyle falls back fumbling for his pants and slinks his hand into
the pocket where he pulls out a foiled condom, a concerned
look of question in his gaze.
I stare deeply into his eyes as his teeth grasp the foil, tearing
the top, stopping before it fully splits, and popping the plastic
ring from the foil.
My breath hitches as I watch it roll down, securing it with a
slight pucker.

Anxiously, I straddle him quickly, fearful, anxious, but also
desperate to find a new normal.
 Someone to love.
Someone who will love me right.
This act cements that.
If I do this, I won't be his anymore.

His girth sits right outside my heat.
Knocking.
Forbearance.
Slowly I kiss him, and move my hips, rocking back and forth
with indecision.
"Laurel," painfully he groans.
His member loiters awaiting invitation.

I am ready, at least I want to be ready.
Want to feel that first stroke.
Need to bind myself to him.
But the fear and doubt creep back in, putting me in a
chokehold once again.
"Kyle, I…" I trail off.
There are no words to describe the whirlwind of intrusive
thoughts swirling through my brain.

What if he can tell I'm not a virgin?

I had lied and told him I was when in reality I am damaged
goods.
There would be no indication of my purity.
Damned cultural expectations!
What if there was some type of irreversible damage?
Physically that is.
The thoughts continue to flutter, battering the innards of my
brain.
Intrusive.
Making me want to pull my hair out.
Increasingly intimidating.
Then I think the worst.
What if I am repulsed by Kyle's touch?
What if the feeling of his body in mine makes me sick?
There was no coming back from that.
He waits teetering on the edge of potential bliss.
Patiently.

"Laurel," he groans, hands tightly wrapped around my lower
waist.
Tears pooling in my eyes.
Dark enough that he wouldn't see but they are there.
They threaten to fall, to ruin what's supposed to be a beautiful
moment.
I can't understand the conflict within, but the tears feel like
home as one trickles down.
"I'm ready," I lie, brushing my tears away.
This is my last chance to get this right.
"Yes. Kyle please."
He hears yes but he can tell that it really means no.
"Maybe not yet Laurel…for me," he dares lie, but it's a lie I
can forgive.
I nod yes, "Ummm… maybe in a second then."
Agreement.

I'm scared, a weeping tremble falls around my body and I
have to coax myself down.
My father has robbed me of my ability to touch and be
touched without consequences.

My inability to fully accept his touch without thinking of him.

Instead of pressuring me he waits, putting safeguards in place
and he presses his hands between us.
 Cupping at my jaw he graces me with a litany of sweet kisses,
and between embraces he breathes words of affirmation.
He tells me I am beautiful, that he cares about what I need,
and that he loves me despite not using the *L* word.
"We can do whatever you want Laurel, I'm just happy to be
here," his hot mouth repeats, tickling along the cartilage.
"I want this," I say just as he lets go of my face.

Nodding, he presses a chaste kiss to my cheeks.
Together we teeter.
A place between probability and promise, nails pressing into
the meat of my thighs,
The moment of truth.
I can do this.

His body responds to the feeling of my ache for him.
"It's ok," I tell him abruptly, my breathing heavy, the moon
glow scattered across my dampened chest, "I want this…I
want to feel you. Us. Together."
He nods, hesitation still heavy along his brow, worried that he
might do something wrong with me, and for some reason, his
concern is all I need to affirm my decision.
This right.
He is safe.

With a simple maneuver, I find myself at home, letting him in.
He had knocked first and waited for my invite.
Lingering, taking it all in, eyes ironclad, breathing in sync as
we share in the initial pleasure and surprise at the act we had
just committed in partnership.

With an inhale, I provide assurance, his movements halting.
"I'm ok," I promise.
Reaching between us, I move off and pull the condom free. I
need more.

I need all of him.

His breath hitches, "Is that a good idea? I mean I want that,
but are we safe?"
The question barely makes it out of his mouth as his tongue
catches all the anticipation.
 A man is still a man.
My head says yes with a slight nod," I don't want anything
between us. Just be careful, " I assure all chattering lips and
swaying hips.
 I'm playing with fire and yet not giving a damn because the
flame warms me perfectly.

Together we harmoniously find the spot where I end, and he
begins.
Moving beautifully, we choreograph each sway, and kiss, the
essence of our hearts pouring forth.
My ears buzz, his hands wrap around my waist, a shudder
expelling itself violently as the dual pleasure takes me closer
to the edge,
Our breaths are heavy.
Proclamations vibrating along the hard-shelled walls.
The sounds of our lovemaking as beautiful as the sounds of
the night outside.
Crickets, the sifting of gravel, the shudder of his mouth.
Our lips weep like long lost lovers when we are forced to take
in air, ransoming one another when they return.
The price is too high for anyone to pay.

My soul aches, ravaged by his tender movements.
The spark that had started the fire has now grown
exponentially, oxygenated by our desires.

"Kyle I-" I start to cry out, quickly losing the ability to speak.
In vain.
Fireworks.
Tiny explosions culminating into a big bang.
Perpetual bliss.

He feels my body echo as I ride my wave, and takes advantage
of my vulnerable state, never abusing his power.
Laying me flat, he follows me to nirvana.
My name is the last thing he says.
We fall into a cloying stupor.
What had I just done?

...

"Stay."
Kyle kisses me, hard and long, fingers tangle in my hair.
Wasn't keen on ending it there.
We have all night.

He is quiet after that, but I know the silence says more than a
million words can right now.
Daddy usually passes out or cries after.
This is so different.
I had a taste of what lovemaking really is.
Hooked, much like our fingers as Kyle kisses me once more.
I decided right then and there that I never want my father to
touch me again.
I never want to feel anything other than this.
The uncomplicated.

His head is resting between my slightly sloped breasts, my
back against the sleeping bag, his hair pulling through my
fingers.
A cool strand falls between the slopes of my chest, his fingers
tangling in it.
Shiny.
"I broke your chain, I'm sorry," Kyle tells me, handing me the
cool metallic pile that coils like a snake, holding a vicious bite
for the right moment.
I run my fingers through his hair, strands escaping the comb
of my fingers, "It's ok, it's not important anyway."
"You sure?"
I wave it off, still riding my high, tossing the chain and not
giving a damn. What Kyle doesn't know is that he broke more
than a chain, he shattered the shackles that bind.

I feel free.

Mikey

Realization.
The realization that men don't have the control we think we have.
One that I find in Gale's eyes as I penetrate her.
Deceiving.

Women always start a fuck either weak and whimpering or completely disinterested, but then comes the realization.
They find it somewhere mid-thrust when we are at our weakest.
Vulnerable men.
They understand that even though they are getting fucked that they have all the control.
They don't need this. Don't need us.
That is true power. Independence.
Being so fully needed by someone they simply use and tolerate.
Another thrust, harder this time, maybe an attempt to assert a slowly dwindling feeling of dominance.
Losing our grip.

They see it.
They always know, and it does not matter if she is on her knees, or if her hair is wrapped tightly in white knuckles, she knows her potential.
Then comes the look.
That look.
It's a smirk, followed by the first real moan.
Not the first moan, the first one that is not faked.
The only one that counts.
That's when she lets go.
The look intensifies, powerful, her eyes barely opened, but highly focused on yours as if she wants you to know.

When she decides she may as well utilize her hold over you to
feel good.
Her choice.
That evil look. The look of power.
Then she meets her end, and you sit there feeling
accomplished, good about yourself.
You have possessed her, fucked her, demeaned her.
Or so you think.

Laurel

I run my hand through his lustrous hair once more. "You
alright?"
He asks, authentically caring.
Swallowing hard, I reply affirmatively, bending my head and
kiss the top of his head.
He looks up and catches my neck with his mouth, and kisses
away the sheen of sweat, the night warm, the cab stuffy, air
polluted with the smell of sex.

I look up at the truck's ceiling, Kyle tangles his fingers in
mine.
Peace fills me, our breathing dancing in unison.
Eyes flutter then shut momentarily before being interrupted
by his voice.
"Laurel."
The cave-like enclosure catches light.
Flashing patriotic lights. Red and blue lights.
For a moment I am confused, still lost in bliss.
I sit up fast causing Kyle to roll off me, reality hitting me like a
ton of bricks to the face.
He says my name again, disbelief in his voice as if he can't
quite put two and two together, or more like he does not want
to believe it.
"Shit!"

Kyle sits up with a jerk and looks back, the glimmering glow
bouncing back and forth in the iris of his eye, "Get dressed," is
all he says in a serious tone that almost scares me.

He doesn't need to elaborate.
No time.
Quickly I pull my dress up and over my shoulders, my panties long gone, probably lost outside the truck.
I hear him rustle around me, struggling to pull his pants up, the clanking of his metal buckle echoing, teasing at the little time we have to get decent or get caught.
I look around frantically, covered but lacking my underwear as they close in and figure It will have to do.
Kyle pulls himself into the driver's seat. I hear the car chime as the key makes contact.
"Laur, are you good?"
I move forward, his hand ready to guide me to the passenger seat.
I land on it awkwardly with an audible clunk, my knee smashing into the glove box.
The pain shoots up my kneecap all the way to my hip, yet I don't make a sound, instead, I rub it with my palm hard, teeth gritting.
Kyle rushes to smooth out his ruffled shirt not a moment too soon.

The lights hone in on us and I am certain our faces glow with guilt.
Trapped.
I have barely caught my breath, and now anxiety fills me.
Dread.
"If they ask, we were just leaving," Kyle states, not a hint of stress in his unwavering tone, but I know he feels it.

The car comes to a crunching stop next to the truck, pebbles clinking on the side of Kyle's truck, an orchestra of clinks.
I look ahead, outside the trees sway softly, the breeze picking up, allowing the sound of an opening car door to travel with a creak.
Blinded suddenly by a bright light.
A flashlight, a rasping at the window.
Kyle pulls the key from the ignition and twists, rolling the windows down, inch by inch.

About halfway it sticks momentarily before falling quickly
into its cage.
Falling like a gate protecting a lone city.
I keep my eyes on my feet.
I hear the voice.
I recognize the face.

A southern tenor made raspy by the hands of tobacco.
Our eyes meet, the dark brown eyes and sloped forehead.
The thinning wave of hair sat half combed like a rooster's
crown on top of his head.
Balding and only in his mid-twenties. Officer Lawrence.
David Lawrence.
My Dad's friend.
Always around for a game and a couple of beers.
Sometimes whiskey, and sometimes more than a few drinks.
More often than not it's a few drinks too many.
I could distinctly recall one occasion when Mom was still
alive.

David and my dad had had one too many and had both
passed out in the living room like a bunch of kids.
I had asked my mom if they were having a sleepover.
That made her laugh.
She made pancakes that night, sticky with a mountain of
maple syrup, the sweet sopping the cooked batter.
Crispy edges and soft centers.
Maple perfection.
Mom had been one hell of a cook.
Sometimes she made her pancakes with a special sauce.
Butter, peanut butter, and syrup in a bowl, all hot and blended
and served piping hot.
It was creamy and sweet. A peanut butter dream.

I feel simultaneously sick and hungry just thinking about it.
My stomach churns audibly.
"Laurel, long time no see," he lamely jokes referring to the
birthday just that afternoon.
I nod back feeling sick.

"You out here partying with all these kids? We got a call about a bonfire and drunk minors; it's been a slow night so we figured we would come up."
We? Shit.
Dads here.

I shake my head yes, "We were just leaving."
"Is that all you were doing?"
The implication is heavy in his voice.
I nod yes, "We haven't been drinking or anything and we were just heading out."
My eyes are big, I'm pleading with him to just take my word and leave it at that with my stare alone.
"I believe you Laurel, but your Dad's here helping break this up and I think it would be best if you just stick around," the words ooze from his mouth.
I can see a speck of green in his teeth.
Broccoli?
Lettuce?
It didn't matter, yet every time he spoke it shifted as if it was desperately trying to escape the little barriers between the tobacco-tinted smile.
My stomach churns as I look on.

"I was about to drive her home," Kyle interjects.
"Well, let her father decide when he gets here. Just sit tight," he adds, tapping the pillar.
There is no arguing with him.
I look over at Kyle whose eyes knit together with anxiety.

We wait, painstakingly for several long minutes, until he pulls up, all the while neither Kyle nor I say a word.
In the mirror I see him strutting from his car, the outline of his hat bobbing up and down as he navigates the uneven dirt.
I suck in a deep breath, catching his eye through the windshield.
The man I call Dad glares, a fire in his eyes that no one else can see, "You been drinking girl?" he asks as he walks up.
No hello.

No smile.
He instantly cuts me down to size with a "Girl."
Making me feel so little, no different from how he always makes me feel.
"No, I wasn't drinking," I informed him, feigning calamity.
Meanwhile, chaos stirs within, my eyes cast down.
My dad nods, his eyes now burning into Kyle, "And you?
Have you been drinking up here with my daughter?"
His voice drops when he refers to me as his.
Possessive.

Kyle's fingers fall from the steering wheel, mouth tight before answering," No sir, we were just heading home."
My dad shakes his head yes, "That's right. That's where Laurel should be, since she isn't at Natasha's like she told me she would be."
His eyes burn into mine "I don't like being taken for an idiot, Laurel," he adds in a snide manner.
He nods slowly as if agreeing with himself.
"I'm sorry, we got invite – " I start to say before he pounces, tone harshly cutting into me.
"Save yourself the trouble and just be quiet Laurel."
His words are controlled, burning beneath was a rage that was on the verge of becoming untethered.
A rabid dog on the last inch of leash.
He is domineering, his grip on the window causing his already pale knuckles to appear ghostly white.
"Drive my daughter home Kyle, then get back to yours," he instructs in a tone he probably used on delinquents, his stubbly chin barely moving.
Kyle's eyes meet his and although I can't see them, I know they carry an air of defiance in them.
He sees it too.
"Did you hear me?"
Kyle's head bobs, "I'll drive Laurel home," he mutters with little to
no intention of following through with the second set of instructions.
He has no obligation to do so.

"The house is still a wreck from the party, I want to see it clean
by the time I come by on break. We'll talk then. No excuses."
"I'll get it done," I reply, avoiding his stare.
My mind is racing.
I could usually read him, but not tonight.
I don't think I had ever seen him this mad. "Go on."
Kyle twists the key, the engine sputtering to life.
"Twelve thirty, Laurel," he adds, the window slowly
distancing him from us as we slowly drive off.
He would have me sweating with every tick of the clock, with
every mile of the road.
Tonight, I will be alone.
Mikey out.
Rachel and my grandmother in the city.

I shift in my seat uncomfortably, pulling the buckle in and
clipping it, the reminiscence of Kyle caked and cracking as I
shift in my seat.
"Take me home."
Kyle takes off, we retreat into silence.

The minutes pass, the town's glow approaching, the intensity
waxing and waning till we pull up to my house. Familiar
bumps from the long dirt driveway shake me to reality., it's
not a place I want to be.
No more city lights, instead the glowing ghost of my kitchen
lights, peering hauntingly through the flowing curtains.
The front door beams under the harsh yellow porch light, a
low buzzing emitted from it, random static crackles as the
bodies of unsuspecting insects meet the intense heat.
They had been drawn by the light,
Lured to their demise with the assumption that the clarity
would bring peace, forgetting the safety of the darkness.
I never feared the dark, I feared the light.
Was terrified of what it revealed.
Scared of what people may see.

A light breeze moves the porch swing.

I haven't found words since our retreat.
Kyle breaks the silence, "Are you going to be ok?" He poses, breath hitching with some violence.
I keep it simple and deflect, "Thanks for the ride… and everything else," I state, hitting the buckle release sending it flying into its storage.
"Laurel, hold on," his hand takes mine, fingers tracing my palm.
I breathe in deeply and humor him falling back into my seat, it envelops me like a hug.
"I got to get going," I murmur, strands of hair falling over my eyes.
"You know you don't have to go. My mom will be home in the morning, and you could stay over till then."
My nose tingles, "I can't do that."
"I think it might be for the best, and my mom won't care."
"She wouldn't like that," my voice crackles.
I took notice hoping he hadn't.
I see his shoulders tense as if he wants to say something, he knows he shouldn't, but I don't give him the chance.
"I'll be alright Kyle," I lie.
My vocal cords deceive me with their crackling.
My eyes deceive me with a hot tear rolling out.
I wiped it away quickly.

Truth is I know what is coming.
Truth is, my memory of Kyle and what we had shared is about to be tainted despite the vow I had made to myself that I would never let him touch me again, despite the chains that had broken moments earlier.
"Please."
I am tempted. Tempted to take refuge in his bed, tempted to give in to his pleas and tell the world what he had done, but…there's always a *but*.
But I can't let anyone know what I have done.
But I love him. But he loves me.

I could go with Kyle.

Never come back, but the truth would have to come out, and I would become something for Kyle to fix rather than to love.
If the thought of my father's anger, and the potential repercussions makes me sick, then the thought of being something to fix far surpasses that dreadful thought.
I force a smile, "You worry too much, Kyle."
With a heavy sigh, he pushes forward, "He seemed mad…maybe it would be good to give him some space." This time he's a bit more forceful, his hand ripping my chin to face him.
Briskly, I pull away, scared his touch will convince me.

My hands graze along the door handle, I am ready to run, but I can't just abandon Kyle's concern, his pleas falling on deaf ears, his air of concern on my shut eyes.
"Look, Laurel, I just don't want to see you get hurt is all. Not when the two of you could easily discuss this in the morning when the air has cleared."
Relief fills me. It's the last thing I should feel, but it's there.
Relief that Kyle thinks that Daddy would put his hands on me out of anger.
I inhale, my lungs puffing, my fingers tracing his palm now, nails following the shattered heart line up to his thumb, "My dad has never hit me, and he isn't going to start tonight, so just do me a favor and stop worrying about me. Kiss me," my fingers ease along the tense cliffs of his jaw, "Just once more before I go."
He looks at me disapprovingly, "I know that Laurel, that's the problem."
"How is that a problem?"
Sincere eyes narrow, full of care," If he doesn't hit you, then what are you worried about?"
Red-handed.
Trapped. I could see the worry in his eyes.
I won't let him worry.

My hand wanders absentmindedly to his jaw, and I pull him into my kiss allowing my lips to linger before offering words of reassurance "I am not worried," I stroke his face, he turns

himself onto my hand kissing my palm with great tenderness, "I'll be ok, I promise," I lie before I make my retreat, the door slamming behind me.
I tread slowly, the crunching of the old truck tires leaving me with my thoughts and an empty house.
I don't dare look back till his lights are past the tree line, that's when I know I won't change my mind.
Tonight, I take a stand and although it won't be a strong front I put on, there will be a front.

...

The house is in disarray when I walk in.
It stinks of burnt meat and stale beer.
I bolt to the laundry room, a load of dry laundry signals completion with its blinking light, and the dryer has run its cycle, telling me with its silence.
Clean.
Wet.

When I open the door, a strong aroma of lavender fabric softener cuts through the unclean air, and struggle to find a clean pair of panties in the mess of brightly colored clothing and baby socks that seem to have come in singles rather than pairs.
Rachel swears the washer eats the socks.
Neither Rachel nor my Dad were particularly good at sorting before they washed, and I was constantly finding Ava's little socks in my sweater sleeves.

I dig through heavy jeans and dainty dresses, baby socks, and still-stained bibs that would remain so.
No luck.
I dig, nails catching on fabric, the lavender dryer sheet entangled along a bib.
My fingers wrap around a handful of clothing in the hot center, and I find what I am looking for.
Cheap white cotton that had shrunk in the heat.
Or maybe I had gotten bigger.

I slink into them.
Time to conquer the task at hand.

Soda cans litter the counters, sticky rings had formed beneath
the tin bottoms.
Condensation and sugar.
Ants looking to please the queen would make their way in if I
am not quick enough.
Thin, grease-soaked paper plates, that had lost their structural
integrity are strewn about haphazardly, streaks of ruby
ketchup and brown crumbs cling tightly.
The trash can is already filled to the brim, the flies buzz
happily, which has my stomach lurching, and my hands
working to locate a new one before pulling the full one free.
I tie the top tight and walk the bag out of the house avoiding
globs of ketchup that had dripped off the plates and formed
jellified dunes on the floor, then move to swing the bag open,
the air parachuting the sheer plastic.
In my head I recite my workflow, the words flashing through
my inner eye over and over as I work, my anxiety melting like
butter only to return when I dare check the clock that sits
above the stove.
The hands are quickly approaching the peak to greet.
Ticking.
Teasing.

Counters.
Dishes.
Cabinets.
Sweep.
Mop.

Repeat.
Repeat.
Eight times I recite my list trying to soothe myself in the
perfection that is eight.

Sweep.

Mop.

Breath.
Every second lasts a lifetime, and it leaves me beyond
exhausted and I urge myself to focus on the tasks at hand.
So I scrub, mop, and wipe till my hands are red and burning.
I fill the sink to the brim with water so hot it feels ice cold,
scrubbing tediously, taking pleasure in the control I have for
now.

It would be short-lived.
That much I am certain of.
Managing the literal chaos, all the while ignoring the
figurative chaos within.
I turn my attention to my final task. A deep scrubbing of the
kitchen counters.
Absent of trash and crumbs I now had to focus on removing
the lingering stains.
Quickly, I pour the powdered cleaner watching it fall.
A periwinkle snow landing in lotus-like forms all over the
cheap counters.
It was always stained.
I hated it.
Mom had wanted to change it.
"Granite, and fresh stains on the cabinets."
Her request to my dad for her birthday gift, she hadn't made it
to that day.
Daddy had pulled off the cabinets and begun to sand them.

After she had gone the cabinets had sat out in the garage
unfinished until Rachel came along.
Instead of honoring her request he slapped some cheap paint
on them and hung them back up.
It would have hurt too much to see it every day, stained in the
color she had chosen, a deep oak.
It was much easier to forget her when the cabinets were
painted white.
In a way, we had all forgotten.
Pushed her to the back of our minds.

Mikey seemingly unaffected, my father reluctant to face anything that would remind him of her.
As for me, I had too much on my plate to process, and every time I started to swallow down a mouthful, the next course would appear, and I would force down a half-chewed gulp painfully.
So it piled up until my stomach was on the verge of bursting.
The eventual vomiting of truth.
Guess I wasn't full enough yet.

Mikey

Crickets sing.
Taunting little tunes to remind me how fucked up I was.
Gale is murmuring beside me, satisfied and still tripping.
My mind was becoming less fuzzy.
Soon reality would return, and I would return to the bore of sobriety.

Laurel

Crickets sing taunting little tunes outside the open window.
The chemical smell had become overwhelming, my stomach had begun to churn.
It could have been different.
Tonight, that is.
Instead of listening to the song of the night from the fume-filled kitchen, I could have been in his arms, the rhythm of his heart holding a duet with the crickets.
Now my hands are raw from scrubbing, my feet ache, and my mind is jumping between random bouts of anxiety and inexplicable serenity.

The singing continues through the breeze stirred curtains, floating like a floral ghost in the darkness of the living area.
Darkness disturbed.
A crack of light flickering from behind the swaying curtains.

Another round of anxiety hit, and I hadn't even entered the
ring yet.
A heavy percussion fills my head, and my throat feels as if a
noose had a neem tied around it.
I glance up at the clock; five to one.
He had said twelve-thirty.
My father was never late unless he meant to be.
Just another way to toy with me.
Testing my obedience.
He knew I would wait.

I resume scrubbing the counters, a dark stain I presume to be
spilled coke and chewing tobacco sits in the corner between
the sink and the countertop.
All of Dad's friends dip.
Thin lips perpetually swollen with a ball of nicotine.

I try to ignore him as he comes in.
Feign ignorance in hopes that he would leave, or even forget
about tonight.
Belt and keys plopping on the kitchen table.
"Looks better," he comments, instantly pulling me into his
web.
I start to reply but I don't do it as fast as he would have liked,
so he repeats himself, something he doesn't like to do.
"I'm about done," I reply, continuing to work.
The faster it was done the faster I was out of there.
"We need to talk about tonight, Laurel… look at me."
Right to business.
Never an eloquent speaker.

With tears already swelling, my frame turns to face him, lower
back pressing against the counter, a fat dip tucked away in his
mouth, the remnants being disposed of in the coke can he had
set on the table, our eyes meet, mirroring our relation.
I see myself in them.
Giving him a once over, his brow furrows, feet propped up on
the table with a soda can pressed to his lips.
Smug. Calm. Authoritative.

"I'm sorry."

I try to get on his good side and fast.

Truly, I am sorry, just not in the way he wants me to be, that much is a guarantee.

Hooking his finger in his lip he pulls out and presses into the can before getting up, his work boots hitting the ground with a thud, one that must resemble the pulsing that lies beneath the badge of justice pinned to his chest.

"I don't think so. I think that you are sorry you got caught."

My lips tremble, "I am sorry, though."

His lips meet the can downing it before crushing it, he tosses it towards the trash, tin landing with a clink, "You lied to me, Laurel."

He paces, asserting his power.

"I never thought you would lie to me; you have always been the one I thought I could trust, between you and Mikey."

Embarrassed, I look at him, "You can trust me, I just wanted to have some fun is all," I protest, crossing my arms over my chest.

It makes me feel foolishly safe and my voice makes me feel powerful.

Preemptive and stupid.

"That's what you call fun? Drinking, with those future degenerates," he scoffs, an air of superiority dripping off his serpent tongue as if he hadn't just been drinking that afternoon.

"Natasha's dad has two DUIs and is probably only days away from a third and Dean is no altar boy."

Heavy with guilt, my eyes turn down.

"No Laurel, you need to hear all this. I need you to know who you spend your time with, have you ever heard the saying, show me your friends and I will show you who you are… So, who are you, Laurel? Are you a degenerate too? I thought you were smarter than that."

I nod knowing I wasn't getting out of hearing his defamation of the people I cared for, "I didn't do anything, though."

"Natasha and Dean were high as kites on God knows what, and this is not the first time I have dealt with Dean. Far from it. "

I already knew, but I was ready for a refresher course.

"That boy beat the hell out of some freshman last year for seemingly no reason."

He pauses to make sure I'm still present, his hand twirling along the air, "Then there's Emma and Kyle, and all I can say is their dad didn't kill himself for no reason."

I grimace at that knowing how much his father's death hurt him.

It takes all my power to stifle the urge to scream at him just for saying it.

"Ever since you started hanging out with Kyle, you have been pushing the boundaries," he adds, acting as if we hadn't been hanging out since childhood.

It wasn't a lie.

Lied and deceived.

All I had wanted was one night.

"I'm disappointed, Laurel,".

There's a look of disdain in his eye, his mouth prolonging the words, words that pierce through my ribcage and burrow themselves in my fucking heart.

The sponge in my hand is oozing snowy foam now, small trickles falling to the floor, foam mounds.

I am on the verge of exploding, I am feeling something I had never felt till now, a deep hatred of my father.

"I am the sheriff of this damn town, and I already have your brother running around making me look like a fool, and I don't need you out there acting like some cheap little bitch," he spits.

Daddy had never talked to me like that.

Had never dared.

"I'm not," I mutter, "I promise it's not like that Dad."

Cruelly, his lip curls in a half laugh, "Do you think I'm dumb Laurel? You think I believe that you and that boy were just heading home?"

He approaches me slowly, one foot in front of the other.
Heel, toe, heel, toe.
Like a DUI suspect walking the invisible line, his square
shoulders bobbing and weaving.
"You know what I think, Laurel?" he questions.
I can hardly breathe, let alone talk so instead I shake my head.
I'm not afraid, I am ashamed, humiliated even.

Quieting down, my body jumps into self-preservation mode.
"I think you were letting that boy have his way with you. Is
that right, Laurel? You and that boy were having sex, weren't
you?"
It's more of a statement than a question.
I had.
I had been so wrong. Dirty and lustful.
Still, I lie, shaking my head no.
His hand pulls through my locks, "I know you were I could
smell it all over his truck when I walked up…and I saw that
condom wrapper. At least you used your head for a second,"
he shoots begrudgingly, unaware that it hadn't stayed on for
most of our interaction.
"I'm sorry, Dad," I have no idea what else to say, my face red
with humiliation as he brought up things a father shouldn't.
"Sorry doesn't change what you did, and If you think the guys
at the station are going to keep this quiet, then I have a bridge
to sell you."

Again, I apologize, hoping this would end it, that he would let
it go, then let me go.
"It reflects poorly on me Laurel, do you understand? All my
coworkers hearing about my daughter getting fucked in the
back of a truck at some party, high on God knows what. If
you're all grown up now, then act like it. You share your body;
you act like a woman! So be a woman, Laurel, leave this
house, and make your way out there since that is what you
want. I hear you loud and clear!"
Practically yelling now, his face in mine, he points his finger at
the door, a drop of spit hitting my lip.
I feel my body quiver with shame, I try to stifle it to no avail.

A tear rolls down my cheek, "That's not what I want, Dad…I just want us to be normal, can't you give me that?"
A sign of his victory, another falls, he swipes at it, thumbing it roughly against his rough fingers, "Nothing about this is normal Laurel, but I love you and I know you love me. I am not the only one who pursues you. Might I remind you that you touched me with the intention of letting me love you that night…I thought I told you, what we have is special. It's something only we can understand… but you go, and you share that with someone else while I sit here stupidly loving you."

It shouldn't, but it hurts me, he is hurting me with words alone.
I catch my lip between my teeth and let the heat leave my face," I- I'm sorry Dad. You're right."
"If you were sorry then you would stop all of this now. No more Kyle, no more lies, no more parties," he snarls, taking me by the shoulders, his nose grazing mine.
I shake my head in agreement, my earrings catching hair as I do and I press a kiss to his cheek dutifully, "I'm sorry."

I'm not such a good girl, am I?

Obedience meet rebellion.
Isn't she pretty?

Laurel

I lie in bed, replaying the acts, flickering like fluttering found
footage.
Snapshots like rapidly fluttering polaroids.
Kyle's touch is gone now.
Replaced.
My body aches.

It hurt badly, my body was already tender from what Kyle
and I had done and sore from the way I had contorted myself.
When he tried to kiss me after I planted a warm one on his
cheek, I refused, yanking my head away, not wanting to
further taint such an intimate action.
He didn't like that, hands cupping beneath my hair holding
tight, my scalp screaming when I tried to pull away.
Teeth bared like a beast, he had set his mouth against the skin
of my chest and clamped down with brute force, stealing my
breath, his lips curling back so I could see what he was doing.
Skin in his teeth, flesh in his palms.

It took everything in me to swallow down a scream.
My lip puckers and I plead for him to stop in an effort not to
turn it into something it wasn't.
With a silenced cry, my eyelids flickered, eyes rolling back,
displaying the lighter side of their moons.
Marking me, he pressed until he got the desired effect; my
voice and the pained cry I struggled to omit finally broke
through.

That's when he spun me, jerking my dress down, his hand
molding my ass, spreading me as if he was trying to find proof
of my betrayal.
He had made it hurt on purpose to punish me, making sure
the memory would be forever with me, even leaving another
biting bruise along my shoulder.

It would be hard to forget.
The way my head had lain in the cave between the cabinets
and counter, his baritone twang telling me I was going to be
ok.
The way my pelvis had dug into the metal cabinet knobs, a
pain that had penetrated deep into my bones.
The way my wrists ached as he had tightened his hand
around, fists clenched.
The way my skin sits hot along my cheek from the friction we
had created a sea-foam puddle of chemicals that had bubbled
against the fragility of my face.
The way my soul aches.

Something primal had risen tonight.
Anger. Anger at the memory he had tarnished, the way he had
replaced Kyle's touch with his own as a reminder of his
ownership, his brand on me.
Anger had bubbled over as I had pushed back against him
until he held up my arm and tightened it like a constrictor
before gripping it at the elbow and jutting up, a blinding pain
forcing me to bite down my hatred.

Silent battle.
My refusal to stay compliant, resistance futile as he assured
me, I was fine, and that this was just something else we
shared, even though it was nothing more than a power
struggle.
I knew then that I would not win.
A part of me decided that I was not going to lie down and take
it anymore and for that, he had punished me.
Pushed with all his masculine might until he felt that he had
truly conquered me, and I was more than wet, I was hurt.
The feeling of illness instantaneously as he left me oozing, our
sin dripping on the freshly mopped floors, tinted with ruby,
smudging my inner thighs.
He had never made me bleed before, not even my first time.

When he pulled out, he spun me and eyed me, as if he hoped
to see tears, and when I offered no salt of repentance, my

father's eyes shone with rage until he swiped those same angry eyes down, the stain of my pain apparent in its crimson tint.

A satisfied look crossed his lips then, while agony was perched on mine, and as much as I begged it to leave it refused to fly.

I didn't dare pull my underwear back on until he told me to, sucking my lip between my front teeth in an effort not to start sobbing as he examined his handy work, my shoulders climbing and falling with small furious pained breaths I prayed he wouldn't see.

"Get upstairs and get all that makeup off," my dad hissed, leaving my space to click the TV on, my dress still rolled up past my waist.

I had lost the battle. Hell, I had lost the war, and I retreated completely defeated.

Trekking slowly up the stairs, I had caught snippets of several channels before I heard him settle on fish and game programming.

The hunt was on, a man callously preying on a weak doe, the TV blaring as I slowly walked up the stairs.

Feminine prey.

The masculine apex.

It wasn't the first time he had fucked me.

But it had never been like that.

Not forceful.

It had always been coy, convincing, and seemingly innocent.

A secret.

Maybe that's why I had never connected the dots.

This wasn't our little secret anymore.

No special bond.

No sweet whispers of love.

This was the first time it had truly felt it for what it was.

What it had always been and still I can't bring myself to call it by its name.

Mikey

As it turns out, Maureen is pregnant, and currently tripping.
"I don't know what to do!"
Seeing her in this state makes me want to tell her that an abortion was her best bet.
A woman who could not even take sobriety in her first trimester was in no place to be a mother, but I am in no state to tell her that.

Laurel

Disgust.
The only way to describe the breathtaking emotion running through me in a simple manner.

I sit up from my bed as I hear his truck rumble to life.
Back to work.
Time to clean myself up. I had gone and sat on the floor, too stunned to make a move to the shower, making a concerted effort to keep quiet so he wouldn't come up.
White cloud-like puffs line the counters, each evenly spaced to the next.

I squirt a generous amount of oily pink makeup remover onto each ball, almost soaking them through.
A dollop of greasy makeup remover and cotton serves to wipe up the caked-on makeup.
Red spots my cheek like the Japanese flag.
Chemical burn.
I swab a cotton ball over it, wincing as I wipe the beige that surrounds it till the ball is in a disintegrative state between my polished fingers.
Not enough.

Quickly I strip to nothing, his calling card streaking down the inner bend of my shaved legs.
Dry.
I run a finger down my body, trailing to the flaked mess, and cringe as it begins to scale off and turn the shower on.

The room fills with steam, spurts flowing out from the crack beneath the door into my bedroom, a seductive ghostly swirl wrapping me into its embrace, balmy on my skin.
Tingling.
I step in, the water obviously too hot.
It doesn't stop me. I turn my back to the stream allowing it to beat down along my shoulders.
I feel.
Physical pain.
My fingers scrub against my skin, hard, frantic.
I scrub everywhere except where I am most stained, the space between my thighs, afraid that my touch would drive me to tears and instead I allow the water to flow and cascade between.
I exit the shower, my legs violet from the blood pooling, skin as red as a lobster tail.
Warm to the touch, makeup is long gone.
Still dirty.
Where do I go from here?
It is all so anticlimactic.

What's worse is what comes next.
The act itself was always painful in some ways but it was nothing compared to the aftermath.
Like being stabbed.
The retreat.
When the shine leaves you and you're bleeding out, that's the most painful part.
The desperation to plug up the seeping wounds.

Then comes the intrusive line of questioning.
Assumptions that I shaped into questions in an attempt to ignore the obvious answers.
What if it doesn't end with me?
Does he feel bad about what he does?
Is that why he drinks? Is that why he's so heartless?
Why can't he love me?
Really love me?
Why can't he just fucking love me?

I hid in my room for the next few days, my body aching, my femininity sore.
He had harmed more than just my mind this time.
The only release I have is to lose myself in my notebooks, trying to find the words equivalent to my hurt.
After he fucked me, he came to my room before returning to work and found me crying. That made him angry, and he told me to stop, but I just couldn't.
Trying to lessen his guilt, he claimed that he did what he had to do to show me just how much he adores me.
That's it's all he ever does, highlighting the risks he takes to love me.
Telling me to be more accepting of it.
"They could take my freedom for loving you girl, and you sit here and act ungrateful. Tonight was a lesson learned, girl. You are mine and mine alone. Is that clear?"
Again, all I say is yes.
He tries to soothe me then, tells me how valuable I am.
"You look beautiful right now."
And.
"You don't need all that makeup, angel, and I'm sorry I brought it up."
I shiver at the implication I was anywhere near those near-perfect beings with how tainted I felt. I probably resemble the more biblical version.
"Thanks."
It's all I had the strength to say.

His voice cracked, "I- I thought this would end with Rachel, but you do something to me, Laurel. You make me want to love you and it drives me crazy... it makes me do crazy things," swallowing he moved his hand along my waist, "I need you to take responsibility for your hand in this...for loving me back."
The dominating words had such a strangling hold on me.
He thinks I'm porcelain.

That he will be able to reassemble me when in reality I'm glass, and soon someone is going to look in and see right through me.

...

Please come down below.
I'll let these lips talk.
If you know the code.
Don't be scared.
Praise this temple.
Treat it well.
They say. Oh, they say.
Body. Body is a temple.
I'll invite you inside this temple.
My body is a temple.
So I'll decorate these walls. Let these curtains fall.
So you can see. What lies beneath?
Because baby.
I wear my heart under my sleeve.
Here you come. Knocking once more.
Didn't I tell you I can't take any more?
Shake me down to my core.
My hands fold together. Shaking on my knees. Set me free.

They say. Oh, they say.
I'll invite you inside this temple.
My body is a temple. So I'll decorate these walls.
Let these curtains fall. So you can see what lies beneath.
Because baby, I wear my heart under my sleeve.
I'll open my door to yours. Let you explore.
I'll show you what's in store.
Ring you up. At no cost.
They say. Oh, they say.
Body. Body is a temple.
I'll invite you inside this temple.
My body is a temple.

...

It started with Nick,
Nick with a K.
Potential, a dirty copper stain
He would leave me breathless.
If I would just dig deeper
Revolted, pushing him away.
Temptation running
Through that red, white, and blue.
Secret, pugnacious patriotism.
He pulls me back. Kisses like iron
Evidence on my breath
Wet. Obsession courses
The result of my sin
Obsession. Becomes possession.
As sharp as a pin. His kiss in pain.
Cold steel, superficial
A fire beneath
It's always been lurking.

He is rational. Like the moon and sea
I am wild. Like fire and breeze
Knick makes love.
Only to me
Bringing me to the edge. Teasing the fall
Behind sealed lips
I keep my peace.
Only one bite, can't help but release.
His embrace fast and venomous
The strength to my weak
He helps me.
Deceive
Lips spread to ear, as I utter.
"Great,"
Still, I believe I can take the reins.
Control the flow.
Drops of who he is.
Reflect on the floor.
Ruby   Hibiscus

Chasing away Azure
Bringing Light to the Fog
Always Coursing. Dark as slate
He puddles beneath
A love so focused
Driven. Privy
His love. Flawless. So distorted
His touch is greed.
His handle, lust
Not focused on hips
Or curves of the breast
But rather the skin of the Limbs
He falls from my grace.
Falls from my grip.
All the while entering fathomless depth.
How deep is my love?
The only judge, the mirror
Reflection deceiving. Warm fluid easing
I like what I see.
As Knick falls over me, his release cakes quickly.
As wet as the Amazon
Precipitously Morphing
Dry as the Sahara
Again and again, I let Knick fall over me.
And when Knick knocks, he requires no invite.
He is dopamine.
Serotonin
The cure for the dull
A break from the monotony

Knick bears down.
Back flash revoked.
Brittle fractures spindle
He is carbon steel. Organic and Raw
Knick is of heart. Made of obsidian
And I am of mind.
I am owned, branded, and claimed.
Knick cannot be caged, Knick cannot be held.
I am Knick', but Knick will never be mine

Ode to my inner hedonist.

...

It's not a safe time to be alone.
It's not a safe place, loneliness, that is.
Yet, there is something that keeps me here.
If there wasn't someone in the distant future waiting for me, I might be tempted to stay under the water a little longer and this time.
Not for the sake of comfort.
Or maybe for the sake of it.

I did something stupid…crazy even and no one can know.
Does dying hurt?
I would like to believe that the precursor hurts.
But that final moment.
I chose to believe it's incredibly peaceful.
Nirvana.
To finally be at peace.
Almost as soothing as the way the hot liquid flowed over my body at that moment.
It's a funny thing.
And if anyone walked in right now.
It wouldn't be so funny.
Not when they saw what I had done to myself.
The stain of hurt I can't explain away.

Mikey

Dad squawks over lunch about the bum I had tossed the rock at, completely oblivious that the culprit was sharing a grilled cheese with him.
"I can't let things like this happen under my watch! Just last week, too!"
Rachel beams impressed at his desire to find justice.
In a bigger city, not a soul would care about some schizo-crackhead.

I watch as he dabs the crunchy bits of crust in the piping-hot tomato soup.
Canned.

I get a glimpse into their "Case."
The rookie officer had spent his morning doing the grunt work, interviewing and transporting the injured bum to Willow County hospital with a nasty gash on his head.

"That poor man," Rachel cries out as if she cared for him. Those pretty ivy eyes grow big, her hand pressed to her chest.
"Mr. McKenney will come out of this ok," my Dad assures, grabbing her hand reassuringly, "Just a couple stitches and he will be back at it, drinking at the quarry," my father assures her also pretending to care.
Mr. McKenney stood five foot five and weighed about a buck twenty, with dirty mangled hair, and a chipped front tooth, and now he was going to have an awesome scar and a couple of stories to tell around his trash fire, or on one of his daily excursions to the fry hut where he would sift through the trash for stale fries and burger bits.
 Rachel reaches for another sandwich from the center of the table and bites into it, a string of gooey cheese bridging her hands to her mouth next to a too quiet Laurel.
"That's just awful. I can't imagine who would attack someone who is already so down on his luck?" she asks, fingers busying along the table to help Ava.
Just a couple of teens who were tripping balls and being harassed by some washed up asshole.
I wish I could tell them the truth, but it would have made Dad furious and I'm finally back on his good side.
Honestly, I am not in the mood to deal with his wrath.
"Well, you know there are always kids partying up on the quarry. Maybe it was a misunderstanding," Rachel ponders, always so innocent.
Or oblivious?
"Laurel, do you want some?" Our stepmother motions to the creamy coleslaw she had just scooped onto our father's plate, in abundance.

My sister shrugs as if she hadn't even registered the question.
My father tenses at her perceived ignorance, "Rachel asked
you something, Laurel."
She comes to attention at his request and takes the bowl into
her own hands, thanking Rachel before returning to a land of
dissociation.

Laurel

The fourth of July appears with a boom, Mikey already setting
off fireworks in the backyard despite the burning sun.
An air of celebration clings in the air like a child to its mother's
skirt.
Heat sits heavy, only intensifies with the quickly spiraling
day.
The morning parade had left the streets littered with an
assortment of rainbow candy wrappers and missed catches,
half of which had melted on the sidewalk.
Streamers from various poppers stuck on the black asphalt,
my feet catching on to them.
Blistering heat. Hazy.
Beads roll down my breasts as I help clear the trash, the slight
swell where my face had been burned taking in the heat as it
heals and fades.
A handy reach extender that I was utilizing to keep our town
pristine is wet in my palm.

Dad had signed me up for pick-up duty, much to my dismay.
Punishment disguised as the sheriff's daughter's dutiful
service to the town.
There had been no department float for me this year.
I had been a spectator, a blisteringly painful punishment that
he disguises as a gift to me. Telling Rachel before dinner last
week that I was too old for such things, and that my sister
would prefer it.
Rachel had glanced at me then with question in her eye, a
spoon stuck in her hand as she stirred the goopy mess of
cookie dough she was making.

The chocolate chips pure through the vast sea of dough, she hadn't put enough in, these cookies would fall flat, much like my response.
A feeble word of confirmation fell ominously from me, my soul yearning for his attention and our tradition.
Peering on from the sidelines I smiled at my sister, trying to abate the chagrin surging, tingling along the top of my nose.
Ava adorned his lap and won the crowd with her little waves.
Another punishment.

Dad had made a whole show of it, even announcing it at dinner over a mediocre meatloaf last week.
It was a dense conversation served over an equally dense hunk of meat.
I flicked a piece of crusted ketchup off the top of my helping, hunger absent.
Rachel seemed so excited at the prospect of showing beautiful Ava off and accepted my earlier affirmation that I didn't want to partake.
Mikey didn't seem to give a damn as he shoved a spoon full of dry box potatoes into his mouth. Brown gravy drizzled down his chin, as he devours it hungrily.
Rachel wasn't much of a cook, but that night, I was particularly reluctant to dine, the brown gravy curdling along the silver rim of the chipped spoon.
Dad smiled at Rachel as they discussed what Ava would wear, going as far as to consult me on my opinion as if he hadn't robbed me of the pleasure of standing by his side.
He loved it, dangling morsels at me, no one aware.
Teasing me, always cruelly. Putting me back in my place.
I jabbed at a flat cookie then, the chocolate chip streaked in its melted state across the slight swell of its head.
"Ava is going to look so sweet up there, isn't she?" My father cooed her way, beaming at me.
"Handsome dad, and my beautiful daughter."
I swallowed hard then, my eyes finding his, interlocking.
My head tilted down with such speed then, fear someone might see the way we looked at one another with exploration.

Rachel wasn't lying, my father was handsome, devilish, and ruggedly so. All man, with soft yet imposing lips.
Looming, dark, and expressive eyes that seem to drive into your soul and read you. They were set narrow, beneath his heavy brow, hair as black as onyx. He was strong, tough shoulders, square and intimidating, a height women want to feel safe, the arms he works hard on vascular, veins always bulging. My father's hair sat abundantly on his head, always glossy with product and well taken care of. Despite how masculine he was, he was usually groomed and well-put together, part of his career description.
His frame would be imposing, perfect against criminals, not that any were particularly volatile out here, and he had a tattoo done along his inner wrist after mom passed, giving him an edge of danger.

When he wasn't dangling bones, I would never taste in my face he was blatantly putting me down.
Constantly commenting on my appearance.
Requesting that Rachel make some healthier choices for our meals.
I was living under a microscope of disapproval.
"Your hair looks better down," he half said, half ordered before the parade, pulling loose the braids he had set earlier with careful precision.
"Save some for the rest of us," he had joked at breakfast the other day.
To the family, it all seemed like a joke.
To me, it was nothing more than a rejection, a way to hurt me.
He was blowing me out, a feeble flame.
He knew how much I was hurting, and he liked it.
To make me as sad and sick as he was.
Misery loves company, and I was miserable.
Depressed. Sick.

The days leading up to the parade I fell into a deep dark pit.
 A depression I felt I would never escape, and no one would ever know what was behind my smile.

No one asks anyway, and if they did, I would lie.
I certainly wouldn't want to burden anyone with my hurt, not even Kyle who I hadn't seen or heard from since that night.
He knew better than to call.
I had hoped to see him today.
He usually rode the hospital float with his mom and this year he would be driving.
"Ava ready?"
I nod yes to Rachel and begin to unbuckle her stroller.
Dad sits on his throne, his chair on the department float, full uniform, and a big smile on his face.
He waves consistently when he isn't throwing candy to the kids.

Ava is adorned in a festive red, white, and blue gown, glitzy streamers braided in her abundant locks.
My sister hates dresses, frilly, lacey, big enough to swallow her, she cries.
I had done her hair for the occasion, her burnt auburn locks curling with the humidity.
With the right amount of brushing, it fell perfectly into place.
I had lifted her to see the mirror, and she cooed with glee at the baby who smiled back.
She was perfect and ready to go.

I kept my eyes fixated on the back of the parade all morning, knowing the order.
When I caught a glimpse, Kyle smiled, driving slowly his mother in her scrubs tossing candy out of a shopping bag.
He sees me, smiles, and lifts his hand thumb and pointer spread to his ear.
"Call me," he mouthed.

...

We spent the rest of the day out by the ponds, swarms of buzzing insects grouping wherever food was abundant.
There was an overabundance and sadly most of it would go to waste.

Gluttony at its finest.
Fruit salads sit uncovered. Half-charred hotdogs courtesy of the police department lay shriveled in buns softened by the wet air.
Globs of potato salad, bits of fat jellified from the overabundance of the mayonnaise.
I could feel droplets roll between my breasts before catching on the cotton bridge and my feet and back ache from standing all morning.
I was ready to be home, knowing full well that I would be alone for once if I could convince my Dad to let me skip the fireworks.
The shows had lost their brilliance since my mother passed. Instead of awe, they always left me melancholy, like I was missing something.

A breeze introduces itself instantly, threatening the heat, slow dark, looming clouds from the north had begun to move around us.
Then I hear it.
My name? The breeze?
Then I hear it again and look over behind a rather large oak tree, a diseased tumor lumped at its roots, it sprawled over the fishing pond.
Galls.
Probably full of squirming larvae.

Again, my name moves through the breeze to the drum.
That's when I see him, Kyle.
Butterflies flutter up from the pit of my stomach, trying to force their way through my sternum.
These aren't the butterflies he usually gives me.
The butterflies weren't born of attraction. They were a warning.
A warning that he may be watching.
I look over my shoulder at the crowd.
They are all gathered by the sand pits, horseshoes glimmering in their hands.

Rachel blends into the crowd, cheering him on, Ava's head
bobbing up and down as she moves.
Trying to confirm, I glanced back, a come-hither motion luring
me to him.
I make haste, without so much as a hello he takes my hand
and leads me over the small bridge and past the restrooms.
A dense patch of poison oak-filled forest sat behind, building a
barrier between the small creek and the stagnant ponds.
Further into the brush, he leads until we are at the creek bed.
Upstream I can hear children playing.

"What are you doing here?" I ask nervously, the trees bringing
us cover, the croaking of a toad not far off of the babbling
stream.
I glance around, paranoid.
"Haven't heard from you since- well since we," he trails off,
his handsome visage spreading to a smile of remembrance,
"Since your birthday," he hints, waiting for an explanation I
don't have.
"I was worried is all," Kyle states, brushing a strand of hair
out of my eyes.
A child screams a delighted screech in the distance.
Simple.
Content.
Just a day by the creek.
The scream breaks the silence once more followed by the
yelling of the supervisor.
"Don't worry about me," I protest, focusing back on him.

I hadn't been aware of how long I had stood there without
offering a response, but it was long enough that Kyle's eyes
had filled with worry.
Telling him not to worry wouldn't change anything.
He would just do the opposite, but it's really all I have to
offer.
So I continue to feign normalcy for as long as I can.
My eyes dart, a branch cracks across the creek, a bird chirps in
a nearby tree.
Every sound is a threat.

I couldn't take the repercussions if my father saw me.
"I just wanted to see you, maybe catch a movie, have some
dinner. I miss you, Laurel," he states, fingers slowly looping
into mine. "And I want to kiss you. God, I want to kiss you."
I want him to kiss me too. I haven't stopped thinking about his
mouth.
Memories of what we had shared had been the only thing that
brought quiet to my perpetually racing thoughts.
All I offer is a simple kiss.
Kissing to soothe the guilt.
I kiss him to ease the hurt.
Committing theft with each swipe of our lips.
I am robbing him.
Robbing him of his love.
Robbing him of his trust.
Robbing him of his happiness simply to appease my hurt.

The saddest part is that if I would only allow it, he would do
everything in his power to take the hurt.
He would make it his own, and it was at that moment that I
realize that he is too good for me.
Too kind. Too loving.
There is no future where I won't bring him pain.
Where I wouldn't demolish him.
Never intact.
But in my selfishness, I kiss him.
In his embrace, I let go.
I let go of the tension, let go of the pressure, and the belief that
this has any permanence.
I accept temporary bliss.
If only for that moment.
That's where it ends. Abrupt.
The deep voice of ownership calling my name.

I pull away fast, "I have to go." painfully I whisper as if
leaving him might maim me.
Short-lived peace snatched away with the tenor calling.
He shakes his head in an unspoken understanding.

"Before you go," he begins as I turn from him, "come to Dean's tonight."
"You know I can't."
"His parents are having a barbecue and fireworks. Tasha will be there."
I hear my name being called again.
"I'll see what I can do," I reply as a nervous sweat cascades over me.
"I'll pick you up at the end of the road at eight, and if you aren't there I will wait, and if you're still not there, I'm going to knock on your door," Kyle says with an air of defiance, "please don't make me wait," sincere eyes plead.
Nodding I shift to turn away quickly to make my exit, as my name echoes once more.

Making it to the beige building just in time to poke my head in, then walk right back out, pretending to shake my hands dry, and sucking in air deeply once to even out the air I'm emitting.
"Laurel?"
I feign innocence and confusion as I hear my dad call my name from the other side of the building, where the gravel road meets the facilities.

"Where were you?"
Impatience is tight in his mouth as he reaches for me, taking me by the arm.
My foot catches the dip between the sidewalk and the black tar, causing me to stumble as he tugs me back up.
 "I had to use the bathroom."
"It sure took you long enough, "he snaps, a scowl on his lips.
Secretly, he had hoped to catch me doing something I shouldn't have been doing.
Any reason to keep me in the house so he can pull my strings.
"Sorry."
It's such an automatic response.
Programmed.
"Well, don't do it again. I don't want to spend my day looking for you."

I pull my hand from his and fold my arms across my chest. He takes notice and I expect him to say something but the look of resistance that sits on my face deters him.

…

The car ride home is spent feeling emboldened and trying to talk Rachel into letting me skip the show.
"I was hoping to go hang out at Dean's instead."
My father had always liked Dean's father Martin, a well-respected businessman and fellow gun enthusiast. His emotion was much cooler when it pertained to Dean.
They weren't friends per se, but they never had a shortage of conversation.
"We go every year, it's tradition," he interjects, using our family bond as a tool for manipulation.
We had attended every year for as long as I can remember without exception.
"Come on babe," I hear Rachel come to my aid, "What's one year?"
His fingers tense on the steering wheel, the turn signal flashing yellow.
My timing was deliberate.
Rachel acts as a buffer.

I knew he would be apprehensive to deny me an innocent barbecue if Rachel was involved. Rachel would be open to the idea to not tarnish what she hoped could be a good relationship between us.
I am desperate.
"It's just a barbecue, and Laurel isn't going to have any fun sitting around with us and all your friends," Rachel sides with me.
Daddy takes a sharp left, his grip giving his hands a ghostly shade now, "Well she is grounded Rachel…might I remind you," his tone tenses eyes darting back between the road and the rearview mirror.
A menacing glare radiates outward like a flare, "Plus, that's not really the issue Rachel."

"Well then, what's the issue? "
I could tell he didn't like her line of questioning.
Questioning him and his authority as my parent.
I can tell he is about to snap at her.
"The issue is that she is my daughter, and I don't want her running all over town on the fourth," his tone raises with each word, "There are drunk drivers all over, it's just not good news."
I can tell by Rachel's body language that she is hurt.
Angry that he won't allow her to have any say in the way we are raised despite the fact that he expects her to be a mother figure.
He had completely disregarded her and taken advantage of all her hard work and had in those few words torn away the familial obligation she had worked so hard to fulfill, and she didn't take it sitting.

"I can't believe you would say something like that after everything we have been through," she cries out, tossing her flaming red hair back.
He had crossed a line, and instead of showing an iota of humility, he went on the defensive.
"Well clearly we haven't been through enough for you to think you have a say in this matter," he spits out.
I can feel the car pull right onto our street.
My stomach lurches, breath quickens with regret.

A haunting quiet fills the car, a void between Rachel and my father.
I glance up when I feel the gravel of our driveway, Rachel is silent, an angry tear rolling down her cheek.
Ava whimpers next to me, her little hands balled into fists.
The car stops, he tries to comfort her, to apologize but the words stall behind his pride.
Rachel clicks her seatbelt open and storms in, leaving Ava in the truck.
I reach over and begin to unbuckle her, little coos ripple from her lips as the teeth pull from the metal latch.

My father sits still, silent, his hands still clenched to the
circular controller.
I set Ava free and pulled her to me protectively planting a kiss
on her head.
This had not been part of the plan.
"See what you did," I hear him mutter under his breath as I
leave the car.
I so badly want to mirror his words.
See what you did?

Mikey

They argued, which isn't unusual.
Argued about Laurel.
That part was unusual. The fights had always been minor,
usually about how to do the dishes right, or who would pick
up Ava from daycare.
This is different, true colors were leaking, and the fight was
something much more catastrophic.
Small fights over Ava and her diapers.
Bickering about who would get up when Ava cried.
Arguing over money and bills.
Curfew, grades, my knack for sleeping till noon.
Long drawn-out talks around the table, whiskey blurring their
better judgment.
But never about Laurel.
She had never been a point of contention.
She always did the right thing, until now.
The reason he was so upset wasn't because Rachel was trying
to parent.
He had never complained about it until now.
There was a simple way to describe what was luring Dad into
such anger, Objectification.
Laurel was his.
His toy.
His property.
You don't tell a man what to do with his property, or how to
best maintain it.

In this moment he is wearing his heart on his sleeve, his
jealousy and possessiveness as red as scarlet on white wool.
Face contorted in anger.
The caricature of a tell.
A weak poker face.
I can't wait to see it all blow up in his smug face.
The anticipation makes me giddy.
Between the two of us, there was absolutely nothing more
than genetics and shared living space.

Laurel

Poppers burst all around me.
Mischievous children letting off stink bombs.
Patriotic clouds of red, white, and blue flutter all around me in
unpredictable sparks.
A popper lands at my feet as I make it to the front porch, two
cemented steps leading up to a double door with large
cylindrical handles.
Two long rectangular windows run the length of the door
between the handles and the intricately carved patterning.
I jump back almost losing my balance on the ledge only to feel
Kyle's hand pressed firmly against the small of my back.
A series of giggles erupt from behind a large birch.
Three little faces poke out, a little boy with hair that hangs
wild tosses another at my feet.
Behind him, a little girl in a gaudy and overly patriotic dress
smiles and whispers into his ear.
I am ready this time and dodge it easily, a smile encouraging
them to continue their attack.
 My hands are clenched tight with anticipation, a spark that
never comes as the door swings open.
The three screech and run to the side of the house.
Hand in hand we step into the house, loud music throbbing
through the house.
It felt good to be away from his grasp, I still couldn't believe
he had let me out and I was going to take advantage.

Dad had resorted to sulking in the kitchen, Rachel's
triumphant smirk beaming from the living room.
When I heard Kyle's truck rumble up the driveway, I made a
quick disappearance, not bothering to tell him goodnight for
fear he would criticize anything that he didn't deem
appropriate.
There was nothing inappropriate about the white virginal
dress, and scarlet cardigan that was two sizes too small.
It's what lies beneath that daddy should worry about; tight
navy lace gracing my pale skin, and red pouty lips to top it
off.
Patriotic.
Full of good ol' unrepressed American sexuality.
Kyle took notice when I stepped into his truck giving me a
tender peck on the cheek.
He smelled like aftershave even though his face was slightly
scraggly.
I had blushed at his affection and allowed the waves of tingles
to lift me up.
"You don't look bad yourself," I replied as I took a good look,
the gray beanie still on his head.
I gently tugged it off as he drove, hair falling over his eyes
only to be quickly brushed away, "Hey!" he complained.
"That's better," I teased the truck veering up Summer Lane
and into a beautiful summer eve. Large pines hid away most
of the large houses.

Looming mansions that overlooked downtown, a small creek
bed separating the two.
We had driven up the cemented driveway, my eyes gazing
upon the trees, each sitting in perfectly spaced increments
until the top where we were graced to see a big sprawling
lawn.
"This place is huge," Kyle whispers now, my hand squeezed
in his.
I breathe it all in, food and booze, Dean's mom runs up to us
clearly inebriated.
I feel claustrophobic despite the vast entertainment space.

The room is adorned with bright yellow wallpaper patterned with eclectic spheres, that seemed a decade too old despite an almost new build.
Its effect was dizzying.
Dean pops up next to his mother, quick to greet us and spare himself of her embarrassing drunken rambling.
He wraps an arm around his mom's shoulder, standing a head taller and three shades lighter than her streaky tan.
A large letterman's jacket is draped over his broad shoulders, navy blues beneath.
We greet her, pupils dilated, "Well I am just happy Dean has all his little friends over!"
Slurred words, swaying frame, all I can do is smile and thank her for having us.

Kyle's grip hardens as we push through the crowded foyer trying to match Dean's pace, who made it apparent that he wanted nothing to do with the drunken middle-aged crowd that was growing more horizontal by the drop.
We enter an equally crowded dining room, this one dim, a large family portrait hangs over an equally large mantel; adorned with trophies and certificates.
Parental pride.
Pressure.
Tasha lounges in a large chair, her knees tucked to her chest, always manicured nails pressed against her perfect lips.
"Hey."
"Didn't expect you to make it," she states, attempting to stifle her surprise and excitement.

I watch her get to her feet and swipe a finger over the mantle before grasping a sweaty drink that seemed to be more cherries than actual booze.
Dean makes his way to her and gently kisses her neck," let's go," I hear him instruct, a command she easily falls into in her state.
"Let's go to Dean's room," she suggests, a bounce in her step.
  I could tell they were already drunk or close to drunk by the constant swaying.

"Got some green?"
Dean nods to Kyle, "Always."
I follow the happy couple down the long hall before veering
right away from the music and the crowd and find Dean's
bedroom.
If you could call it that.

It was the size of a living room and pristine, much like Kyle's
had been but his was paid for.
Trophies and medals line the floating shelves, a large TV
situated beneath a TV stand, not a speck of dust in sight.
Pressed firmly on the wall opposite the TV sits a king-size
four-post bed with a navy comforter and one too many
decorative pillows all lined with a dark gold edge.
"Sit wherever," Dean motions to nowhere in particular.
Kyle and I plop down on the loveseat at the foot of the bed,
direct view of the TV, an old western playing.
I sink right into the brown cushion next to Kyle, who quickly
wraps in his arms, my eyes darting all around the room
jumping from bright poster to the next most football.
Green Bay, Cleveland, Dallas, all clung to his walls.
Team photos of mostly burly, sweaty men trying to find just
the right half smile for their NFL pictures on display in
various frames.

Dean has a slight obsession, but as far as obsessions went it
was an acceptable one.
Odd how there is a rank for addictions from acceptability to a
travesty.
The cult-like following brought about by sports, the praising
of the television, the expensive paraphernalia, and monetary
loss was all viewed in a positive light.
The loss of finances on the poker table was viewed as a skillful
addiction that could offer some positive potential if one only
bluffs or pulls a lever ever so perfectly.
Alcohol ranks high as one of America's favorite pastimes;
drunken nights that bring out laughter and open doors and
beds but use any other drug and you become scum.

Drink a handle of vodka and people judge you, but they don't demand a reason.
Deviate from drugs and turn your addictions to your own devices and you may as well be certifiable.
How could someone starve themselves, binge, or purge?
Why would someone run a blade against their skin, or tie a noose around their neck just long enough to feel alive or cum harder than they ever imagined?
When people spot that weakened state, they feel so entitled.
Entitled to answers, entitled to feel hurt by the internal pain you wear externally as if you betrayed them.
Entitled to answers.
To ease their hurt.
To humiliate.
Entitled to disgust and judgment.
But bring out a twelve pack and everyone thinks they are having a good time, and if your head ends in a toilet bowl and you spew chunks of vomit all night, it turns into a good laugh come morning.

Tonight I move towards the acceptable, a swig of beer here, a shot there, just enough to give me a buzz without blurring the lines.
I smile and wince at the burn as the bottle goes around, dark amber waves shifting in the cylinder.
A smile is always acceptable, a tear is an awful thing, so I drink to forget that just beneath my grin I am moments away from a complete meltdown.

...

Two shots and a beer later and I ventured back out to the party with a healthy buzz.
I was going to have to let that fade if I wanted to have an appetite for Kyle.
I enter the noise and shut off my brain allowing it to go fuzzy.
Adults swarm over every inch of the large living areas, most completely inebriated.
Booze.

Food.
Weed.
They thought they were being sly, blowing clouds out of the glass patio door.
It was easily swept back in with the bustling bodies.

I want something sweet, and I make haste to the dessert table where an older blonde with heaving breasts crowds the dessert table, hard nipples threatening a tall mound of ambrosia.
Her skin looks painful, stretched beyond capacity, her lips a childish pink, cheeks puffed after one-to-many lifts.
She smiles, or at least I think it's a smile, unaware of my still judgmental thoughts.
Bad teeth flash at me, yellowed by smoking, tight, and overly crammed in a too-small mouth.

I excuse myself, grabbing a plate.
Waxy, with a floral pattern that surrounded the edges.
It maintained its structural integrity remarkably well under the weight of the sweets I had been stacking.
A brownie overflowing with walnuts, a handful of sweet trail mix, a lemon square.
I eat every bite savoring the sugar on my tongue, not bothering to take it back to Dean's room.
Ravenous.
Not just for food, but for Kyle.
Again.
I want to feel right.
Normalcy.
To gorge myself.
To empty myself.
To allow him to fill me then emptied again.
I am conflicted.

I inhale one last fudgy brownie hoping and begin to pace back to Dean's bedroom, my buzz getting me turned around.
Was it left?
I feel so warm.

Really need to stop drinking now as I have no intention of
stumbling in for my dad to see.
Officially turned around.

The house is much larger than I thought and suddenly it dead
ends.
Dean's room had not been at the end of a hall.
I begin to turn around, a light creeping out from under the
closed door, pulling me to the voices that argue behind the
oak.
I hear it.
Anger. Hurt.
Orange light streaks across my foot.
A man's voice; Dean's dad.
A woman's familiar voice.
Crackling. Crying.
The man's voice grows weary.
Annoyed at her pain.

"You promised at the Christmas party that it was going to be
done," she complains, "and it's July now. How long are you
going to make me wait?"
I press closer, careful not to press my weight on the door in
fear of it falling open.
"Things are different, I can't just up and leave, I have kids to
consider," Dean's father replies, his voice crackling like one of
the fireworks outside.
"Please, Martin."
 Something was unsettling about hearing his first name, which
made him less of an authority figure and more of a person.
Martin.
"Martin, I did my part. I left my husband, and it killed him,
I'm still fighting him for alimony. I can't keep sneaking
around like this. These after-school meetings aren't enough for
me and –" her voice trails off.
Did they hear me?

I take a step back into the darkness and try to slow my
breathing praying I wouldn't have to bolt.

"Look Carla, just give me until graduation," he pleads.
Carla?
The voice sounded familiar.
The name did too.
I catch my breath and step closer.
The room has gone silent now and I peer through the cracked door, a woman I know sitting on the edge of a masterful king bed, its pillared beams gracing four posts, a red satin quilt tossed haphazardly, trussed as if they had just tumbled around the bed.

Carla.
Goulding.
Mrs. Goulding.
That was until recently.
Mrs. Goulding and Dean's dad were having an affair?
I press my lips tight, praying I could keep them that way.
Pacing down the hall quickly and making my way back to the crowded atrium, disgust fills me.
I see Dean's mother, drunk on the couch, laughing with her friends.
Completely unaware.
Naïve.
Maybe not?

She lurches forward, her eyes barely open, much like most of the crowd.
Family pictures line the hall as I find my bearings.
Seemingly happy.
The perfect family.
They gave to charity, ran fundraisers, and worked hard.
They had three kids; two of which were team captains, one of which graduated as the valedictorian just the year prior.
They looked good together with the women's bottle blond hair and pearly whites.
The men's tough builds and full heads of hair.
I thought they were happy.
I feel like I might burst, and a thirst has risen in me.
Perfect pictures for a perfect family.

We all thought we had to keep up with them.
My stomach churns.
The grass is only greener on the other side because it's turf.

I enter the bedroom that sits mostly silent.
Lit by the glow of the TV.
The glow of sex.
I hear it.
High-pitched squeals and low moans.
Dean is on the bed, his arms wrapped around Natasha,
oblivious to his father's transgressions.
His mother's hurt.
Blind.
So close, yet a mountain between.

I can see movement beneath the satin sheet that covers them,
little giggles erupting.
My stomach aches, anxiety rises in my throat.
I am full.
Too full.
I feel out of control.
I want to leave.

Kyle sits a foot beneath the loveseat at the foot of the bed, his
eyes awkwardly looking down and away from the screen.
 I see two other young men sitting on the floor just in front,
their eyes glued to the screen.
Deans cousins.
 I had met them once before at some fundraiser; they were
crude and persistent with their advances on any girl who even
looked their way.

...

A large-breasted blonde lies on sweat-soaked sheets, her arms
are tied to the cheap metal bars of the bed, head jutting
between an awkwardly spaced set.
Her breasts, real loll to the side, eyes focused upwards.
Men gather around.

They use her.
One by one coaxing fake moans from her mouth.
She knew how to act.

The group congregates at the end in a circle, dicks in hand all
beating at different rates, personalizing their styles.
"I want to leave," I whisper to Kyle.
To my horror, I can feel myself growing aroused by the
helpless situation.
It makes me feel sick.
My eyes pull back, no control, and watch as a large man with
bad tribal tattoos slaps her face.
His release. The last one.
The end.
The clip cuts and fades to black.
I pull closer to Kyle, "I know. I'm still buzzing a little so give it
a few more minutes and I'll be good to drive."
My arms cross and I try to calm myself.
Kyle takes my hand and moves me close to him, "This feels so
weird."
Narrowed eyes tell me he is uncomfortable with the situation.
I squeeze his hand.
Affirmative.
"Very."

Above us the bed shifts, lips smack as spittle is exchanged
from one mouth to another, only the sound of the fireworks
that had begun going off masked the sounds of awkward teen
love.
Boom, a streak of red glimmers outside the window followed
by cheering.
Crack, a burst of white light.
My heart begins to race.
My mouth is dry now.
There is a weight in my belly that is beginning to make my
heart skip beats.
Overwhelming.

I try to ignore it and stifle it down, my human instinct kicks into gear and pulls my eyes back to the screen.

She is young and ripe.

Pigtails that are a bit on the nose.

Perfect for gripping when he shoves his cock into her mouth.

I watch her gag.

Fixate.

I feel the all-too-familiar ache move between my legs.

Can feel my stomach grow tight.

Too full.

My pulse begins to quicken with every crackling outside the glass door.

"Oh Daddy,' I hear her groan.

Daddy.

Daddy.

Winding ivy twists in my throat, the stress triggering the slimming.

She climbs on top of him and proceeds to ride him hard and fast, "Daddy, daddy!" she yells as he praises her every move.

This wasn't the type of horse they used to play.

My body holds no secrets.

Babbling brook.

I need to get off.

I need to empty my gut.

"Yes!" she cries out as if she was about to come, clearly, it's bullshit.

"Oh, please Daddy! Fuck," she squeals as he takes her from behind now her hair in his hands like reins on a horse.

Kyle squeezes my hand," OK can we just go wait it out in my truck, this is too weird."

It is and I have seen too much.

My eyes begin to pool with tears, head shakes, "Please."

Kyle's eyes fill with concern.

He knows.

He knows.

How could he not?

...

I end up at the bottom of the sleek hill with Kyle pacing
behind me, hands in his pocket rummaging for his keys.
"Laur, wait up," he calls out.
Another burst of light, green this time.
It falls back to the earth, an insignificant willow.
I don't want to face him.
Don't want him to see me cry.
Hot spittle fills my mouth, bile in my throat.
My stomach tightens on its own now and I fall to my knees.
It's coming now.

I fall to my knees and vomit: cheap drink and sweet cordovan
mush.
No control.
I pray it ends there, but it doesn't.
My hands push into the soft grass, bits of dirt clinging to my
palms.
A red bang lights up the sky, but my heart is beating so loud I
can barely hear the fireworks.
Nose tingles, tears thunder out with my throaty breathing as
the high of my release courses through me only to dissipate
faster than rain on the desert ground.
This is different.
The tingle spreads to my ears and my lips.
I touch them.
I can't breathe.
Suffocating.
Drowning.
My head is pounding.
"I can't breathe," I cry out.

...

 A tapping like bits of hail stirs me from a hazy sleep.
Utter confusion washes over me, silence.
Had I been dreaming?
I lie back down, knees tucked against my chest.
The tapping.

My window.
Mikey?
Sneaking back in?
Feet meet ground, the hot night only kept at bay with the rotating fan on my desk.
I pulled back the curtain, annoyed that he wouldn't have warned me before his departure.
I am stunned to find a familiar face.

Not Mikey.
Kyle.
Balanced on the roof ledge, his usual gray hat perched on his head, and a somber gaze.
I pull the latch, bits of old dust flaking under my nails, it creaks open despite the gentle push.
The cool air from my room escapes as Kyle enters, his hand in mine, careful to step down as gently as possible.
"I saw him leave," Kyle whispers, a loose strand of hair over his eyes.
"He works overnight this week," I confirm," You'll have to leave before eight."
I go to my desk and lift the chair jamming the door, stressed at the idea of someone walking in, while simultaneously imagining the look on his face if he were to walk in on Kyle fucking me.
It brings a smirk to my face, one that quickly dissipates at the thought of the repercussions that would ensue.
My father would use all his power to exact his revenge, Kyle was after all older than me.

"Just keep your voice down," I plead, planting sloppy kisses along his neck with each word before pressing my mouth to his, Kyle's hands wrapping around my waist, guiding me towards the bed.
The kiss breaks, a web of spittle bridging us.
"Scouts honor," Kyle tells me, his finger pressed vertically against his lips as we part.

"Come lay down," my voice quivers with lust and demand, my fingers looping through his, tugging him along, plopping down on the foot of my bed.
The moonlight catches my nightgown, kissing me with light in the eerily quiet air.

I motion for him to sit, and he does, telling me how beautiful I look in the light, and I refuse to believe it knowing what I look like.
The days proceeding my birthday had been hard, devastating even, and my face told the tale of depression and emotional burnout.
My strength, which I didn't have much of, to begin with, is now draining more rapidly than I could have ever imagined and I can hardly do anything more than sleep.

Haggard.
Eyes glazed over and puffy from the lack of sleep the night before.
My hair frazzled and disheveled, a sheer seashell-toned nightgown hardening my nipples as the fabric rubs against them.
I feel the mattress shift with a small squeak as he plops down beside me without as much as a word.

Silence.
I welcome her.
Because to talk would mean to discuss what had happened last night and I don't want to talk about last night.
I have no good explanation, only the oath to my father.
Bound by love.
I recall his bulging eyes when he had appeared in the hospital, all red and puffy, Rachel at his side, Ava on her hip passed out.
"Who brought her in?" he asks with an air of entitlement in his tone.
The Doctor, a wiry man who behaved as if he was working on his tenth cup of coffee for the day, simply shrugs, "Not sure."

My eyes meet his, feet dangling over the bed I had refused to lie back on.
I felt too vulnerable given the circumstances.
I watch as he palms the pen, reading through the discharge instructions, Rachel plops down on an empty chair stuck close to the sink.
"Laurel, what's going on?"
I didn't want to disclose what had just transpired and simply stated that I wanted to go home and forget about the whole embarrassing ordeal.

All the questions.
How old was I?
Did I feel safe at home?
Did I have a history of panic attacks?
Mental illness?
Last period?
It had been a couple of months.
They made me pee in a cup in the bathroom.
Negative.
When's the last time I had sex they ask?
I answered honestly, telling them it was a little over a week ago.
Then came all the observations.
They point out a mark that was very clearly created by teeth.
I explained it away saying it was from my boyfriend, my breathing slowing, each lie sucking the life from me.
Stealing a beat.
They point out that my weight and blood pressure were both low.
Recommendations follow under the bright lights.
Weight gain.
Therapy to help keep from having another panic attack.

"Ammoreah," he called it all the while tapping his foot.
"Therapy," he suggested.
He would never go for that, too risky.

The doctor handed him discharge instructions and then proceeded to angrily twist the lid of his pen.

"I understand how stressful being a teenager can be," I heard him confide in my father afterward.

He then suggested to Rachel that she get me on birth control. Dad looked uncomfortable, "Isn't that encouraging her to sleep around?"

The doctor scribbled something down on the notepad shaking his head no, completely ignoring my presence.

"Hon, wouldn't it be better if we did?"

I sit still, a ghost.

"I just don't want her running around town, jumping from boy to boy like some tick."

Rachel took his hand "When have you ever known Laurel to be that kind of girl?"

The doctor chimed in, glasses that teetered on the edge of his crooked nose, "I understand this isn't something you were expecting, but I think the best thing the two of you can do is identify the stressor and if possible, get rid of it. We don't want to trigger another attack. This type of thing is not uncommon, but we don't want to exacerbate it."

A resident popped in then, nervous, paper in hand.

He eyed her, "Sign these please Dr. Hudson," she had stuttered as if she feared the man.

Long hands ran over the paper before she scurried away, the curtain rubbing, closing like the zipper on a tent.

"Let's just not make a habit of this," he added before handing me a pamphlet that I was obviously going to toss.

I still remember his face after we were discharged; cold as ice, with a fiery anger in his heart, "Get dressed, Laurel," he snapped as he had shut the curtain, the wavy pattern making me dizzy as it swayed, "We are going home."

The staff had left me embarrassed, and with no real explanation as to why, only a few hours prior I had felt like there was no air left in the world.

They whispered the entire drive home, the city's light posts flickering rapidly as if I couldn't hear them in the metal box.

"He is bad news, Rachel. He could have stayed with her but all he did was dump her at the hospital and run off," I hear him hiss as if any action Kyle took would be pleasing to him. Truth is he had left after I begged him to go before my dad saw him.

When we pulled up to the house Rachel had made a quick escape with Ava leaving Dad and me to walk in the dark alone.

Silence only broken by him telling me to never embarrass him like that again.

I hadn't left my room since.

Kyle takes my hand and brings my palm to his lips kissing it, "We don't have to talk about last night."

I shudder with relief, our eyes greeting.

He smiles, a smile I know is masking a world of hurt.

My hand skips up to his jaw, fingers splaying to caress him, right now I want to take care of him.

His fingers join mine and this time he angles his lips to my wrist and sighs as he meets my skin.

A sigh that is indicative of something more.

Deep.

Heavy.

"Take your shirt off Kyle."

Brave move.

Rewarded as he obeys, not even skipping a beat.

He wants this.

Needs to be touched.

Needs to be held.

I sense it.

So I take charge, trace my fingers up his chest and to his chin before pulling him into another embrace.

Full of longing and need.

Never progressing past a kiss.

Love over lust.

"I know you don't want to talk about it right now and I'll drop it… but you scared me last night Laurel… and you didn't let

me be there for you…I understand why, but it still made me
feel useless. All I want to do is take care of you," he tells me.

He kisses me gently.
Guilt floods like an early monsoon.
Kyle doesn't understand why, not really.
I pull my arm away, his mouth breaking from mine, and place
it on his chest, laying him flat and hovering over him with all
the dominating power I have.
Our feet dangle.
My gown rides up exposing my hips.
I don't care, it's my body and I want Kyle to both see it and
adore it.
"I know, and I'm sorry… Someday it will all make sense… but
right now, I want to talk about you. Is that ok?"
There's something more there.
Something else is bothering him and I know what it is, his
silence only pushing me to ask further.
"What's on your mind?"
He stays quiet.
I feel him shift away from me, his fingers resting on my
exposed skin, slowly dancing up; middle, pointer, middle,
pointer never resting simultaneously up my waist, and my
stomach.
He stops at my breasts and lays his palm flat on the hard
peaks, the cotton of my nightgown rough against my delicacy,
hand resting on my warmth before sneaking under my chin
and cupping my face.
Slowly he leads my lips down to his and gifts me with a kiss
that is full of hope and hints at longing, turning me to lay with
him.
An antidote to the hurt.

"I'm so selfish Laurel."
He isn't selfish and even if he was, he had every right to be.
The anniversary.
His dad.
His passing.

"Mom's been on edge all day, because-. "
He sucks in a deep breath that only leaves his lips as chatter.
Sitting up I lean against my headboard and gently pull his
head to my lap, pulling his hat off in the process.
It topples as silky waves that smell of pine.
"And," I coax as he falls into my touch.
I push my fingers through his hair, nails massaging his scalp
encouraging low pleasured groans to grace me.
Tension melting away.

"Tell me, Kyle."
"Then she brought some guy home, and I just didn't want to
be in the way, and I just wanted to see you," he whispers.
I lean down and kiss his forehead, "I'm here," I assure him.
"Does it bother you?"
He shrugs, "What?"
"That she brought someone home?"
"It doesn't."
I hold him tight, dare to question him, "You sure?"
An affirmative bobbing of the head, "She deserves to live her
life," he sighs.
With a shaky breath he continues, "But it still hurts. This
wasn't how it was supposed to be. He was supposed to do – "
his voice breaks off, in fear that he may crack.
I can tell he doesn't want me to see him like this, "He was
supposed to love her till the day he died. He was supposed to
love us," he states, voice a raspy whisper.
The only way to keep the tears from falling.
But then his voice breaks, the mirage of strength he had
portrayed fading in the heat of hurt.
It almost breaks me right then and there.
 I want him to feel his pain, while simultaneously making it
disappear.
Why should he have to be hurt?
I know what to say but I don't know if it's right "Do you ever
think that he did love her? Maybe he thought he was doing
what was best?"
I instantly regret saying it, but he surprises me with not a hint
of anger.

"I do all the time, but if he loved us, he wouldn't have left us.
At least not the way he did."

I pull his hair back with my finger's strands separate between
each finger like rows of grain.
"He was a selfish man, Laurel."
He begins to cry this time and it's beautiful, quiet, and
composed.
No way to keep it in and I can sense his embarrassment but to
me this was beautiful.
The way his tears glimmer like crystals in the moonlight
leaves my heart aching.
I hate myself for thinking about it.

"Hurt can make you selfish," I reply.
"Hurt people hurt people," he murmurs, reciting the church
talk.
I feel him quake in embarrassment.
"I don't want to hurt anyone. Not the way he did" is all he
says before pulling me down to lay with him, his face
smothered by my chest, my arms wrapped around him.
In that moment of pure unadulterated emotion, I knew he had
my heart.
"You are not your father, Kyle."
I mean it, holding him to my truth.
Time seems to fade.

...

I hadn't meant it.
To fall asleep that is, but I had.
Panic kicks me into action.
Darkness of night outside my window, the glowing numbers
across the room assure me that I am ok.
Just past midnight with hours to go till dawn.
Safe.

I step over to the clock, setting an alarm for four, knowing it
would give us the darkness needed for Kyle to sneak out.

Kyle has fallen into an emotionally drained coma, does not stir
at the lack of my head against his.
Not even as the mattress shifts as I return to my bed pulling
myself into his arms, my face set against his chest.
I fall hard.
Into his safe embrace.
Into comfort. Into sleep.
The safety of darkness kills me.
Away from the light, where the real monsters hide.

I wake to the buzzing of my alarm and become alert, pushing
my hips into the curve of Kyle's pelvis to wake him.
Bristles irritate my neck from his beard.
 A beard he had not gone to sleep with, scruffy and rough
against my porcelain skin.
I never recalled him growing facial hair so quickly.
I turn my body, my face meets his, his eyes leaving me
stunned.
Caught.
Not Kyle. Kyle is gone.
It's him. My father.
"Morning mouse, "he whispers through an insincere smile.
A smile full of power and glee at the position he must have
found me in.
I don't reply. I can't breathe.
Where is Kyle? Where is he?
"What did you do?"
It's a cry that only earns me a crooked smile, no clue leaving
his mouth.
He has conquered me.

Pulling myself on top of him, my thighs splay on either side of
him, asking to no avail, "Please! Please…where is he?"
Sobbing weakly.
I'm a fucking mess and not because I'm caught but because he
had taken the man I loved from my grasp.
My fingers meet, jab at his sternum, tears falling down my face
now.
Cold tears.

He catches my wrist, holds on tight, I try to pull away, his hand catching the corner of my mouth, the sting of iron against my nose, warm and comforting.
Blood.
Bloody crescents under his nails, and under my own and down on his chest sits torn skin from where I had swiped at him.
The smile is gone, a blank stare replaces it.
"Give me a kiss, Laurel."
He orders it again and grabs my wrists hard pushing me off, hovering just above, "What did I say?"
"Kiss me, little girl," he demands his tongue out, ready to taste me.
Not my lips.
His mouth parts, tongue slithering out, long, flattened, forked like the devil himself.

Too strong.
Mouths meet, iron clashes, mixing with my taste.
My arms run over his arms, scaly, rough skin, his tongue sucking mine to his.
I try to push him away, but he begins to fill me, my throat tight.
Regurgitation, a veritable purge.
Ending just as my vision begins to fade.
I suck in the air, gasping, his mouth retreating before catching at my neck with a bite, scaly face running over taboo skin.
Delicate.
The snake's tongue slithers, my whole body is taut, each forked flick leaving me burning with indignity.
Humiliation.
On fire.
Wet hot fire.

A dream, just another dream.
But this was no dream; it was a nightmare of epic variety.
Nightmares plague me, peaking at the height of my cycle, peaking every time he touches me.

They never make sense, but the main theme is straightforward.
Trapped. Out of control.

My skin is on fire, my neck is tense, a dull pain travels down to the lowest parts of my belly.
Kyle is awake, I can tell by the way his breathing has quickened.
I look back to confirm that he has escaped the realm of sleep and that it's really him.
Fluttering eyes meet mine in my undignified state.
My heart is racing, my mouth is dry, hips are aching from my constricted position.
"You're burning up," Kyle groans along my neck, pulling me closer to bury his nose in the canyons.
I don't reply, my body stiff, mind frozen in paralyzing fear.
Wouldn't know what to say so instead I breathe, remaining still for a long time, the terror of the nightmare abating.
"Laurel?" Posing my name as a question, he tries to draw my attention back to him, all in vain as pulling myself from a hold that feels more like a clutch I practically jump from the bed and my skin.
Wish I could crawl out of the damn shell that keeps me here, or at the very least molt into a new one.
Bigger and better walls.

I swing my legs over my bed and make haste to the small ensuite bathroom, clicking the buzzing light on, making sure Mikey's side is locked.
With my head under the sink, I drink deeply, mouth brushing against the cool metal tap, and with a jerk the cool silver clanks against my teeth.
The waters cool, and I lap it up until my belly threatens to burst, and when I pull my head up to grasp at air, careful not to meet my reflection.
Wouldn't want my inner critic to pop up this late in the day.

The floorboard creaks at the doorway, goosebumps jolt along the back of my arms.

Kyle stands there, arms spread from one side to the other,
stretching, his toned arms rippling as he moves.
I gaze up at him, his face already scanning me, suspicious of
my current state and I fight back a smile that bloomed from
my annoyance with myself and this ridiculous state I was
finding myself in.
And over a dream!

The look falls away with a yawn, arms gripping up now, body
taut as he stretches.
I watch as his sweats shift lower on his hips, the strawberry
birthmark stretching to claim new borders.
"Can I," he asks, his arms swinging back to his side.
He doesn't specify but I don't resist.
I shake my head yes before twisting the icy water off. The
chrome of the faucet creaks, expanding and narrowing with
the cold that blasts through the old pipes.
Kyle takes it as an invitation to come in, eyes caressing my
own from a distance before sauntering my way, hand reaching
out in hopes mine would meet his.
Testing the waters.
Spindly fingers reach back out, dancing along the air until
they wrap like tangled vines that lure us into a tight hug.
"Thanks," he says as one of his digits caresses the tresses of
my loose hair lovingly.
My brow pushes into his strong chest, collarbone hard against
my forehead.
Temporary comfort.
I don't want to leave his grasp, so I squeeze him tight against
me.
Disarmed.
The urge to cry threatens to drown me in a flood of tears that
put me in a chokehold.
Strangling it down I allow the sunshine to chase doom-riddled
clouds to the back of my mind.
I won't let it.

Tears fade, anxiety arises instead.
Another hunt.

A bloodthirsty hound, the fox retreating into its winding home.
I don't want him to see.
Don't think.
Just become.
If I don't think it will go away.
For now.
I can revisit this later.
Find another reason to stifle it all down.
Focus.
With great force I focus on the beating of his heart, tilting my head up to eye his response.
I want to see a smile, anything but concern.
I don't have time to gauge his reaction as he leans down and kisses me with all his might, lips parting to taste him.
Focus on his lips.
His taste.
My hands stay wrapped around his waist, his arms cupping beneath my chin pulling my eyes to his.
"You, ok?"
Focus on the lie.
Recite.

"I'm alright."
Forever a lie.
He rests the back of his hand on my forehead, "You feel hot,".
"Bad dream," I tell him.
"You have a lot of those?"
I shrug him off, "No more than anyone else."
He kisses the tip of my nose, little sparks flowering through my face.
I can tell he doesn't believe me, eyes narrow, reading my gaze.
Too close.
Focus on the walls.
They fly up.
I pull away, my lower back pushing against the quartz top with a jab, causing me to wince at the feel of the cool leaking through the fabric of my light gown.

"Let me chase it out."
Focus on his words.
The ones that fill me with indescribable warmth.
Focus on his respectful distance.
Kyle is good.

There's a choice to be made, laid out in front of me.
Left, or right?
Fall into his arms or push him away?
The space he maintains, only his hand daring to reach out to mine.
I reach back, stroking his fingers along my palm, his spindly fingers all spidery.
"Can you?"
A dashing smile spreads along his lips, "If you let me."
I mull the offer over, knowing exactly what he means.
My head shakes in reply, "OK, show me how."
Focus on what is to come.
Grazing finger's part.

Kyle paces, disappearing behind the small wall that separates the sink from the shower.
The glass door rolls along its tracks with a creak, followed by the squeaking of knobs.
Water pellets fall, pattering along the plastic bottom like little drops of rain.
I remain still anxiously awaiting his return with palpable anticipation.
When he does, he is stark naked.
Unbashful.
Beaming with confidence, with strong legs and squared shoulders, and that thing that only makes him more man, beaming and alert, at attention.
His hair is loose, tickling his neck, leaving me aching with anticipation, and I find myself licking my top lip, his free-swinging member glistening at the head.
I want to be those hairs, the ones grazing his bare flesh, but I don't dare move despite the hard evidence of his desire for me that is nestled beneath.

More than anything, I want him to want me.
Need him to touch me the way I so desperately want, but I
want him to touch me first.
Chase me.
Prove to me that he wants me too.

My body is aching for it, for him, and only him, heat running
down between my thighs, my sex filled with hazy warmth.
"Let me make it better?"
There's no answer on my end, not wanting to seem too eager,
but I'm also hesitant with how much I wish to take advantage
of our vulnerable state; a vampire, sucking the life from him.
Kyle steps forward, graces me with another deep kiss, my
tongue falling between my lips to meet his, as if he knows I
want to say yes.
His mouth is soft, velvety, I could die in that kiss, oxygen
leaving my body, and I am left panting, mind racing.
I can't keep quiet.
"Please…help me quiet my mind, "my lips crash against his.

My only response is to hook my teeth against his trembling
mouth and embrace him, letting my tongue slide past his lips
to stroke along his and we mash. The taste of his saliva mixes
with mine, a chemical reaction following along the synapses of
my brain.
They all tell me one thing; I want him.
No.
I need him.
I groan along his mouth as the bristles of puberty graze my
own.
My thighs wrap easily around him, his hard length rubbing
deliciously along my opening.
Woman.
Man.
That's all we are, nothing more and nothing less.
Not our problems, not our hurt, just two people who need
each other.
Focus on his kiss.
Our kiss.

Shared, one we both take ownership over as he sets me in the stall, only dying down into embers when the water of the shower falls over us like cold darts.

Still, the icy flow soothes the heat that I had awoken to and keeps alive the Kyle induced warmth, the contrast stark and pleasing.

"Please," I whisper, thighs still wrapped around him.

There is no hesitation, no need to build it up.

Certainty.

A low groan, my name.

Hands on my hips.

He makes love to me, and I lose bits of myself.

When all is said and done, he reposes me, assuring me I'm alright.

We catch our breath, and he runs his hands through my hair, then brushes my lip gently.

"Can I?"

Motioning to the body wash I swallow hard with agreement, the idea of such an intimate act frightens me.

I'm terrified to fall in love with him and this would only make it easier.

A comical amount of my favorite wash comes out, golden and subsiding on my shoulders, his hand happily working and soothing the knots along my shoulders.

A touch that is both tender and tough, a perfect combination.

When he's done, I'm panting, the nucleus of my chest crying out for him.

Reaching back, I coil my hands around his neck, pulling his chest harder against my chest, and kiss him.

"My bed," I beg with fervor, eyes trained on him.

Wet, and shivering Kyle carries me, licking off droplets of the shower from across my chest, before he lays me on my back with a small squeak.

His hand falls between us, femoral grazed by his touch.

We become one.

Damp sheets tangling around us messily.

Kyle kisses me, "I'm not leaving, yet" he assures me, adjusting to spoon me from behind.
I push into him, pull his arm around me, nails gently pressing against the bone of my hips.
He stills and I encourage him pushing and working him in and out.
I feel everything now, and I don't want to be alone, even if it means telling him everything. .
Someday.
Focus on these fleeting moments.

"Are you alright?" Love's strong voice whispers into my ear.
I nod "With you…always."
I mean it, even if it felt wrong to let him out a foot in the door.
Doesn't mean I'll come out yet but at least it's an option.
"I won't always be here Laurel, and I want you to be ok when I'm not around."
The words cut deep.
Truth hurts.
My eyes cloud.
"Promise you'll never go too far?"
His hand moves over my flat lower belly, resting palm down, his nose in my hair, tangling with the scent, his mouth slowly parting as if he isn't sure if he should continue.
I stay silent for a while, and he slips from the clutch of my core.

After a long moment he continues, "Are you really ok, Laurel?"
I stay quiet and roll my hips back, our bodies threatening to morph into one again as if I instinctively want to silence him with pussy rather than talk to him, and that alone makes me feel disgusted with myself.
Slowing my movements, I pause and still.
I need to regain control and that is not the answer.
Don't you dare cry.
One. Two. Three. Four.

Eight, I end my counting at eight because it feels safe, and I converge my eyes to look intensely at the leaking light of the moon.

Words escape my tightly pursed lips and for once they contain a smidge of honesty, "I don't think so."

The tears came hard and fast falling into damp sheets, and my lip trembles before parting in a small gasp as I try to stifle the flow, but it only makes it all the more apparent, my fingers moving up and curling against the upper cheeks of my face, catching the damp.

I hate myself for crying.

Hate that he knows, but he doesn't make me feel ashamed or wrong for letting it out.

"It's ok if you're not," he whispers reassuringly along the shell of my ear, feigning ignorance, but knowing full well that I am a weeping mess.

I feel his eyes fixate on my shoulder, one of the spaces where his teeth had broken little blood vessels, along with my chest leaving a mark just nights before, and he doesn't pry.

Yellowing pools of evidence.

Soon to fade.

Destined to stain eternally.

"I'm not ok," the words bleed from me, draining my strength.

"It will get better someday, Laurel, and when you're ready to tell me I'm right next door. You just need to take that step and I promise I will be there for you."

Someday will never come, and despite the small distance that sits between our homes, there's an ocean between our minds.

...

It's a hot day and I wake up completely spent.

Sheets tangle, rolling to my side I find a familiar ache nestled between my legs, a reminder that last night had not been a dream despite the absence of his frame in my bed.

I don't want to get out of bed and yet the birds are almost demanding it.

They sing loudly.

Louder than I can recall, or maybe my head just hurts.

I had come to a sick realization last night.
One I wanted to push down deep.
I am in love.
Mutual.
Unselfish.
Unblemished.
Love.

What we did together, my father has only ever done to me.
I had been so blinded by the bright sun that I hadn't been able
to see the blue sky that surrounds it.
But how do I live without sunlight?
I don't.
For now, all I can do is draw the blinds.

I reach over to the bedside and twist the white lid off the
sickly orange, it comes off with a pop.
Valium.
The little round pill that would take it all away.
Or so I'm told.
Rachel had brought me some of hers yesterday.
"Don't tell your father she warned," her eyes full of guilt.
I agreed and placed the orange tube on my nightstand and
waited about ten seconds after she had gone to inhale one,
desperate to feel nothing.

Big mistake.
I was on my ass within a half hour.
Had barely left my bed.
Floating.
I felt nothing.
Fell into a trance and when I came through the other side, I
was left desperate.
It all came crashing down and everything I had pushed down
with that little round pill came back tenfold.

Ideation creeps in, bred out of desperation.

It wouldn't be that hard to take them all and go to sleep.
A deep sleep.
I take another.
This was followed by a period of manic giggling and intense crying.
The type that leaves you hyperventilating curled in a feeble ball.
I took another and floated.
All the way up the ceiling.
Freed of my fleshy cage and into a deep sleep.
A deep forced sleep interrupted only by Kyle strumming his fingers against the glass.
Kyle who was no longer in the bed we had shared.

He had made love to me again last night, kissing at my breasts plucking blood to the surface of my nipples before falling between my thighs headfirst and kissing at me, feverishly. Tenderly he lapped me to orgasm, and then, only when I was shaky and falling apart, the tears still coming did he share himself with me.
Morphing into another release.

My waist is absent from his protective grasp now and I want him more than I have ever wanted anything.
His breath is no longer climbing up my neck.
All I feel is loneliness.
He was gone.
Gone until September.
Working at his uncle's ranch.
I take another pill.
Let the birds sing.
Let the day fade away.
Let it all go to hell for all I care.
I don't want to feel a damn thing.

Mikey

I watch as she chokes down two Valiums like candy.
Dry.

I can't say I blame her.
She had, after all, climbed a peak last night only to fall into a lonely canyon today.
I had heard the shower late into the night, followed by whispers.
It was easy enough to put two and two together.
I had kept my mouth shut, opened my eyes, and caught a glimpse as they crashed onto her bed, a pile of wet hair and dewy skin.
She was so beautiful as the night shone on her.
So free.
Strong.
I had never seen that side of her.
Kyle saw it too, fueling himself with her touch, taking what he should not, and yet, Laurel was enthralled and hopelessly lost in it.
I never want him to touch her again.
I am selfish.

Laurel

I overdid it and for a moment knowledge had been instilled in me, and I felt as if I might die when the pills peaked, and I could hardly stand upright.
My heart was faltering, skipping beats and my legs were numb.
I had tried to get up and make myself vomit, get rid of it, instead, I faded out and away with an acceptance that disturbed me.
If it was the end, I was glad to embrace it, perturbed only by my ease in accepting it as so and hating myself for making them take care of the aftermath.
Spent the next day dizzy, my vision blurring with each step.
I can't tell anyone, and while staying away from my family was the best option, it is not in the cards.

He was home for the next three days.
Wanted to spend time as a family or whatever we are.
He had been so enthusiastic and excited at breakfast.

My first appearance since my fuck up.
I almost feel bad about his childish demeanor.
The way he was trying to rile us all up for our family outing.
Left without a choice I prepare for a long hot day.
Jean shorts and a long black-sleeved shirt cover me, and I
make haste to the bathroom then, shocked by my reflection.
Bags had formed under my eyes like small ripe plums that
were begging to burst.
My hair sits lifeless on top of my head, knots forming at the
bottom.
So unappealing.
I am filled with disgust as I pull my jeans up further up on my
hips.

There was no one to impress.
But there was no one to appease.
My father.
He would absolutely care about the way I look.
The way we all look.
The whole family had to look perfect so to avoid his criticism I
brushed and pluck and paint myself into the perfect daughter.
Makeup perfectly applied, light, and natural.
Hair brushed and pulled back with a virginal white
headband.
Nails painted a non-threatening light pink.
I am put together just the way he likes.
The final touch comes in the form of a light floral mist.
Lilac.
Imagine, the glass cube read in black Buffalo script.
I close my eyes.
Imagine what?

Mikey

A rodeo.
My father's idea of a fun family day.
Of course, a man like him would enjoy viewing such a cruel
sport.
The way they slap the horses on the backside.

The way the spurs dig into their flesh.
How quickly a helpless calf could be knocked down and
forced into bondage.
The control.
The stress that little calf was put under.
His idea of a good time.

Laurel

Instead of watching the show, I pace the dusty grounds, a
whirlwind of brown dust floating at my feet with each heavy
step.
Armed with a pocket full of cash, courtesy of Rachel, I make
haste towards the concessions and get in line.
I stand behind a heavy-set man, my stomach demanding
nourishment now.
The man steps up closer to the counter, his jeans falling loose
around his backside.
Unfortunately, I catch a glimpse of a severe case of acne that
was ballooning under the strain of infected skin, sweaty, beads
rolling off what little hair he had across his sunburnt skin.
I take a step back utterly disgusted as if his acne might jump to
my skin.

I'm ashamed of myself.
Sickened by my judgmental thoughts.
After what feels like an hour, I make it to the front, cheering
erupting from the stands.
Roars and laughter erupted all around.
I glance past the rickety fencing and spot gaudy flashes of reds
and yellows all around.
Laughter erupts.
Seems like the clowns had made their appearance.

This part I may have enjoyed but not as much as the food I
was about to devour.
I order half the menu, nachos, chocolate bars, and a large
slushie, in hopes to fill myself to the brim.
Want my stomach to stretch.

But only momentarily.

"You plan on sharing," a voice interrupts behind me.
Mikey.
I eye him, his moss hair perfectly quaffed, button up wrinkle
free and one size too small.
Wrestling was paying off for him.
"I guess," I reply as I hand a couple of bills over to the pimply
teen that worked the register.
He hands me back a few coins and promptly waves us to the
next window.
"Are the clowns out?" I ask, trying to make conversation,
aware that they were currently performing.
Mikey nods before leaning against the shiny ledge.
He begins to strum his fingers impatiently.
I look back towards the stands, waves of people constantly
shuffling to and from.
A little girl drops her ice cream cone behind us, her mother
scolds her and she wails in perceived agony.
I look back and watch Mikey begin to gather our order that
had been slid haphazardly on the counter, the nachos
threatening to fall.
"Help me!"

Lurching my fingers grasp at the edge of the nacho tray,
orange, fluorescent goop clinging to my fingers as I struggle to
get a good grip on the flimsy tray.
Mikey piles the rest of my food into his arms and begins to
walk away.
"Where are you going?"
He turns back to face me, "Just follow me."
Like a lost little sheep, I trail behind.

Mikey

Laurel fits right-in under the bleachers.
Part of the unused fairground, far away from the watchful
eyes of supervision, yet close enough for a swift return to my
father's side if he came calling.

Gale and I had planned it all on the phone last night, a moment to get high.

Laurel

Gale looks different today.
Her hair is darker, makeup not as intricately applied as it usually was.
Her demeanor had also changed.
She was clingy, yet seemingly uninterested.
She instantly grasps onto Mikey, long dirty nails daring to dig in if he dared walk away.
To her left is another couple I recognize from school, Maureen and her boyfriend.
Gale seems more interested in the groping pair than my brother.

Maureen eyes me suspiciously, gangly and petite with now bottle blond hair and bad teeth.
I watch her suck down a beer.
Rumor is she is pregnant.
My source wasn't necessarily reliable though.
Tasha loves to talk.
Without as much as a word I wave.
The gesture isn't returned, and Maureen scowls, Reese cowering behind her.

Despite the spiked collar, ripped black jeans, and long black hair he seemed nervous.
Almost as if he was waiting for someone's disapproval of his style, the goal to reinforce his perceived rebellion.
I lean against a metal beam and listen to them all gossip, but don't really have anything to add, not when my nachos are getting soggy.
Gale lights the joint and passes it around taking long drags.
When it reaches me, I am apprehensive.
What if dad noticed?
"Don't bother," Gale interjects as Reese holds it out to me, the cherry red and crackling.

I glare at her.

"What's that supposed to mean?"

Tonight, I am in no mood to be the meek girl next door today.
Angrily, feeling tested I grab the joint and suck it in deep, the
smoke gently spilling from my lips, Gale glares, the smoke
wafting in her direction.

"Looks like little Miss Perfect has a bad side," Maureen
comments, a grin glued to her mouth.

Gale nudges her hard with a warning.

Maureen however ignores her and presses into me, "What else
do you do with that mouth?"

I like the attention, don't care for the line of questioning, but I
can't let on.

"I don't know what you mean."

My brother looks uncomfortable, "Leave her alone Maureen."

The petite blond rips the joint from my finger taking a long
drag, "I just hear things ya know?"

I don't.

"I have no idea what you're talking about."

My brother shifts, eyes zooming in on mine, questioning if I
need him to come to my aid or not, "Maureen! Just stop."

"Kyle," she states simply, the sound of his name makes my
knees weak.

Reese tenses behind her as if he might pounce at any moment,
"Your sister is a grown woman, let her talk."

Maureen waves him off taking a deep drag before sauntering
to me, her face inches from my own.

I can feel my muscles tense, my blood pressure rises.

"What did you hear?"

Maureen's lips part, sweet smoke flowing into my open
mouth.

A grin spreads across her glossed lips, "Just that the two of
you were fucking at the bonfire...in Kyles truck."

Mikey squirms, "Come on Maureen!"

I begin to feel a buzz flush through my body, and I am filled
with confidence, "So what if we were?"

She doesn't reply, instead, she takes the burning joint and
presses it to my bare lips, "I had no idea you were such a slut

is all," she states playfully as I grasp the wet joint sucking in deep.
The smoke hits, annoyance making my mouth part.
"Well Maureen," I start before taking another long drag coughing as the smoke exits, "I guess it takes one to know one, and what Kyle and I do is really none of your damn business."

The group sits quietly.
Painfully quiet.
That is until Maureen, who is red in the face and whose demeanor has grown unconfident, replies with a meek proclamation that she had just been messing around.
I am tired of getting walked all over.
Tired of being the sweet girl next door.
The good girl.
I push my luck a little further, "You know what, this is great and all, but I have something better than weed…that is if you are game."

All eyes on me.

Mikey

This was a new side of my sister.
The sister that had presented the group with an orange
prescription bottle.
Laurel rattles it.
All eyes turn to her as if she had rung the dinner bell.

A side I like.
The side of my sister that watches Reese crush up the pills into
a fine powder, using the bottom of the bottle.
A side I had never seen as she snorts up a thick line with no
questions asked.
I watch her in the corner giggling.
I'm not going to stop her.

Instead, I support her and join in.
Take my hit, the burn is instant, the poorly crushed pill tearing
up my sinuses.
A slow climb.
To an unforeseen peak.
High.
So high.
I laugh.
We all laugh.
I scream.
They scream.
We all scream.
Falling into a powdery white dream.
Everything feels so strong. Heavy?
I can feel again. Feel everything.

Laurel

I don't feel a damn thing.
Not the hot sun on my skin.

Not the pangs of hunger in my gut, money wasted on
concessions.

I barely feel myself walk into the house at a quarter to eight,
my dad instructing me to put up the dishes before peeling out
of the driveway, clearly anxious to fall into a whiskey good
time.
Off to get his fix.
He would probably stumble drunk after two, Rachel sober,
Ava asleep in her seat.
I'm happy and it shows.

We barely made it through the door before I burst into a fit of
uncontrollable laughter.
The peak is in sight. My ambitions are just out of sight.
There is always a higher crest to summit.

The car ride had proved difficult.
I had to focus on the passing trees just to stifle my laughter.
Mikey somehow maintained a full-blown conversation with
Rachel about his job at the feed store.
Maybe it didn't affect him as much.
"Got any more?"
I nod and hand Mikey another that he proceeds to swallow
dry, his pupils huge already invading and conquering his
colorful pupils.
"We could take it up a notch," he offers with a grin that tells
me he has something up his sleeve.
"What do you have in mind?"
I throw my purse down on the couch along with myself, shoes
flying off in opposite directions, my skin tingling, head heavy.
"Do the dishes and find out," he teases, motioning to the sink
full of breakfast dishes, thick syrup, and mountains of
congealed powdered sugar.

I agree, curiosity and the promise of further inebriation getting
the better of me.
The task is painstaking.

The cabinets blur, and the soap feels comfortable as it stinks and sinks between my fingers, my mouth frozen, captured by the heavy buzz.

The unfinished plastic plates are tossed into a sloppy pile and keep working on the pans.

A couple of greasy trays from chicken parmesan, and last night's dinner plates, sit in the water, a layer of grease rainbowing across the top with the soap, and here I had thought I only had breakfast dishes to do.

I twist the knobs on the double sink once more as the other side drains, ready to refill, the water drowning the grime that caked the dinnerware.

Scrub, rinse, and dry, all slowly, careful not to let my seemingly huge hands grip too tight, or too loose depending on the wave I ride at each moment.

I save the best for last: a fresh sink of piping hot water for Dad's precious new whiskey glasses, courtesy of Rachel on his birthday.

The water stings, steam rising.

Paper-thin, hand-blown glass, with his name precisely printed along the center of each glass in a light caveat font.

Crystal clear.

Allegedly, it helps to "Let the spirit shine," my father had said happily when he opened the gift and admired Rachels's generous gift.

I dry and stack them next to the double-walled glasses: perfect for sipping the pricey stuff.

He did much more than sip that night. I remember pretending to cheer as he blew out his candles, snow dumping on the cold March evening.

His real gift didn't come until later that night from Rachel.

I rinse the last glass and place it gently on his bar tray, little streaks of water still present from my sloppy work.

He would absolutely complain come morning.

"Next level," Mikey calls out, drawing my eyes to where his voice came from.

I hear him sprint down the stairs, hitting each step with a loud thump, before leaning on the door frame.
There is a bottle in his hand, clear liquid sloshing around from its previously opened state.
"Vodka," he announces, hopping my way excitedly, shaking the plastic gallon before popping it open.

Mikey takes a long swig, barely reacting to the burn before pressing the lip to my own.
I allow the liquid to burn down the length of my throat before gagging and pushing the bottle away.
"How do you do that?" I pose the question, perplexed at his under reaction and my overreaction.
I realize how loud my voice is, the drugs and booze blurring my senses.
 "I'm a man," he jokes, arms contorting into an obviously fake flex, "I already got hair on my chest."
"You look ridiculous!"
Again, he clenches his fists, then rolls his pant leg up, flexing his calf.
"Like what you see?"
There's a crazed look in his eyes, a devilish look across his lip along with some little hairs.
I wonder if he might grow a beard like our father.
Without a word, he pounces, tackling me to the couch, before laughing maniacally.
I laugh, shove him off to the floor with a deep thud.
"Give me that bottle," I demand, trying to catch my breath, giggling, my head falling over the edge of the couch, legs and butt still on the sitting portion.

...

We lie on the couch drunk and lazy, the TV insignificantly playing. Not an image registers long enough to disrupt my buzz.
I am distracted by my body, which is loosely spooned into my brother's, as we lie on the couch.
My twin.

The way we must've lain in the womb.
I don't imagine we ever touched quite as much, or that my
eyes would flutter with drunken sleep, heavy and
comfortable, certainly couldn't imagine what came next, and I
stirred much later judging by the paid programming on TV.

A man struggling with his blanket clumsily on a sofa on the
screen, my brother also quietly struggling behind me, moving
his hand from its draped position along my waist upwards,
running lazy strokes along the ribcage beneath my breasts.
Frozen, I utter not one word, but I hear every word he
whispers into what he believes is my unconscious state.
He is so careful, loving really, weary not to grip too hard, and
never to explore too low, and while it feels sick, I can't help
but keep my silence and fall into the novelty of his touch, the
truth of his love and just how to run it deeps canyoning like a
crafting river.
It's not sexual, the exploration all I feel is adoration, cherishing
me with love.
What is this if not love?

Love coursing through his body, tinted red, filling and
hardening only the orifices that passion can fuel, driving him
wild and willing to risk it all simply to touch me.
"You're so perfect Laurel," hot words, spoken with so much
honesty.
Risking my waking just to feel me.
Intimacy, and if I was willing to give it to our father, why
shouldn't Mikey take it too?
So sick.
I love him but acknowledging what I had allowed him to do is
too much and I won't let him live with the guilt of moving to
hazardous territory.

With firm resolve I sway, murmuring feigned sleepy nothings
before turning to nuzzle myself into his chest, his fingers
forced to leave me, my breasts pressed there as I pretend to
sleep to guard his heart and pride.

He slowly pushes me away to give space, but not before
kissing my cheek, understanding the error of his ways.
For that, I have love for him.

Mikey

The morning sun hits me dead in the eye.
The light seems rather vengeful this morning.
Punishing me for last night's events.
But I couldn't help myself.
She drove me crazy with her innocence, her need for a savior,
and if I could be that savior would it be enough to keep her
around?
Would it cement my love for her?
Would it pull her into its web of love, silky strings wrapping
her and holding her in place?
If it was my web that she became tangled in, what did that
make me?
The predatory spider, set on devouring her completely,
reverting her to another form of victimhood?

Or perhaps she would think of me as her hero, one who would
swoop her up into his arms and fly her to safety.
Maybe she would swoon and fall to her knees at my feet like
no woman had ever fully submitted before.
The price of freedom was just another form of enslavement.
People just don't notice when the light shines a little too
bright.

...

I don't have to wait long to face my sister.
A groaning sound rises from the floor next to me. I glance
down, the box spring rustling beneath me.
She rises straight up like some type of disturbed vampire, hair
strewn messily around her face, her lips pouty and traceable.
Granted she might accept my lips to meet hers.
"We slept past the alarm."

She ignores me, groaning something about her head and
water.
I reach over to my nightstand and toss down the crinkly
plastic water bottle.
We had some cleaning to do.

When we have the house pristine, she seems lighter, happier
in fact, and she keeps smiling my way.
"Last night was fun. I missed hanging out."
Skipping my way despite her hangover, she hugs me tight,
pressing a kiss to my cheek, a kiss that makes me shiver with a
demand that only further deteriorates my soul.

Laurel

I am proud of my brother.
His control.
His love for me.
His ability to draw a line and for that I love him.
I tell him as much.

...

August makes me dizzy, the heat too intense and I grow
almost excited to be back at school with its industrial air
conditioning units.
Kyle is doing well, working hard on the ranch, four-wheeling,
stacking hay bales, rustling up livestock, and enjoying evening
campfires with his cousins.
He misses me.
So he says.

It would be another couple of weeks before he flies home.
We agreed to talk again on Tuesday at nine o'clock. My
stomach clenches at the thought.
Making something that should excite me makes me feel sick
instead.

I hate sneaking around, but if my father were to find out, there would be hell to pay.

Mikey

Rachel had been distant.
Wouldn't let me hold Ava.
There was always room for an excuse.
At times, I wonder if my father had said something to her.
After Laurel's episode that is.
Whatever he had said or done it quickly found its way back to me.
What was worse was the fact that he continued to push me away.
Didn't want to take me hunting like we usually did in the summer.
Nothing.
Up until this last year, we had always spent the week after the fourth upstate with his work pals, drinking beer, tracking big bucks, talking about women, and sex.
Mostly they drank beer.
Dedicated the first couple of days to getting that prized kill, then it was off to drunken oblivion.

Dad always allowed me a couple, but once he was blacked out drunk it wasn't hard for Todd and me to guzzle what we could find.
Todd was Officer Spence's stepson.
He was a year younger than me, but just as fun and driven to have a good time.
Good times we had, stumbling around the campsite drunk, the men yelling out obscenities, sharing stories of their latest fucks.
I am honestly surprised my dad never slipped up and said her name over the last few years.
Never mentioned his daughter and the unspeakable things he does to her.
The man can keep and protect a secret like no other and to keep his secret safe he has to keep Laurel complicit, either

through actively showing her how much he loves her, or by
shunning her so that she desperately wants his love.
Master manipulator.

His dedication was back on her which makes me question
what the newest development was.
What had he done to her?
Was it so bad that he had to buy her a car?
He had promised to take her after the ceremony.
The wedding, that is.
So sudden.
He is up to something.
That or he is finally unraveling.
I'll have to sit back and watch it all unfold.
Till then it was three nights in the city leading up to the
wedding and a week in Mexico.

Laurel

The wedding passes by fast in the small venue, Ava serving as
the flower girl, red ringlets bobbing as she strolls clumsily
down the grass aisle, from a dirt wooded path.
I knocked some dead blades of grass up; they cling to the
bottom of the tight V-neck Rachel has me wear.
Fern colored, long, and flowing at the bottom.
Mikey sits in the audience, no place for him in the wedding.
The venue is beautiful, especially with the last-second
planning.
A large flat field of Kentucky bluegrass in front of a picture-
perfect red barn, a thin patch of forest from the parking lot to
the clearing, tall trees that seemed to have been meticulously
placed to let the sunlight beam through them surround all
sides.

The barn had been an option but with the perfect summer
weather they had opted for a large white-pitched tent in the
field complete with a dance floor, and Rachel's cousin as the
entertainment.

Rows of white chairs line pristinely just beyond the tent, which was occupied by staff quietly setting up a buffet. An arch sits to the east, adorned with white clematis and vines. She looks beautiful, her red hair curled, tumbling down beneath a ballerina veil, her dress a skintight floral lace, opening to a beautiful waterfall of ruffles at the base. Off-white, of course. Perfection. Dried white rose petals fall over the grass path, a bouquet of tall lavender and blue thistle wisp in the breeze. It was Indiana after all.

There's a gaggle of family and friends huddled on white lawn chairs, white bows tied around the backs. I am amazed they had made it on such short notice, but family was important to them, or so they said. They all stand and beam as a slow ballad plays across the speakers. Down the aisle, towards a life of commitment and happiness. Married into secrecy. Lies. Infidelity. I set Ava in Rachel's arms as she reaches the end, careful not to damage her chiffon dress. My dress feels too tight now, my breasts have gotten bigger, which is to be expected at my age. The growth wasn't welcome and seeing my breasts fill out...well that made me cry. Something I seem to do a lot lately.

Mikey

Dad stands tall and proud, clean-shaven in his fitted gray tux. Completely comfortable proclaiming his love for one woman as he stands between the two women, he regularly beds. His pocket is adorned with a few scraggly bits of lavender. Fragile, simple, two things he is not. I listen to him proclaim his love for Rachel.

Tell her that she has touched him, how important she has been
to us all.

"I didn't think I would find love again after my late wife's
passing, but God has blessed me. Above and beyond."

Rachel blushes an indecent red, gripping Ava against her
booming bosom, her free hand caressing him in a simple
gesture.

"He has provided me with a beautiful family, my daughters,
my son, and a chance to call you my wife."

The crowd audibly swoons around me.

I want to blow chunks, but my gut won't allow it, not at such a
regal event.

"Edmund," she begins, her voice crackling, emeralds wet with
happiness. "The first time I laid eyes on you, I never would
have imagined that I would be so blessed with the gifts you
would bestow on me."

Maybe he does love her.

Rachel continues, "A new family, a love that has only
continued to blossom through drought and torrential rains
alike. There is no man I could want or need more than you. A
dedicated father, a dutiful officer, a man of his word, and one
heck of a handsome man if I do say so myself."

My father smirks at this, his friends whooping all around.

"I want to spend every minute of my life with you. The good,
the bad, and everything in between."

She doesn't know how bad the bad really is.

"Today is not the best day of my life, Edmund, because I
refuse to believe that this is as good as it gets. That's not
possible with you."

I look down at the blades of grass between my feet.

Tickling.

Growing.

Threatening to swallow me down.

Bury me six feet under, where there really is nothing to feel
but worms eating away at me.

Let the earth swallow me whole.

Let me find some use.

Their words.
Disgust.
Irritation.
Shrinking.

Laurel

Large pinecones decorate the white tablecloths, green napkins,
and silver-rimmed plates.
Beautiful.
Too bad it was all bull shit.
Much like that kiss that leaves me seething.
Scorned.
Elated.
Clarification.
This is far from over.
My heart aches.
I'm not sure why.
My belly groans.
I know why.

I want to cry.
I know why.

Jealousy.
Rejection.
Suspicion.
I can't find the tears.
This is not the time.
It's never the time.

Mikey

Uncle Cal and Rachel dance a dance full of smiles and decent
talk.
It was the first time they had met, but it was going well.
Grandma dances with her son.
Crying.

Full of joy.

I have no desire to dance, and clearly Laurel doesn't either so after a slow dance with Cal that she seems to have mixed emotions about, probably because he looks so much like our father and she is unsure whether to kiss him or shove him away, we opt for a quick walk in the woods, a scent trail of weed sucking us in.

Cal's stepdaughter sits on a toppled birch, the sky blue, sun fading along with most of the wedding party's inhibitions. Mara's hair sits short and spiky, her dark makeup smeared, a joint pinched between her fingers.
"Got any for us?"
Shoulders jolt at the sound of my voice. The still smoking apparatus held tightly behind her back.
"You scared the crap out of me!"
I had hardly recognized her when she first appeared. Last, I had seen her, we were fighting over a magazine after my mother's funeral.
Her dad had scorned her, told her the right thing to do would be to give in to my tantrum.
It was her magazine.
She had protested as much, but grief won.

Cal had legally adopted Mara after her mother, Cal's ex-wife, had left him for another man, leaving her daughter behind.
The woman had no motherly instinct and had spent the majority of their short marriage drinking and participating in a chain of ongoing ladies' nights.
She left one day with nothing more than a phone call.
There was someone else.
Someone more exciting.
By that, she meant a man with money, a forty-foot yacht, and a huge cock down in Florida.
Cal hadn't dated much since.
He looks like dad.
Just a little younger, and with sharper angels and darker eyes.

Cal is a good man.
At least I assume he is.
Mara hands me the joint.
My night is a tumbling blur after that and a few swigs of her
flask.

Laurel

Riding on a marijuana-triggered cloud I find my playful side,
the cold night airing the smell from my now freed hair.
It falls over my shoulders, the friction along my neck flashing
back memories of Kyle's lips on my neck.
I smile.
Feel out the music.

Mara and Mikey laugh around the cupcake table, taking finger
swipes of white frosting off random tops and rearranging the
fluff with a spoon as no one would take notice.
I snatch one and inhale it, my stomach yearning for something
sweet.
Dad asks me to dance, the cupcake still lingering on my
tongue.
I can't say no, instead I take his hand and beam.
Words blur as he makes some announcement about how lucky
he is to have me as his daughter.
I feel uncomfortable.
"She is going to make some man very happy someday," he
ends his little speech with a lie.
He would never let that happen.

Everyone claps.
I retreat within myself, sporting a stupid smile that screams
insecurity.
Gears jam.
Thoughts fizzle.
This bridge is up.
A slow song pours out, the lighting dimming around, bluish
lights glow and twist all around.
The sun has bid us goodnight.

His hand falls to my waist, encouraging me to sway.
It makes me wonder.
Wonder if he will be there the day, I walk down the aisle.
Will he be green with envy?
Cry because he is losing his hold on me when they should be
tears of joy.
I wonder if I will ever walk down the aisle.
Wonder if he will ever let me go.
All around, Dad's friends are reigniting lost moments with
their partners, while my mind flares with anxiety.

As the crowd tightens, Dad's bristles run along my ear.
"I can do better, Laurel."
That's all he says. Five words.
Five words that make me feel violently ill.
It's too late for that.
There was no doing better.
He had pulled too hard, and I had already snapped.

Mikey

Dad and Rachel spend the night alone, Ava hanging out with
Laurel in her room much to my sister's dismay.
She had a bottle, a handful of diapers, and a heart full of
longing for her mother.
I leave Laurel to tend to her.
Go chase the night away with a few shots of whiskey and a
hard-on in my room at Rachel's quiet insistence.
I quench both my thirsts on the empty bed, imagining Laurel
asleep next to me, unable to protest if she ever dared.

My sister was never one to fight.
To scream and end her misery.
Instead, Laurel found warmth in the cozy little box she was
put into.
Was exhilarated at being doted on like a little doll and only
cracked when the real play began, but she was always so
easily glued back together that he didn't stop.

No one ever really took notice despite the obvious damage and lately, it seemed like the glue was no longer holding firm. So I chase another shot of whiskey and grimace, the mirror presenting a sad portrait of an almost man alone on a large bed, with blankets that did nothing to warm my body despite the summer heat.
The mirror doesn't lie, but the mind does.
It shows me all the things I desire, and I thank God that no one can see into the brain, or I would be locked up for good.

Laurel

Sunday.
The dealerships are closed, and Dad is meeting his friend for a drink tonight.
Monday we would pick up my used car and drive it home, my heart and a down payment already set on one.
All he has to do is sign.

I'll just have to make it through the night.
I pass off a still sleepy Ava who had cried all night to a dazed Rachel and meet Mikey over a continental breakfast.
My stomach churns at the sight of a dense waffle that Mikey was stabbing at.
"Wanna take a swim?"
I don't.
"Ava kept me up all night."
"Come on!"
I roll my eyes, "Fine, but let me at least finish eating."
Coffee, with lots of cream.
A bite of Mikey's soggy waffle and an orange later and I am wading waist-deep in chlorinated pool water.
"So, how's Tasha?"
I roll my eyes, "Any reason why you may be asking?"
Cold water specks across my shoulders, freezing me to the core.
"Really!"
His only reply is to splash me again.
"Just trying to open up a conversation is all."

"Whatever," he mutters, turning red.

I descend, the water wrapping me in its chilly embrace.

"Mikey and Tasha sitting in a tree…K, I," I finish chanting much to his annoyance.

My brother lies back into the water next to me, allowing his ears to sink, and I mimic him as he answers, with muffled words but I know what he's saying and when I ascend, I look over at him, "Don't let Dean catch you. He would kick your ass up the street and back again Mikey, and I say that because I love you."

My brother stands and joins me.

"It's not serious anyway. We just hooked up, so don't get your panties all twisted about it."

My tongue shoots out at lightning speed, his own coming forth with another slew of words, "And for the record, Dean could not kick my ass."

The conversation turns serious very quickly.

To the fact that I was staying an extra night.

I tell him I will be ok and jump to another subject praying he will drop it, Mikey, insinuating that he knows without ever telling me so.

"It's fine Mikey. So, are you going to take my friend out on a proper date or what?"

Instead of a yes or no, I am met with silence and decide he has soured against me at my lack of participation in what he wants to talk about.

I dunk myself under the water, enjoying the weightlessness for a moment, hoping that as I resurface Mikey will have dropped it.

No luck.

He leans against the wall in the shallows, goosebumps lining his body.

"I'm just worried Laurel, I know you can't say anything but-."

I cut him off, "I don't get what you are so worried about," I snapped hoping my anger might be enough to deter him and this line of questioning and talk.

Eyes gaze down at the water; I feel bad for being so harsh but what choice do I have?

"I'm… I'm sorry, just don't worry about me, ok? There is nothing to worry about Mikey."

"I'm not stupid, Laurel."

"You might be," I kid, his eyes angry, telling me to shut it and take him seriously.

"Laurel… I'm not fucking stupid."

I have no idea how to respond to his biting words, but my heart stills for a second.

"I can't do anything to help you if you won't let me help."

"Don't need help anyways. I'm going to be off to college soon… it's only another year and a half, and- and we will be away from this. From all of it. So just drop it ok?"

My brother smirks a smirk that isn't pretentious but sad, "Yeah, you think that little bit of distance is going to protect you?"

Doubt rises like bile in my throat.

Leaves me unable to speak.

I cannot speak.

Not now.

Never.

It would only serve to destroy the family.

"Maybe I don't want to be saved. It would just make a mess of everything."

Maybe I had been naïve to think that graduation would be the end, that it would put some distance between us.

The realization that I had been mistaken hits me like a ton of bricks, my chest tight.

"It won't do anything, Laurel, not unless you tell me to. You need to let me help you," the words curl sensibility around me.

He wants to help.

Maybe he can.

Blinking my own stupidity away, I sturdy up and moved to the deeper waters, standing on the tops of my toes.
I don't know where this is coming from, but it's unwelcome, it's confusing and is tearing down my wall, threatening and weakening me.
I want to tell him everything, what could it hurt if he already knows?
"There's nothing to tell, Micah," the tremble of my voice lies.

Momentarily the topic is dropped but my brother is a persistent person.
Something I had always admired about him, but now rue.
Even when we were children learning to ride our bikes, I had fallen and called it a day, my bloodied knee motivation for me to go in and pull close to my mother.
Mikey, on the other hand, spent till the sun was well past its showtime to continue to practice on the long driveway.
He only gave up when our mother dragged herself to the porch and called to him, luring him with fresh chocolate chip cookies and milk, her face dropping when he made haste for the house completely tattered and covered in cuts.
My mother spent the rest of the evening coddling him tight against her bosom to the disdain of my father who had accused her of making him soft.
The next day, he was back on the bike.
It took me a whole two months to get it down, as I was too scared to earn my scrapes.

"Laurel, do you trust me?"
He grabs my hand, pulls me close to him, the water sloshing around us.
"Do you trust me with your life?"
I have no reason not to, so I tell him as much, ready to squash this conversation.

Mikey

Round eyes scream yes, her arms heavy with hesitation as they cross above her chest protectively.

"You can trust me, Laurel," I lure, taking her by the hand and
tilting her back into the water, her eyes widened with
confusion as I pressed my lips to her forehead before grasping
her and allowing her to float gently.
I need her to understand that I will never hurt her, not really.
Putting my weight on her shoulders and I push her under.
Hold her there.
She doesn't do much at first, plays along with my game.
But as the seconds tick by she refuses my touch, throws her
arms up out of the water to clasp, her eyes shooting open as
her nails dig around my wrists.
Still, I don't release, not yet and the fear takes over, just a part
of the process, her body twists, hair tangling chaotically.

She can trust me, even with her life.
The water begins to splash around her body, trying to push up
for air.
I hold her.
Waiting for her to give in and let me take the reins.
When she does give in and relaxes under my grip, water
settling, I jerk her up, her face breaching with a loud gasp.

I pull her to me and for a moment she pants in my arms frantic
for oxygen. Just as I think I got through to her I feel her shove
away with fear-fueled anger.
Her face is beet red, chest heaving violently clinging to each
morsel of oxygen I had so deprived her of.
"What the fuck?" she screams it, her hair draining of water,
blood from her face.
Yelling between endless deep breaths, she tells me off.
 She is yelling now, pushing me away from her as I reach out
in hopes of holding and comforting her, "Don't fucking touch
me, Mikey!"
Water sways around as she tries to escape my grasp and get
out of the pool.
My hands wrap around her wrist, and I tug hard, "Laurel, it's
ok," I try to assure her.

"What was that?" She almost screams the words, yanking free as she desperately moves towards the blue tiles of the wall.
She is crying.
Crying harder now than I think I had ever seen her cry.
I can barely differentiate between tears and droplets of pool water.
"I just wanted you to see!"
"See what? See that-," her breath hitches, ending in a hiccup, "You're fucking crazy!"
Hyperventilating trying to inhale but only finding a trickery of breath.
Breasts pulse with anger, chlorine-shot eyes searing my gaze.
"That you can trust me! I could hurt you and I didn't!"
Saying it out loud sounds crazy, the logic is lost.
It had made sense only moments ago.
Laurel makes haste to the ladder, climbs out, dripping onto the deck, passing the towel rack she pushes the door and storms out only to slam into Rachel.
Perfect timing.
"Laurel, what's wrong?" My new mother asks concern etched on her groomed brows, her arms full of pool toys, and my sister.
Laurel hyperventilates, face red as a cherry, hair mangled.
With a "Nothing," she shoves past Rachel, who doesn't buy a word of it.
Rachel is suspicious eyeing me with Ava on her hip in a tiny suit, ready to take a dip, Rachel clad in her own daisy patterned one piece.

"What did you do to your sister?"
"Nothing," I shrug, aware that this would bite me in the ass if she found out.
Summer wasn't through yet and I didn't want to spend it grounded.
"Micah?"
Eyes roll, "I dunked her underwater and she didn't like it, that's all."

Laurel

We cut the bill down and Dad settled us into one room for our last night.
"No sense in wasting more money."
What a crock.

He plans to meet a friend who had attended the wedding at the bar before he flies back to Chicago.
The shower rumbles on, I sit on the bed anxious.
Expecting the worst.
I only look up from the patterned comforter of the queen when he prances out in a cotton towel that was much too large.
He had said he could do better.
Had promised, but promises don't mean shit.
I know better.
This way I have a say.
He can't take what I will give.
Whatever I have to tell myself to get through the inevitable.

"Dad?"
I lie on the bed, my stomach pressed firmly to the freshly pressed sheets, the ugly pattern of triangular peaks peering through my spreading legs.
My hands are rigid, tucked beneath my chin, feet twirling childishly.
Aware of the effect I have, especially when I up my feminine wiles and lick the top of my lips slowly, I play him.
The previews of a movie I had been wanting to watch loop in the background.
I guess I hadn't been loud enough when he doesn't respond, and I watch his reflection as he slaps on some oily deodorant.
"Dad," I called out once more, regressing to childish antics.
Tonight, I am the lure, and he is the unsuspecting fish.
My body is the juicy writhing bait.
I am the water he so desperately yearns for.
In the end, we'll both end up flopping and gutted in the most grotesque of manners.

Remote, clenched between my fingers, I aimlessly wait on a purchase-only channel, flipping to my back now, propping myself against the headboard.
I watch as he struggles to feign ignorance.
Deep tan. Unmotivated.
"Dad, can I order this movie?"
Remote presses to my parting lips, base clenched like a dove in my fist.
This time I see the effect my calling has on him as he doubles beneath the hotel bath towel.
He likes it more than he should.
The way I called him dad.
The childish flannel pajamas.
He has a type, and I am nothing less than a kink come true, and nothing more than a toy.

Tonight, my desire to fuck with his head is tantamount to his desire to avoid me.
The pedo disguised as law enforcement, using his power to aid in his perversions.
Am I the only one?
I push the thought deep, and pursue him, not allowing myself to be clouded with jealousy.
Roll the dice of my fucked-up game.
Unzipping temptation and he is no Job.
How eagerly he falls into sin.

Mikey

We ride home in complete silence, Rachel's eyes jumping between the road and Ava every couple of minutes as if I might just jump and attack them both.
I find myself relieved when we finally make it home.
Close the car door behind me, careful not to wake Ava who had finally given up on crying for release and settled on sleep, drool seeping from the plump creases of her lips.
It stunk of soured milk.

My room is hot. Too hot.
I try to dial out to Gale.
She doesn't answer.
I'm wound up and utterly irritated at her lack of attention.
Guess I would have to settle on a few shots from my flask and
a quiet night in.
God knows Laurel's night was going to be anything but
restful.

Laurel

It doesn't take long for the towel to fall along with my flannel
bottoms.
I was bare beneath, shaved myself clean.
Every inch of skin that sits beneath my neck is bare for him.
Expecting the typical fuck, I shut my eyes and wait for him to
take me.
But tonight is different.
He wears a condom. Never has before.
Different.
He shuts his eyes.
Shielding himself from my aging face, no longer round, no
longer innocent.
Not his little princess.
Too much of a woman, for so little of a man.
Different.

I bite down on his shoulder hard as his pelvis grinds into me,
groaning.
I am different. Full of rage. Distress.
Different.
He can't take what I give.
They dig in further, threatening to puncture his skin.
I want him to hurt.
Good luck explaining it to Rachel.
I can imagine him coming up with some weak excuse as to
why he had to keep his shirt on when he fucked her.

Snapping back to reality, he pulls me off by the hair, not uttering a word.

His eyes hold enough warning in them, telling me not to do it again.

"Sorry, Dad," I feign innocence, chasing it with a smirk he doesn't see.

The gaze changes to disgust at my mention of his familial title.

"Edmund…right now you call me Edmund."

I nod.

"Let me show you something that's going to make us both feel really good," he coaxes, pulling the desk chair and setting it in front of the mirror.

Smiling wide he grips two rubber bands that had been wrapped around his work papers and tosses them to me, "Use these."

He doesn't specify.

I know.

Looping half my hair through each I braid it quickly, just the way he likes, frayed ends caressing my breasts.

Smiling, he plops down on the chair, causing it to sway. With a "sit," he pats his lap motioning me to him, and like a stupidly obedient pup, I obey.

I don't deny him anything, violent thoughts creeping from the back of my mind with every swaying of his hips, my back to his chest.

Hands tuck beneath my chin, "Look at how beautiful you are Laurel," he whispers, his grip tightening.

I keep my mouth clamped shut.

"So beautiful."

It's shocking.

He won't let me look away, not that I can, I am fixated on the grotesque connection, his body deep in my own.

Entering me, pulling me apart.

So beautiful, I see it now.

My demise pleases me because I deserve this.

I know I shouldn't look but I can't help it, and somehow the
viler the action the less control I have.
Can't pull away.
A lion taking down its prey.
A horrific car crash. Mangled limbs.
The scene of a crime.
The way skin parts with the pulling of a scab.
A needle piercing a vein.
Tantalizing. Intriguing. Disgusting.

I had always worked hard to keep my eyes shut, to pretend,
and when that didn't work it always led to my ultimate
demise.
There is no smile on my face, his fingers run over my open
top, exploring before falling between us.
Trying to make me complicit.
The image is coaxing me.
I don't want to be here.
There's nowhere I'd rather be.
I don't want to feel this.
I want to feel this.
Not his shame. My shame.
Not his hunger. My hunger.

"Didn't you hear me, Laurel?" he asks slowly, retreating from
me, only to return with a gasp.
I shake my head "Yes."
"Yes- yes, who?"
"Edmund."

My response drives him back to work like a whip on an ox.
I am the carriage, and he works hard, his eyes clamped shut
now.
It climaxes with a please as I kneel between his hairy legs as he
towers above me.
I watch him peel the condom off and drop it on the forest-
colored carpet.
Sweaty.
The fibers of the carpet are rough on my knees.

Specks of dirt and sand that had been neglected dig into the skin.
Gagging as he thrusts in and out briskly, fingers on the tails of my hair, my palms on his thighs.
Warmth coats my throat in spurts that I choke down contracting my throat.

Once I am good and humiliated, he releases me, tells me to get some sleep like the good caring father he pretends to be when moments earlier he had invaded private chambers.
I stay there for a moment and watch him pull his clothes on.
Not skipping a beat, he tosses me the room keys, leaving me to my own devices.
I never ordered the movie.

...

Waiting in front of the building, the hot concrete beneath my bare thighs burns.
I pulled at little bits of grass and weeds that had emerged in the cracks of the walkways, traffic bustling at the intersection that lies just beyond the hotel's vast parking lot.
Check-out was at eleven and I knew it wouldn't take long for housekeeping to make their rounds, seeing as we were situated on the bottom floor.
I leave a five as an apology for the mess knowing full well room service probably often dealt with sticky masculine globs and discarded condoms, but, nonetheless.

The buzzing of a vacuum in the room whose window sits feet from my back causes me to jolt, the handyman lingering outside the exit, a cigarette in hand, foot in the door, defeating the self-locking mechanism.
Taking a long drag he turns his face to me, yellowed by years of smoking, wrinkled from the sun, he nods as if to acknowledge me.
I nod back feeling it would be rude to ignore the gesture.
"Ya know you can probably wait inside ma'am."
"Thanks, but my dad should be here soon," I smile.

The man nods again as if to tell me to suit myself and stamps out his cigarette with his foot before grabbing the butt, bald head reflecting the burning sun.
"You have a good day now."
"You too."

As the concrete grows increasingly hot, I am forced to sit on the duffel bag instead, leaning against the stucco wall, sweating profusely.
The roar of the vacuum grows distant with time, replaced by the chirps of a lone lingering cricket.
Mocking me.
My eyes flutter with exhaustion and not much else.
I'm too tired to feel.
It's not as if I hadn't slept.

The minute he left I pulled myself into the shower and caught my deplorable release as if I would lose breath if I didn't get off.
I spent the rest of the shower questioning what the hell was wrong with me while scrubbing myself raw before falling into the king; hot, red, mentally drained, without a queen in sight, the crisp white sheets fondling my hot skin.
I clamp my eyes shut, willing amnesia, and am met with a comforting loss of consciousness.
Darkness.
Not stirring till the alarm screams consciousness at nine.
Back to reality.

My head was pounding, eyes and mouth dry as old bones.
A hangover without the bliss of drunkenness the night prior.
Outside of the physical, my fragile emotional state has chosen complete numbness as today's defensive line.
Getting stronger.
My mind attempts to protect me.
You can't cry when you feel no pain.
Can't feel pain when your mind is a static buzz.

The rumbling of an engine comes around the corner, a small
black sedan with my father at the wheel.
My car.
A gift.
A bribe.
The man I call dad steps out of the car, almost tumbling as his
foot catches the curb, alcohol still absorbing from the night
prior.

"Get in Laurel, you're driving," he whispers as if his voice
might trigger a teasing headache.
Behind his sunglasses, I imagine the red eyes of a bloodhound,
droopy and bursting with dozens of microscopic blood vessels
that had become irritated.
"She's a beaut!"
Attributing femininity to anything he can drive or control.
I hop in, buckle up.
It was probably all in my head, but I instantly felt comfortable
behind the wheel, as if the car had been made just for me.
Smooth, never jerking like Dad's truck.
I make a right onto the ramp, nervously merging behind a
white van, dad sits quietly next to me, his head leaning against
the glass.
"Know the way home?"
Nodding yes, I flick my blinker off.
"Good."

We spent the next twenty minutes making small talk about the
upcoming honeymoon.
A week in Mexico, Rachel's parents taking Ava.
The conversation felt forced as if we were two strangers.
It was unnatural, like wearing socks to bed.
rocking senses this and allows the hangover and the rocking of
my car to put him to sleep.

Mikey

We had been assigned a journal this summer that we were told to write in every day, even if all we did was write down what we did that day.
Two weeks before summer break comes to a stop I glance down at a near empty journal.
The English department thinks that journaling can help open our minds.
Self-awareness or some bull.
All it did was make me clever.
I snatch an assortment of pens and pencils to not make it too obvious that I had done all my writing in a day.
Mostly I fill it with bullshit snippets of work, and hours spent at training or with my friends.
Then a thought forms, creativity flows from my fingers as the sun sets.

I am air.
Great strength, light in the feet.
I drift, never content enough to remain.
Soothing at times, hard to agitate.
But when moved I unleash complete chaos.
Self-control becomes as lost as a man at sea.
Blinded by the nothingness that surrounds me.
No one can see me.
I agitate, stir up water, stir up fire, flatten earth, gain color with traction.
Opposition swirls in every direction.
Formation of a storm. Threats of destruction.
Then there's the aftermath.
Beautiful songs. Whistling.
Smooth lapping of my tongue. Words drip off like honey.
Calamity for all.

She. Woman.
Another nature.
Misunderstood by all.
Fluid and graceful, she is of water.
Giving life or ceasing to provide it.

The earth cries out for her touch, gashes form upon its skin
when thirst rises.
She is a morning mist giving to all.
Melancholy as she taps upon your window.
The light of Eve.
Depths unknown.
Temptation to plunge deep within her.
At times so controlled, forming, crashing, and retreating like a
wave.
Adaptable; malleable, she comes in many forms.
Solid, cold as Ice.
The particles of herself pushing further apart.
Hardened.
Deep freeze brought on by the fluttering of seasons from the
heart of the Earth.

He. He is Earth.
Shifting. Growing.
Claimed by many and owned by none.
Created by the strong barleys and grains he harvests.
The minds of man who inhabit him.
Dying without the touch of water.
Awaiting her gentle touch.
I have seen eyes full of desire.
 I have seen his eyes wander.
Seen him move to the edge of her touch, plunging into her
shores, mingling beneath, sifting sands.
Lost within her. Petrified to drown in her.

I can't turn this in and crumple it between my fists and pelt it
into the wastebasket.

Laurel

Summer journaling, I have no interest.
Half of what I would have wanted to write couldn't be turned
in, but I had been diligent to scribble down some random
tidbits of my day every morning.

This morning's passage gets tossed into the waste bin, along with a couple of popsicle wrappers.
I jot something new down hoping it will satisfy Miss Jennings' desire for a full journal.

Is it strange that I have a favorite word?
It describes my mind to a T.
Ambivalent.
Adjective.
But you already know that it's an adjective, Miss Jennings.
I'm not sure why I just addressed you.
You will never read this, not with the twenty-plus journals you have to grade.
I assume you just skim through and check for filled pages.

The word ambivalent describes two opposing states of feelings that are contradictory.
It is my constant state of mind although I am sure you would never believe that by looking at me.
From the outside I am perfect.
I get good grades. Don't stay out too late. I respect my parents, always.
Never do I question authority.
Always come to school, hooky's not my thing.

Believe it or not, it's all a facade.
Thick as it may be, it's beginning to crack, much like my torn mind.
Ambivalence in every part of my life.
Always contradicting.
I miss my mother.
But I am also happy she is gone.
I loved her. Hated what she did to herself.
Her slow suicide.

I love my father.
Love the way he holds me.
Love the way he breathes me into him.
One form. Love.
His touch.

I hate my father.
Hate the way he breathes air into him.
Hate his touch.
Love my strength. Love the silence that keeps me safe.
Hate my strength. Hate the complicity of that silence.

Want. I want so many things.
Want so much for Kyle to know me. All of me.
Hate that I can't give him that.
The thought of his knowledge makes me sick.
Need. So full of need.
Need Kyle by my side.
Want him gone.

I am. Love. Loved.
Full of hate that should be indifference.
A harbor of lies.
Tides that never fully recede.

I finish with my daily writing, the ink sinking deep into the
sheets beneath.
Can't turn this in either.
The paper tears away with all its truth.
The ones beneath must go too.
I pressed too hard.

...

Last night I heard Dad and Rachel talking about Mikey.
Rachel's suspicions.
The sad part is that my father went along with it.
Mikey was to be punished for his sins.
My brother is no saint and nowhere near comparable to Christ
himself, but he was utterly crucified in that short
conversation.

"There is something seriously wrong with him, Edmund!"
He hadn't said anything, just nursed his drink, upper lip
curling over the rim.

"And as for Laurel, it's clear that this isn't just about her mother. Something is going on with her."
Still, he didn't reply, Rachel's gears turning as quickly as her fingers do through her warm locks.
"Someone is hurting your daughter Edmund, and I think it's Micah."

The time had come for him to reply, to tread lightly through the field of lies, lest he set foot on a landmine of truth and Boom!
No. More. Secrets.
Just horror.
My father mulls over his drink searching for a needle in a stack of needles, the words never quite forming.
"Edmund!"

My father finally snapped to reality.
"That's a rash thing to say, Rachel. We have no proof that anything like that is happening to her."
Eyes dart to him, "Is it not apparent? She barely eats and when she does, she fucking gorges herself. Then we get phone calls about her having panic attacks."
Rachel paused, voice crackling under the stress.
After a moment, she regained her composure.
"I haven't seen her smile in days. She won't look me in the eye, and you want to sit there and act like she's ok?"

I watched on as her frame tensed with realization.
Suspicion about his lack of communication.
"Edmund?"
Tense, his eyes darted to meet hers, locked in with intimidating confidence.
I watched from the crack in the patio door.
I saw it in his eyes, fear.
Tension. Panic. She doesn't know him well enough to read it.
He knew what was coming next and began turning gears in anticipation.
Script forming.
She says his name again, lips trembling apprehension.

"What is Rach? What are you asking?"

Nickname used an attempt to pacify.
The tone was stern, full of vindication and pride.
"I don't want to start a fight, but I have to a- ask," she cried
out, the words shaking loose from her.
Was met with cold wrath.
Appalled.
"I can't believe you would ever think that of me."
His voice didn't rise then.
Turned it on her instead, "How could you think that? Have I
ever done anything to make you feel like I would hurt my
daughter? Do I not provide for this family? Work my ass off
for my children? Do I not treat you with love and respect?"
Filled her with guilt.
Doubt.
Begging.
"I'm sorry."
"I love her for God's sake, she is still a child! My child!"

His voice rose then.
Flair for the dramatic.
Making it more real.
Indignation.
Unrighteous.
Rachel began to cry then, "I just don't know what to do,
Edmund."
"You know me, Rachel, I always try to do the best I can as a
man and as a father, and I have fallen short lately, but I would
never lay a hand on my own daughter. Not Ava, not Laurel."
 He was so convincing then, eyes full of fake tears, hands
stroking her long hair, so her tears didn't catch them.
I watched as he pressed his whiskey-laced lips softly against
her forehead filling her with belief.
Reassurance.
"I love you Rach, I love this family and we are going to get the
kids the help they need for our family."

He offers her a drink.

Mikey

They make a few brisk decisions.
Therapy for Laurel and me.
I can tell it makes Dad anxious, but he has to trust that his grip
is strong enough to keep my mouth clean of any of his
transgressions.
Saying no to Rachel's request would be too suspicious.
I enjoy watching him squirm.

Then there's Laurel.
That one not only makes dad squirm, but it has also him
outright complaining and trying to sway Rachel against it
without being too transparent.
"I don't know if we can afford the copays for both of them and
Mikey needs it more."
Rachel graciously offers to put in more hours.
Trapped.
Saying no would only raise suspicion.

What comes next leaves me irate.
I am forced to trade rooms with the guest room that lies
outside the living room.
Not even technically a bedroom as it has no closet, and we
rarely have guests.
The lack of closet space motivates Dad to purchase an oak
drawer set for my new quarters.
Rachel tells me that a boy my age needs.
his own space.
What she means by that is that they want me as far away from
Laurel and Ava as possible.
Diligently, we lift, and paint, and pull posters and paintings
off what used to be my walls.
I patch the hole in the closet before they notice, grapple with
some spare paint samples in the garage to match.

Rachel eyes my every move now.

Criticizes everything I do.
Questions me anytime I leave the house.
They even reinforce a curfew.
Midnight unless we are staying the night.
She is such a hypocrite.
Blind to my dad's sins.
I tell her as much after she gets on me for not doing the dishes
just a few nights later, making it clear that I am not the
enemy.
That I love my sister.
I tell her that she knows the truth.
That she is willingly blind.
"I'm not the one you should be pointing fingers at!"
Hands on her hips, "Then who is Mikey?"
She yells, clearly infuriated by my lack of elaboration.
"Him," I spat, literal drops flying across her face as I
emphasized.

For the first time ever, Rachel puts a hand on me.
Slaps me hard, her ring pinching my cheek.
"How dare you, Micah!"
How dare I?

Laurel

Back to school.
Another year closer to freedom.
I was going to make this year count.
I was going to be strong.
Push through.
Get the hell out of that prison some might call a home.
I hate it there.
School is a safe space, and I intend to spend as much time
there as possible.
I signed up for the book club, and the school government.
Nothing big.
Just the person who manages the setup and tear down of the
after-school activities like dances and the talent show.

Speaking of the talent show, Tasha is full speed ahead on performing a dance for the school.
She claims it will piss all the parents off.
"First, I have to get through the auditions with some bullshit dance, so we don't get flagged. You in?"
Risky.
"No, my dad would kill me... but my lips are sealed."
"Wuss!"

I also pick up a babysitting gig every Wednesday evening.
Three to seven.
Then therapy on Thursdays.

Dad picked me up from school on the first day to drive me to Dr. Martin's office, even though we had gotten my car insured and registered.
He insisted.
I already know what his intentions are.
Desperate desire for my silence.
I don't let on that I know exactly how nervous he is to take me, so I watch on silently at his mounting stress.
Seeing him squirm ignites a certain sense of power, even if it is fleeting.

Nails pressed to his lips, little flecks of blood dripping off the edge of his thumb.
"You ok, dad?"
I know he isn't.
His turn to lie, "Yeah mouse, just been a long day," his cuticle fills with blood, finger taut against his teeth.
The truck veers left, taking us away from the office and driving me through the little coffee shack.
"Get whatever you want, Laurel."
Generous.

He settles on a coffee with two sugars, no cream and I order a spicy chai latte, hot.
The barista hands it to me, steam escaping the lid as I squeeze the flimsy cup.

It burns through the processed paper.
Slowly, baring the heat I maneuver the cup into the holder, a splash of hazel liquid dribbling over, leaving my fingers throbbing and sticky.
Dad takes a sip, grimacing at the intense heat, still the car doesn't move in the right direction and instead creeps into the wooded slopes.
He doesn't stop until we are well over the bridge and in the national forest and he scans his pass.
Into the void.

Dark woods, far from the beautiful yellowing of the sugar maples, and the soft glow of small sequoias.
These were the type of dense dark greens that cluster warding off the sun.
The type of woods where the red riding hood had met the big bad wolf.
I sit in the rumbling truck with my own wolf, silent, watching the sky above quickly morphing to a slate, teasing rain.
Ominous.
His hand gripping the wheel tight, face scrunched as if he can't exactly get the words out of his mouth.
Instead, he slumps in his seat, calloused hands tight at his eyes, a sob escaping his throat.
This wasn't expected.
Manipulation?
It sure doesn't seem authentic.
I see right through him.

"Are you ok?" I ask.
Silence broken.
He wanted me to make the first move, so I did.
Traps me in his sticky web of deceit.
"Dad..." I don't know what to say next, "Are you-."
Words go interrupted, his hand jumps to my arm clasping tight, the other one slowly falling under my chin, tucked, ready to pull me to him if the moment calls for it.
"Laurel, I'm sorry."
Not for what he should be though.

"Laurel, I love you, I really love you…and I don't say it
enough."
His words are fake, yet I blush reddening like a plump beet.
Quickly his tears dry as I softened to him.
Vulnerability makes the tears redundant.
"I love you so much, more than anyone ever could. My love
for you… its… well it surpasses what I feel for Rachel even,
and I don't mean to hurt her, but what we have is so special, I
just want you to understand."
I grow increasingly more nervous with each predictable word.
"I think that therapy will be good for you. It's going to help
you grieve your mother, and sort yourself out."
He takes no responsibility for my hurt.

I'm not the one who needs sorting, you are dad!

I want to throw the now warm chai in his tear-streaked face.
Make him hurt.
"Getting your help is important but there are some things that
need to stay private."
Of course.
"Like what?"
Faked naivety.

"For example, our relationship, that's private. That's
something special that you and I share. Something no one can
understand."
Oh, people would understand, just not in the way he wants
them to.
"You are so special and beautiful. I just don't want to lose you,
Laurel…and that could happen. "
Guilt drowns me, I grip my drink, the lid beginning to unseal.
"I. Love. You," tensely he sputters in a tmesis.

It's vile, pulls me under, into its muddy darkness.
I can't let him get hurt.
As much as it kills me to admit, he is special to me too and I
love to be loved more than anything.

To feel like someone.
A treasured little secret.
Another calculated tear falls, my stone face facilitating their necessary return.
He is pathetic. Disgusts me.
But so am I.
He loves me. I love him.
I feel sorry for him and for myself.

"Don't cry, Dad," genuine tears begin dimming my judgment like a heavy fog on a lonely road.
A road that has only one destination.
"I just can't lose you baby."
He wipes away a tear that is bred more out of fear than actual love.
"You are so strong Laurel, and I need you to keep being strong for me."
I don't feel strong, but I can be.
I can be strong for him.
Could continue to be that vessel.

"I just don't want to lose you."
"You won't lose me. I'm right here,' I whisper into his ear with assurance, my hand pressing against his leg.
His chest barrels out erupting into a violent tremble, "I would never betray what we have. I promise," fingers cross over my chest.
"I know."

His mood changes swiftly, stiffening, hand tight on his coffee, the black tar threatening to escape its corral as he presses it to his lips, coffee pours into his mouth, like a wild horse, released, before returning to the cup holder.
"That being said Laurel, I want to make it clear that I will do anything to keep what we have quiet."
His voice is stern, hand over mine gripping tight, "I mean anything, and that's a promise."
The change of tone has me on edge, there's a fire in his eyes that was threatening to burn me to ash.

We are alone.
Secluded.
"What do you mean?"
Tight hands around my own, there is a tension that comes
from outside of the muscles of his arm in the way he grips me.
"Whatever it takes, Laurel."
It's coming to light, and it's beyond dark, the shroud of control
is slipping, as are his reins on me.
"Do you understand?"
My hands grip tightly along the car door, rain pattering wildly
against the pane as the trees zoom past us, clouding, and
meshing together.
Crystal clear. Every word.
"I do," I admit, the words heavy on my chest.
It all makes sense, every extra mile he had driven into the
secluded woods.
Every syllable was meant to intimidate me.
To make me submit, and he hadn't even needed to intimidate
me.
My innards twist, the bits of my soul that were still
untarnished quiver with understanding.
He would do anything.
Hurt me even.
He would never hurt me!
You just misunderstood.

"I promise."
My father and I are one and the same; we keep our promises.
With the unspoken agreement, he quickly starts the truck and
drives me to the brick two story without another word.
The truck rumbles to a stop, stomach in knots, the chai teasing
a revisit.
I bit my lip.
He pulls me close, eyes still rimmed red, "I love you."
Threatening reminder.
One I don't need.
I had taken that vow of silence so long as he lived the first
time, he ever kissed me.

…

For a long time, I refused to look him in the eye when our
bodies met, fearful that I would see a man and not a monster.
When I did start to look him in the eye my fears came to life.
 I saw the man.
One whom I loved so deeply and earnestly.
But when I was made to reach my climax, he would try to
meet my pleasure with his wicked stare, so I wouldn't forget
who had brought such pleasure to my body.
I wish I could tell the therapist that.

Mikey

Back to school. Another year closer to freedom.
I will do better this year. I will participate.
Keep up with wrestling.
Get an after-school job just to get out of the house.
Therapy on Mondays, Dad would drive me, lips tight, eyes
angrily pointed ahead the whole drive.
I slammed my door on the way out to his disdain.
The sneer was threatening enough to make me keep my
mouth shut.
My lips are sealed.

Laurel

My lips are sealed.
Well not exactly, but I don't divulge much to the frumpy
therapist with bifocals that could host their own stand-up.
Dr. Martin.
She is nice enough, tries to read me, I pick up on that in my
first session.
 I wouldn't be able to stay silent.
So I came up with a plan.
Silence was futile.
Blabbing was a death sentence.
Say too little and suspicion will arise.

Say too much and suspicion will become speculation,
speculation morphs into a hunger for the truth.
Too hot.
Too cold.

Instead, I settle for a porridge that is just right and munch
away.
Topic of focus; my mother's passing.
In a way I needed it.
To talk about her as I still hadn't truly grieved her passing.
I didn't have time to.
Too quickly I became a drink to quench his thirst, one he had
too quickly become drunk on.
My pain had faded, placed into my box of grievances that I
would somehow cope with at a more satisfactory time.

Mikey

Therapy is bullshit.
School is a snooze.
Laurel is pretending that she is full of life and joy just to keep
Rachel off her back now that she has gone to a few sessions of
therapy.
Ava is Ava.
Dad walks around with his pin on his chest, making me want
to gag every time I see him.
Normalcy.

I know I said I was going to make this year count, but my
enthusiasm fades as quickly as the sun sets.
Apathy.
Gale wants adventure, a thrill. "You used to be fun," she
scolds me as I drive her home from a sub-par dinner date.
Shrugging her off, I focus on the road, Laurel's car screeching
to a halt in front of Gale's house, "I am just tired, Gale."
"Too tired to come in?"
I was never too tired for that.
She leads me into the craftsman, kisses me hard on the porch,
her mother probably at some church function.

Time for some sub-par dessert.

Laurel

Kyle doesn't show up the first few weeks of school.
 He calls when dads are at work, Rachel picks up and calls me
down.
Either he is fearless, or he knows for a fact that Dad is gone.
"You really shouldn't be calling. I will call you," I hear myself
almost scolding him.
I soften, his breath heavy on the phone, melting the negativity
away.

"I'm sorry, I didn't mean for it to come out like that," I stutter.
Disregarding my warning, he quickly accepts the apology
with a gentle "How are you?"
That was quickly followed by an alluring, uncaring dialogue.
"I miss you and I really couldn't care less what he thinks."
That settles it.
I appreciate the thought, "I just don't need him getting upset
with me when you are going to be home soon is all."

The thought of his return panics me.
I hadn't been eating much.
The little I did consume it was in binge-worthy amounts and
did not often reach my gut.
He would notice.
Yet my brain tells me the opposite.
Yeah, because you look like a cow!
A fat slob! Shut up!

"Well, if he gets mad, I can always climb back through your
window and join you in time out," my man teases a tempting
offer, all thoughts of self-depreciation quickly sizzling away
like butter on cast iron.
"That's tempting."
It really is.

I could imagine it now, Kyle falling through my window, climbing into my bed, his arms tight around me, nose nudging along my nape.
The thought drives volts throughout my body.
I twist the cord between my fingers, the thoughts increasingly becoming more sexual in nature, "When will you be back?"
"Last week of September, just in time for the talent show, I had it cleared with the school. My uncle just really needs the extra hand this year."
The talent show was going to be held at the end of the first week of October.
"Who told you about the talent show?"
"You think you're the only one I call," he teases.
I can feel my lips spread to a smile, "I was hoping that I was the only girl you were calling."
I glanced nervously to make sure no one was around.
The coast was clear.
"Nah. There is another pretty great lady I like to talk to from time to time."
Silence on my end, waiting for the punchline.
"She makes the best damn green bean casserole too."
Face growing hot, "Are you trying to make me jealous?"
He snickers, "Nah. My mom may make a mean casserole, but she has nothing on you."
"You got me!"
Pause, as if he is trying to get his thoughts together.
"Really Laurel, I'm just ready to be home."
Heat crawls across my chest, flushing red.
"Why are you so excited to be home? Do you have some damsel in distress you need to tend to?"
I glance around making sure no one can hear my teasing.
Coast clear, Rachel long gone with Ava.

"Not a damsel per se. Just a beautiful girl next door type, who is very much in distress."
Fluttering in my gut, like a million little butterflies were trying to escape.
"Does that make you a knight in shining armor?"

"No, I'm just the boy next door in a beat-up truck who is desperately trying to prove his worth."
Tears well in my eyes. I can't explain it.
Maybe it was how sweet he was being.
Maybe it was how wrong he is about me.
Maybe it's the price of being a woman.
Either way, it causes a cry to fall from my throat, hot warm tears tumbling to the freshly mopped floor below.

"You have nothing to prove," I struggle to say through my crying.
Silence, a sniffle on my end breaking it. My fingers intertwine in the cord of the phone, the tan rubber bounding lightly as I release.
He knows I'm crying but doesn't mention it, "That may be true, but trying to show you my value keeps me honest and motivated."
Bawling now, I slap my hand over the receiver.
This time he mentions it, only out of concern, "Laurel, are you ok?"
A levy in my brain has shattered.
This is beyond my control.
"I'm fine I just-"
He waits.
"I'm sorry, I'm just feeling emotional lately, and I miss you, and" I tremble, "And I need you. There's a lot I want to say to you, I just don't know where to start."
Someone calls out behind him, "You can tell me anything, Laurel. When I get back, I am going to make every minute we have together count. I want to take my time. Remember how to navigate you. Court you the right way…the way you deserve."
Gentlemen as always, "What does that entitle?"
"Well it means that I'm not going to kiss you or get you naked the minute I see you no matter how badly I want you and I do want you, make no mistake Laurel. I want to do this right. Take you to the movies. Have dinner. Go stargazing in my truck and let the romance fill the air between us. I want you to tell me everything, no matter how scary it may seem."

The tears begin to dry along the creases of my face, "Can we hold hands at least?"

...

Kyle stays honest.
Picks me up after school on his first day back.
Dad is at work late. Rachel believes I have a study group.
I hop in the truck, nervous, his lips looking particularly kissable at that moment.
"Where to?"
He flashes a couple of bills my way, "Arcade?"
"Give me a minute to take you all in," I tease, eyes scanning over his strong chin, dimples drifting endlessly, his usual hat on top of his head.
"Do I get a turn?"
My head shakes no, "Not a chance, you said you would be a gentleman, and a gentleman doesn't stare."
"Maybe not, but a gentleman does admire his lady," Kyle complains, his eyes running over me.
Teeth dig into my bottom lip as our eyes do what our lips should, he feels it too, quickly starting the car to gain back some control.
"So…. arcade?"
I roll my eyes, "So you can bankrupt the claw machine companies?"
"Exactly."

Kyle was strangely good at extracting toys, plushies, and electronics for the claw machines.
It got so bad that the owner of the local arcade traded him for free laser tag hours just to keep the machines stocked.
"Nah, I'm going to watch you struggle, then being the gentleman I am, I am going to swoop in and – "
"Make me feel like a total idiot?"
Truck pulling to a stop sign, his eyes darted making sure the intersection was clear before turning right.
"Nope, I'm going to get you whatever your heart desires."

The arcade comes into sight, and I feel a surge of excitement, powerful electricity climbing to my fingers.
It had been a long time since I had been here.
Mikey and I used to spend hours at the arcade while our parents would go out to the movies, leaving us to our own devices.
We used to dig under the machines growing up, my mother only ever allotting us a couple of bucks each.

"Well, right now what I want is not in any claw machine."
Something had come over me today.
Blame it on the weather. Blame it on the distance.
The lights of a red arrow flash and flicker off us and I can't help but stare at him, biting my lip, the blossom blooming exponentially under the pressure.
Kyle takes a deep breath, clearly bothered by my statement, in the best way.
"That's not on the table tonight. Never on the first date," sweetly reminding me of his true intentions for today.
I jam my tongue out of my mouth and aim it at him, it doesn't go unnoticed, "Spoken like a true gentleman."
"Let me treat you right…please. I want to court you, the way I should have. You deserve nothing less."
It's serious, his tone, full of pride, his voice rasp and low.
 "I won't stop you; I just like to tease."

We pulled into a spot in front of the little strip mall.
Pizza joint at the end, arcade smack in the middle, neon lights flashing, the windows completely painted over, surrounded by a hair salon, and several small outlets.
"Two can play at that game, Laurel, and you won't like the ending when you go home flustered."
"Tease."

Shutting up I allow him to treat me the way he believes I should be, despite the fact that I deserve none of it.
Kyle, acting like a true prince, clad in a beanie and forest green hooded coat despite the still warm weather.
Every door opened, car, building, and so on.

Hands kept to himself as I made my way in.
Met with an icy blast.
The jacket makes sense now.
I hug myself, clad only in a black rose-patterned baby doll
dress and flats.
Attentive as always, he takes pity, "You want my jacket?"
I tell him no at first, an answer he doesn't accept, peeling it off
his shoulders and allowing my arms to push in.
Now that I had it, there was no way I wanted to return it.
"I have this under anyway," he motions to a long-sleeved
shirt.

Kyle turns and begins to pay at the front counter, I can't help
but press my nose to the fabric.
It smelled like him, his pheromones kicking mine into
overdrive, an ardent tingle settling beneath.
I chew on my lip, trying to draw the pleasantness out before it
mounts into a painful need.
That's not what you are here for.
Reminder.

We make haste, a cup of coins jangling as he makes haste to
the air hockey table, a neon-burned orange puck dropping
into the slot, fed by the coins.
Kyle's hands swirl over the striker, my hoovering, trying to
grab it at the right time.
It floats like a phantom right into my grasp, I was ready.
"You, my dear, are going down."
"We will see about that," I retorted with unwarranted
confidence.
I had not played air hockey in years and when I did, I hadn't
really been any good.
Case and point Kyle creams me six rounds to my one, which I
was almost certain he had allowed me to win.
"For the record, I know you let me win that round."
"I would never!"
Fingers vine together, contorting to meet the others' touch,
little sparks jolt through me.
I want so badly for him to kiss me, but I know he won't.

Instead, he swipes his mouth against my ear, his muggy breath trickling down the nape of my neck before whispering, "You ready to lose some more."
This ignites my inner competitive side, my hands pull from his, moving him aside, "In your dreams, Kyle."

Flashing mauve lights attracts us to a car game that he completely creams me at, and a street fighting game that he absolutely destroys me at.
I talked a big game and was left trophyless.
Well, unless you count the time I got to spend with Kyle.
"How are you so good at this?"
I watch him plop a brass engraved coin into the slot of the motorcycle game before he straddles it. "Lots of practice," he tells me motioning to the empty one next to him.
My leg swings over, eyes running down my body as I mount the wobbly vessel.
The hard plastic rubs against my lonely nub, causing me to shift back.
We drive over mounds of animated dirt, and somehow ultimately finish by cruising over a pond that ends up being a mirage.
Well, Kyle does, mostly I swerve and bounce off mounds of sand and rocks the entire journey, retiring before the finish line.
Morocco.
Level… easy.
"You do suck at this," he teases eyes glancing up at the flashing digital clock.
The tickle of truth leaves my nose tingling, a slight pang of embarrassment pitted in my belly, "I tried!"
Little chuckles bubble, his arms wrap around my waist, sparks flying across my chest.
"I'm just teasing."
"We should probably wrap up soon, I don't know of many study sessions that run later than six."
I know he is right. I don't want him to be.
But the clock already reads fifteen after five.
"Just one more thing."

Flashing green echoes off those deep eyes, "What's that?"
"I want that," I pointed to a cheap necklace, black pebbles
beneath it, encased in a plastic fortress.
He winks at me as if to say no problem.
Pulling my eyes forward I focus on the glass box, the looming
metal hand swinging after a prior failure not moments ago.
A little girl, pouting at the loss of the unicorn earring set no
doubt, her father scrambling to find more change.

"Your wish…my command."
 I watch him maneuver, drop the claw down three times, bring
it back up.
Completely confused, I stand in awe of the intricate process.
"What are you doing?"
I watch as his finger slides over the joystick, with a certain
elegance, his hand grasping the stick, lip between his teeth,
pupils honed in.
"Almost there," he murmurs tensely as if he were cracking
some vault, the claw wrapping around the slick plastic box.
Pulling up it clicks, shivering, threatening to drop the
package.
My eyes widen visibly as I watch the claw travel on its rail, a
little bump right at the end.
Plop. Down the chute.
I feel my entire core tighten, full of adoration and lust.
Not really giving a damn about the necklace that is now being
clasped behind my neck, his lips grazing the goosebumps.
I shudder.

"I can do that all day. Replication is a good way to prove your
ability," he informs me, snagging another box, this one filled
with a man's chain.
So nonchalant, eyes kissing my gaze.
He winks, clearly aware of the effect he has on me.
"I thought these things were rigged."
"That's the thing, most rigged games can be beat with a little
manipulation," hand busting the box open, the light chain
slinking out.
"Help me?"

Nails graze over his collarbone, pushing his loose hair out of the way.

I feel it clasp shut, the cool touching my fingers.

"Tell me how you do it?"

There's a sheepish glint in his stare, his shoulders squaring as he beams with pride.

"My dad taught me. See the claw only stays tense part of the time, so there's a method."

My eyes widened, childishly, "Tell me…. please."

Turning to face me, hands clasped tight, "The trick is a rule of threes. Let the joystick spin for three seconds, locate your victim, push up three times, and then down three times. But to be clear it's not a hundred percent effective," letting go of my hands he begins to demonstrate.

"Toggle left and right, then let it come up and down three times and," his claw closes around a stuffed animal this time, his tongue between his teeth in concentration, "and voila."

My mouth drops.

He grips the black cat, "What do we do with it?"

He shakes his head, "Not a clue, I was just showing off."

I want his hand back in mine.

…

On our way out I take a quick trip to the bathroom, check my hair and my makeup.

I don't like what I see.

Can't understand what Kyle sees in me.

My hair is so plain, my face just as plain, not even my eyes hold any stunning color.

My full lips are too big for my small face, eyes too round, always filled with a certain sadness.

My breasts are unwomanly even now that they have filled out, I still find them too small while my body feels huge.

The scale doesn't agree.

Self-pity fills me.

He deserves so much more.

Shut up!

This isn't the right time to wallow in self-hatred.

I step out, with a lot of motivation, my eyes darting searching for Kyle.
We needed to head out.
I couldn't be late.
My stares gazed just beyond the prize counter at Kyle who eagerly handed the stuffed cat to a little boy, no older than four who had been eyeing it.
I pretend not to see.
My heart is filled to the brim.
I don't deserve him; my selfishness eats me up.

Kyle and I make the short drive back to the school where Rachel would pick me up soon.
I had ridden the bus to school, anxious to take my car out, but Rachel had needed it for an appointment today.
I thank him for the nice time, expressing gratitude.
Smiling that striking smile he turns his face to mine, a long strand of hair whispering over his eye, "Can we go out again soon?"
"If you still want to."
His head bobs a yes, warmth puts me on mute.
I want to kiss him.
Rather, I want him to kiss me. I like being taken. Told what to do.
As if he can read my mind, he turns, eyes to my lips, "I want to kiss you, Laurel."
I feel his hand cup my chin, slowly pulling my lips millimeters from his, a male gaze, full of lust and potential predation glossing over me.
There's a sweet shudder, the sight of his lust driving me to the edge.
An edge I am not allowed to go over.
"Can I?"

We sit, lingering until I move my nose slightly upwards and begin to rub against his, before I trace my lips down the strong bone of his jaw, tilting down.
He presses a kiss onto my forehead before pulling my chin up, grazing mine, "Please?"
"Kiss me."
The graze transitions into a slow dance.
A waltz turns into a smooth salsa, heat rising between us, sensuality fueling our lips, pressing passion into one another.
Palpable tension.
A yearning for more.
I want so much more.
We part, breathless, the clock on his dashboard reading five forty.
"Rachel will be here soon."
He nods, fighting with his breath, "Yeah."

One more kiss, quick this time, his hands tinkering with the little star on the cheap necklace he had clawed, replacing the chain he had broken.
Replacing my father.
I smile against the kiss, Kyle takes notice, returning the gesture as he parts with me.
"You have no idea how hard it is to stay in control right now."
Eyes roll, "I doubt that."
"Why?"
There is no answer he won't refute so I slap my mouth shut.
Don't have an answer that would be appropriate to give.
"When the time is right, I am going to make you feel so good," I purr, running my hand along his cheeks.

The time is now, Laurel.
Throw yourself at him.
Tell him!

"I have been thinking about it all summer. I want this to be real. I want to be able to call you my girlfriend."
This is real.

Then he shakes me with one simple request.
One I cannot fulfill.
To trust him.
With all of me.
Not just my body.
"That's what I need, Laurel."

…

I spent the rest of the night thinking about what Kyle had said.
He wants the impossible.
Shooting for the moon.
Where would I start?
What would Kyle do if he knew the truth?
Would he keep my secret?
Come on, Laurel! Kyle would lose his shit.
He would tell.
No one would believe him.

Kyle would never stay quiet, not because he wasn't trustworthy, or because he didn't care.
Quite the opposite.
A tear stings my eye. Anger.
His genuine good heart pisses me off because it leaves me in a place where I have to choose silence.
I want to tell him everything.
Want to fall into his arms and feel the sweet relief of having the burden lifted from my chest, and onto his shoulders.
I want him to save me.
No matter what that means.
I am so selfish.
But I also want to keep my father safe, no matter what that means.

Mikey

I am so selfish.

Gale on her knees, kissing my thighs, telling me how lucky she is to have me.

It had only taken a gas, dinner, and a movie to get back on her good side.

The cycle will probably repeat next week.

I stand up, Gale landing on a large pile of laundry that eternally surrounds her bed.

"Are you ever going to pick that up?" I criticize her nose crinkles with rejection, like some over-baked chip.

"Fuck Mikey, is that all you can focus on right now when you have me on my knees?"

I reach over to her nightstand, take a swig of flat beer, wincing as it goes down, "Tastes like shit."

Gale shoots up appalled at my lack of interest.

Truth is, I'm not disinterested in sex per se, I'm just not interested in Gale ever since that night I spent with Tasha, and it was slowly getting harder and harder to pretend I wanted her.

Tasha made it so hard for me to ignore her, always glowing and bouncing down the halls, large hoop earrings and intricately decorated lips down the hall, passing me as if I was a ghost, winking when no one was around.

Dean was none the wiser.

The memory of the way those lips had felt wrapped around me is enough to leave my pants tight.

I always manage a casual wave that she reciprocates, before slobbering all over Dean, who would probably pummel me to death if he found out how I had pummeled myself into Tasha.

"I'm sorry…I'm just not in the mood."

Scoffing, she bounces to her feet, throws her legs over my thighs, pinning my lack of interest between her legs, "Any reason why?"

Her voice is husky, flowing from her tongue like cayenne and honey.

I know better. It's venom.

"No reason."

"Come on, tell me," She purrs, tongue flushing against my ear, "It's someone else, isn't it?"

"I'm just not in the mood," I spit my heart sputtering with annoyance.

"Fuck you, Mikey," her fingers clench against my jaw, nails digging. "Also fuck your excuses."

Pain shoots along my jaw, a drop of blood ribbons down, falling between us.

I shove her off as gently as I can onto the lumpy mattress,

"Geez," I clench my face.

"Hurts, doesn't it?"

"Crazy bitch!"

Gale squeals, delighted with my reaction as if this was a game, "Did you just call me a bitch?"

"Well, you did just claw my face!"

Gale flips onto her knees, little skirt riding up, "That's just foreplay Mikey, give me a minute and I can show you just how vicious I can be."

Clawing my face had never been a part of our warmup.

"Come get me," she teases, skirt hitched above her hips, fingers slipping beneath her panties.

She groans, dipping a finger in, "That could be you babe."

My cock stiffens at the crazy woman's actions, but I am still too mad to let her have what she wants.

"Come on Mikey," pouting she flips herself onto her back, spreading her thighs for me, a trickle of blood begins to dry under my chin.

As much as I do not want Gale right this moment my predacious man brain kicks into caveman mode.

The woman wants to be claimed.

Why not?

I move to hover over her, eyes big as the moon, "You made me bleed," I comment as I pull my hand back.

It makes contact with her cheek with a loud smack, and a loud cry from her.

"What the fuck Mikey?"

"You are not the only one who gets to have fun Gale," a cold
voice I recognize as mine says.
Cold satin pours through my tense lips.
"Asshole!"
Her arms cross over her chest, as if to try to hide herself.
It does the trick.
"You started this Gale; Let's see if I'm still boring to you when
we get done."

Fear clings to her iris, lust chatters across her lips, body tense
and I'm not sure if she wants this, but I am also not sure she
knows what she wants either.
I can fix that.
She had asked for this.
I flip her onto her stomach, yank her cheap skirt down to her
ankles, her voluptuous ass in full view.
Running my hand across, goosebumps erupt violently like
Vesuvius along her soft skin.
Keeping her on edge, yanking my hand back, slapping her
hard.
She cries out beneath, my knee now pressed into the back of
her knees, hands scrambling to cover the spot I had just
contacted.
Again, I draw my hand back, harder this time on the same
spot.
"No more!"
"Shut up, Gale," I hissed, yanking her hand away, holding it
in mine.
Another.
Another, till she is crying real tears.

Despite the violence of my hits, it has done nothing to
dissipate my anger, in fact it's burning stronger now, and
embers fanned by the wind.
"No more, Mikey! I'm serious, that hurts!"
I greeted her with another slap, harder this time, "I said shut
up!"
She wants to fuck with you.
This is the price she pays.

I am tired. Tired of getting walked on.
Getting dominated.
It's my turn.
I imagine the thoughts that must be running through her mind.
What was I doing to her? Why did it feel good?
Had she asked for it? Why is she turned on?
I flip her to her back, pinning her hands above her head, not much fight in her.
My cock strains against my pants, I free one hand and rip myself free.
"Stop you psycho," she struggles beneath nails pushing into the tops of my hands, yet I catch a small smirk along her lips.
"Am I still boring?"
A tear shakes loose, "No! I didn't mean it like that!"
Too late
"Good."
Her fight gives, and it makes me feel powerful for a moment.
Before I can rationalize, I pull my hands to her throat and squeeze gently.
Is this why he likes it so much?
The fear, the way her whimpers are a confusion of pleasure and despair.
I imagine her. Laurel. Writhing under his bulk.
Moss stared up at him, pleading for him to stop.
Begging him to drive further into her. Internal struggle.

It must be exhausting for her.
I released realizing I had squeezed too long.
Gale gasps. No, not Gale.
Laurel.
Laurel with her beautiful budding lips, and silky hair.
Laurel telling me no.
"Mikey, I'm close to passing out…please."
A grossly faked groan, fluttering eyes that hide the void, and her fear.
Liar. She just wants this over.
I want so much more.

Someone had once said assault, if that's what this is, was not even about sex itself, and although I wasn't doing that, I was assaulting her.
It was all about control.
Power. Dominance.
Maybe it was, but it was also very much about the sex, and it certainly is for my father.
Sex and power.
If it wasn't then it would end before orgasm.
Pleasure would not be a motive.
My voice quivers as I let go of her feeble neck.
Body is on fire, vision spotted, little stars of pleasure bursting all around me.

I am brought back down, hands shaking, hands spasming from the prolonged grasp on her.
"Mikey, oh… baby," my woman fakes kindness beneath, unaware her name had not been on my mind in my weakest moment.
Glancing down, marks line her neck, a tear slides down her cheek into her fearful smile, "Mikey that was…" trails off.
"Sorry," taking my turn lying as if I had not just choked her.
I try to play dumb, "Did you like that?"
My hand pulls her to me to pacify her.
She rubs her wrist; I can feel her pulse barreling in her neck like the hooves of a dozen wild horses.

Lying behind her I pull her to me, focusing on the TV, so I can ignore how hard she's breathing.
Gale doesn't dare move.
If I just feign innocence, what could she possibly accuse me of?
"Love you, babe."
"I love you too."

Laurel

I seethe at dinner, refusing to acknowledge my father who is blubbering about some party he broke up with.

Quickly he moves on to his and Rachel's plans to go to their friends for a small get-together tomorrow.
He hadn't done anything to deserve my newfound anger, recently that is.

It's me.
Resentful.
He had tarnished me.
I couldn't even proceed normally with the man I longed to love.
There isn't really room for love, my heart has lost its volume trying to minimize what my father could take.
Not now. Not like this.
It's his fault that I'm this.
It's your own fault.
You're weak.
He can smell it.
As if he could read my thoughts my father glances at me with a smile, almost as if he had something up his sleeve.
What do you have planned?
What are you going to do to me now?
I can't take it!

Negative energy tightens my stomach, a noose looped around it.
Can't function.
I shove a pea around my plate, allowing the puddle of soupy potatoes to absorb it beneath.
It drowns quickly, only reappearing when my fork presses down on the pile, green oozing into the white mush, tinting and bubbling like a morning sea foam.
"Laurel, aren't you hungry?"
Rachel is trying to coax me into a conversation.
I'm not interested.

My stomach feels jumbled, crowded like the comparatively empty spaces of a hoarder's quarters.
It's almost to the ceiling now and I feel trapped.

Thick knots in my abdomen and the burned chicken Rachel is trying to pass off as dinner that stinks to high hell leave me feeling nauseous and frazzled.
"I don't feel well," honesty fills the air, with a hint of disdain.
Dad catches the attitude and a hint of a sneer, and shoots me a look that tells me to watch it or else…
"Sorry, I think I'm coming down with something."
 He glares again, this time worry stings his look with questioning before he averts his eyes back to Rachel and smiles with encouragement.
Rachel had bought a new cookbook to improve her kitchen abilities.
It wasn't working.

"At least have some of the chicken. Rachel worked hard on it. Right, babe?"
Rachel beams at the compliment, "It's been marinating since last night."
Dad moans as he spoons a large forkful of breast into his mouth, seared skin and all.
I watch him chew, eyes shut, a throaty groan escaping as he the shallows of his gut as he swallows, "That's great, babe."
Many times I heard that groan when he was sitting between my thighs and based on the out-of-control look on Rachel's face, she had heard it too.
It's the sound he makes moments before he orgasms, face scrunching, lips pursed tight, body taut.
Then boom.
It was finally over.

Rachel blushes red, splotching her persistently mottled skin at the sound that she also knew to be primitively his.
Heat floods my mouth at the thought.
Breath in.
Another low groan, "It's perfect, Rachel."
She is glowing now, "Thanks, honey. I just feel like we haven't done this in ages, and I just wanted dinner to be special."
It's special alright, my father gets to play head of house with both his lovers, and only one knows about the other.

"That would explain the candles and the tablecloth," Mikey jokes, breaking his silence, fork stabbing into the hard meat.
Her brow furrows clear disdain for my brother's interjection.
"Pass the salt," dad requests, unphased.
My finger hovers over the container, hand slowly tightening around the glass before running down its shaft, my eyes meet his, locking in as I grip more tightly.
My tongue swipes over my lip graciously as I toy with the near-phallic tube.
I could make him uncomfortable too.
"Thanks, hon," he almost chokes out.
"Do you need the pepper too Dad?" My voice squeaks with faked innocence.
I could tell it was flustering to him and I revel in the power I feel.
He wasn't going to let this fly, that much I know, but damn if it doesn't feel good to spoon-feed him some of his own medicine.
Best not to let him overdose on it.

My nausea is slowly fading, being replaced with a hint of vindication.
Watching him squirm and growing more uncomfortable by the second is good medicine.
"So there's a dance on Halloween," Mikey starts but is quickly interrupted by my father.
"And you want to go?"
"Yeah."
Dad's cheeks grow as red as Santa's after a long night of deliveries, "Can I have the salt back please Dad?"
Hesitation heavy in his buzzed lids, that drink must've been good.

Mikey

I wait for Dad to turn me down, but he surprises me with a big smile, "Yeah, and take your sister."
"Dad, the salt?" Laurel asks for the second time.

It's just salt, but his entire body tenses as he reaches across to
hand it to her finger loose almost as if he is purposefully
trying not to make any contact with Laurel.
Laurel is playing him right now, I hadn't been blind to it, and
his acceptance of our going out is his way of telling her to stop
without having to say it.
A bribe of sorts.

Rachel is busy cutting up Ava's chicken into micro-sized bits,
her eyes zoom in on the knife, I watch as my sister wraps her
fingers around his hand, taking hold of the shaker.
She grips, a little too long before pulling away, her pinky
which hadn't been wrapped around the container slowly
caresses his hand, elongating as he pulls back.
"Thanks, dad," pouty lips whisper.
There's a moment of silence that goes unnoticed by Rachel, his
eyes averted on his drink which he was nervously swirling.
"Can we take Laurel's car then?"
I watch on as he snaps out of whatever sick thought was
playing in his head, hand relaxing around the glass, "I don't
see why not."
"I can't wait," she interjects, "Oh, and Dad, can I have twenty
bucks? I know you only owe me five, but it would be nice.
Mikey and I could pick up dinner."
Rachel's eyes flash over at my father almost warningly.
She was a firm believer in making us work for our cash flow.
He visibly gulps, Adam's apple begging to burst with the
heavy swallow.

"I owe you five bucks?"
She nods, "Yeah, remember at the hotel Dad?"
Must have been bad.
Her words are round, smoothly flowing with implications that
Rachel somehow is oblivious to.
He doesn't acknowledge her right away, his mind probably
racing, recalling what had happened at the hotel.
Must have been something appalling given his ashen face.
"Remember how you couldn't find your pants and your wallet
was in them?"

I want to laugh, his throat tight, as if he is about to choke, "Ermm yeah, I think you are right, Laurel. It just slipped my mind."
The words chord, catching on the inner ridges of the column of his throat.
Her tone was heavy with insinuation, words elongated as they left her mouth all buttery and female.
An air of power and sexuality breezes through her, like wind through a screen door.
I had no idea that my sister was a woman capable of manipulation and lust.

"Good thing I packed a couple of pairs, or I would've had to have met Larry in my birthday...or wedding suit," he jokes diverting attention from Laurel's revelation.
"Sorry about that, hon. You're right, I do owe you."
Nervous swigs of whiskey fall down his hot throat, I imagine his esophagus squeezing every last drop of booze willing it into his system to ease his anxious state.
Laurel's eyes haven't left him, in fact, they harden like cooled metal, a drill hammering against concrete, "Can I get it before the dance then?"
He gives easily.
"Yeah sweetheart, that sounds fine."
"I have some cash now," Rachel offers only for my dad to wave her off.
 "I got it, honey."
Wouldn't want his wife to pay his ransom.
Honorable really.

My dad paws his wallet refusing to let his wife pay for the soft emotional and petty financial blackmail.
Laurel grins and pouts out a "Thank you, Dad," before sliding the twenty to herself and slowly pushing it into her bra.
Dinner ends quickly after that.
Laurel seems quite pleased with herself.

...

Stowed away in a baggy under my bed is a secret.
Dad would kill me if he found it.
Three hits of acid courtesy of Corey who sold them to me
cheap after our last trip.
I'm anxious to take a trip, knowing this wasn't the right time,
and I certainly didn't want to engage on my own.

Laurel

She is up to something.
"It's my birthday, so I chose what to do today!" she exclaims
from the passenger's seat.
I pull up to Tasha's house, my fingers tight around the
steering wheel, my first solo drive.
I am instructed to pull up to the local salon.
Selena's.
Owned of course by Selena Marrow, the envy of the town.
All the men fawned over her despite her happily married
status and her two children.
I can't say I blame them.
She is beautiful; tall with full breasts that always spill over her
cheetah print attire.
Her teeth were perfectly straight, white as freshly fallen snow
never hidden long beneath her always tinted full lips, lips that
often barked instructions at her husband who owned the store
in Spanish.
It only made her more gorgeous, the way her R's curled from
her tongue in anger and bliss.

"Come in ladies," I hear her shout from the back, gently
smoothing the bottom of a customer's feet, her dyed
mahogany waves flipping with her head.
The shop was small, with three-foot baths, two nail stations,
and a small waiting area that housed a fish tank filled with a
small school of Dwarf Gourami's.

They flick around nervously in flashes of red and shimmering
blues captivate me with each move.

Their tank is clean, adorned with a white pebbled bottom,
plastic plants floating all around.
Selena's husband catches me eyeing the display, "You like
them?"
I nod yes, "Very pretty," I compliment a sudden wave of
nerves claiming me with the sudden closeness.
"Where do they come from?"
I try to keep the conversation going to ease myself into a
feeling of safety.

He steps out from behind the desk, crouching before the tank,
the dim bluish light streaking across his stubbled face, his nose
grazing the glass, "South Asia."
I imagine them in the wet tropical waters, bobbing around
before being torn out and placed in a plastic container,
whisked away from their home, then again, I can also imagine
them in a polluted river, flopping around in murky water and
trash.
"Want to know something else?"
He smiles up at me content to have someone show interest in
his tank, almond eyes filled with anticipation at my answer.
My head bobs, "Yeah."
"They are what you would call um, what was the word?"
For a moment his brow knits as he searches for the right word.
I wait patiently.
"L-labyrinth fish…that's it."

My knees buckle forcing me to crouch next to him, focused on
the patterns the group swims, darting back and forth, "What
does that mean?"
Unpainted nails splay across the glass, palm flat, the coolness
traveling to my core, he eyes them as if he's trying to figure
out what to do with them and fails to answer.
Instead, our eyes fall on the glass, mesmerized by the school, I
remain silent not wanting to interrupt the viewing, Tasha talks
to another worker just a few feet away.
I hear her request a manicure and pedicure combination
treatment.

"I'm sorry," he breaks the silence, "how about it
then…manicure for you?"
"Oh, it's ok," I blush, not accustomed to a man expressing any
shame or guilt for his behavior, not that he should harbor any,
"And yes. Maybe a darker color?"
"Of course, and to answer your question before, a labyrinth
fish is a fish that has a lung-like organ…and that lets them
breathe air. That's why we have the top opened."
My mouth opens slightly in awe.
"It's rare."
I hear his wife's voice command him.
Pulling himself back to his feet with a tired groan, Selena
barking orders in Spanish from the other side of the room.
"*Si! Si!*"
"*Ayuda a registrar los y dejar de fumar con esos malditos peces!*"

With a grin he waves her off, "The boss says to help check you
in," smiling warmly, he hands me a clipboard, "But what she
means is quit messing with those fish," he winks.
I nod with acceptance, mouth a timid thank you.
An hour and a half later my feet are as soft as a cloud, nails
trimmed and painted a smoky gray that I was certain my
father would not approve of.
My toes match, little rhinestones pressed along the top of my
large toe.
Tasha emerges with long clicking nails, white with an intricate
geometric pattern swirling across the center.
"You like?"
I nod, "What's next on the agenda, birthday girl?"
"Oh, you are going to love this."

I didn't love it.
Didn't love being dragged to the next town over to meet some
crook palm reader who she claims is the best in the state as if
you could be good at an art that had no basis in the realms of
science and reality.
I guess lying is an art form.
Tasha had me sit next to her, a middle-aged woman with
newly graying strands sits across from us in an uncomfortably

relaxed manner, almost as if what she had to say was going to
be completely honest.
"Cards?"
I watch my friend nod as if she had done this before.
"So, I'm going to explain to your friend what we discussed last
time."
She had done this before.

I am subjected to a short speech about how psychics or
mediums or whatever she wants to call herself aren't always a
hundred percent accurate.
"It's not like what you see in your movies, with a crazy lady in
a purple robe who is convulsing after she reads someone's
palm. It's far more subtle than that. A tickle in my belly, a little
spark in my palm. I don't see things, but I do feel things.
Energies, emotions…" she trails off looking me deep in the
eye, "Just get comfortable."
Rigid, I am anything but comfortable as she reaches over and
runs a long red nail along Tasha's smooth palm, "This is your
lifeline, it's long telling me you will live to a ripe age. This has
a basis in Hindu palmistry."
I watch as my friend smiles, gloating at her possible long life,
relieved at her believed confirmation of such.
"Your lifeline begins at the mount of Jupiter; this shows me
that you are a very ambitious person. Full of hope and dreams,
ones you will accomplish if you stay on the right path."
The grotesque earrings dangle loudly as she beams at Tasha's
palm, "Here we have a parallel line running with your lifeline,
we call this a parallel line of Mars. It indicates good health."
My friend looks at her in awe, "And my love line?"
Tasha's hand is enveloped in the woman's larger hand,
"Hmmm see this?"
Her usually narrow, feline eyes widened, head shaking yes.
The woman's long nail caresses it, "This curve here signifies
warmth, or your desire to love and the ability to be loved."
Anyone could tell you that about Tasha within five minutes of
meeting her.
What a load of bullshit.
It's not your day so shut up!

"And here I see only one marriage and two children… a slightly older partner."
She sighs with happiness, her eyes twinkling with flashes of her future.
Not Dean or my brother.
I still hadn't let on that I knew she had slept with him, but I guess they won't be together forever so…
It didn't really bother me anyhow.
"You are a libra, aren't you?"
What tipped her off?
Couldn't be the intake form that had her birthday scrawled clearly on the second line.
They finish up, every aspect of Tasha's palm a picture-perfect indication of a life that would be well lived.
When they wrap up, I tuck my hands deep in my pockets, uncomfortable.

"It's your turn, Laurel."
I try to shrug her off, "I'm ok."
"Oh no you don't. It's my birthday, isn't it?"
I sigh, making sure she could hear my disdain.
"It'll be fun."
My hand lies flat, a slight tremble at her touch, hands much colder than I had anticipated given the way she had stroked Tasha's always warm digits just moments ago.
"Let's see here," her eyes scan, "You have a very expressive palm. You have already lived so much despite your young age."
My hands fight the urge to yank free from her clammy touch, "As I told your friend this is your lifeline, see how it begins at your headline here?"
I refused to look down, ears buzzing, something about this was making me uncomfortable.
"This signifies that you tend to live in your mind, that you have a tendency to repress your emotions."
Still, I remain unimpressed at the bull she was feeding me, Tasha, however, is at the edge of her seat, her mind's gears turning at an uncomfortable speed.

I was definitely going to hear about this the entire drive
home.

What tipped her off?
The long sleeves.
The crossed arms?
The fact that I won't make eye contact with her.
Phony.

"See the difference between the shape of your hands?"
She has our palms touched, "A clear air hand and a water
hand."
"How can you tell?"
The woman's eyes smile, "It's all in the shape.
Tasha's hand is long in the fingers, her palm square. She is
balanced but prone to stress."
My palm sits on the table, ready for her to continue rambling
about my supposed water hand, or whatever.
"What's your sign, my dear?"
My mouth is stuck shut, for some reason, I feel a deep
animosity towards her despite her sweet voice.
"Let me guess then…maybe a Pisces, or a cancer."
I hear my friend squeal, and rat me out, "She's a cancer…and
a twin."
A look of annoyance is shot her way without a second
thought, already aware that the woman knew when we were
born, annoyed that my friend was falling so easily.
"Well, while the Gemini sign is known as the twins, the
symbol for cancer is a crab's claw, or some might say a
woman's breast, but there are some who think it symbolizes a
balance of sorts. Yin and Yang. Female and Male."
The chair grows harder beneath my bottom, pressing too hard.
"Her twin is male!"
Psychic hands grip mine again, lying it flat, "I would be so
curious to see his palms."
Yeah, it would be nice to squeeze some more money from me.

Breathing deeply, she hums, "I feel so much life in you, Laurel. You're swelling with it and soon you are really going to live life the way it's meant to be lived."

Daggers are bow being shot at my friend, and I cringe, burying the words deep.

My marriage line is read, next, again she hums, "Three loves, one of which is stronger than the others."

I try to silence my desire to strangle her.

"How about her love line?"

Ignoring her, I wait, slightly intrigued, "A very straight line. This shows me you tend to be passive in love. Now I can get far more into depth on all of this, but let's stick to the general indications for now."

Tasha bounces, "What about kids?"

"The child lines read four strong ones and one weaker line. Perhaps a loss?"

Gulping at the notion I have to remind myself what I am doing and how there was no proof for what she was telling me.

"Heart, Heart, head. Let me see that wisdom line."

I offer my hand up once more like some sort of sacrificial lamb, lay it on the gaudy purple silk that lines her circular table.

"It is certainly short. This can mean that you tend to be indecisive, and possibly impulsive."

Fair enough.

"A slight curve. Gentle and tolerant. So different from your friends that sit completely straight, which tells me she is practical and tends to be good in the fields of science."

In all her intelligence, Tasha couldn't seem to see how fake this was, but to be fair she was pretty good at math, something I always struggled in.

We spend the next half hour watching the woman shuffle her large worn tarot cards, spreading them in a half-moon on the table.

"Let your heart and mind guide you. Feel the card's energy and show me which one calls to you."

Tasha breaths in, eyes shut, fingers glossing over the cards that lay sprawled along the deep purple silk, like some worn lover post-coitus.

"Tarot is an art, it doesn't always tell us exactly what it will be, it lives more or less in the realm of possibility. The path you chose daily and how you chose to respond will always shift where you may end. Rather it gives you a chance to respond." She pauses, sucking in a deep breath, exhaling loudly, "Clear yourselves," she orders.

I do not do such a thing, my eyes peering through to see them breathe in deep and sharp; like some laboring woman trying to manage her labor pains.

What they can't see won't hurt them, and I find myself inhaling deeply when she burns the tip of a bundle of sweet sage, fanning around us for its "Spiritual cleansing capabilities."

I have to stop my eyes from rolling; however, it is soothing.

"The appearance of a major arcana card will influence the whole reading. Think broad lesson. Now the minor cards," she makes a show of grazing a lengthy nail over the cards, "The minor cards tend to be specific to daily challenges."

Silence fills the room, anticipation looming over Tasha's head, lip between her teeth, "Can I go first?"

"You can take both readings if you want."

I feel her foot nudge mine annoyed, "No Laurel, we are both doing this."

With those words I find myself trapped.

If I was being honest maybe I am a bit afraid of what she would see.

"Wands, cups, swords and pentacles," my friend recites.

"I see you know your suits." excitement rests scrawled across her lips, with a tinge of frustration, she wouldn't be able to bullshit us.

"Suits?"

"Yeah, like when you use a normal card deck, same idea."

My mind flashes images of hearts, and spades dancing in a blank room.

The woman reshuffles, "The energy has changed since I laid out," she explains.

Her fingers search randomly, pulling a card from each suit, "The wand for energy and sexuality, the cups represent love and emotion, then you have your swords, these represent your intellect."

I wait for her to tell us about the last suit, clearly having a hard time locating one, "Here are the pentacles. We use these for readings on finance, career paths… well, you get the picture."

"Then there are the court cards, but we'll get into that another time."

"I'll reshuffle, and I need the two of you to get a question and place it in your mind's eye before the reading. This will help the results make more sense to you."

The cards intertwine, Tasha pulls three cards and places them face down, her trembling fingers filled with excited energy.

"I have a feeling that you are looking for illumination about a particular situation."

She nods, "In terms of my relationship. I have been torn lately."

My eyes burn into her, I hate that she was talking circles around me as if I didn't know.

Well, as far as she knows I am clueless.

She is my best friend; it hurts that she won't just come out and tell me.

To be fair, I wasn't as upfront with her as I could be.

"This first card represents changes to be made."

She flips it over revealing a woman holding the head of a lion hand above its snout.

"It's time to gather up your courage and make a tough decision. Do not waste your strength on someone who doesn't deserve it."

We are told the second care offers direction on how to care for herself during the decision-making process.

"The chariot."

I glance, a pharaoh hovers, ruling with a long staff over two sphinxes, castles looming behind, symbols I cannot understand.

His empire.
"What does it mean?"
"It suggests you chase after a past ambition with new intensity. Perhaps a new outlook."
Clearly, Tasha was imagining her short-lived past fling with my brother.
Is she about to start dating my brother?
I do not want to hear anything about their sex life.

She flips the last card, a knight riding a white horse.
I recognize it immediately as death.
"Major arcana."
Her face lightens, the smoldering glare fading to withering ash.
The usual honey-smooth skin looks much more corpse-like.
"Don't worry dear, death isn't always a negative. I think in this case it represents the end of something you once cherished. A start of something new."
Trembling lips part, "Major arcana meaning this card should overshadow the others?"
Guess Tasha was about to start sleeping with her brother.
Not that it bothered me if she wasn't ditching me for him.
The heat of insecurity swells in, my heart rate rising like a hot air balloon, ready to escape.
I realize this is not the time.
If I wanted to be an ideal friend, I was going to have to give in and feign interest.
So far, I had clearly missed the mark.

"It's your turn," my friend informs me, a glimmer of both hope and fear wallowing within her gaze.
The dealer reshuffles the cards before slapping the base onto the table to even them out.
"Just take a deep breath," she requests, the cards smoothing into an arc.
With her eyes busy on the cards, I ignore her and breathe normally.
Spindly fingers hover over, "The energy is strong in this hand."

It takes every shred of strength I harbor to ignore the plain silly behavior.

Maybe I was just being a bitch, because I was the only one not having fun.

I remind myself it's not my day and I just need to grin and bear it.

"Did you take a deep breath?"

My head shakes a lie.

"Alright, tap the first card."

My fingers randomly graze over to a card at the top of the arch, hovering, "This one I guess."

"Why?"

I shrug.

"Did its energy call you?"

It sure did, just like my brain is calling me to get out of this stupid place.

A simple nod suffices despite the rude interior dialogue.

"What are you seeking?"

I piggyback off Tasha, "Clarity on a situation."

Snickering, "Always."

I sit still as a portrait, awaiting to be painted as she turns the old card, "The emperor."

A man in a red robe with a pained expression sits rigidly on a chair, handles two carved rams heads.

My eyes gloss over his, he seems troubled.

Pained.

"It's time for you to take control of the situation at hand. But be wary of your energy towards the problem. Too harsh and you will stumble, too weak and there will be no resolve."

My biggest problem is the emperor.

The man who rules my home.

My life.

The one that had been hovering since my mother passed.

"The emperor is a major arcana card; this card will play a heavy role in this reading from here on out."

Her stare is a serious one, one that makes me uncomfortable as if she can sense my resistance.

Hesitating to pick another card, unsure if it was appropriate to do so, yet I hovered.

I take the hint as she motions, my thumb caressing the card at the bottom of the arc.

Supporting the weight of the rest of the deck.

"The moon, another major arcana card, and your ruling planet my dear."

The moon I see is not the unassuming gentle one I seek in the sky on a warm night, but a bright yellow-faced ball with creatures gathering beneath.

Not what I had been expecting.

"The moon has many faces and phases, people ruled by the moon are oftentimes layered and complex."

"That's Laurel alright," Tasha snickers, earning her a look that could kill.

"The moon tells me that the answer or the path you must take to resolving your problem will not be found where you had expected, but that the result will be freeing."

Cool, I am being urged to solve an issue quickly but with absolutely no guidance.

Sounds promising.

Finally, with great pleasure I pulled the last card, "Three for three, all majors."

She is beautiful, the emperor's companions lounging in a gown, femininity oozing from her pursed lips, fertile wheat growing at her feet.

Her eyes stare off into the distance as if she is ready for whatever may come next.

"The empress. She is calling you to approach your problem with openness, but within reason. Your good faith and soft heart may be a place of weakness that some may take advantage of. I say set up firm boundaries in the most loving manner possible."

Clearly, she hadn't met my dad.

If only the cards had clearly spelled out how to get through this.

The reading doesn't sit right with me the entire ride home.

Attacked.
I felt skeptical. It was all a farce.
So why was it so intriguing?
Why did my thighs feel heavy?
Why does my throat feel tight?
Why does my skin itch for freedom?
Why was I riddled with anxiety?
Unsettled. Drained.
Every fiber of my being wants to escape.
I want to start over.
I want to sleep.
Tasha, feeling emboldened, demands information on
something that ultimately doesn't concern me.

"Ok, I'm sorry I came across so harsh…but I just want you to
know that I'm not upset about you and Mikey."
She sits silent, guilt etched across her brow, "Laurel…"
She stops not knowing what to say, fingers tight on the wheel.
"Tasha, it's ok…really. I'm not upset. I just wish you had told
me."
"How did you know?"
Turning up into her driveway I killed the motor, facing my
friend, "Well, I saw the two of you."
"It was just a one-time thing, and nothing really happened."
"Well, it doesn't have to be, if you're trying to make
something more of it. You're my best friend and I don't want
you to keep things from me, and for the record I know it
wasn't a one-time thing."
The car rattles a bit as she shifts around, reaching in the back
seat for her oversized purse, stuffed with random bits of
makeup and old receipts.

"Do you really mean that?"
"Of course. Two conditions."
The purse plops onto her lap with a jungle, the keys
somewhere deep within, "Well three."
"What might those be," the sass had returned to her voice.

"First, I don't want to hear any explicit details about your sex life with my brother."
Agreeing with a nod, "Ok."
"Second, you still have to promise that whatever may happen between the two of you, that it won't affect us."
Our pinkies hook together hard, almost as if they were fighting a silent battle.
"What's that third then?"
"Will you cut my hair?"
Slinking back into her seat," "What? We were just at a salon!"
Shrugging with indifference to her annoyance, I struggled to locate my own bag that had fallen in the crevice between the foot of the backseat and the back of the drivers.
I feel her eyes burn into me, "Oh, I see. This is about the tarot reading, isn't it? You're shook, aren't you?"
"No!"

My fingers clasp around the band of my bag and I tug it to my chest like some type of comfort stuffy, emboldened with disbelief that she would say that.
It certainly bundles in odd spots like a teddy bear would when you squeeze it too hard.
"Laurel, it is! Admit it!"
I was.
Stupidly so.
Never will I admit it.
"You talked so much shit the drive up!"

I roll my eyes in embarrassment rather than annoyance, "I just need a fresh start. Maybe put some stuff in the past, is that so wrong?"
"Not at all, but just so we're clear I am not a hairdresser, so you aren't allowed to get mad when I butcher it."
Fear sits in my throat; I hadn't even considered how silly I would look if she cut it poorly and I had to shave my head.
"If you do, you aren't allowed to date my brother," I tease.
"Fair enough."

A half hour later my hair tickles the middle of my neck, my face shines.

I feel lighter.

"You know in Korea it's common to get your haircut after a breakup?"

"Fresh start?"

Silver shears descend from fragile fingers onto a poorly painted nightstand, "All done."

I see her pause in the reflection, her soft lips parting, "You aren't breaking up with Kyle, are you?"

Head bobbing no, "I mean I'm not even sure if we're a couple to be honest, like we haven't used those defining words, although he did say he wanted me to be his girlfriend, but it was more of an implication than a question."

She is right about one thing, and end was coming, just not with Kyle.

"Well, this is a fresh start, maybe the new look will motivate you to make a real move and get that boy wrapped around your finger."

That's much less than I want, a finger wouldn't do, I want him wrapped around every part of my body, other than my finger, and as for my father he was going to have a hard time wrapping his disgusting fingers around my hair or any other part of me from here on out.

The power is momentary, but for a moment I feel alive.

For now, it has to be enough.

Mikey

We bid them goodbye, Ava already in a bad mood in Rachel's arms, "No parties and get to school on time tomorrow. We will be back tomorrow evening," she instructs, tossing her new black leather purse over her shoulder.

The smell of fresh leather stings my nose, I can almost hear it mooing.

"Scouts honor," my hand shoots up, fingers pressed together like some type of hand symbol for a sacred oath.

"You aren't a scout," a voice reminds me; Laurel, descending for the first time since yesterday after she and our father had gotten into an argument over her new look.
The chin length cuts sways effortlessly, void of its original heft, the burden of years of growth that had harbored me were gone.
"What did you do!"
Shouting had drawn me down to the kitchen where dad was putting up dishes and Laurel was coming home from her day out with Tasha, clunky purse still strapped over her half-bared shoulder, baked by the kiss of the sun.
"And what are you wearing?"

Everything she did was clearly an offense to him despite the hot weather and seemingly appropriate outfit to combat it.
The loss of control clearly affects him on some personal level.

It picked up from there snowballing into a screaming match only simmering when Rachel reminded my father that it wasn't his hair, and it would grow back.
"I like it. It makes you look more well… womanly," Rachel defended.
Maybe that's what triggered him.
"You didn't even ask for my permission! What's next, Laurel??"
"Oh, you know, a tattoo" my sister had replied, her tone heavily laced with stifled aggression.
"That's not funny!"
Hands tightened around a soda, a small pop emitting under his stress.
"I'm sorry, dad, I just wanted a little change," I heard her tell him after a clearly forced apology.

A little change?
Wonder what that entitles?
That fresh start she was referring to probably didn't include him, and in some ways that's worrisome.
Losing power was not an option, he was only going to grasp more tightly from now on.

He must've sensed it, pulling her tight as he hugged her and offered her an unbelievable apology, he made sure his wife would hear.
"Your right honey… I apologize. "
Rachel looked on; smitten with the loving touch he had been forced to provide.
What she is blind to is restraint.
Laurel smiles, thinking she has won some sort of freedom.
That pretty smile is short lived, as he lingers in his embrace, Rachel rushing to a fussy Ava.
I watch on from the kitchen, his mouth lingering near her ear, her straight face quickly shifting to a wet eyed distant stare.
"Ready, babe?" Rachel calls.
Laurels face tilts and she pecks his cheek dutifully.
It seems so out of place.
"Yeah, hon. Be back soon," my father replies, winking at Laurel, "Night son," he adds passing me, beaming as if he wore a crown on his head.
My poos sister fell silent then, combating tears eyes glued to her feet.
Victory short lived.
Wonder what he said.

It must have terrified her.

Laurel

Vile.
He makes me so sick.
The way he whispered in my ear.
The way he could cut me down to size right, as I had felt I was free.
Strong.
Able.
I am none of those things.
It only took five words; "Don't forget, I love you."
Dread sucks me down into its dark funnel.
Those words seem normal, but they are anything but.
It's a warning.

Stop loving me.
Please. Please.
I hate you.
How can you love me when I hate you so much?
But you do love him.
So, so much.
I want to scream it out, but my lips only allow me to kiss him goodbye.

Mikey

An idea strikes me, and only once like a hot rod of lightning.
Why not?
What could it hurt?

Laurel

Weary eyes, looming at the small square of potential.
Yin and yang.
Fitting.
Cancer. My twin. A sign?

It's not a sign.
Are you insane?
Acid?
There is not a being in or out of this universe that would try to give
me a sign to use acid.

I tell Mikey no.
Actually, it's a "Hell no!"
He persists.
Tells me it would be freeing.
That he had done it the other night at the quarry.
"I felt so free when I took it Laurel. For the first time in years, I
felt powerful. You want to feel that don't you?"
I do…but.

"Mikey, No!"
"I felt so weightless, like nothing mattered. Please. It would be
good for you," Mikey pushes his bottom lip out for good
measure.
"No! This is a serious drug. I don't want to do something
stupid."
He taunts me, "Didn't realize you were such a fucking drag."
Hot bile like anger threatens to leave my stomach. "And I
didn't realize you were a fucking drug addict."
Scoffing, "I am not an addict. It's acid, not fucking crack."

Mikey

I watch longingly as she stalks off, desperate to not ride the
high alone.
My calls leave her uninspired to take the journey with me.
Somewhere above a door slams.

…

Laurel turns me down for the hundredth time and inhales a
poorly constructed sandwich, consisting of the bottom scraps
of jelly and chunky peanut butter, her legs childishly dangling
over the edge of the island.

It had been hell to coax her out of her room in the first place, but I was no quitter.

The idea keeps creeping back into my mind, the clock only reading a little after five.

I don't want to start too late and feel rushed.

Resorting to begging, I press my hands together, tucking them under my chin, "Pretty please Laurel," I fall to my knees and playfully plead.

Laurel

Idle hands are the devil's plaything, or so I was told by every adult who was trying to lure me into outdoor activity.

I try to keep my mind off Mikey's offer, despite a gut gnawing desire to try it.

To combat the temptation, I take a shower, paint my nails, and chew them down to a nub.

I want it.

Want to feel everything. Want to feel absolutely nothing.

I desire to soak in its strong masculine energy and fall in the sweet yawning thighs of the feminine return to reality, or so I imagine that's what it may feel like.

Darkness flipping to light.

Light fading to darkness.

Confusion and enlightenment morphing into one.

Chains broken into momentary freedom.

Unlocked, if only for a moment.

"Take my hand."

Mikey offers it up like a cocktail platter, my fingers folding into his, kneading his knuckles like dough.

"You promise this is ok?"

My hands have begun to shake in anticipation and fear.

"I wouldn't hurt you, would I?"

I didn't think so, but then again, I never thought those I loved could have inflicted the wounds they had, and because of my love for my brother, I gave him the chance.

Heavy lashes coated in too much mascara flap shut, breath
fills my chest protruding it before rapidly retreating, "Ok."
"Then open your mouth."
Tongue out, still apprehensive, the bit of paper he presses
down on the ridges is barely noticeable as it curls up along the
edges of my tongue, releasing its slightly bitter taste.
Familiar, like a dandelion and summer
The way a man's release tingles with life, an acrimonious
residue.
"Tastes like a dandelion, huh?"
"A little."
And something else.
"Just give it a half hour or so and you will start to feel it."
With that, he presses two tabs onto his own wet, red, tongue.
"Bottoms up."
"What if I don't want to anymore?"
Anxiety wafts over me, a dust storm in the once-calm desert,
threatening to bury me in gusts of destructive fear.
Grinning, "It's too late now."
"No!"
It was too late.
I suck in what feels like my last breath and take a seat on the
sofa.

Mikey

Laurel giggles, eyes widened, pupils boring into my own,
"Ok, so this is it right?"
"This is just the start sis."
Laurel falls onto her back laughing hysterically, "That's good
then. I'm good, right?"
My vision temporarily blurry only catching her frame
shooting back up, "Yes."
"Your eyes look so big," slow words trip slowly along with the
air from her lungs, each syllable bouncing as it slams into the
hard concrete of reality.
She breathes hard through her nose, causing her nostrils to
flare like an angry bull.
"I'm not wearing red," I joke.

Self-consciously, she pinches her nose shut. "Shut up!"
The effects of the acid must be hitting her like a train.
It was hitting me too.

Laurel

Feeling it. Feeling everything.
Everything. Everything makes no sense, but nothing makes
sense.
Wait, I think this is it.
Nothing makes sense.
What?
The walls of my home have softened somehow, the patterns of
our wallpaper drip like wet paint, curling and curving the
ridges of the flawed wall.
I readjust my eyes.

It's not real.
Or maybe this is reality and I have just been blind to it.
"They can't stay that way for long Mikey."
My brother looks at me, clearly feeling similar effects.
"What?"
I point to the walls, my body upside down, my calves flat on
the couch, no recollection of contorting my body into such an
odd position.
"What do you see?"
His words are slow, his head now dangling next to mine.
"I see you, " he laughs out as if I would understand, and I
guess in some way I do.
"I see you, Laurel."
He is almost impossible to ignore.
His fingers triangulated the spot on the wall where the flowers
were most cluttered. "They are getting bigger, aren't they?"
Not bigger, just stronger.
Pulsating.
Throbbing with such strong pigmentation, they threaten to
bleed.

I climb the high and it quickly loses the subtle glow it had
teased me with.
Maybe this was almost the peak.
The slow steadiness I had felt is spiraling fast now.
My heart throbs with fear of what comes next.
Mikey hums a painfully familiar tune next to my still dangling
head.
I pull up as if to get away from it.
Cindy Lauper.
"Stop it!"
He doesn't respond, keeps humming obliviously.
"Mikey, stop!"
My words must be nothing but a slurred mess to him.
Jolting upright, I cover my ears, disoriented, my hips swaying
towards the kitchen.
I need a drink. Desperately need some air. Water.

Reaching into the sink, I tightly grasp one of his special
whiskey glasses and overfill it, ice running over my fingers.
I squeeze the smooth, hear it begin to lose its structural
integrity with a deafening crack.
Another gulp.
Mikey is still humming in the living room.
That song.
We are not alone anymore.
He is there in the front of my mind.
In me. Shuddering. Loving me. Hating me.
Taking. Always taking.
Chanting now.
I want to silence him.
"Please."
The voice.
My voice cries out now.
"I don't want to have fun! Mikey shut up!"
I can tell that I'm screaming it out now, but Mikey doesn't take
notice.
It floods in.

Daddy.

I love you.
You will always be my number one.

Heat pummels me onto the ground and I sob.
Mikey's voice.
No. His voice. My father.
"Laurel, look at me."
Look at me, mouse.
In my head, it's in my head.
It's all in my head but it doesn't make it any less real.

You like it…tell me you like this so I can help you feel good.

Slurring. I feel him, his weight heavy forcing me apart, tearing
me apart.
Blood and alcohol.
I can smell it.
I can feel it coat my inner thighs in a hot, sticky manner.
Triggering.
Under her nose. Under his eye.
Drying. Crying out.
Flaking.
Blood. My blood.
I smell her.
She is here. Copper. Iron.
Stinging my nostrils.
Fresh.
"Laurel."
Not his voice.

My vision shutters like a blind being drawn urgently.
He is gone. She hasn't left.
Swishing coldly in my belly, the water begs to expunge itself.
A boat rocking in my gut.
I had held on. Too tight.
A dozen little scarlet drops on my palm, warm and dripping.
My blood.

"Laurel!"

He isn't singing anymore.
Concerned.
I bring my palm to my eyes, a little too close, the liquid
tickling my lash.
It begins to imbrue the sleeve of my shirt.
But I feel no pain. I feel the warmth.
The way it drips, earth quaking across clean skin.
Only relief.
Wiping the wound against my dress, the pain becomes real.
Rubies glimmering with diamonds of glass.
Cavernous.
Wondrous pollution on the recently mopped floors.

I pick the shard up between my fingers, dancing into my
grasp.
Run the cool edge of potential along with my fingerprints,
patterns of my composition so unique.
That much is mine.
Teasing.
Tempting.
So much potential for relief in one little piece of broken glass.
It would be so easy.

Mikey drops back down, pressing a rag, the shard falling
beside me unnoticed.
"Jesus, Laurel, get up you're making a huge fucking mess!"
He offers me his hand and I take it without question.
"You broke his favorite glass," my brother laughs as if he
found some pleasure in it.
"Yeah…I did, didn't I?"
"Fuck him."

Mikey

My fingers skim over the dial on the stereo, unleashing a fury
of intricate and complicated notes.
Each note is like an individual opera roaring into my mind.
I don't talk, but the music does.

Each song is a novel story, ones that recount love, pain, heartache, even emotions we cannot quiet grasp.
Unexplained.
Serenading me to a new world.
Vibrating through to my core.
I need Laurel who has seemingly disappeared.

Climbing this high alone should be illegal.
I mean technically it is.
In the kitchen, I hear the thunderous crash of glass, pinging like pins.
Falling to my knees I realize it's my sister and treacherously trek through the mountain range of the couch.
Bluish light assaults my already dilated eyes. A splash of blood and water mixed in a milky pink around her splayed thighs that had seeped from her hurt hand.
She leans against the counter, hot tears falling down her face despite a crazed smile, uttering nonsense and guilt for breaking his favorite glass.
"I think I broke it."
She had her hand bleeding, a small bit of glass clenched between her fingers dangerously.
"Mikey, I want you to stop singing that song!"
Laurel's eyes are crazed, pupils alert, widening further as if to devour her entire iris.

Worry threatens to turn to panic, but my sister needs me and I'm not sure I can truly find the ability to panic at this moment.
Not when everything throbs and echoes so wondrously around us.

"If I stop singing the song, will you wash your hands and come sit with me?"
A smile spreads to her lips, opening far enough to catch another tear.
"Wash it for me!"
"Jesus, Laurel, you're making a huge fucking mess!"

Seeing her blood annoys me knowing we would have to clean it, what's worse is what she broke.
"You broke his favorite glass."
"Yeah…I did, didn't I?"
Giggling, I eye the glass, the sharp edges morphing, becoming soft, just like Laurel's voice.
Alien.
Unrecognizable.
"Fuck him," she whimpers, filling me with pride.

Gathering her strength and taking my promise to stop singing we wash her hands, allowing ourselves to be distracted by the swirling shifting waters as they vortexed their way to the freedom of our old pipes.

Laurel

The internal storm materializes itself in the evening skies as if it knows what I need.
It begins dry, lightning threatening to spark a fire as it crashes all around.
But it won't be alone. Rain is threatening landfall, employing the right moment to hit.
I fall painstakingly slowly off the peak, reaching the comforts of the more subtle high.
It kills me into submission.
Content with her tender grasp.
Mikey hands me a bottle of vodka. I drink greedily, thinning blood spitting from the hand we had so painstakingly washed only to be carried away in the flamingo beauty of the mixing liquids.
The crackling of lightning encourages my hips to rock from side to side, my brother catching glimpses of my show as he lounges on the lawn chair lost in nirvana, really peaking now.
Rain begins to drizzle, warms across my chest.
Suddenly, it all makes sense.
Emotions have lost their strength.
Layers had now become two dimensional…or is that the first dimension?

Wait…

I'm numb.
Lost.
Anger was just anger.
It wasn't layered like a saucy dip, a crunchy upper layer of
hurt, or the soft underbelly of fear.
The building blocks of anger.
Hurt was just that; hurt, primal shooting through my body,
void of the fear of the unknown.
Happiness.
Contentment.
They had no dimension.
No place in my world.
These things don't exist in the realms of my reality.

Mikey

She is wild.
I had never seen this side of her.
Her animal.
The beast that lingers deep within all of us.

The tears are still coming now violently, but she laughs
through them, the lightning powerfully striking all around us.
Those momentary cracks and flashes of light reveal a twisted
smile.
Each roll of thunder feels like it's vibrating through to my
core.
Invading my soul.
She is invading my soul with each twist.
Breaking my heart with her bleeding hand up in the air now,
her body slithering as the wet drops clean the blood that has
faded and blended into her white top.
Her hands scream surrender the way her lips should, running
up to feel the static that's coating the air.

Laurel

I finally come down in the early morning hours, my racing
heart catching back up to the beats it had missed over the
years.
The couch wraps me in an embrace. The glow of the TV
numbs my mind.
When it finally fades, so does my consciousness.
Into the comfort of lack.
Darkness.

Mikey

I shake my sister awake and we scurry to pick up the bits of
glass and scrub the blood off the baseboards and pack
sandwiches for lunch, pulling into school just in time for the
lunch bell to ding.

Laurel

"Your hair," he points out, stroking my neck before retreating
to his touch and dousing a cheap burrito in red sauce.
Kyle.
His smile looming over me.
"I just had a strange night."
"Tell me about it?"

I do.
Leaving out the little meltdown I had.
"Please be careful."
I bite into the stale crust of my sandwich and chew painfully
on the dried bits.
"I will probably never do it again."
Can't help but feel slightly irritated at his desire to control me.
Or maybe I was just sensitive to it.
"Hey," his finger brushing the bulk of my lower lip with a
slight sting, "I didn't mean for that to sound controlling.
I nip at his finger, the spice bringing life to my tongue, almost
happy that he had read me so easily.
"I know. I'm just being sensitive."

His finger doesn't leave me, but my hand travels to his pressing it to my lips to part.

Kyle's eyes widened with lust and apprehension, "You aren't sensitive," pressing his mouth to my ear, "I just kind of like you, and I worry."

Pulling away, I mutter, "Don't."

"I can't help it."

...

Kyle and I spent the next weekend sneaking off whenever Dad was at work.

Saturday morning it was breakfast at the local diner.

We chose a booth towards the back to avoid any familiar faces.

Sticky syrup and French toast make for good conversation and at the end of the meal he plants a maple kiss along my bottom lip.

Trembling.

"So, the dance?"

"Yeah…the dance."

A long sip of soda, "I'm looking forward to it."

I lick the sweetness off with my tongue.

"You promise to wear a costume?"

"I'll be the Fred to your Daphne," he jokes, dabbing his French toast in a pool of amber before clamping his teeth around the stick.

"I don't think red hair will suit me; plus, where do we get the rest of the gang?"

Pressing his thumb to his pointer and twisting, he zeroes in on my face, squinting an eye shut.

"Oh, I can definitely see you as a redhead."

A smile invades my face for a second before I take notice and force my lips into a grimace.

"There it is," he teases, pressing his hands against my cheeks, holding me to his stare.

I so badly wanted to kiss him, but the diner was probably not the place, so I chased the temptation away. "I am pretty sure that Daphne and Fred will never end up together," I educate.

"Touché."
Letting my fingers fall to my pocket I dig out a wad of bills,
and plop it on the table between us, "This one's on me."
I can tell he is about to protest but wisely chooses to leave it as
my eyes meet his fiery intensity.

Out by the car, he gives me one more kiss before pulling me
into his arms, hands wrapped tight around my waist, my
thigh slightly pulsing up to feel him against me. "What are
you doing?"
Blazing lust unfurls into a tingle along my hungry folds.
"Kyle."
I wait with frustrating anticipation for him to kiss me again as
I lightly feather the flowering buds of my mouth against his.
"I think that Daphne and Fred are definitely going to end up
together this time."

...

Sunday.
Church went over, which means less time for family lunch and
a quicker exit for Dad.
Rachel drops me off at the park, Tasha waiting for me by the
swings, Dean's arms linked through hers.
"Be home by eight," she reminds me, Ava screaming in the
background.
"I will."
We spend the afternoon tossing rocks into the pond and
smoking poorly rolled joints until the laughter can no longer
be contained.
When I'm just high enough, I sit on the swings, allowing the
breeze to course through me to rid myself of the stink of
weed.

By five thirty Kyle and I are sitting by the ponds, hands
intertwined, my head leaning against his shoulder while Dean
and Tasha are somewhere out in the woods doing exactly
what I assume they usually do in the absence of a watchful
eye.

"So, when do you start sneaking back into my window?"
He tenses, a bullfrog calling out somewhere in the lengthy
reeds for its mate.
"Well-" the masculine to my feminine clears his throat,
adjusting his hat nervously as if we had never had sex before,
"I think we should keep building on this," hands interlocked
with mine, his tongue sincere.

It doesn't bother me.
To be fair, I hadn't even come clean or been honest with him.
My body was probably the last thing I should give in my
state.
But I'm also well aware of the healing effects of our binding.
His soothing kisses that had led to healing climaxes.
"You're right," I admit with a certain throbbing in my chest,
followed by defiance.
I want this weight to be lessened.
I want Kyle.
But I don't want to wait to let him in.
Not anymore.
Just once I want to be victorious.

"I can trust you, right?"
Kyle shifts, moving me to face him.
Those eyes.
Piercing into me.
"Of course. Anything Laurel," dragging a finger along my
cheek, "If I tell you something, I need you to make me a
promise and I need you to keep it."
"What if I can't...like morally keep that promise?"
Alarm grumbles in my gut.
Shut up.
Now.
This doesn't end well if you don't stop now. Not for you or Kyle.

My toes skim over the top layer of dirty pond water, swishing
the dirt beneath, clouding in the little creatures that fed within.
"Never mind," I mutter solemnly.

I feel desperate to free myself from the chains that had so tightly bound me.

"I didn't mean it like that…I just don't want to make a promise I can't keep Laurel, and if you tell me anything that makes me feel like you might be in some danger, I can't morally keep quiet."

"I'm not in danger."

He wouldn't hurt me.

Right?

Sincerity crinkling along his lips, my head ducked down, refusing to meet his gentle eyes, "We can't have a relationship based on broken promises and lies. So no Laurel, I can't make you that promise."

Chin tucks down, back up, "I understand."

I understand it all.

That he is too good for me.

That I will never be good enough for him, even though he will always believe in my worth.

Will always praise me.

Treat me like some feminine deity.

Adore me.

Adorn me.

But I will always know.

That knowledge will always hurt.

The truth is Kyle can do much better and he should.

But I am selfish.

I don't want him to do better. I want him to want me while I maintain my secrets, only when and if my conditions are met. What I need is for him to settle, despite my unwillingness to bear more than just skin.

His arm wraps around my shoulder and pulls me into him, his nose digging into my hair, taking in my scent. "Sunshine," Kyle says, his words tickling my ear, putting me at ease.

"What?"

Enjoying the closeness, I just about purr.

"Your hair, it always smells like what I imagine sunshine would smell like."

The words sting with a sharp tear to my eye. "Sunshine?"

Nodding, he moves away, takes my hands in his, and searches my face, trying to decipher what sits in my gaze.
"Yeah, sunshine. I know it's cheesy, but I want to share everything with you…but only if you let me."
The way he speaks is almost as if he had just made the decision to accept his words.
Tangled fingers in my hair, clenching and pulling my neck to his lips, gently nibbling the skin, teasing the lobe of my ear.
I soften with a sigh.
"I just-," pausing I try to gather my words, Kyle patiently waiting, "I don't know where to start, but I do want to be honest with you…about everything," I whisper.
Not knowing what else to say with my brain, I allow my heart to take over, and she is not half as rational as the head, a heart that is galloping rapidly now.
"I don't know how to get past this part of my life. I just feel so…so stuck. Like no matter what I do, I'm hurting or betraying someone and it's easier to allow myself to be that someone. No scenario leaves everyone unhurt."

A sudden sting pierces my chest, crawls to my eyes.
He pulls away clenching his hands "I'm sorry, I didn't mean to-."
"You didn't do anything wrong. You do everything frustratingly right."
"It's my secret talent," he smiles, trying to comfort me, gently setting his thumb to my cheek and stroking.
"Ok, Mr. Right, how do I fix this?"
There's a sigh and a certain heaviness in his tone, his finger swiping across my cheek before I see his hands pull the hat off his head and fold it onto his lap, combing fingers through his shining hair.
I look out at the water, ripples of life below disrupting the smooth water table.
"Guess it just depends on what it is that needs fixing. Different tools for different problems."

My heart begins to pulsate at the speed of a dozen wild freed
mares trudging through an open field.
Is this it?
Honesty?
My brain is screaming at me to stop.
This is not the way.
My mouth has a mind of its own, separate from my logical
self. My tongue is sharp, stupid, and completely unhinged.
"He's not who everyone thinks he is," I unleash, the anvil that
had been crushing my heart easing off.
"What do you mean?"
I myself, am not sure. I desperately search for the words, eyes
scanning out at the sparse tree line across the pond that begins
to shuffle and sway.
"Laurel?"

Out of the trees step Tasha and Dean, each with frazzled hair,
a quick pace, and a panicked look.
Dean calls out, "We got to go," his hands flailing violently,
trying to get our attention.
I glance over at the two before hopping to my feet, Kyle's
hand in mine, the way they pace urgently.
They call out our names.
"What do you think is going on?"
Kyle and I jump to our feet and make haste towards them,
reaching Tasha to hear her say, "Your dad's out on the other
side of the park with his partner looking for a loose dog or
something, let's go before he spots us."
We are on a mission now, trying to get to Dean's car and get
out of the park.
A mission to disappear.

...

Dinner. Monday night.
School passed by slowly today, Kyle leaving early for a visit to
the dentist.
I wave him off after lunch and spend the rest of the day
doodling and daydreaming.

Little flowers line the outside of my notebook, vining from the bottom to the top, the center filled with random notes about the industrial age.
Sounds dirty and exhausting.
Factory work and fires.
Lack of basic hygiene and pay.
Power-driven machines.
Steam engines.
My eyes scream, focus, my hands give away a complete lack of focus.

"Laurel, am I boring you?"
I shift my gaze away from the tattered sheet of paper, sparse notes beginning to be wrapped up with little buds and stems.
"No."
"Then I guess you can tell me when the industrial age began?"
Glancing down at my notebook, I caught four digits, the only four I had bothered to jot down. "Umm, seventeen sixty?"
Dr. Caddell wrinkles his pudgy nose, almost annoyed that I had replied, "Very good, now if you don't mind getting out of your head and joining the rest of the class it would be appreciated."
People snicker around me, my eyes shoot down to my tagged desk, crude carvings of initials and hearts throbbing at me as my anxiety tops.
I even hear Katie Greenburg whisper to Kat Erikson about me and it's less than nice.
"Too busy thinking about fucking Kyle I bet," they both giggle.
I'm not the only one who hears.
"Miss Greenburg, care to share?"
Cheeks flush red just now, realizing how loud she had been.
 "No. Sorry professor."
Dr. Caddell turns his back to the class, his khakis wrinkling as he writes on the green board.
A man with a doctorate degree stuck working here.

With his back turned, I feel Katie toss something at me; a wad of balled-up paper.

I pry it open beneath my desk and read.
How does it feel to fuck my sloppy seconds?
Crinkling the paper back into a tight ball, annoyed, and stuff it
deep into my bag before glaring her down.
Her almond eyes meet mine. "Just remember who had that big
cock first," she whispers.
Kat chuckles stupidly, her fat fingers gripped tightly around
her gaudy bag.
"And he couldn't get enough," she adds the mushroom of her
pencil playing along her lips.
She is trying to get a rise out of me and it's working.

I wait till the bell rings, pace out slowly behind Katie and Kat,
their skirts swishing as they try to hurry away from me,
whispering and giggling, shooting back menacing looks.
"Clearly, he could get enough, or you would still be together.
Guess someone can't get over being dumped," my tongue
slips without my permission, and I know that I should have
shut it.
Their heads snap as if they were somehow conjoined, "Oh hon
you misunderstood the situation. He only dumped me
because I found someone much better, and he didn't like
that…broke his little heart."
Moving my fingers to the dial of my lock I begin to spin it
right, "It's your loss I guess."
The lock pulls free, and I push the lever up to open it only to
be stopped by glossed nails. It slams with a thud.
"Laurel, I like you," she lies, "And that's why I'm going to tell
you that you could do so much better than pining over the
same guy I got rid of. I mean shouldn't that be enough of a
hint? That he isn't worth it?"
"It's kind of pathetic," her dumb friend drawls slowly, a string
of drool falling accidentally from those venomous lips.
"Plus, Kyle is kind of a baby. It's been years, and he still cries
about his daddy."
Behind her, Kat balls her fists and pretends to rub away fake
tears, "Boo fucking hoo."
Her pink lips pucker on the B, falling flat as a plateau on the
final O.

My heart aches hearing them attack the sensitivity he allows
people to see, knowing full well it takes a lot for him to cope
every day.
I feel annoyance begin to build in me, eyes focusing on the
hand that was still pressed to the metal of my locker, the
crowd rushing by as the bell for next class was getting close to
ringing.

"You sure are full of yourself Katie, it's starting to show…right
there," I point to her stomach knowing full well it would stick
with her and eat her up, given her rapid weight gain the last
few months.
Maybe I should have been kinder or been the bigger person,
but I feel defensive.
Protective event.
Kat gasps, "Oh my god, we were just playing Laurel!"
"No, you weren't."
They stalk off, Katie with tears in her eyes and Kat telling her
I'm just a bitch.
 "Didn't feel like much of a game," I muttered, burying my
head in my locker.

…

I am thankful.
Thankful for the loose dog that had kept me from spilling my
secret.
Thankful that Kyle had not dared bring up my half-
confession.
My thankfulness is short-lived.
I can tell Dad is mad when he stalks into my room, sweat
beading across his forehead.
He is nursing two fingers of whiskey in a spotty glass, his
favorite glass shattered and glimmering in some dump.
His day off wasn't going to plan.

Ava had woken him up before he had intended, and Rachel
had been pestering him to do yard work that he had half-assed
based on the random piles of leaves littering the backyard.

Rachel is downstairs doing dishes, Ava somewhere in the
house destroying bookshelves and dumping toys.

"What gives? No dinner again?"
Dinner had stunk to high hell, and my encounter with Kat and
Katie had left my stomach in knots.
Cheddar broccoli, rice, and burgers that smelled bloody even
from a distance were not my idea of a good meal.
"Not hungry is all."
I was hungry but I also wanted to avoid him as much as
possible, this was not in the plan.
"Been hearing that a lot lately."

I try to ignore him, pulling my math homework from the
sheath of its blue folder.
Blue for math, yellow for history, orange for geography, and
of course red or green for science depending on what Dad had
bought that year.
It had been that way since the third grade.
Eyeing the equations, I grow increasingly nervous at his
reluctance to leave and let me work.
Flicking the light on my desk on, I pray he will take it as a sign
to go.
The stream of light sheds no clarity on the problem at hand, so
I give up, shoulders tightening, "I have a lot of homework to
do Dad," I hint.
"We need to talk."

I hate those four words.
Words that held so much emotional control.
That made my heart skip several beats.
"Did you hear me?"
An unknown amount of time had passed as panic held my lips
shut.
"I'm trying to talk to you Laurel, so give me some respect and
turn around."
My chair turns with a creak, "What's going on, dad? I have a
lot of homework to do tonight and-.

There's a twitch on his upper lip as he takes a sip of the amber as if the alcohol was the only thing stifling pure unadulterated anger, it's a look that tells me to shut it.
"I was at Willow Park Sunday. There was a dog there running around scaring the shit out of people," he chuckles at the notion.

I imagine the mangy mutt snarling at the pedestrians, my Dad holding a gun to it screaming for the canine to comply.
Sit.
He would put its short little paws behind its back.
Little dog cuffs, tight on its grubby ankles.
The humor is quickly chased down with the heavy burden of the closeness that he wants, hands patting the soft spot on my bed next to him.
I know he wouldn't dare be so brazen with Rachel right downstairs.
Would he?
It wasn't as if her presence had stopped him before.

"Come sit," he proposes again, his voice rasp and heavy with stifled anger.
I begin to wilt as I traverse the room, with each step my legs grow heavier as if a million tiny creatures were springing up from the floorboards and holding me down.
Trying to keep me away from him.
The bed shifts, eyes glued ahead, my shoulders met with a strangely tender touch.
My mind races, and I try to figure out what he might say next, all the things he would perceive as wrong popping up in my mind's eye.
Dad reaches, pulling me into a hug. One I don't reciprocate.
"I thought I made it clear that you were not to be hanging out with that boy alone."
Heavy on the boy part, his voice dipping as if it had fallen into some dark unseen pit.
Pulling away the wilting of my soul turns to rot, leaving me a bare twisted stem of caged defensiveness.

"I was with Tasha and Dean…we were just hanging out. Am I not allowed to spend time with my friends?"
Thorns sprout.
I may have come in a little hot, but it wasn't as if I had broken the rules, we were not alone, at least not then.
Fire meets even bigger fire.
Morphing into one.
"You never asked my permission to go, and you used Rachel to chauffeur you around, so give me one good reason why I should let you go to that dance?"

I hadn't had a choice, Mikey using my car for work, Kyle unable to pick me up for obvious reasons, and Tasha and Dean only met us at the ponds.
"That's not fair," I whine like some spoiled child, whose father had taken her favorite toy.
"I think it's best that you stay home seeing as how you can't control yourself."
His eyes darken.
"Control myself?"
As if he was in control of his urges.
He had spent years controlling me in some last-ditch effort to stabilize his own messed-up life.
Anger quickly blows up, and I seethe at his hypocrisy.
Red tide.
Deadly.
Unpredictable and sure to leave him blubbering like a dying fish, if only I could unleash it, but it would mean fully becoming untethered from him.

"I can control myself fine! It's not like we did anything!"
He stares at me, "You aren't so innocent though are you Laurel?"
I blink stunned at the question that was more of a statement and a damned implication of my sin rather than his.
"You would know!"
My stupid mouth retorts with the truth.
I wasn't innocent.
My innocence was gone.

Taken and abused.
Not lost, as it could never be found again.
It was simply gone.

He smirks, prepared to gut me, his tongue licking the rim of
his drink, dipping in slowly before lapping it up like a cat,
before pushing his claws from their hiding spot.
More than happy to toy with the little mouse I am.
I look away.
Dead tell of my guilt.
Devil on my lips.
Can't bite the devil on my tongue.

"It's not like Mikey hasn't been running around doing
whatever he wants, whenever he wants, fucking anyone he
wants! It's none of your business, anyway!"
I didn't mean for the word to slip, especially not with the
infliction of cruelty behind it, but regardless I double down in
my defiance.
"We have raised you better than that, Laurel. Cursing? At me?
You think you're some precious little angel beyond reproach
but let me tell you something. You're no angel, you are
anything but innocent, and if you think you have any value to
any man who is going to come into your life, then you have
another thing coming. The fact is Laurel," his voice hardens
around my name, face red, "You lost your value to any man
the minute you let that boy touch you. You are nothing but
another worthless girl."
Claws pierce the skin now.
Blood pours like some torrential rain, my words along with it,
"You never seem to care when the fucking pertains to us.
Wasn't I worth something to you then?" I hissed.
My father's hands shot up, pressing my wrists hard in his
grasp, squeezing with anger and something else, fear.
I had played my hand, maybe too well.
"Is that what we do Laurel? Fucking? Here I thought it was
special. I thought you knew better to question my love for
you."

"You're only upset because you can't keep me as some obedient pet anymore. The fact is you're the one who did this to me…you took any value I held the first time you touched me."
"And you never turned me down, not once did you tell me no."
The look in his eye says he wants to hit me and honestly, I wish he would.
Let me feel the pain.
Better violence than his loving touch.
"You know what? You are nothing more than an ungrateful brat. After everything I do for you kids," his hands fly," I mean look at all this for God's sake, all the clothes, the roof over your head, and this is how you speak to me? I should slap your smug little face for being so ungrateful, Laurel, but I won't." He peers at me, a glint of anger in his cocoa eyes, a forcefulness as powerful as a tornado there. It meets the hurricane of defiance in mine.
Why pray tell?

"Why not? Scared that Rachel might ask me why you slapped me?"
I pull his hand and press it to my cheek.
Invitation coming across as a threat.
His only response is to squeeze my cheek between the fingers of the hand I hold, "Do it," I whisper.
Tightening muscles, teasing landfall only to pull back to his side, "You tell her whatever you want, Laurel because no one will ever believe a little tramp over the town's sheriff, and that's a promise."
He struts out leaving a storm wider than an F5 swelling behind him.
I feel victorious.
Deluded in thinking that this is over.
But it isn't.
Far from.
He is right.
The girl who cried big, bad wolf.

The only difference between Peter and I is that my wolf had been there all along.

...

An icy blast greets me at the dinner table the night of the talent show, Mikey gone to prep for the wrestling team's demonstration.
Tension sits tight in the air, invisible strings tethering the two of us to one another in anger.
Pork chops sit in front of me, dry and tough, matching the scowl on his face.
Our bitter battle was not as invisible as I had thought, and Rachel tries to pacify us.
"Won't you two just kiss and put on makeup?"
I assume he has more than kissing on his mind.
Rachel seems exasperated as she flings a spoonful of wet noodles on the eggshell-thin plate.
They seep boiled water and steam across the flat surface onto my chop.
"Stubborn the two of you."
"Like father, like daughter," I chanted, hoping to get under his skin.
"It's ok Rach, we just hit a rough patch and Laurel isn't happy about having to miss the dance."

Damn right, I wasn't happy.
His jealousy was clouding his judgment.
The last bit of control he could exert was to lock me up, watch my every move.
Rapunzel without the hair.
He had gone as far as to tell me to put something nicer on for the show and when I dared make myself up with darker colors in defiance, he handed me a makeup wipe and made me start over, telling me I looked cheap, and I was better than that.
How absurd.

"Yeah, what's next, are you going to ban me from going to college too?"
I watch him suck up a flat noodle before proceeding, "I will take anything I want away from you Laurel because I am your father, and you lack respect."
Ambiguous.
"You take whatever you want anyhow," whispers trip from my tongue unnoticed.

He had already taken everything; my self-respect, my value, my virginity, and my honesty.
"Just eat, you two," Rachel barks, popping Ava down in her highchair, her fists grabbing greedily at a noodle.
I shove the overly peppered noodles down my throat, eat the dry pork, and top it off with two slices of pie and milk, to his disapproval.
Unbeknownst to him I would revisit it later.
"You best hurry up and get ready for tonight," he calls out as I leave the table urgently, my anxiety building hot from my close to bursting belly.
I slam my door hoping he can hear how mad I truly am and swallow down the last two valiums I hid in my nightstand.
I am allowed to feel this.
Allowed to hurt.
At least I think I am, and so I sit wallowing in self-pity, my back pressed hard against the door, lungs urgently sucking in air, drying tears that had not yet fallen.
Tonight, it will rain.

Mikey

Chaotic.
That's the only way I can describe the talent show tonight.
What a clusterfuck starting with Tasha and Gale's performance that they had changed last second, to the half-nude bodies of teenaged girls thrusting and dry humping the stage in typical eighties aerobic clothing, parts of the crowd gasping, the rest hooting and hollering.
Gale looked good up there, but cheap as well.

Then there was Laurel who was hellbent on pissing Dad off.
Her makeup was too dark as if she had pressed harder than
necessary at application.
Dad wasn't pleased.
Had her change the dark boots to flats.
Had her tie up her mangled hair, or so she complained to me
when she came in.
She seemed off when we saw each other in the lobby.
Probably high on her last valium.

...

Gale.
What a BITCH.
Bitch.
Making out with Reese behind the gym between our sets.
Like I wouldn't find out.
As if I hadn't cheered her on as she danced like a skank on
that stage in her ridiculous outfit.

It had started innocent enough, six young women on the stage
in skirts and shirts, long neon stockings beneath.
Then the music hit, and the clothes fell only to reveal too-
bright eighties aerobics attire, lime green, and hot pink
leotards with skin-toned tights, teased hair, and cuffs.
Then there were the bouncing bottoms and heaving still not
fully grown breasts that gyrated in a manner a young
woman's shouldn't.
My cock was stiff before the first chorus of Kim Wilde's cover
finished and I'm sure there were many unwelcomed thoughts
in the stuffy auditorium, the rain outside causing the humidity
to swell.

I felt shame burn red.
Shame on myself for not tearing my eyes away.
Still, I wanted to congratulate her; a single flower I had picked
tight in my palm ready to present to her.
Then I saw her, her tongue fighting Reese's, propped against
the rough bricks.

I couldn't help but think back to the way she had teased the floor from her knees, breasts caressing before, flipping to her back, hands pressed firmly to help her hips rise.
Feet clapping together at the top as Kim Wilde whined into the speakers.
 Keep me hanging on.
Suggestive. Luring. Tempting.
I was going to let go.
She was the one who had kept me hanging on, all the while doing Reese behind my back.
Unless this was new but judging by the tonsil hockey, I doubt it.

I rode the anger into my performance and used it to crush the show.
The crowd was enthused by our maneuvers, both content and bummed to have lost seminude dancing girls on the stage in exchange for some guy-on-guy.
I start with the Granby roll.
Dean takes charge performing a tight waist on a poor freshman who has to pay his dues.
Hip throws to take downs, the mat clapping at each visit of our frames.
The last maneuver, anger flooding me, thoughts of what she had said.
So unphased, Reese is desperate to move her off him only to have her pull in more tightly, smiling wickedly.
Proud of her handiwork.
"You were fucking boring, Mikey."

Laurel

Hips swing, fingers fall over mountains of pubescent breasts, the crowd whoops and cheers.
My eyes won't focus.
Body floats into the banisters, my arms clinging.
I don't want to come down.
I watch.
Outside of myself, a mellow high running its course.

Whatever Gale and Tasha were doing must've been out of this
world given the whistles and jeers from the young men in the
crowd, that clouded over some hushed gasps.
Clearly, my father is siding with the young men, totally
focused on the dance while whispering disapproval to Rachel.
The way he beams at the girls.
The way he focuses on their contorting.
The way they simulate sex in a "Dance."
The high isn't enough to keep me there.
I stand up, make my way out of the crowded auditorium, with
several hushed, "Excuse me's," and near falls, I make it to the
welcome silence of the bathroom.
Graced with a lack of women I take my chance to gather my
mind before it runs off on me.

The blue light crackles over the mirrors, a faulty faucet drips
comforting the buzz in my ears.
I pick the furthest stall and shut it, rolling my panties down
around my ankles.
Don't even need to pee but I force it knowing it would seem
odd if I had to leave again before the talent show was up.
I wash my hands, suds scraping the grime out from under my
nails, black bits of eyeliner caught beneath from when I
rubbed my eyes.
Meeting my gaze, I find myself on the verge of tears, I barely
recognize myself, pupils darting, "Get your shit together," I
whisper turning the knob shut.
Stepping out the door catches with a heavy thud, a long hall of
lockers and student-made banners stretch down the long hall
towards the cheers and loud music, Coach Riley's office
nestled between a break in the rows of storage.

"Laurel," his voice calls me to him.
The man I call dad.
Arms crossed over his chest.
Looming at the end of the hall, eyes burning into me.
I walk to him dutifully as I should.

"Your brother is about to be up on that stage, couldn't you
wait?"
I shrug, his hand clasping around mine.
Unprovoked.
Tightening his hand to show how displeased he is with me, he
grits his teeth and snarls, "That's it? Can't give me a proper
answer?"
I yank myself from his grasp, fire in my eyes, his own
growing, "I had to go to the bathroom," my chest heaves the
words.
"Don't test me right now, Laurel," ignoring my explanation he
takes my hand and holds it tight, "I have enough on my mind
right now, and I don't need to have to worry about you too.
Now get your ass back in that auditorium."
I want to scream, but settle for a scowl instead, "You don't
have to control my every move!"

Guess I had crossed a line, and he snaps, cinnamon, cayenne
heat pours into his touch, fist sitting around my wrist.
Disarming me.
I don't pull away this time, knowing it would be a mistake.
His face is like a stone, my body mimicking his face.
Still as a statue I stammer, "I'm…so…sorry."
The anger quickly subsides into something new.
I am not sure what he is capable of anymore and that puts me
on edge.
Releasing, "Don't ever talk to me like that again, Laurel, are
we clear?"
"Yes," I nod in agreement, watching rage flare his broad chest
up and down, his nose, so similar to mine moves towards me,
nostrils fanning.
"Good."

We make it back to the auditorium and watched as my brother
displayed his wrestling maneuvers, face red as Santa Claus.
Then came the choir, singing an a cappella version of Don't
Stop Believing.
Some magic tricks. A disorganized garage bands.
Muffled.

The baton team, twirling and dancing.
Everyone laughs and claps, giddy and impressed.

Silence clouds me as I fight a battle no one can see in my
head.
Little blob like characters trying to take control of my brain.
Blue characters of sadness bobbing around, red hot blobs of
anger meeting those that were green with envy each totting a
sharp blade of destruction.
Seething. Fighting.
The war is bloodying us both.
Forgetting they are all the same flesh.
Taking swipes at those they perceive as others, blood pouring,
skin falling from bones like butter on a hot skillet.
We all bleed as one.
Had forgotten that I am not the enemy.

When it's all said and done a crowd gathers in the foyer to
enjoy cookies and cheap lemonade in the football team's
cylindrical dispensers, yellow bodies stained with little flashes
of black from countless hours on the football field.
I take a sip of poorly mixed lemonade, sweet crystals catching
in my teeth fading from sour too sweet as I wash them away,
the crest of my high wavering.

Kyle waves from the other side of the room, trying to draw me
to him.
Watching on, my father sits distracted at the wrestling booth
selling shirts.
I march right up to Kyle and plant a kiss on his cool cheek,
"Hey."
He looks taken aback, running his mouth to my ear, "Careful,
your dad will see."
Skipping fingers, jumping to his jaw, pulling his mouth to
mine, "I don't care," my heart speaks into the kiss, his spittle
mixing sweetly with mine.
A fleeting feeling of fulfillment and power makes me smile, it
may be short-lived, but it fuels me to take his hand and press
my back to the wall next to him.

"Laurel, I don't want to get you in trouble," doe eyes look over at me full of surprise and apprehension.
"I missed you and I want to enjoy this…please, let me touch you."
With a shaking head he grips more tightly.

We spend the next hour joking and just enjoying each other's company, his sister jumping in towards the end.
"Can you believe that dance?"
Her hair bounces, fake curls tight around her jaw.
"Tasha is getting suspended," I half joke.
She definitely was, I had already seen her getting walked to the principal's office, as the ringleader she was going to get buried, the other cowards dispersed like cockroaches as if the staff didn't know who they were.
"I told her it wasn't a good idea."
"Well, I thought it was great, a big fuck you to the patriarchy and the repression of female sexuality."
Kyle cringes at hearing the words come from his sister.
"I didn't think of it that way," he says.
"I don't think Tasha did either, she was mostly just pissed about the new dress code and her dad…to be fair, I get it."
His sister eyes me, "Please do tell."
"Well, first they put ridiculous lengths on the skirts we could wear, then they banned tank tops. It gets hot, but no one says anything when they guys play skins on the court."
Kyle shakes his head, "It really is bullshit…meanwhile we as guys can wear wife beaters and play skins."
"Then change it," his sister suggests.
"You're the rebellious one."
She jabs him under the ribs, "Enough!"

We stand quietly enjoying each other's body language, in those moments he tells me so much, hands tight, lips pursed, at the end of the get together he walks me to the front of the building and kisses me goodnight, his arms as tightly wound around me as the air of the dark, seeping into every pore.
It leaves me smiling, "Goodnight."

I watch as he departs, interrupted by my father barking at me
to help him grab the leftover boxes inside the atrium,
"Coming."
Dad looks my way lips thinned, full of disgust and
overflowing with jealousy.
Jealous.
Green. Algae. Grass.
Money. Stash.
Stashed away so no man could ever touch me.
If only he had his way.
To hide every inch of my skin, so that he may be the only one
to feast.
White. Pure.
No longer.
Tinted by his hand.

Mikey

Poor circulation blood leaves my pinky thrumming.
Brick wall one.
Micah zilch.
I watched as Gale hopped into his car, grumbling.

Maureen was nowhere to be seen, not that I expected to see
her after Reese had so swiftly dumped her when the truth
came out.
Guess the second trimester wasn't treating her well.
I sat on the step waiting for Rachel who promised me a ride to
William's place after she helped with tear down.
My eyes drift to the car that Reese and Gale had entered, they
weren't going to get far.
I had quickly decided after viewing their grotesque display
that she was going to pay.
Not because it hurt, I mean I could get another one of her any
day of the week.
It was the humiliation that stung me.
For that I had been driven to leave her and Reese a little gift,
one I had concocted during the intermission.

I had paced past the loud gathering in the foyer and watched
on as the line to the bathrooms began to snake.

Using the light from the stadium that was flowing into the hall
windows to guide me to the back of the school where shop
class was taught, I searched.
The room was dark, a little flashlight that was kept for
emergencies sat next to the extinguisher and fisted it, the
deceiving heft taunting me to drop it.
Rummaging through toolboxes to no avail I grow flustered,
only then recalling the wall of nails, each type meticulously
labeled and filed away in clear cubes that were pulled from
their resting places.
Ten-gauge duplex nails.
Perfection.
I pocketed four and marched out, bubbling with revenge
driven excitement.

Gale had parked just beyond the parking lot in the grassy
outskirts.
The lot had been packed early in the night.
Taking the first nail, I pressed it to the side wall of an already
worn tire.
The head burrowed into my thumbs the way men burrowed
into women, with some resistance.
Gasping at the unexpected pain, sucking my thumb, and
repeating the process on the next tires leaving the nail deep
within, I found fulfillment.
I had then patted myself on the back and returned to the
school quickly to blend into the crowd.

Gale and Reese march back to the school demanding to use the
phone so they can contact a tow truck, and all I offer in reply is
an innocent look.
One spare certainly wouldn't help when all four tires were
flat.
I want to laugh but have to
 remind myself that it would be a dead giveaway.

It was obviously me, but they had no way of proving it, so
they kept their lips shut.
The battle was won, a war was brewing.

Laurel

Dirt stings my nostrils as they flare haughtily, my cheek to the
bare ground.
Earth seeps into every pore.
Moist, putrid, worm-laced earth.

Above. Somewhere above me little drops of rain fall easily off
the sheen of red fall leaves, taunting me as they slide off the
fleshy horizons of my lower back.
Exposed. One leg hiked up onto the knee on a hiking trail.
Then as soon as it begins, it ends.
I can tell from the shudder above me.

No lingering.
Spasming rejection on my end.
Then comes an offering. A humiliating one.
He hands me a rough tan napkin as If I had a runny nose, it
had once been crumpled deep in his coat pocket, unused after
a drive thru lunch.
Sandy against my flushed and angered sex, rubbing me the
wrong way.
He watches making sure I'm clean, as I turn to my back and
dab the pleats before lingering on my elbows.
Another offering; his hand.
I have no choice but to take it.
On my feet once more, shoulders hunched.
Impossible to stand tall after being knocked down so swiftly.
I hadn't fallen.
Had laid down willingly knowing what was to come.

Isaac. Sacrificial lamb.
God had not intervened.
I was in my body. Aware that I had grown numb, and that
made it all the stranger.

I didn't close my eyes, but I had become blind.
I didn't close my mouth but was muted.
The click of a button. The undoing.
I hadn't become deaf.
A sense that remained painfully in tune with its surroundings;
creaking branches, the little breaths he sucked in from
exhaustion, the rumbling of deserting thunder beyond the
small hills.
Roll of thunder.
No one hears my cry because it never left my lips, and for that
I am to blame.

I am nothing, no one, nowhere, but also painfully present and
aware.
All alone.
If a girl cries in the woods and no one is around to hear, does
she hurt?
Does God hear? Is he gone?
Was he ever even there?
I scold myself for thinking it when I know the truth.
He was never there to begin with.
Only an illusion of comfort, that refused to bring me even a
hint of solace.

I let go and tried to give myself to reality.
Wet dirt. Thundering skies bellowing greedily all around.
The way the clouds tears feel like wet kisses against the goose
fletchings.
They spider along every inch of my flesh, bubbling, and
ranting with sickness.
Mother earth had abandoned me.
Ignored my wish for her to unleash her roots and swallow me
whole, choosing to watch on in its stead.
Going as far as to taunt me with the call of an owl.
Shunning me with the chattering of insects; gossiping of my
indignation.
Haunting me with the slipping of wet leaves that threaten to
keep me down.

Yet, I had tried to force myself on her with each swaying of
my body that had drawn me closer to her.

So badly I wished to be her,
To be in her. Writhing within six feet of her deep comfort.
I walk back to the truck we're Ava is snoring.
Only metal doors had separated her from a glimpse into the
future, and only time from the pain.
Only a wall away from Rachel.
 A tongue batting away from truth.
Clothing from touch. Skin from organs.

"Sorry," he motions to my clothing, folded in a neat pile on the
passenger seat, my frame shaking and dirtied, "Didn't want to
get your clothes dirtied up."
God forbid.
I pull them back on, dirt scraping against the innards of the
cloth covering my shame.

...

I had been riding my wave on the ride home, or what had
been a ride home at first.
A little detour.
"You can't act like that, Laurel!"
Referring to the kiss I shared with Kyle.
It had been innocent enough.
"I have your best interest at heart, Laurel. I wish you could see
that."
Submission, "Sorry."
.

I felt no fear. Only prominent helplessness.
It wasn't as if I could disagree, being in his truck and all.
His tongue spewed vulgar remarks about Kyle, from the way
he had held my hand, to the kiss.
"Disrespectful. All he wants is to fuck you! You're smart
enough to realize that aren't you?"
Ironic given his own desire to do so.
Then it changed.

Vulgar talk of my beauty, the way I looked, how much he loves the way I smell and taste.

"Laurel, don't you see how beautiful you are? It makes me crazy sometimes seeing you waste what you have."

Auto masochism.

Followed by the lies.

"That's all he wants from you, Laurel, nothing more than your body."

Steering hands pull us off into the wet hills.

Mention of our special bond convinces my thighs to part as his hand slinks against my inner thigh, applying the pressure of a pull.

Calloused hands pulled me from the warm cab.

"Take your clothes off," he had whispered along my neck, hot mouth eliciting a chill to fall down my spine, twisting at another piece of my sanity.

I strip to my undergarments but it's not enough, it's never enough.

 "All of it…the grounds all wet," he had pointed to the saturated leaves.

"Ok."

Cold. Stripped.

"I can't do this anymore," I whisper to myself alone, baring my body to the cold elements.

"I'm going to tell," I cried out, in my head at least.

Pretending certainly alleviates some of those feelings of complacency.

I can't take it anymore.

I'm going to tell.

I can't.

Tell.

I can.

Never tell.

I can take it.

Will never tell.

I can take it all.

The rain picks up, the thoughts wash away.

The dirt slides off my knees, creating a landline of coffee-colored water to slip down my leg as the rain pummels into me, erasing any proof of the night's activities.
Dad sings under his breath at first then more loudly, Ava cooing.
"My little mouse, lost in such a big house," he begins, smiling widely as if the song he used to comfort me would still have the same effect now.
That smile is illuminated by the flashing of light posts as we get into town.
When I ignore him, he takes to heart, "You used to love this song, Laurel! Cheer up and sing with me."
He wants to lighten up the mood and I have no choice but to sing along, muttering solemnly, the words piercing through my sanity.
Tonight, the salt burns my cheeks, hot like acid.
I'm disgusted that he would think this was helpful.
Further perverting what once had been so soothing.
When the song ends, he silences himself, fiddling his hand in his pocket.

...

We're out of milk.
Dad gives me a fistful of bills, through the window, watching as I shake, his hand slow to open, "And get yourself something too."
Trying to buy my silence again.
It's cold inside the market, the AC blasting through the store as if they had forgotten to kill it for fall.
Sterile, flickering lights guide me to the coolers in the back, rumbling in delight as I run my fingers over a couple of expiration dates.
I settled on one that would give us three weeks, knowing full well the gallon wouldn't last one week.
It takes all my effort, and I can barely close my fist around the plastic handle, hands shaking, palms weak.
My high is long gone, I'm now lost in the valleys of low, Death Valley.

I set the gallon on the belt, avoiding the cashier's eyes.
A small wet jumbled ring of some unknown substance sits
dead in the center of the belt.
 "It's sure coming down out there," the feminine voice
comments.
Shame tells me not to look the cashier in the eye, droplets
dripping onto the belt from my mangled hair.
Can't help but wonder if she can smell sex on me.
I struggle to give her some polite acknowledgment, and offer a
nod and a few words of agreement, "It really is."
Paying, I hand her the first of the bills, hands grazing before
returning to my side.
"Thank you, Miss."
There has been no way for me to grab anything but the milk,
taking him up on his offer would have only left me feeling
cheapened, tarnished even.
Tonight, he didn't have to buy me, I had been free, and I'm
sure knowing that wills satisfy him, and I refuse to let him
cheapen me further.
"Bag?"
I nod watching her hide the milk away in plastic before
wrapping it around my hand and stalking off.
The cashier calls back before I make it even halfway to the
door.
A groan leaves my lips as I turn, waiting for some sort of
enlightening revelation or accusation that I had forgotten to
pay despite the rattling change in the pocket of my skirt.
"Your knee is bleeding."

My moss eyes pull down.
A single water drop runs down to my talon from the scraped
skin of my knee.
Offerings of a band-aid. I decline.
Let it bleed.

...

The house Autopilot.

Rachel. Putting up dishes.
Ava. Cartoons. Too loud.
Laughing.
He is laughing.
Rachel. Dad.
Lies.
"I had Laurel run in and grab milk. It was pouring!"
The rain that is.
"Take a shower."
He urges. Demands it. Eyes stern.
Wants to erase all evidence.
Then he embraces her, for arms wrapping around his neck like
an octopus. His eyes never leave mine in that embrace though,
taunting me, playing with my heart, and trying to incite
something sinister within me.
My eyes pool with a potential puddle of pained water.
Devastation is painted all across my brow, but he doesn't
notice.
Or maybe he just doesn't care.
Requests a drink.
The glow of the fridge. Rachel reaches in.
Blur. All a blur.
The creaking of the stairs.
Squeaking of my mattress as I sit on the end.
Nothing. Nothing.
Breathing. Alive?
Nothing. Was my heart no longer beating?
Then, that organ in my chest that acts as a vessel to my being
jumps, snagging in my throat.
Rasping on my door. Knuckles in wood, so familiar, but
forgotten these days.
Father.
A reminder. The dangers of my truth.
My lips must seal.
He would do anything to protect us. Anything.
Even hurt me. He makes it clear.

I am special.
"I love you."

Nothing. Sigh.
Repeats his lie.
Facing the window, I dare speak, "Do you really?"
Unanswered. Door shuts.
Crumble. I want to cry.
But I am *too* big to disintegrate.

Mikey

Green with envy with pale white skin.
Seafoam, crashing blue waves pull me in.
Red throbbing heart. Blackened by sin.
How could she?
The same way I did.
This is different. I'm a man.
It's not my fault, I can't help it.
Not the way she can.

Something snaps.
Fists collapse against the wall.
Rachel walks out a little later.
Silent turns, and frequent stops.
A nod. A shake. Ending, a polite good night.
Rain oozes, the drains slowly bending to small creeks as they
reject the incoming fluid.
Gutters tattered and overfilled, like my mind.
William falls asleep one movie in.
One last cry from the sky.
My chest is heavy.
A tear falls.
Hello. Hello stranger.
Suddenly overcome with dread. 0 to 100.
Needing relief. To calm the chaos in my head.
Sneaking out. Looking for a fight.
Hide and seek.
Barely hidden.
Dropouts and stoners. Skateboarding.
The abandoned car dealership.
They cut me into a hit or three.
The weed feels right.
"Ain't your dad the sheriff?"
Who's your daddy?
This can go one of two ways.

They may kick the shit out of me. They may bail, after all, I could be a narc.
Either way, I welcome the reaction.

Laurel

Green with sickness, pale white skin.
Blue waves pull me under.
Crimson from beneath lost in absence.
Red silent heart, beating to a still. Darkened by sin.
I don't want to feel clean.
Don't deserve to feel clean. Can never be clean.
 I feel nothing because I don't know how to feel.
I feel nothing until my fingers press against my knee.
The sting. Hot like the bite of a fire ant.
I feel. I like it.
Push just a little more.
Filled with relief.
I need more.
This I want to feel.
Still wet. Still muddy. Tattered. Dirtied.

I run the cool edge of the scissors against my outer thigh.
Tip-toeing around my logical brain.
Self-preservation in a state of slumber.
Goosebumps confirm life.
I push.
You wouldn't know it but skin doesn't just break or so I had learned.
Previous run-ins.
It has strength and equal give.
Then there's your stupid brain.
This isn't right.
It hurts. That's kind of the point.

Back to sleep. Shut my protective brain off.
Close my eyes.
It hurts so good.
Push. Push hard.

Drops of red as I press my agony down.
The fruit of my labor. Dilating.
He is leaving me now.
Draining myself of him. Of his touch.
I push again, feel warmth caressing as it escapes the veiny
cage it was restricted to.
His kiss fades. His words are slow.
Crowning. Dig deeper.
Ring of fire. Push.
Deliverance.
I want to fully drain myself of him, but to do that would mean
exsanguination.

Mikey

Hungover.
My clothes smell like smoke and little memories spark across
my vision.
Will tries to shake me awake.
Perplexed, no recollection of my return.
"No way," I protest, turning myself away from incoming light.
He doesn't push.
 I sleep my day away, on the small pull-out.
Last night had proven eventful.
Had to show them I was no narc.
A hit here, a shot of something that burns there. Then came
the pills.
I don't even ask.
Just down one with a swig of vodka.
Take the lighter, torch the pile of newspapers we had gathered
in the center of the old building.
"Guess he's cool," their supposed leader barks, his hands tight
as if he is forcing his cool demeanor.
I guess I'm cool now.

Laurel

As the weekend passes, Rachel allows me to talk to Kyle on
the phone while Dad is out running some errands.

"I'm still grounded from the dance," I inform him, leaving against the aborigine wallpaper that Rachel had picked out. I think it's ugly, but she's pleased so who am I to burst her bubble?

"And I'm not supposed to be going out." Just another way to control me.

He seems disappointed, "I know, but it doesn't make me miss you any less."

Shared sentiment.

"Me too, but I think I'm going to go to the dance, anyway."

No response, I sway, my bare feet pressing into the linoleum tiles, pinky spreading.

"Did you hear me?"

He breaks the silence, "Maybe it's not such a good idea."

"Kyle, what's going on?" I ponder, my gaze locking in the mess of alphabet letters strewn about the white fridge face.

I can only question the hesitation when I was sitting here excited at the notion of spending an evening dancing in his arms.

Kyle is keeping something from me.

"Please talk to me."

The line grows fuzzy for a moment, and I hesitate to push him. It hurts for me to plead, I'm a hypocrite wanting his full-blown honesty and returning none.

On the other end, he sucks in a deep breath.

"Um… so your dad showed up at my house to talk to my mom the other day. He told her that I need to stay away from you and that I'm a distraction… I think he hates my guts."

He didn't!

Of course, he did!

I feel queasy, cold sweat pulsating and seeping from every pore.

"Kyle, I'm so sorry."

Guilt rises speedily in my throat as acidic bile.

"He was acting weird, then he pulled me over and gave me a ticket because I had a taillight out…he seemed pissed… and well I shouldn't say it," his breath hitches over the line.

I can't believe it.

Can't believe he would stoop so far into his blatant and now obvious jealousy.

This isn't just disapproval, it's control.

"And what?"

I wait as if what he wants to say is too hard to get out.

"I won't be mad, Kyle." *Just furious.*

The assurance is all he needs to open up.

"Like jealous."

His mask was starting to fall, coming undone, and people were taking notice.

I can't allow that to happen.

"It was really weird."

"I'm sorry Kyle, I really am. He is just under a lot of stress at work."

He doesn't mention it again, instead, he gets ballsy, and we plot.

"How about we hang out the night before the dance? I can take you home from your babysitting gig."

The Moore kid. Super sweet. Early bedtime.

"That would be nice."

"Maybe after that, I can drop by and knock on your window after your parents leave for the night?"

I had been thinking about it since his last visit even if it was just to cuddle, it would be worth it.

"They aren't going out until the night of the dance, I remind him."

I twist the long cord in my fingers, a grin crawling on my lip, the wind whistling happily outside the cracked kitchen window.

"We would need to be careful Laurel, which means you'll have to be quiet."

He was right, I couldn't imagine the nightmare that would unfold if Dad walked in hoping to use me to chase some sort of sick release, only to find Kyle and I crossing that line already.

There would be no way to explain away the presence of either man to the other.

Mikey

The beauty of being single is the lack of guilt I feel sneaking
around with Tasha.
We had maintained our distance since the night, up until
now.
The day after Gale and I split, I called her up and to my
surprise, she agreed to meet me at the movies.
Of course, that meant driving to the next town over to
minimize any interaction with people we know.

A long majority of the evening was spent with her looking
over her shoulder as if Dean might just be standing yards
away with binoculars and a notepad ready to bust us like
some crazed investigator.
She only stopped when I kissed her hard, the rain drizzling
around us, her body pressed along the door of her car.
"William was my ride up, can you spare a few minutes," I
asked.
"Yeah, but let's be careful…Dean," she panted my tongue,
flicking along the sensitive flesh of her collarbone.
I couldn't care less if Dean saw.
Yeah, he would probably kick my ass, but Tasha was certainly
worth it.
All woman, never stifling her heavy panting and kitten-like
groans that spill from those luscious painted lips every time
my head dips below.
I could read her like a book, an easy one that had little script
but packed a lot of volume.
Unlike Gale, Tasha is straightforward with what she wants,
and what she wants is to be treated like a princess.
No, not a princess, a queen.

Just last night, I picked her up after her dad left for work and
took her to the next town over in Laurel's car.
The price was a heavy one.
Weeding the garden, which had been her chore, but I would
do close to anything to get laid.

Worth every penny I dropped on dinner that night which consisted of steaks and sides and set me back a couple of days' work.
"So."
Eyebrows rise quizzically, "So, what?"
Tasha pushes the knife into her rare steak, blood and salt oozing from various pores.
I wish she would cut into me like that, make me bleed, expose my rawest bits.
A tiny morsel pushes past her lips, teasing at dessert.

Chewing on both steaks and thought she swallowed hard, "So what exactly happened with you and Gale?"
The question should bother me, but it does not.
Sure, I'm pissed, but it's nothing, a couple flattened tires and roadkill had not fixed.
It was such a thrill picking up that dead raccoon off the road knowing full well what I intended to do with it.
The poor creature got a proper burial in a cardboard gift box, topped with a gaudy pink bow.
A little parting gift suited for a spoiled little bitch like Gale.
Hearing her shriek was the cake, watching her uneasy stomach heave and chunks fly from her lips thin lips was the ice cream on top.
I laughed the entire drive home. Hope Reese knocks her ass up too.

"You haven't told me anything other than she was cheating, which to be fair… so did you," the woman takes a long sip of soda from her straw, cheeks staying plain and golden, not a blush in sight.
Blunt, my own cheeks grow red, "Ouch!"
I take my own drink, "Fair enough. I did cheat…as did you."
"I'm no better, I know that," she mumbles, sawing another bite of steak before pressing it against a sugary sweet mound of maple sauce, "I mean Dean, he's great and all but…" she trails off.
"But what?"

This is what I want to hear, Tasha tear into the golden boy, those deadly arched brows climbing steadily.
"But… I…" she pauses to gather her thoughts, deep breath, "There's something about you, I can't really describe it other than it feels…dangerous."
I bite down on my own juicy steak, "Does that turn you on?" I ask knowing full well I was no hard ass.
Fire ignites in her honey orbs. Need.
I feel it too, mounting, my need to kiss her, consume her.
"You might find out just how dangerous I am after dinner…but not before dessert," eyes darting across the dessert menu, "and paying that is."
I was going to need to pick up some extra shifts to cover this.

The date ends in the back of Laurel's car, foggy windows and heavy breathing.
We nestled ourselves between some trees up in the hills and I quickly nestled myself between Tasha's already parted thighs embracing her harshly. Her outfit has no give, and I respect that.
She says she isn't ready yet, but I still want to taste her and find some intimacy.
I'm not sure If I can love but I imagine it might feel something like this.
Wet, compact, her kissed traveling along the bridge of my nose, pausing on a sun created freckle.
We spent the next half hour snuggled uncomfortably along the back seat of the car, old rock droning through the stereo, talking happily.
We split a joint, the bottom too small, and we have no clip.
Throwing it out the window does not seem right; God forbid some kid finds it or some animal scurries away with it.

"How's Laurel? " Genuinely concerned, she asks.
Buzz kill.
Who the fuck wants to think about their sister after making out with her best friend?
Still, I entertain her. "She's ok, I guess."
Truth is she barely leaves her room.

Refuses to talk to me on anything other than a surface level.
"I've been so busy lately, being grounded and all that I haven't
been much of a friend, I admit," Tasha begins planting a kiss
on my neck, it roots deep, filling me, "But she also seems
withdrawn. Like she's hiding something."
I have no idea what to say.
On one hand, I cannot betray Laurels trust, but I want to share
everything with Tasha so it will stop weighing on me.
"I'm probably just reading too much into it. That or I feel
guilty."
My fingers run down her spine, one vertebra at a time, "You
definitely did not feel guilty a few minutes ago," I tickle along
her ribs now, cupping bare breasts, giving her a squeeze.
"Seriously."
A huff, a sigh, knowing I could not ignore her concerns when I
had the ability to keep this night going, I give.
"Also how are you out right now if you're grounded?"
"Dads at work," she reminds me, annoyance in her glare.
I huff, knowing I could not ignore her concerns when I had the
ability to keep this night going.
"Ok, you want my honest opinion?"
I decided not to lie but lying and omitting are not equivalent.
"Laurel is just under a lot of stress lately. She and my dad are
butting heads."
"What do I do?"

Longingly she runs her fingers over the cool of her necklace, a
bronzed Libra sign.
Genuine concern presses her forward.
I think it out, debating how to ease my way around the horrid
truth.
"Just go say hi tomorrow…she could definitely use a day out."
Little drops of rain knock along the top of the car, reminding
us it was time to head out, "Let me get you home."
With a groan she slinks up, pulling her leopard print tube top
up her waist to cover her bouncy breasts, gold rivers of her
earrings dripping down into her messy hair, "Will you come
by soon?"
"If you want, I will sneak back over tonight."

Pushing my luck.
"I would love that."
Smiling, she throws her hair in a bouncy bun, thick strands begging to snap the band.
"Ok, one condition though."
My hands grasp loosely at my shirt, discarded in the darkness between the seats, "Well actually two. The first being you promise not to hog the blankets."
My woman arches her back, letting a small yawn slip through her pretty lips.
"No promises…what's the second?"
My fingers grip the butt of our joint, her lanky fingers topped with golden flecks and black bands like bits of nummite cover her natural nail, clasp it.
"Get rid of this."

Laurel

I am exhausted.
Can't stand the thought of getting out of bed, let alone actually get out of bed.
Overcome by the heavy boulder of depression that seems to perpetually crush me.
Even breathing is difficult.
My brain is taking over.
Confusion.
I was overcome by the perpetual crushing weight of depression from the heavy boulder. Overwhelmed by the heavy boulder of depression that perpetually crushes met nothing more than to disappear but instead I stick out.
Everyone describes depression as blue, the darkest blue.
But it isn't blue, it's red, deep red and violent.
Overpowering.
Strong.
Bright and searing into me.
Keeping me down.
I hide my pain, draping it in fabric.
No one would understand so why worry them?

I had tried to convince my father to drop Kyle's charges or just to revoke the ticket, but he claimed it was too late and then things got really strange.

His jealousy brewed then hit with the violence of a hurricane, blowing everything out of proportion.
"What about me, Laurel? Don't you care about me and how it would look if I just dropped my daughter's boyfriend's ticket?"
"He isn't my boyfriend!"
His eyes grew wide like an owl then, his lips tight like an angry gash that bled only foul dialogue.
"If he isn't your boyfriend then what is he? Tell me, Laurel! You slept with him, didn't you?"
A blur of tears clouds my vision.
 Anger was driving him mad, jealousy, spitting, "Don't you dare lie to me Laurel! Just because you let him disrespect you and you have a little crush, doesn't mean I have to help, that boy is not above the law," he dropped his tone for a moment as if he had to prepare himself for what came next.
I freeze, no way to answer.
"If you love me the way you say you do, you will let this go."
With that he had slammed the door shut, leaving me alone in my room, then the house, his car starting up and peeling out in a cloud of dusty smoke.
I spent the rest of the day between bouts of crying and angry pouting.
That night I apologized to him after dinner and placed a gentle kiss on his cheek, the type a wife would offer her husband after a fight, full of anger and understanding that this was the way to peace.
"I love you."
He huffed a "sure," that made me long for his true forgiveness and the love he had once offered.
"Dad," I half whispered, "I said I love you."
He didn't reply with a confirmation of shared love, rather he ushered me to bed leaving me desperate for his approval, knowing full well that withholding his love would drag me right back to him.

I know what he's doing and still it hurts.
I'm tired of being his toy, but I so badly want him to wind me up and watch me dance.
Instead, he slams the lid shut.

...

Rachel knocks before entering my room with offerings of a peanut butter and jelly sandwich cut into rectangles.
"You missed lunch."
"I'm tired and my head hurts."
She sighs, sets the plate down on the white desk, "You've been saying that a lot lately."
"I'm sick…probably just a bug," I changed my story so she would leave.
None of it is a lie.
Sick. Tired. Bloated. Depressed. Uncomfortable. Anxious.
Rachel is sweet, and it makes it hard to get her to leave and seeing as how she is so kind, I can't just tell her straight up that I just want to be left alone.
"Can we talk?"
"I did the dishes already, and Mikey is doing the weeds for me."
Head bobs, "I'm not here about the chores, Laurel."
Too bad.
"I'm just worried."
I wave her off, "There's nothing to worry about, ok?"
My voice is bitter and cold, hands perched around my robe clad body.
"I think there is Laurel, and I don't want you to feel like I'm trying to force anything out of you," stopping, she fights back a tear, "I'm trying, Laurel, and I'm worried about Mikey, too. The way you stormed out of the pool at the hotel, it scared me."
She pulls the vanity chair and plops down, I turn from my unkempt bed to face her, "That was nothing. We fight sometimes."
"Twins," Rachel tries to joke.
"Something like that."

She can tell this is getting nowhere, stands to her feet, hoisting the barely full plate up, "Eat this and bring the plate down when you finish."
Conversation avoided.
I instantly chirp up, "I will, and I'll probably get on pulling those weeds then."
Smiling as if she had accomplished something, she begins to strut victorious, "Leave the weeds to your brother."
Daughter stepmom bonding and all that.

Mikey

I catch Laurel doing my agreed upon chore, hands digging through the dirt, nose wrinkling as I kneel next to her.
Completely spent from the night I had spent with Tasha, I slump.
After I had dropped her off, I parked Laurel's car, made an appearance at the house as proof I was home at curfew and excused myself to bed.
Once the house grew silent, I made my escape and jumped out of my window, checking to make sure dad and Rachel's room was dark.
The roads had been slicked with rain, darker than night, and my bike skied quickly through the slippery top with a goal to reach.
I pedaled the required distance, each mile bringing me closer to Tasha and her soft skin.

Tapping on her window her shadow shuffled behind heavy curtains, rain dripping from my hair, heavy on my clothing.
Extending her hand, I climbed in, pulling my coat off, before shuffling through my pant pockets for the joint I had brought for the occasion.
"Get showered," her nose had crinkled. "You smell like a wet dog."
My body met the shower with speed, tossing some of her body wash across my chest, drowning it along my length, before rinsing off and killing the water.

When I got back to her room, Tasha was sprawled across ruby satin sheets, completely naked, hair falling loose, my joint pressed to her lips.
Little billows of smoke clung to her.
I did not hold back, climbed over her, nipping every inch of bare skin, focusing specifically on her tender spots; the curve of her breasts, the left one being more tender, the spot right below the lobe of her ear, her inner thigh. Kissing sweetly, I want her to know how I feel.
In real life she's all-powerful, in love, she's sweet and submissive, a delicious, stark contrast.
That one always left her gasping, pleading for me to give her more.
I always give her more.
"I'm sorry."

A couple good moments with my sister's best friend and I was feeling a twinge of guilt. For many things, I apologized to Laurel before I left, including pool.
Starry moss bores into my own, lips parting to accept my apology, "OK."
Plunging fingers descend beneath the roots of some ground ivy before hooking and pulling up, Laurel tosses a dandelion into the pile behind her.
"Dad's pumpkins are getting big."
Five bulbous, fairytale pumpkins lie only yards away beneath a sprawling spruce, with a few more weeks to go.
Their tops hadn't exactly rounded perfectly but they would be perfect as Halloween decorations.
"When do you think we should pick them?"
"Whenever they round out, I guess."
I catch her focusing on them, "Is that how that works?"
With a shrug, we retreat into silence.

...

Simultaneous hall passes lead to a delightful accident.
Kyle, pacing down the hall from chemistry as I leave math.
"Follow me."

I do.
Excited hands pull me under the gym bleachers, "Fancy meeting you here," he jokes, inciting a furious strawberry blush to spread across my chest.
"Are you stalking me?"
I push us further beneath the bleachers as a precaution, "Not at all, I would never be able to watch you silently from afar.
"You are much too tempting," hands pull through my free strands of hair, my own hands mimicking, pulling his beanie free into my fingers.
"Good, because this is much better than watching," I say my nose gently nuzzles his as his fingers scoop beneath my chin, sending sparks floating.
I feel him nuzzle back, our lips brushing ever so gently.
He teases me, the seconds ticking by our lips so close yet worlds apart.
I can't take it anymore.
Yanking his hair I press him against me, my lips parting with no struggle and I find myself lost in the sweet kiss.
Nothing sexual about it, just loving and it feels good to be loved.
Truly loved.

Hot cinnamon liquid mixes with my mouth, my tongue pressing against his.
I love him, but I won't say it.
Wish he knew just how much.
He pulls away planting another kiss on the tip of my nose, "We should go," the words jumble out of his mouth as if he had forgotten how to speak.
Desire is laced beneath my ribs, and I wish we were somewhere quiet so he could hold me.
Above us the bleachers shake, his hand clasping mine, a grin along his lips, "Like now," sheepishly he whispers.
We ran out avoiding capture, and giggling.

...

I dream of Kyle.

A warm field, cotton candy sky above us, filled with puffy
peach and strawberry clouds that seem frozen in time.
Watermelon flashes across my exposed chest, warm hands like
the sun hiking the curves of my body till they meet sweet
cherry mounds.
He is the sun.
I am a sunflower.
My growth depends on him and the wet rains my body
releases at his beckoning.
Body turning to him. Dependent.
Tracing his every move.
Swallowed down.
Pitted, blushing raspberries, ripe for picking between those
snow-white teeth.

He works below, harvesting the golden silk crop.
I feel like I might lose it, fully aware that I am dreaming.
Sadly, I welcome it.
Just a little more would have me shaking, another lap of the
tongue, another sly grin.
But the sky turns away from the colorful painting that had
lingered above mere moments ago.
Slate. Silence.
The air is heavy.
Sweet bluegrass now crawling with vermin and pests.

Kyle is gone now and the warm sweet wet that had been
trickling from between my thighs had changed into a torrent
of polluted water.
Above a crescent shadow covers half my face.
Lingering.
The cool metal of a scythe glimmers with intention.
"Time to harvest," the figure moans slowly, sweeping the
metal against my helpless skin, and the flowing water of my
sex thickens and runs as red as the devil.
"Time to harvest." I nod.
"Time to get up."
I'm not sure what it means so I stand on my feet, my toes
caressing now bristling grasses.

"Time to get up," a familiar voice chants above, it lingers in the swirling clouds, only this time I'm not dreaming anymore.

Alarm blaring, flat on my back, barely able to breathe.
"Laurel get up, you're going to be late," my father tells me from my door frame, fixing his badge against his puffed-out chest before reaching to fix his belt, smiling widely as if he knew something I wasn't privy to.
He grins teasing implication, my nightgown still on, panties intact, and yet I find myself paranoid with assumption.
I flash him eyes that beg for answers, void of any strength.
Content with the way I squirm he leaves silent.
Fear. Unknown.

I proceed to break down the moment he leaves the room.
I'm sure, even now, he's smiling.

. . .

 There are all sorts of whispers going around the school about Mikey.
"Did you hear he threw rocks at some bum?"
What was that about?
Dean whispers, "Some dropouts said he set fire to the old car dealership."
Tasha scoffs, "They ruled that as an accident."
"I totally heard from someone who was there that he was beating up some poor hobo," Christy McCallister stutters to Manuela who feigns interest, her eyes jumping to Tasha as if she knew that she and Mikey were sneaking around.
I leave the group, uncomfortable, arms tight against my chest.
"What's going on?"
It comes across as a hiss as I stand by his locker, right next door, eyes filled with fire.

The morning had started rough, the day not getting any better.
Mikey glares at me as if he had no idea what was going on.
My fingers wrap around metal, turning the dial on my locker, waiting for some justification or denial on my twin's end.

"Well, it sounds like people are gossiping, Laurel," my brother
tells me, grinning a toothy smile, "as they always do."
"What if dad hears?"
My eyes scan for my history book and the references that I had
completed just the day prior.
It was time to apply to colleges, but Mikey didn't seem
concerned or even motivated.
"I figure I let them talk and eventually someone does
something stupid or embarrassing and it will all blow over."
Down the hall Gale begins to strut towards my brother, cheap
burgundy boots and tight jeans squeezing her shapes.
Trouble.
"What about the fire?"

Sucking in a breath he sees her a smirk growing across his
mouth that says a lot more than I can decipher from my
position.
"Quit it," I snapped, warning him to quit causing trouble.
He rolls his eyes, "They can't prove anything, plus, the fire
was an accident," my brother winks the words, "and nothing
is tying me to it."
"And if dad finds out?"
I pull the book and jam it into my book bag.
"What's he going to do anyway?"
I shudder at the thought.
"Hmmm… I don't know, maybe throw you through another
table," sarcasm drips, laden heavily on my tongue, "or worse
yet he might just lose his shit for good this time and take
things further. You need to stop getting into trouble because-."
He cuts me off, gripping my free hand, shocking me,
desperately I try to rip my hand away, but he holds tight.
"Because what?"
I feel selfish saying it, so I shut up.
"Come on Laurel, you were about to say something," his voice
drops low, eyes suspiciously gazing out in case anyone was
rubbernecking. "Just this once save us all the trouble and use
your voice."
Quick to reply, low, my voice half muted.
"He might take it out on me, Mikey," weakly I whimper.

I think back to my wake-up call.
He had just been able to waltz in and fuck with my head.
It makes me sick.

"Nothing?"
I don't come right out and say it, but he already knows,
pleading eyes searing into him, "Please, just stop."
"I can't fix it, Laurel, not if you don't let me."
He releases my hand; I don't mean to but the salty waters of
pain form and sit on the edge and for the second time today I
find myself crying feebly.
"Maybe I don't know how to ask," my wobbling lips spout.
I don't even know what I'm asking.
His head shakes, "You just did."

Mikey

My father does not find out about the fire. I doubt he would
give a damn unless it directly affected his reputation or
embarrassed him somehow.
Most of the time it seems like it may be easier for him to just
ignore the problems rather than confront them head-on.
Lately, he has been pushing college brochure after brochure
my way urging me to start applying.
I tell him I will or that I had when the truth is that I spend
most afternoons messing around.

I don't get what the rush is, there's nothing to worry about, I
go to wrestling, his stupid therapy sessions and my grades are
remarkable, I'm holding down a part-time job.
My grades are a good reflection of him and his status.
Not a B in sight.
All too easy.
The bigger issue at hand is Laurel worrying about my
extracurriculars.
Worrying about what I was spending my weekends doing
rather than learning how to stand up for herself.

Shit, if she doesn't do something quick, I might have to, I mean she practically begged for my help.
The way she looked at me this afternoon was sad, gut-wrenching even.
So fragile.
Fragile things tend to break, and she is beginning to crack.

Laurel

Sneaking off with Kyle to the movies makes my heart race erratically.
A cheap comedy that incited nothing but equally cheap laughs, that was aimed to help the producers break even.
The real film was the one that was developing between Kyle and me and Dean and Tasha made out ferociously in the row behind us as we chose to hold hands and let the anticipation build for the post-movie.
Sad that she still felt the need to balance Dean and Mikey.

Midway through I get up, make my way to the bathroom.
My pants pool around my ankles, I free recycled water from my bladder and glance down.
Pride fills me as I beam down, my handiwork begins to scab.
Four jagged lines run my outer thigh.
I dance my fingers over them.
Raised.
It fills me with excitement. Turns me on.
Soothes every ache. Triggers my guilt.
This isn't normal.
This will not be my norm.
Never again.

As I wash my hands, I see a shadow behind me.
My heart jumps three beats.
"God! You scared the shit out of me Tasha!"
She giggles, pulling out a phallic tube and applying a shade of electric purple that made the cheetah print dress jump out.
As if her look required any more attention.
I feel so plain next to her.

She offers the tube to me, "I doubt I can rock that," my hands decline the offer, gently nudging it away before I throw soap on my hands.
"Suit yourself."
The soap foams, building with each move of my hands, a flatulent sound escaping the squeezed palms, Tasha giggles.

"So, what's the plan after this? I was thinking maybe we could all take a quick trip up to the hills. Maybe let me and Dean sneak off into the woods, I'll leave the car to you and Kyle," she winks.
I think about how risky that would be.
"I can't, I have to sneak home before my dad realizes I'm out with Kyle. Rachel is covering, but she is only willing to take that so far."
Tsking, "Fine but can you at least do me one big favor?"
She pulls a piece of stiff brown paper towel and dabs the corners of her mouth, puckering and releasing with a loud pop.
"Sure."
"Can you come with me to the clinic tomorrow? I'm fresh out of refills of my pill and they want to do a pap before I get the refill and honestly, it kind of scares me."
My turn to tsk, "It's not like you're a virgin."

As if the two correlate.

Her box braids swing as she faces me, "It's totally different. Plus, you're my friend and we should stick together."
She's right.
"Plus it wouldn't hurt for you to get on the pill yourself."
Incredulous at her usual invasive tongue I turn to her, "Kyle and I are not having sex right now," I blurt, instantly regretting my admission.
Her eyes roll, big with big eyelashes, "But you have had sex Laurel, and you will again. It's not like we plan these things out, and right now being pregnant would be an absolute nightmare."
I agree.

Consider her offer.

...

The clinic is cold and sterile, overwhelming even.
If he somehow caught me here, I would probably never leave
the house again.
Worse yet, he might find a way to humiliate or punish me, and
I had been desperate to hold my ground, but it's all crumbling
now and I just don't know how much more I can bear.
All around are posters depicting the female anatomy and
displays for all sorts of birth control methods.
Resource pamphlets litter the stark white counters of the
freezing lobby.
Across from me, a young mother cradles her swollen belly, her
foot tapping, fingers mindlessly swiping through a glamour
magazine.

They call Tasha back She jumps to her feet with anticipation.
"Can my friend come back with me?"
The insurance card gets handed through a glass window, a
metal box lining up with the frail receptionist who nods a
simple yes.
Her lips were brown and thin like some sort of dried-up
worm.
The thought makes me shiver.
Those nasty squirming, eyeless, phallic insects, it makes my
gut churn and always has me dreading the rain, when they all
find a way from the dirt and find themselves suspended in
stinking, retained water.

I follow Tasha back a quarter of an hour later, her hips
sashaying down the narrow hall in her denim skirt,
completely unphased by our environment and the charts of
the female anatomy.
When her time came, I held her hand through the pap, feet
pushed hard against the metal stirrups, her body dangling
down.

"It wasn't that bad. I think I was just nervous is all," she tells me after my car pulls up to the drive-thru window.
"Yeah, but the cramps will kick in soon, that's the hard part," I tell her, recalling my pap, and how bad the post-pap cramping had been that evening, or how bad my heart ached when I found out I was sick.
Salivating at the thought of a burger and fries I push thoughts of the afternoon from my brain and grow excited.
"I mean I'm glad it doesn't need to be done again for a few years, but I was expecting much worse."
I disagree.
The first sight of the speculum and the light were enough to make me wish I had a penis; the thought alone has me flushed.
It was hard accepting being probed and dehumanized for some test I figured was useless for someone my age.

We stop and grab coffee at the market as we wait for her prescription to be filled.
I had been tempted to get my own but the fear of my dad finding the packet in my room turned my mind back to sainthood fairly quickly.
We sip from cheap steamy cups dressed in brown sleeves as we wait for her number to be called.
"Damn."
"What is it?"
Tasha's face scrunches up, "Cramps…fuck."
"I told you so."
They had made it clear that it was probable for the next twenty-four hours.
Sliding fingers reach into my purse clasping a smooth plastic top. I pull a pain pill free, "Here, take one."
"I knew I chose you as my best friend for a reason!"
That brings a smile to my face.

Coffee and a painkiller are all it takes to get her talking.
The gossip was that her dad had now found God and quit drinking.

"He joined these groups, can't complain. I mean he quit
drinking, which makes it hard to sneak a few swigs of his
quote-unquote emergency bottles. It's pretty annoying."
The hot bitter bean swoops over my tongue, "Why?"
She downs the rest of her coffee and tosses the cup just
missing the bins opening, "He is boring now, always trying to
drag me to church and shit and it's only been like a few
weeks."

Finishing my cup, I toss mine to join hers, "What, you don't
like church music?"
My best friend teases right back, "God is dead, even the Times
knows that, and for the record, church music does suck."
"Speaking of men and their desire to worship things that don't
matter, can I complain about something?"
Not as if she hadn't already been complaining, but I don't try
to stop her, I just listen as she recounts how little appreciation
Dean has for her body and how he isn't glorifying her in the
way she most desires, oral sex.
"I just feel like he doesn't want to go down on me, and I have
no idea how to ask because," she blushes furiously, noticeable
even under her glowing dark skin, "because it's embarrassing,
and with Mikey-."

Tensing I envision my brother and my best friend, no idea
how to respond as she stops just short of telling me that my
brother is a giver, which makes me blush.
I work hard to muster something up to assure her that I care,
"Well, if he doesn't want to go down on you just quit going
down on him. I promise he will notice, and he won't like it."
"You are a genius!"
Curiosity drives me now, "Are you telling me that he has
never done it?"
She shakes her head affirmatively, "Couple times…and he was
so quick about it."
My bottom starts to grow numb on the rigid plastic.
Her face scrunches again, "I hope they hurry, that pill isn't
cutting it."

She begins to say something else when the pharmacist calls her number through the speaker system.
By the time we head home, we end up skipping lunch, her cramps hitting her hard.

Mikey

The rumor mill catches fire as word gets around that I was at the quarry.
Gale.
It had to be Gale planting petty seeds of revenge.
Dad flips.
"Gale called and told me everything."
Confirmation.
Explosions of anger flare out, he accuses me of being less than a man and a liar, which is rich coming from him, and I imply as much.
Rachel is not in sight; I can be honest, and my knowledge scares him.
His arm squeezes tight around my arm as he pulls me in landing a sloppy punch right in my gut.
I keel over into a ball, panting to find air.

When I do emerge anger clouds my better judgment and his chants of my weakness and disrespect leave me with only one choice; to fight back.
My hands press against his chest sending him hurling backwards, back thumping against the wall.
Retaliation, his fist making contact above my right eyebrow, blood instantly spurting into my eye.
That was going to leave a mark, a big goose egg.
It ends right there.
I was going to need to be more careful.

Laurel

There was a definitive shift in Dad's personality.
Spiraling.
Fast.

The man I call dad had put his hands on my brother; although
I hadn't seen it happen this time.
Didn't need to.
There was plenty of evidence.
Mikey wears a beanie that does little to hide the swelling
along his cracked eyebrow for the rest of the week.

Mikey

I feel.
Or at least I think I do.
Not anger. It's humiliation that leaves me writhing.
He had decked me like a coward and left it at that.
I am not keen to end it there.
Yearn to take him man to man.
Well, see who is still standing by the end of it.
He had left me feeling powerless.
Is this how Laurel feels?
No wonder she chooses silence.
Powerlessness leading to the waving of a white flag.
Why put up a fight if the result is the same?
Why fight when there is no winning?
Why swim when you are bound to drown?

Energy lost. But not me.
I am going to fight.
It's time he gets knocked off his throne.

Laurel

Hiking in the woods behind my house on a crisp October day
allows me to breathe and clear my head as I make my way to
the small clearing.
Kyle is already there at our agreed meeting spot, his hot
breath steaming up the cold cobalt sky.
Flattened white clouds dispersed randomly.
"I got to be quick."
He nods, "I hate sneaking around like this."
"But I'm worth it though…right?"

It's less playful than he thinks, I need the reassurance. Twinkling with emotion I push myself into his arms, a welcome release, "You are," he says honestly as his nose caresses my hair breathing me in deep.

"How was your trip to the clinic?"

Giggling, I eye him, "Strange," I admit pulling free from his grasp and recount everything from the pill to Tasha's confession.

That part makes Kyle laugh, "I always assumed as much," he says, in reference to Dean.

"Why?"

Kyle sits down, back to the large tree, the sun teasing a disappearing act behind their sprawling branches, "Well the other day he asked me how to give a girl oral."

Laughing I join him, "Really?"

"Hey now, you women can be intimidating and well…. we aren't inherently born to know how to please you."

"Fair enough, but you don't seem to have an issue with it," my eyes jump to him waiting for a reaction.

I get one, his chest puffing as he sucks in cold air, "Tease."

"Tell me more."

"It turns out he has only ventured down below once because he is that nervous about it."

I never imagined Dean being the type of guy that didn't at least try, but now I have two people telling me as much.

In fact, we had watched him excel for years from the football field to the wrestling mat, never giving an inch.

Kyle tries to end it there, but the conversation has begun to turn me on, heat tingling in my core, "Did you tell him how to do it?"

Lips pursed together, "Huh?"

His hands are on my thick sweatpants, poking a small hole near my knee as if he is trying to stay in control of himself.

"Did you tell him how to do it?" I repeat the question with much more assertion.

"A little but I don't think I'm an expert or anything."

"You're good at it," I inform him, running my index finger along his neck before sinking it into the shirt beneath his jacket, teasing his collarbone.

"Laurel," he threatens with a sharp bit of air falling from his mouth.

"At least, I think you are."

Blushing, "I try."

Curling my tongue, I dare ask, "So what did you tell him?"

He senses my intention, pulls my finger to his mouth and runs it over his lower lip before puckering and kissing it, "Just that it takes patience, and that you need to listen. Women don't always tell you what they want directly, It's usually more subtle. So, I just told him to listen to the way she breathes and the sounds she makes."

My heart pace begins to quicken, thumping violently against the too many layers I am wearing.

"It's usually a pretty good indication of whether you are hitting the right spots or not."

I recall the way his mouth felt on me, wishing he was there now, "Is that how you do it?"

"Is your head in the gutter now?"

Affirmative head nod, "It has been for a while."

It's lower than the gutter, I'm flustered.

With my finger still on his lip I feel him vibrate with a growl, "I know…so has mine."

The woods come to life around us, trees crackling from the icy breeze, our breath inciting a veritable smokestack as it contacts the air.

Above a squirrel runs between branches, frantically storing away an acorn.

"I can't help it," I whisper, straddling him, his hands in mine, quick to pin them up against the rough bark of the big elm we find ourselves under.

Small flakes fall like snow as our skin contacts its trunk, catching the fading sunlight.

"Laurel, what are you doing," Kyle poses, his chest rising and falling, lips trying to touch mine, only to find my grasp tightening against his pulse, "Not yet."

He begins to complain but I silence him quickly, using my free hand to pull my breasts free, my shirt still covering my lower abdomen.
"God Laurel, what are you trying to do?"
Palming one of my breasts, the other in my hand I find relief, freedom even.
Momentary, sure.
"Take control. Cherish a rare moment with you," I tease, tweaking a free nipple, rolling it between my fingers, groaning as I do so.

Not my intention but nonetheless it elicits a response from Kyle, his lips tight as if he is trying hard to not flip me off him.
"Ok Laurel, you're in control," he admits.

We play around, but it doesn't take long for him to crumble.
"I'm sorry…it's just been a really long time since we did anything like that and-,"
 My hips are still rocking on the slowly dissipating length, finger pressing to his lip, canyoning them.
"Don't be."
Plucking a nipple between his teeth he sucks gently, his hand plunging back down, allowing me to determine my own rhythm.
Climbing.
Releasing.
"Sorry if that was disappointing."
"You didn't disappoint. Not one bit," my tongue strokes at his ego, and then along his bottom lip.
I move my shirt back up over my pert breasts, the cold air uncomfortable without his soothing swallow against me.
Standing, I rearrange myself and pull on my sweats, running my fingers through my hair.
The hike had likely gone on long enough.

"I was thinking before you go that maybe we should talk."
Hate that.
The implication that something may be wrong.

I have to remind myself that there wasn't going to be anything
back given our activities.
Those words rarely come free of negativity.
The same phrase Daddy had used when he informed us that
Mom was sick.
The same words he used after she had died.
What teachers preface a punishment with.
In those cases, there was rarely a talk, at least not one that
went both ways.
Much more of a listen.

"What about?"
I look overhead, a little squirrel running off a branch, flying to
the next tree over.
"The clinic. Maybe we should consider some form of birth
control?"
He almost looks guilty asking me, "I mean condoms are great,
and I can wear them, but I don't want to risk hurting you if
something went wrong and one broke...and last time we had
sex. That was risk."
Sincere as always.
"Tasha could go with me."
"Or I could... that way we can see what our options are."
 Our?
Is he serious?
"I mean it's both our responsibility but maybe we
should figure something out before we take this any further.
When we last had sex... it was risky."
Puppy dog eyes meet my equally softened eyes.
The fact that he was willing to talk about it showed me he
cares, and I am impressed.
"And if it takes a little time, I can always get some condoms. I
mean I'm probably getting ahead of myself," he rambles.

Not for me.
I want to feel all of him when we finally connect again.
So, I kiss him to shut him up, "You are not getting ahead of
yourself. I want you, and I don't think I can wait much
longer...I appreciate you wanting to keep us safe."

I smile as he brushes my cheek, "Impatient?"
"Very impatient. I can go after Rachel gets back from her mini vacation. She might even take me, and I am almost certain she won't tell anyone, but maybe till then, you should get some condoms… you know, just in case."
He parakeets, "Just in case."
By that I meant until my birth control kicked in for good.
I was almost certain I wouldn't make it another month without having him in me.

"I'm not trying to pressure you to sleep with me for the record. "
"I know."
An uncomfortable look comes across his face, "Also…" trailing off, his eyes darken as his fingers blanch.
"What is it?"
I can tell it's something tough given his choked state, "It's just…I don't want to embarrass you… just wanted to ask about your leg."
I pause to think about it, "My leg?"
Nodding, "Those scabs?"
Flushed of color, I tear my gaze from him.
How had I forgotten?
He doesn't accept, creeps his pointer under my chin and lifts my eyes to his, "Hey, look me in the eye. There is nothing for you to be ashamed of."
"Hey."
Fluttering heart keeps the words from forming, I allow him to speak.
"It's ok, we all do things we don't want others to see, but I hate seeing you hurt and feeling like I can't help. It makes me feel so useless sometimes."
Fingers curling beneath my face, our eyes mix, moss to those baby blues, "Being here with you, that's enough. You are the only one who puts me at ease. How can you say you're useless?"
Turning the script back to him before pressing a soft kiss against his lip to appease him.

 I hate having to manipulate him like this but there was no reasonable explanation for what I had done to myself that didn't end with me blabbing about my dad.
"What I need is this…to be with you," my lips utter, taking his hand into mine, I move his fingers to my lips kissing each individual digit, "It's the only place I want to be."
"I can't tell you what to do, but I want you to remember that I am just a call away and soon enough we will be out of here. Things will get better," his voice teases implied knowledge, "Till then please, let me take care of you the way you take care of me. Let me be the one to comfort you and love you."
Love?
With tears stinging in my eyes, I allow my head to bob a yes before I let him wrap me in his strong arms, my ear pressed to his quickly beating heart, my mind recording its song.

…

I make it back just as the sky morphs into an orange creamsicle.
Rachel is peeling potatoes above the sink, Ava in her small play pen drooling over various toys.
"Can I help?"
Silently she hands me a potato peeler and scoots to the second side of the composite sink, slashing away at a large russet.
Sucking in a deep breath I begin, "Can I ask you something with the promise that you keep it between us?"
Brown spud drops into the sink, eyes greeting mine, still not a word, rather an intrigued and almost giddy smile.
As if she was pleased, I had come to her.
"I promise."

I look back down and begin to peel a small toe shaped legume, "I was wondering if maybe you could take me to the clinic and help me get birth control."
Plopping the now golden toe into the pot next to us, a bit of hot water splashes dangerously across the stove with a hiss, "I can, but I feel like I should discuss this with your dad before we go."

Shit.
No please no!

I shut up immediately and pulled another potato from the bag with a crinkle, "Never mind then…do we need all these?"
Head shakes yes.
"If you promise to be discreet, maybe we can work something out just between us. But I can't let this get in between your father and I."
My stomach spins with relief and annoyance.
Relief that she was budging.
Annoyed that I had to be discreet when all I wanted was to be responsible and protect my body.
"I'm just trying to be responsible."

Rachel steps away, reaching into the fridge, four perfectly seasoned steaks come out with her, "I appreciate that, Laurel. It's very adult of you."
I watch her flick the knob on the stove, butter starting to sizzle on the pan she had set out earlier.
"So are you and Kyle – " she stops there, reddening and looking away.
I don't make her say it knowing it would be uncomfortable for both of us.
My mind drifts back to Kyle in my bed, just above the dining area not long ago.
Tangled in sheets.
Wet and exposed.
Sweat made its own form of love on the low count threads as we kissed and basked in the glory of our orgasms just moments prior.
"We aren't right now, but I want to be ready…if the time comes."
It's not really a lie.
We aren't currently having sex.
"I understand. Kids are a lot of work and you have so much ahead of you. Best not ruin it."
I really pray that she keeps it between us.

Abandoning the steaks, she makes her way to the calendar posted on the fridge, little scrawls of red in the little blocks. `
"I can take you the day after Halloween. I just don't have time the next few days, but I can go ahead and call. Get something booked for the first week of November. Your dad and I should be home by the early afternoon. Something after noon should work."
Right after their night out at their friends lake house.
Partying it up.
Ava was to stay home with me, dads last ditch effort to keep me from the dance that night.
Couldn't drag her along and ruin his fun.

Mikey

My shift gets cut short, an incoming storm and a loss of power causes me to be sent home from work early.
Racing into the house I notice Laurel and Rachel are both gone, dad's car out of the driveway, his boots parked by the front door.
Waltzing in not a moment too late, the rain hammering the roof and the patio, bouncing hard as they hit the solid ground.
I stare out the window for a moment enjoying the music.
My body begins to sing, my stomach grumbling, I had missed lunch, dinner was still a bit out with Rachel probably out picking something up for dinner.

Shuffling above me draws my attention.
My father.
Water running through the pipes ceased, he must have been in the shower.
I sit at the table, pop the top off a soda, the bubbling stinging as it goes down, only angering my hungry stomach further.
Steps above.
Whimpering. Crying.
I can hear him sobbing now, thinking he is alone to mourn some hurt or loss, forgetting he was not the victim, but rather the perpetrator.

In his mind Laurel is a temptress, and he is nothing more than a weak man.

Trying to maintain my composure as I hear him sniffle his way down the stairs, heading right to me and right to a humiliating encounter.
Salt ladened red eyes find mine, peppering anger into them.
I slink down, staring right at the can as the last step creaks, his body fully turning to face the open space.
Jerking himself to his full six-foot one stature he wipes his red-rimmed eyes, humiliation dancing along his lids.
"Thought you were at work," the man I call Dad grumbles swiping at his face, trying hard to conceal the pain he had been greeting.
"Got sent home, the storm… the power went out on the other side of town," I pointed out the window to the rain.
"Didn't even notice, he growls with a shrug, his beard thick and still dripping with glistening buds of water.
Uncomfortably I chug the rest of my soda, the carbonation catching in his throat, exiting as a burp followed by a shaking breath.
"I didn't think you would have noticed. When it rains it pours you know?"
Head shakes, "Yeah."
For a moment, I feel bad.
I know it torments him; his sick obsession that he clearly lacks control over his wicked desires and senseless actions.

My head still hurts.
A small scab that flaked sits above my eyebrow reminding me of our last fight.
"Dad, are you ok?"
I legitimately ask from an almost loving place…not sure that I could love him per se.
"I'm fine. Why?"
Feeling gutsy, "Well, you were just crying upstairs."
Head darts, nostrils flaring, "Micah, don't push my buttons right now."
The shame was probably eating him up.

Gnawing at him like a worm on a rotting corpse, gladly
sucking away at the morsels of guilt, and shame that oozed
from every stinking pore.
"Is it because of Laurel?"
Testing the waters.
I want him to tell me, to admit his crimes, to give me a reason
to really unleash the fury that had been building up inside.
Shoulders tense, knuckles gripping the sink.
"Yeah, your sister is getting into some trouble lately."
His mouth has a mind of its own, its lips curl, scoffing, his
eyes clearly telling.
"Is that really what you are going with?"
Narrowing eyes, dilating pupils.
He seems defensive, as he should.
"What are you implying?"
Shrugging, "Nothing, what do you think I'm saying?"

My father stops, yanks the fridge open and examines nothing
in particular before letting it shut, the light flickering off, "Best
to let sleeping dogs lie son…wouldn't you agree?"
My head shakes no, "Not when it involves Laurel…not
anymore."
I feel brave tonight, emboldened in my desire to save her.
"Son, I have no idea what you're implying but I don't like
your tone son. Your sister is rebelling, and it is taking a toll on
Rachel and I and we certainly don't need any more lip from
you."
I can't tolerate this anymore.
Need so badly to shut my fist tight and pummel his face, to
feel his blood drip down my bare knuckles as the first of many
payments for his sin.
For both me and my sister.
"Yeah, she is rebelling… against you, and she should
be…Laurel doesn't have a voice, you've made sure of that. So,
from here on out I'm going to be her voice."
Snickering, "How about you mind your own business son.
You have plenty of your own problems."

Eyes deceiving me.

I stay silent and feel my courage waver now that he starts to
grow angry.
"Your mouth isn't moving, but your eyes tell me there's anger.
What are we going to do about that?"
Egging me on, trying to regain his power through
intimidation.
"Come on Micah…since you're such a man now…standing up
to me. Telling me how it's going to be."
I am a man. Just like him.
The same beast that flares in him lights my core.
Drives me to do horrendous things.
And yet…here I am, judging him.
I love her.

No! It's not the same.
Gale deserved my hands on her stupid throat. Gale liked it, she said
so!
Yeah…then what about Laurel…the couch when you touched her?
Face it, you're a copy and paste.
Like father, like son.

Drawing air into my lungs I part my lips, "I guess you want
me to shut up and leave so you can continue your sob fest
before Rachel gets home. It would be problematic if she
walked in while we were having this discussion, wouldn't it?"
I witness a bolt of fear flash across his face, becoming stuck as
he sputters more lies, "Son, I have no idea what the hell you
are getting at, but it's wearing my patience thin. Go get your
ass to your room and get ready for dinner or get the hell out of
this house, because Rachel doesn't need anymore drama."
Crunching the empty can in my fist I feel courage rise in me
returning heavier this time, puppeteering me to action.

I love my sister, and I can't live like this anymore.
Complacent, letting him hurt her.
Fuck, I had allowed it to happen.
My twin.
Her pain is mine, her fight is mine, maybe I had forgotten that.

And if I can save her, maybe she will truly love me, forgive me
for my sin.

"I know what you're doing to her, I have seen it …and now
it's tearing you up inside. Isn't it?"
If a human could physically turn green from feeling ill like
they did in the cartoons, my father would have done it right
then, his frameshifting to stare mine down, "Son, you are
treading in dangerous waters right now. Talking about things
that not only are not happening, but that don't concern you. I
would watch what you say next."
I think it over, fists tightening in my pockets, a physical effort
to keep myself from attacking him, wanting to scream his
indiscretion for the world to hear.
Slam my fists into his face.
Do to him what he did to me.

Instead, I stay quiet and allow him to conquer.
It pleases him judging by the smirk he now wears proudly.
"That's what I thought. You have a year and a half left before
you run off to college, thanks to me. Learn to keep your
tongue behind your teeth before you say something you
regret."
I have regrets, plenty, all of which began with silence.
"The only regret I have is keeping my mouth shut."

There is no discussion from there, only raining fists, and
grunts coming from his mouth.
I take the first two to the chest like a champ, the third knocks
the wind out of me, forcing me into the fetal position.
Despite his clear win, he does not stop there, quickly he picks
me up by my shirt twisting the fabric between his shaking
hands.
All I can do is obey my body's instructions; heaving and
searching for the depth of air as I try to control the short raspy
pants falling from my mouth, the pit of my stomach heavy as
If I had ingested a litany of stones.

"Fuck you!"

Wrong answer, he drops me with a thud.
I get up to my feet, his back turned, "Fuck me…Fuck me!"
Chanting over and over appalled at my choice of words.
Taking his distracted state to my advantage, I slam my fists
against his back.
He never expected it.
Never expected us to fight back.
Had always thought himself all-powerful, well, not anymore.
Angrily spinning, I toss my hands up and grab him by the
collar, throwing him down to the ground.
Freezing for a second, stunned.
Not a word.
We are at it like two rabid dogs, tossing glassware, throwing
each other to the ground, my fist crashing against his face, his
arms pressed against my neck.
So enthralled in the throes of angry passion and the masculine
urge to destroy each other that we don't even notice the door
swing open.
"What is going on!"
Rachel.
Dropping a bag of groceries with a clunk, milk dripping all
over the floor, glass shattering, her other hand stuffed with to
go burgers and fries, Ava probably screaming abandonment in
her seat outside.
I release him immediately, but he does not get the message
and grabs me by the collar.
Rachel shrieks, running to the phone, her hair damp.
"Stop it! Edmund stop! Oh my God!"

…

We ended up in cuffs in front of the house, luckily none of our
neighbors' homes were glued to us given the wood line we
had bought on.
My father is humiliated, and clearly nervous, about what I
may reveal.
Rachel is in a panic, trying to explain it away, and blames it
solely on me.

"Kid's been having some issues lately, we have him in therapy but…" her voice trails off as I walk past her, my anger steaming.

My father sides with her, and I have no recourse outside of blabbing, and given the circumstances who would believe me?

"Micah…he just, well he just snapped! I was trying to calm him down so it wouldn't come to this…but he attacked me," my father begins to explain it all away.

"Should we take him downtown? Let him cool off?"

Oh, the joys of having buddies on the force.

Dad looks at me, an air of warning and warmth in his gaze, an unspoken agreement budding.

It's clear, if I keep my mouth shut, I can stay.

Not ready to sit in jail overnight.

Silent.

My voice has a price, staying out of jail.

I am just like Laurel.

Weak. Silenced.

…

A split lip, a re-busted brow.

Blood had dripped down my face and dried, peeling around my chin.

My lip was swollen, as if a bee had stung it, and my ribs ached from where he had slammed his fist into me.

Dad had come to fake an apology and threatened me back into silence, informing me that I was not going to school the next few days and that I needed to sit here and learn my place.

In reality, he wants to keep me here, worried that my appearance may cause people to question our activities.

Rachel comes up with a first aid kit that she tosses on my bed and a look that says that I should be ashamed of myself.

I am.

For not standing up to him.

For not allowing the words to leave my mouth.

So much shame.

A myriad of emotions I had not felt in years fills me to the brim, and it dribbles out.
For the first time in a long time I cry.
Tears of hurt and frustration soak my pillow and my sleeves until I feel sleep wrap me in her warm embrace.

Laurel

Mikey looks awful.
I can't believe what Dad did to him.
Still, he won't tell me what happened.
But I have a sneaking suspicion it has something to do with me.
The way he looks at me.
"Mikey, please just tell me what happened."
I lie next to him on the couch, cartoons playing, the joys of a quiet Saturday.
"Please. I won't be mad; I just want to understand."
Eyes fixate on me, one hidden behind a dome of swelling, guilt fills me as he stares at me with a desire to be held and not questioned.
I can't offer him that.
"You already know, Laurel," he quips angrily.
Head shaking, "No, I don't, please don't blame me," I sputter.
My twin focuses back on the tv, "We are almost out of here Mikey, ok? So, we just need to grit our teeth and bear it."
 "That's not enough Laurel, he can't keep doing this! When are you going to help me fix this?"
"It's too late," I grip my arms, nails digging. "There is no fixing this, you have to see that. We just," I halt, pinching the bridge of his nose, "we have to wait it out."
The couch shifts and he gets up leaving me alone, staring at the neon colored tv show.
"It's not too late for Ava," he calls out, the door slamming behind him.

Ava.
What if its already too late for her?

Mikey

I am not sure where I am going but after snagging Laurels
keys, I know I need to see Tasha.
She had no idea what went down yesterday, and I didn't want
to scare her…but I need her now more than ever.
I want to fall between her arms, allow my head to nap
between her silky thighs, breathing in her womanly scent,
tasting her bountiful pleasure.

Trying to call her from Corey's phone leaves me more
annoyed than anything as she doesn't pick up.
"Dude, what the hell happened to your face," he points out
clearly oblivious to my discomfort with his questioning.
"It's nothing man, I just need to find Tasha."
"Tasha? What for?"
Glaring, "Nothing, just- just, have you seen her?"
Clearly uncomfortable with the situation I caught a glimpse of
knowledge in his stare.
"Do you know where she is?" I repeat, annoyed, my lip
pulsating.
Head shaking, "She was at the ponds with Dean earlier, I saw
them out on the dock while I was out running."
Rattling keys in my hand, "Docks…got it. Thanks."
I take off.

Laurel

He is right, I know he is.
But what if he has no intention of hurting Ava and I rob her of
growing up with a father?

Not knowing where to go, or what to do leaves me dizzy.
It's too intense.
I can feel it coming.
Don't know what it is, but it's approaching, closing in on me.
The end of the line leading to a stick of dynamite.
The last swirl of clouds that build a tornado.
The spark that starts a blazing forest fire.

Mikey

Clouds swirl like soft-serve ice cream in the sky above.
Another evening of dripping rain would soon ensue.
My eyes aim for the goal as I walk briskly.
 Go home.
Don't blow this.
What if Dean kicks your ass?

Pushing my thoughts out I peel into the dirt lot and walk
hastily towards the docks catching a glimpse of Tasha through
the reeds, alone.
"What if Dean kicks your ass?" I mutter in a mocking voice.
Idiot.
Swallowing hard, I charge forward, needing her touch right
then and there.
I might explode.
The dock creaks her head and snaps back, "Mikey?"
Horror on her face, "What are you doing here," she hisses her
eyes scanning nervously across the waters.
"I needed to see you, Tash."
Grabbing my hand, "What are you doing? Dean is here," she
repeats.
I look around, "Don't see him, and you know what I don't
give a shit, let him see," I try to take her hand and she pulls
away stunning me.
Between her perfect teeth that are grit together hard, she
scolds me, "You know what would happen if he comes back
and you're here holding my hand."
"Tasha, I just…" a tear pools in my eyes, stinging, she takes
notice, her hand pulling through my hair and onto my split
lip, horror across her face, "Oh my God Mikey! What the hell
happened to you?"
Her nails sting along the small cut, "I'm ok, Tasha, I just really
need you right now."
Glancing around, "I can't right now, Dean is here, he went off
to the gas station to get some sodas, but I can meet you
tonight…at my house."

Nodding, she kisses my forehead, allowing me to stalk off to wait for the promise of sunset.

I wait until the sun sets before knocking on her window and easing my way in.
"Shower?"
She nods and hands me a towel allowing me to make my way to the ensuite where I find hot comfort, the setting on the showerhead on the full body setting allowing it to pummel against my bruised side.
The pain is soothing somehow so I let it pound into the cluster of pooled blood.
The door slides open, soap falling from my hair, my hands coming through wet locks, Tasha stands there fully nude, eyeing me for permission to enter.
I nod, taking her hand, quickly she sets the shower head to the rain setting, heats up, the mist slowly rising around us.
A kiss blossoms between us, her arms around my neck, leaning down to kiss her softly, iron stinging along my lip, causing me to wince.
Abruptly she pulls away, "I didn't mean to hurt you."
I pull her back lips crashing hard this time, the pain swelling, "I like it."
Guiding her hand down to my back, her hand hits a nasty bruise, fingers feeling hard as steel against it.
Swirling her tongue over lips I cave back against the cold wall of the shower, shivers of pleasure and the shock of the cold wall ripple through me.
Tasha continues moving her hand to cup my chin as her mouth beats against me.
Head spinning, I lean against the shower wall allowing her to work me at a furious rate.
"Stop," I pull her to her feet, feeling my release not far off.
"Let me take care of you."
She shakes her head no, a dew clinging to her thick hair, "You're hurt, just let me take care of you."
Sinking back down I pull her back up under her armpits, the silk of her skin driving me wild, but it's both not enough and somehow too much.

My head spins, "Tasha, just stop ok!" it comes out grumbly and dramatic.

I want control, for her to not argue with me and fight me all that does is serve to take me back home, the exact place I had run to her from.
Anger clouds her face, "What the fuck Mikey? What do you want from me?"
I shut the water off reaching for the towel and start to dry off as it slides from the glass pane, she swipes it from me, "Seriously, tell me what the fuck is going on! You come in here, your face all fucked up and you won't talk to me, or fuck me, so tell me now or get out."
Hopping out of the shower the steam clouds the room, I sift quickly looking for my pants, bundle up in the corner on the floor and I start to pull them on, "So that's it, you won't even talk to me?"
Ignoring her, I pull my shirt on and over my head, leaving her standing in tempting nudity, shivering.
I want so badly to go wrap her in my arms and recount everything that had happened the last few days, years even but I can't.
This was dangerous.
I was too vulnerable to be here and completely out of control.
Running was the best option.
Clearing my head somewhere else.
"Mikey!"
Snapping. I'm at attention. This was hurting her.
"You're worrying me."
Scaring her even.

Damn. Listen to her. Apologize now!
"I'm sorry Tasha I just…"
She is close. Too close. To me. To the truth.
Pulling her fingers through my hair I feel her eternally manicured nails pulling sapphires through my slick locks, encouraging my swollen eyes to drown with salty tears.

I feel like such a loser, letting her see me cry, but I lose control and a single tear twists and curves until it situates itself on the corner of my lip.

Listen to her, do not cry like a bitch!

"I'm here," Tasha whispers, "we don't have to talk, just let me hold you."

I feel less than. Less than a man,

Testosterone fills me, surging, chasing the temptation of tears away.

The bickering in my head finally settles on one simple solution and that is to show Tasha that I'm a man, and what do men do best?

Take. Fuck. With impatient hands I take her by the hair, embracing her hard, ignoring the pain in my lips, the splitting gash that runs above my eye.

"I'm sorry," I pant, pushing her up against the wall, pulsing my lips and knees down before she stacks the back of her thighs against my shoulders.

"Shut up," I order making contact a second time, a slight flush appearing over her bottom, with a third the flush deepens, if her skin had been shades paler it would have been screaming a strawberry red cry by now.

The next time my hand makes contact, I move my pointer into her heat, curling its palm to push down towards the floor, her hips contorting, "God!"

Snickering, "What does God have to do with this?"

This time I don't hold back, with all my strength I slap her other cheek, "There is no God here to stop this, Tasha."

So, I fuck her, taking what a man should, allowing testosterone to convince me of my masculinity as I push into her with no warning, her mouth still asking for God, face flat against the foot of the bed.

She begs me to show her nirvana, her bottom jiggling powerfully against my thighs as they make contact, rolling up to her womanly hips.

Only then do I succumb and relinquish my power, letting her ride me.

When all is said and done, we collapse, her fingers tracing my chest, as I sit propped against her headboards, "So…" her silky voice trails, "You ready to talk to me, because I'm not just good at fucking. I listen, too."
Sighing, I reach into her dresser and pull out a baggy of weed, she gets up ruining the closeness, and grabs her bong from the closet, and her tank top that she pulls on over her mountainous breasts. Quickly I put my shirt and bottoms back on.
Plopping down with a shake she curls her pointer motioning for the flower.
Tossing some dry bud into the glass she asks once more what's going on.
"Grind it, babe," I complained dismissing the question.
"It will get me high all the same."
Eyes roll, "Fine."
Reaching for her lighter she hands me the bong, "Greens…you need it."
Flames hit the sizzling dried herb, white smoke billowing in the glass funnel with a crackle.
I pull the stem and suck hard, the skunk grass circulating my system warmly before I cough out the excess.

"Mikey!"
Handing her the bong, "Yeah, what do you want to know?"
A big gulp of air and an even larger gulp of smoke later and she finally answers, "What do you think?"
I pressed a finger to the swollen eye fighting off the urge to groan as the pain surges, "Fought a bear."
Slugging me before she pulls my hand to hers, "Seriously, I'm worried Mikey."
I sense that "My dad and I got into it, that's all." I dart my state at the boy band poster on her wall, frosted tips, and big sunglasses leering.
"That's all!"
"Yeah," I shrug, reaching for the bong, her hand tightening around it with ease the same way she grips my shaft. I had wanted so badly to find comfort in her and maintain my silence simultaneously.

"If you aren't going to be honest then what are we doing here?
It doesn't make me want to open up to you."
She had opened up to me that night. Cried about her father
when he fell off the wagon, yet again, complained about how
big of an airhead Dean was. Then she cried tears that fell for
no reason other than she needed a good cry, and her feminine
body ordered it before it succumbed to its weakened monthly
bleed.

"I don't know."
Tasha takes another hit, shaking her hand, the lighter metal
too hot after such a long drag, "You don't know what?"
Coughing the words out, smoke sits thick between us, milky
in the sky.
"What we're doing here. You got me running around like
some puppy and still fucking Dean."
"I thought we had an agreement. That I was waiting till after
the football season to dump his ass, so I don't fuck up his
scholarship by breaking his little heart."
Her voice sings songs of ruthless reality.
Snatching the bong from her I begin to light the bowl, noticing
its charred state she hands me the baggie and I focus in on
grabbing a pinch, "Does keeping his heart and scholarship
intact include fucking him?"
Scoffing, "Are you… jealous?"
Eyes darting, "So what if I am? I mean look at you."

An evil smirk streaks across her tasty lips, "I like it, and for the
record, we aren't even sleeping together anymore. Dean sucks
at fucking. All I want is you."
My heart skips three beats, I try to shake it off, lighting the
grass, "Bull shit. What could you possibly be telling him to
keep him from begging to sleep with you?"
Pointing up, "That I found God. I drag him to the youth group
on Wednesdays," her tongue clicks, "I sit through that bullshit
for you."
Ghosting the smoke, I exhale hard, "Have you?"
Giggling, "Have I what?"
"Found God?"

"You are an idiot!"
I am, but I also love seeing her so excited.
"So?"
She tears the glass from my hand and sets it on the bedside table, "No, I haven't found God."
"You sure? You were certainly calling out to him earlier."
Tasha grips a pillow and slaps it across my face, leaving me speechless.
I grab it from her hand and press it to her face for only a moment, pushing her beneath me with a squeal, our chests heaving, kissing, begging to greet without the heavy burden of clothes.
I don't know what comes over me.
If it's the way she breathes or the way her fingers run over my injuries, but I feel a swell in my chest, "Tasha..." I gaze down, her eyes fixed hungrily against my lips, pupils high and dilated.
"Micah," her plump lips utter between raspy breaths.

Before I can stop my stupid inebriated mouth from uttering the words, they come out at the speed of light, "My dad is hurting Laurel...has been for years. That's why he did this," I almost cry, hands falling over my face.
Instant regret, spilling a huge secret just so she will baby me the way I want, I click my jaw shut before I can say more.
If I could reach out and pull the words from the air and prevent them from reaching her ears I would, but instead with both lay still, eyes widening.
"What?"
Heart pops erratically, corn kernels meeting heat.
All I can do is shake my head before she pushes me off her, and I fall onto my back helplessly, my heart thumping uncontrollably.
Shit! Shit!
What the hell Micah? Fix this now!

Lips tight, hers loosen, "Mikey, you can't just say something like that and clam up. What the hell is going on? What are you talking about?"

"Nothing," I snapped defensively.

I can't will the words to exit.

"Seriously? I mean I know he did that to you, but I have never seen her in that state…no bruises or anything…" voice trailing off with realization, horror in her eye.

"It's nothing…let's forget I said anything."

Slumping next to me heavily, her fingers sinking along her hairline, "Is he…" she can't bring herself to ask, but I know the implication, "No…Mikey no."

"Forget I said anything…please," I beg, cheeks hot, limbs heavy.

"What? No Mikey we need to ugh," she sucks in a flustered breath, fingers combing through her hair overwhelmed, "We need to tell someone… the cops… Rachel, I don't know," her eyes fill with tears now, "She's my best friend! Why the fuck didn't she say anything?"

"Tasha… you don't understand there's no one to tell. This needs to stay between us… telling you was a mistake, and I am sorry I dragged you into this."

Violence in her gaze, her voice rising, "Are you insane? That man is fucking…he's fucking…he is abusing my best friend," the word abuse falls slowly from her tongue, too scared to use the "R" word, she sucks in a breath and continues to look for a solution between heavy sobs and all I can do is retreat into silence.

"He beat you to a pulp and you want me to be quiet?"

"I know it seems crazy but – "

Divine feminine rage takes over, "But! But nothing! How long have you known? You let that happen to her!"

Desperation to get her to stop worrying fills me.

Regret.

Shame for having let it go on so long.

Then there's a sense of relief.

Shifting the blame on to me she locks eyes with me before slamming her fist into my chest with a thump again and again, "You let him fucking beat your ass! You let him do that to her!"

Unwinding. Falling apart, finally.
Guilt rises all steamy from my gut, my heart in knots of guilt
and hurt that she was placing the blame on me, anger fills me
as she slams her fist to me once more, catching her arms in my
hands I tense, "Tasha stop! I know. I know, ok! I'm fucking
half a man, and if you don't think the guilt makes me sick then
you're insane."

She thrashes against my hold, but I am stronger, my fingers
pulling her to me, nails creating crater-like crescents in her
satin skin, "You let him… y- you let him," the fiery woman
sobs against my chest.
When her cries finally morph into little chattered breaths, I
loosen my grip.
"I'm going to let go now, and I need you to listen to me," my
voice comes out in a chattering whisper trying to tame her
fury, "now."
I let go slowly, unsurprised as to what comes next.
The retaliation immediate, an open palm that was intended for
my cheek catches my screaming eye, cracking the scab that sits
above it, blood dripping reddening my vision.
My hand flies to the spot as I groan.
Her eyes brim with the realization of what she had just done.
"Oh God! Oh, I'm sorry," she shrieks, grabbing at my face, my
hands trying to create a barrier, fear and lust both heavily
influencing what comes next.
I grab her hand and yank it off my face, using my weight to
press her against the bed then against the mattress, my hips
pushing into her naked bottom, pushing myself between her
palpating thighs, groans of confusion turning to cries for me to
wait.
"What are you doing?"
"Please, I know this doesn't make any sense right now, but I
need you. I need this," I begin to cry, the sting mixing with the
warm iron, blood mingling with saliva as I twist my tongue
along hers.
 "Please, Tash…please" trailing off, hands tight in my hair, a
roller coaster of emotions ping-ponging through my brain.

Burying myself against her a sob wracks my throat, chest jutting up, begging for my lips to suckle her brown flesh, I find safety there. There's an intimacy that's not bound by sex.

I don't deny he emotionally, not a damn thing, but I stop short, needing only her hold.
I don't deny myself the comfort. Emotions blazing; fear, hurt, vulnerability, and sheer bliss.
Comfort. My need satiated.
Then silence. Nothingness triggered by our shaking bodies and our racing thoughts.
Static. An ache across my brow, nervous pounding in my stupid head.

"I'm sorry, I won't say anything…not yet, but we need to do something," she breathes.
Kissing the split skin, rose red cakes over her bottom lip, a tremble, I run the pad of my thumb over it, wiping her clean, "It's my fault. I know that."
"No, it's not. I was just mad and scared. I'm so scared, Mikey."
Resting my head between her breasts I press my lips to the dewy sweat-riddled flesh, "Of what?"
"I don't know how I'm supposed to act normal around you two now-, now that I know."
It's time to act. My eyes are open.
Wide open and determined. I will put an end to this.

Laurel

Liam is a great kid.
Patient. Playful. Obedient.

I had asked Kyle to come decorate pumpkins with us and he agreed.
We sat on the large deck, a cool breeze flowing between us, painting, carving, and gluing random craft bits onto the four large pumpkins his parents had provided.
Liam had insisted on keeping two to himself.

An agreement we had come up with in exchange for a candy bar from the Halloween hand out stash.

I recall his mother, a tall lanky, frizzy-haired woman with the biggest heart telling me he couldn't have sugar tonight and he reminded me as we concocted our deal.

"Our secret," I tease, handing him a fun-sized candy car.

As for Kyle, Mr. and Mrs. McCallister knew him well from school where Mr. McCallister had been contracted to do maintenance work and had no problem with him coming over to carve pumpkins as long as he promised to be a gentleman while I babysat.

That part had caused me to blush furiously.

That implication.

Kyle had taken notice and winked at me from across the room.

I wanted to simultaneously shove him to the ground and sit on his face and make him sorry and kiss him for being so adorable.

The thought of sitting on his face had left a crimson smear across my own.

His teasing had circulated heat to my head, and then below, dampening me with arousal, an arousal that had refused to leave me since.

True to his word Kyle had not laid a finger on me since his arrival... and it left me infuriated.

Only his eyes touch me, caressing, scanning, kissing every inch of my covered skin.

His irises make love to me, nip my neck, stop on my heaving chest.

He was patient though, more so than I was.

When he wasn't teasing me with his stare, he was lending a hand, even helping Liam cut the top off his second pumpkin while I put the finishing touches on my cat; whiskers made of pipe cleaners and a button nose.

"I like your cat," Liam comments, squinting his eyes despite his proximity to my pumpkin, Liam's button nose flaring with excitement, "It's so pretty Laurel!"

I turn the carved-out lump to Kyle who teases me right off the bat, commenting that I had cut the eyes lopsided.
"Well let me see what you made, Michelangelo!"
His arms hover around, "I'm not done yet."
A playful grin meets my happy gaze, the night air perfect for this activity.

It smells like fall, the leaves swaying and raining down on the smooth emerald deck as we work.
Inside, there's a pumpkin pie with a balloon of cream perched on a stand, ready to be devoured. Soon the sun will dissipate, leaving the cold thrill of the Halloween season upon us.
"Lemme see…please," I whimper knowing what it does to him when I beg.
Kyle carves like a maniac, trying to hide his work behind his oversized gray zip-up.
"Please."
Powerless, he turns it and I set eyes on his grotesque creation, and without a second thought, I laugh.
"Hey now! It's no David, but it's better than your cat!"
Kyle pretends to kick my pumpkin, causing me to whine in protest, a spark lighting in his eye.
Gripping my hand he pulls my ear to his hot mouth, "Save some of that whining for tonight."
Biting down on my lip, I press my hand to his chest, "There's plenty left you just have to come find it," I tease before gently creating distance before pacing back to the inside for candles.
"I plan to," he shouts.
"Plan to what Kyle…tell me…please," Liam asks through excited pulls along Kyle's sleeve.
"I plan to devour you."
Glancing back, I see Kyle curl his fingers and roar at Liam who excitedly runs off towards the grass.
Moments like these leave my heart aching, especially when he eyes me and mouths, "You too," my way.
There is no substitute.

Is This Love?

Mikey

Something needs to be done.
But first I need Laurel.
Want her approval.
Want her to guide me.
I would never hurt her.
Even if it meant paying the price with silence.

Trouble is my big mouth and Tasha had put me in a terrible predicament that left me in a time crunch.
I messed up and I know she will not stay quiet for long. She had made that clear.
What I had made clear was my promise to fix this, despite how late we were into the game.
My stupid mouth.
A mouth that was currently sucking down a beer at Corey's, foot tapping anxiously as I tried to find a way out of the mess I had created.
"You look like you need something stronger."
Corey offers me a swig from a bottle of whiskey.
"What's with you?"
Shrugging him off I mutter his direction.
"Nothing, "Just want to clear my mind," I motioned to him to leave the bottle on the table.
"By getting messed up?"
It sounds stupid when he puts it like that.
"Guess so."
Regardless, I take a long swig and let it settle.

Laurel

All said and done, the pumpkins all turn out pretty ugly.
My cat with its wiry whiskers, Liam's alien that was dripping streaky paint, the forgotten pumpkin in the corner who had

been beheaded and left untouched, and of course Kyle's
skeleton that needed to take a trip to an anatomy class.

We place them on the steps to light them up before the light of
day fades.
Kyle's fingers glide along my cheek as I glance at the light
display sending a shooting thrill down my spine, turning I
offer him a gentle peck on the cheek.
"Thank you."
Smiling, I led him back inside by the hand, Liam worked up
and ready for a snack, bounding across the cream cushions of
the loveseat.
"Popcorn!"
 The frantic boy jumps up and down on the couch demanding
his movie treat.
"Dinner first," I remind him, to sift through the fridge before I
spot tinfoil.
Bingo!
Leftover pizza and applesauce.

Liam devours it, still leaving room for soda and popcorn.
I don't deny him two slices of pie even.
I eat a slice too, smearing whipped cream along Kyle's nose
playfully.
His finger swipes and plops it on my nose before he kisses it
clean.

Turning on the tube I let the stream of cartoons flood the
darkened room while Kyle and I snuggle close, my frame
leaning against the arm of the couch, his arm wrapped around
my shoulders.
The cartoon plays through, Liam growing sleepy next to us.
I allow my head to fall into the crook of Kyle's neck, inhaling
him.
Taking notice, he strokes my hair, "Something you like?"
"You could say that."
I feel his mouth morph into a smile above.
"Plus, you smell good…like a cookie," I tease.

"That may be because my mom and I made cookies this afternoon."

Forcing myself not to tease him for the sweet gesture I twist my nose, I imagine him with a little apron on, his nose covered in flour.

His mom lived to bake when she wasn't working rounds at the hospital.

Kyle always had homemade chocolate chip cookies and strudel for breakfast packed away in little baggies.

Maybe that's why everyone liked him.

"You made cookies with your mommy?"

Pulling under my chin he has my eyes locked on his, "Yes I sure did, Laurel, and if you don't wipe that smirk off your face, you won't get any pumpkin chocolate chip cookies."

Gasping, I feel my mouth fall open in indignation, "You wouldn't deny me!"

"Then behave," his voice commands, nuzzling me against him.

"I guess I'll be good then."

I meant it. There was no way I was missing out on those.

Mikey

I want to surprise Laurel with a ride home.

New car and all.

Well, new to me.

Gray. Slick.

A stick shift with a dinged-up bumper but hell it only cost a couple grand, and Dad was glad to pay up if it meant I shut up.

The blue house comes into view, jack-o'-lanterns lit on the porch; an ugly cat and what I assume is an alien lean against each other.

I look over beneath the little ash that had just been planted a few years back, its diamond bark giving it a certain elegance.

Beneath it sits a trashy beat-up truck that I would recognize anywhere.

Kyle.

Dad would be furious, but I will not make a peep.

Laurel

An unexpected knock has us both tense.
"Who is it?"
Kyle calls out before he opens the door.
I glance over the back of the couch, Liam completely
undisturbed, his eyes shut with sleep, the glow of the tube
moving along the wall.
"It's your brother," he calls out.
I hop over, wondering what he was up to, and why he is here?
"Hey."
He seems tense, smells of cheap whiskey, his undamaged eye
glossy, the other one peeking through the newly lessened
swell.
"Like my ride?" He shrugs over to an old beat-up car.
"Yeah, I do."
That's all I have to offer.
"Wanna hitch a r- ride home?"
I don't, he stinks of booze, eyes glossy and red, but I also don't
want to hurt his feelings, and exasperate his drunken state.
"I'll be here till ten. Plus, Kyle is taking me home," I point
back to Kyle who has sunk back down on the coach his neck
craned to listen in.
He steps in. "Warm in here," my brother slurs, stumbling into
the foyer now.
"Aren't you worried that dad is going to ask why-" I watch
him gulp hard, "walking," he adds head bobbing.

Grabbing his hand I pull him by the hand holding onto him
tight, "Mikey, you are drunk, you smell like you fell into a
barrel of whiskey...what are you doing?"
"Just getting ya home."
Almost falling over, the whiskey hits him like a train.
"Mikey, you can't even get yourself home. Why don't you just
hang out here and sober up? Kyle can drive us home."
My brother pulls me into an awkward embrace, my arms
stuck between us as I try to shield myself from his touch.
"Oh sis...I'm good. I'm just so good... I'll make it home."

"So will I Mikey. I told Dad Mrs. McAllister was driving me so there's nothing to worry about."

He begins to protest, tight lips spreading as I yank myself free from his grasp.
"What are you so worried about?"
It comes out harsh.
I can see Kyle begin to grow uncomfortable, dying to come to me, but also trying to resist long enough to let me handle it.
"Just looking out for my favorite sis," spit runs with each word.
"Well I'm ok…but you're not."
Blowing a raspberry, tongue pulsing angrily from his busted lip before pulling his coat pocket inside out, looking for his keys.
"You shouldn't be driving."
My eyes roll, which causes him to anger, his hand around my arm now.
I tsk, clearly annoyed now, "Mikey come on, this isn't funny."
"What? You don't think I do my best for you sis?"
Fingers and nails dig into my wrist.
"Mikey stop."
He doesn't hear me only gripping more tightly the pain searing now.
"I love you, sis. I don't want him mad again," hands tighten with every word constricting like a hungry anaconda.
"Mikey, let go!"
Kyle jumps to my aid, his arm tight around my brother's prying him off as my loyalty to him seemingly rips at its invisible seams.
"Come on Mikey. Just relax."
Rupture.

Mikey

Unable to contain the pain any longer I squeeze tightly, nails popping, skin tearing before Kyle's hand rips me from her.
Tearing us apart.
Always tearing us apart.

The world is against us.
Always has been.
I see that now.
I can't hear what she says.
 I just feel my soul tear as her touch leaves mine.
Glancing down at my nails, I see bits of white flesh and specks
of red beneath.
Shame grips my stomach and twists, prying every drop of
guilt I have to offer from my soul.

"I...sorry Laurel... I-I didn't mean it," I stutter, catching the
painful look on her face.
Facing her, I see Kyle move his hand to her shoulder, gently
encouraging her to him, leaving an ocean of confusion
between us.
It sparks something jealous in me.
Something that leaves me gasping like a punch to the gut.
A knife to the heart.
"I think you need to go," he says, holding her to him now,
chest puffed out protectively.
"Go sober up, Mikey," my sister begs, her hand touching
mine, sending a riveting urge through me.

 An urge to protect ignites.
Kyle is no good for her. He has no idea how to protect
her. How to love her.
This was fleeting, their love only a temporary fix.
An insignificant blip on the radar.
Come college he would be long gone, and I told him so,
yelling it out, my face reddening with rage.
It was me.
Me. By her side.
Dusting her off. Polishing her. Holding her up.
Protecting her to the best of my abilities. And I had failed.
Not anymore, not tonight.
This is where things change.
Where I show her how important she really is to me.
She will see just how much I love her.
Burning with anger I leave, stumbling, my body freed.

On the porch I aim a well-placed kick at the pumpkin I assume
is Kyles, caving it in with my steel-toed boot before peeling
out and driving around town for the next hour, trying to sober
up enough to function.
Once my mellow drunkenness fades to a buzz I know I'm
ready and in the perfect headspace for a confrontation.
Tonight I will keep my word to Tasha.
Everyone is going to find out who he really is.

Laurel

My brother peels out pelting pebbles that bounce and clank off
of Kyle's truck.
"I probably shouldn't have let him drive, considering…" My
words fade into the night, Kyle's arm on my shoulder.
"Guess it's a good thing my trucks have already beat up,"
Kyle tries to joke, still clutching onto me, the warm relief of his
presence slowing my heart, "Try not to worry, ok? Let me look
at your arm."
I have no idea what just happened.
Silence.
I can't joke when my throat feels so tight.
"What was that about?"
"I have no idea."
" He seemed mad," Kyle tells me as if I hadn't been there and
makes haste to the first aid kit where he cleans me up and tells
me I'm going to be ok as I stand in nervous silence before he
leads me to the couch.

Pulling me by the hand he moves me to the couch, wraps his
arms around me, holding me tight against his chest, "I'm
worried," I admit.
Fingers twist in my hair, pushing it to the other side of my
head before tenderly swiping his bottom lip over already
tender skin, coaxing goose fletchings to rise in abundance.
"It's going to be ok Laurel."
Pulling away from him, I push my way onto his lap,
straddling him, our lips mere centimeters away.

 Liam snores just feet away.
"You don't know that. He was drunk and driving…my dad is
going to kill him."

Unbeknownst to me, a wet tear crashes down my cheek, my
face flushed, teeth gnawing at my inner lip.
Nose to nose, Kyle delicately kisses my face dry thumb with a
ginger swipe.
"It's going to be alright."
Shaking thighs pulse and push deeper against his waist,
running over a surprising hard-on, breath hitching along my
lips.

I'm lost in the moment, lost in the comfort his hold has over
me despite the implication of my hands that are now running
along his waist beneath his shirt, "Just take a breath, Laurel, I
hate seeing you flustered like this."
He means it.
I take some air in and relax against him, letting him hold me
for a long while before he starts to move me off him," In the
interest of keeping from getting flustered myself I think you
should get off my lap," he suggests, speaking the words into
my lips, our foreheads still pressed.
"This feels good, though."
 My hand runs up now below his shirt and onto his warm
chest, heart beating erratically beneath the sheet of skin he is
draped in.
"That's exactly what I mean."

Suddenly weightless his hands hooked beneath the underside
of my thighs, I am flipped off, left laying flat on the couch,
Kyle pushing himself to hover over me, his hot mouth hard on
mine, "Don't tease me or I will make it just as hard for you,"
he whimpers along my neck, nipping at the softest bits of
flesh, leaving me aching for more.
My core is so hot it would threaten to burn the house down
had it not been for the seeping wet he had coaxed mingling
with the fire.

"I'm sorry, Kyle," I apologize as he pulls off me, hands to his side, eyes burning into the screen.

Sitting up, I appropriately nuzzled into him, nose gently rubbing along his shoulder before I turned my head to face the TV and control myself.

"I didn't mean to work you up."

Smiling," Don't apologize, I enjoy a good buildup."

"What are we building up to?"

Hand in mine now, pulsing gently, "Be patient and you will find out."

...

"So this is where I leave you," Kyle tells me, at the end of the street, the light flickering above.

I am forty bucks richer and completely worked up at the insinuation that something hot and heavy is coming.

But we are here now, and I am left confused, his hands kept firmly on the wheel, my eyes batting, mascara drawn out lashes at him, "Night then," I say slowly just hoping he won't let me leave too easily.

I want him, but I don't want to tell him so.

Stepping out, I feel heavy disappointment, like a stone tied around my neck. Each step seems unattainable.

Before my second foot hits the ground, Kyle calls my name, causing me to hop right back in like a giddy child.

With a wide smile plastered to my lips, I face him, scooting closer to him in his three-seater.

If I had a tail, it would be wagging it along the seat maniacally.

Good girl. Sit. Stay.

Thank God, he called me back!

"Did you really think I was going to let you go that easily, Laurel?"

Oooh…. Oh God Laurel, he is about to pounce.

Cupping my face, he swipes a finger along my quivering lip, teasing it to part, my tongue firmly flicking along the nail bed.

"Have I been patient enough, Kyle?"

Head shaking a firm yes, but his hands fall back and stay to himself, "I just don't want you to be too expectant…or eager or you could make things hard for me."

This is a side of him I have not seen yet; controlling, dominating, leaving me on edge, making me wait for him. Withholding even.
The minutes tick by before he runs a finger gently up my uncovered thigh, the black skirt leaving little to the imagination, pale silk bearing itself to him.
"Are you going to be alone tomorrow night?"
Shaking my head affirmatively, I speak slowly, "Yeah and Ava goes to bed at eight… I'll be all alone."
"The dance won't be fun without you to hold or slow dance with, so I was thinking of skipping out and coming by."
Snapping my head to face him I protest, "That's not fair to you. You should go, Kyle."
"I would rather see you," he hints, a sinister glimmer sparkling in that smile of his.
"You're bad, plus who says we're doing anything?"
"Don't have to. I just want to come by."

Stress fills me, it would be a risk… one of epic proportions, but he is worth it, a night in his arms was worth it.
"I'm just frustrated that I haven't gotten to hold you for more than a moment and I want nothing more than to spend a night with you, even if all it entails is eating popcorn while you watch shitty rom coms and cuddling up on your bed. I just want to spend time with you, alone," he tells me, pulling his nail along the tendon that runs behind my knee and up dangerously close to my core before he switches its direction grazing the front now.
His words are innocent, his touch less than.

Nimble movements have my fingers curling around the passenger door handle, resisting the urge to take his hand and plunge it where I need it most.

"I uh- I want you… come by," I force myself not to gasp as a new trickle of femininity threatens to prepare me for him, "I want all that and more."
His fingers skip up my thigh, "What does more encompass?"
I know exactly what it means.
"I don't know…maybe a bath, and a good joint."
I watch him flick up the heat to the car, the windows fogging to hide us. "Lying is not a good look on you."
Busted. Not that I was really trying to hide my desires.
If I wanted to lie, I could and well.
Had years of experience.
I begin to blush furiously.
"Now that right there is a good look on you. You look stunning right now."
I should stop being coy,
"Should I really tell you what I want?"
"Please do," he kisses the words along my neck, hand dipping along the outer edges of my knee now, slinking back to his side.

Desire swells in me, nipples hardening against my strapless bra, the swell threatening to tip over the top of my shirt.
"You should start by kissing me," my hand travels to his face, spreading along his jaw, pressing a feverish kiss against his mouth, my tongue battling his for dominance, the taste of his saliva rushing my senses; buttery from the popcorn, fresh from the stick of gum he was chewing.
Pressing my tongue against him, I contort it just right, latching onto the sharp kick of mint, pulling it against my cheek before we part, breathless.
"Then, I want you to put your hands here," taking his hand and control I trail his fingers along the outline of my breasts, "And here," I inform, moving it down beneath my skirt and panty, manipulating them.
My body begins to slink and sink against his touch.
"Damn, Laurel," he chides, tongue swollen with anticipation.
I chewed his gum slowly, savoring the fact that his mouth had been on it moments earlier.

"I need that back," he mutters, pulling his hands up and running them through my hair, taking the gum back, slowly rolling his tongue along my own.
"Then, I want to do this," pulling his fingers to my lips, I slowly suck one down, swirling the tip, pressing it to my cheek before sucking it down into the depths of my throat, my own body attacking my taste buds.
Taking the same finger coated in spit I press it to my heat, allowing it to penetrate me, my back arching against the seat at his touch, "Then I want you," I moan.
Groaning, "Are you sure?" Kyle poses, making me feel as if I lose my mind right there and yet I don't pull away from it, instead I breathe through the sensation.
"Promise?"
I nod, "Yes, I want you Kyle, and I can't wait much longer.

The need is carnal, and despite my determination to stay in control, I falter
Desperation culminates.
 My desire to stay in control falters, and I find myself intwined in him.
It's too much, a full-blown make-out session ensues, steaming windows, adding to the ambiance.
With shaky breath, he checks in eagerly.
 "Everything but?"
Nodding, I find myself unsure if it's a question or a statement.
 I don't have time to ask before he pushes me onto my back, hair sprawled gloriously around my head like a halo as I take a less than innocent position.

Trembling bodies gently lay along the three-seater, arms pinned above my head with one hand.
What was it about female submission that helps men feel more masculine?
The power.
The control.
Knowing there is no way out.
That we live and breathe to serve.

At this moment, that's exactly my purpose, but Kyle also serves, dead set on satisfying me.

Twisting, I move to take the dominant position.
I glance down and see Kyle, only Kyle.
Relieved that my mind hasn't wandered yet, I kiss him.
A sly smirk climbs easily onto my lips as I watch his grin disappear.

We play each other for a long while, twisting and maneuvering, battling for power.
Ultimately, he'll win, there's no doubt in my mind, but being allotted some power, and a voice is freeing.

The game is almost painful as blood continues to course down, pooling like molten lava, sharply gathering.
Nuzzling his face against the shell of my ear, he inhales deeply before licking his lips.
Embarrassment with his enthrallment clouds my mind.
It's almost unbelievable.
He wants me.
Me!
"You smell amazing and it's making it so hard to be a gentleman," he protests.
"Then don't be."
A groan falls from him, hands traveling between us.
Slowly, he circles me, fireworks bursting throughout my vision, so bright that I damn near go blind.
"I don't want to be…but you deserve better."

Silence befalls us.
I have no rebuttal, no words, and even if I did, he would steal them from me.

Kyles mouth has left mine, trailing kisses down my abdomen before settling below.
Straining my neck, I catch a glimmer of hope.
My skirt inched up by Kyles coy nudges.
.

My body is about ready to tear out of its cage, my inner animal
hollering to be released from captivity.
I shouldn't be here, not with Kyle, my rational mind combats.
But it's also what I want.
Normalcy.
To be loved the way I deserve.
It's not in my best interest, but my body incapacitates my
brain and I fall in dangerous waters.

Curiously, and with the utmost caution, he gauges my
reaction as he begins to explore me.
With rapt attention, I focus on his touch.
The way he breathes.
The way his fingers feel against my flesh.
The intense need to be held by him.
I don't think I have ever wanted anything more than I want
him.
It's not necessarily about lust, or even my hormonal drive.
No.
Its more than that.
I want to be more than a body.
Just this once.

Letting go, I allow him to work with my body, finding the
spots that feel best.
Kyle delves deep, kissing, stroking, and teasing me.
When I'm wild with desire, my head shakes wildly, he takes
full advantage and moves me to my end.

When I come down, I caress his head, smiling with relief, my
breasts heaving with a furious intensity.
Crawling up, he presses his lips to mine.
My taste fills me, invading all sensibility.
This doesn't end here.
This doesn't end well.

Pulsing his frame between my legs, I butterfly them out,
making room.

He's eager, and I feel the need to make him feel as good as he
made me feel.
"Your turn," my tongue commands, pushing him flat against
the hard seat.
My lips work gently but steadily south, nipping along the
way.
I set him free, his inhibitions dissipating as quickly as his
bottoms.

"Jesus, Laurel-"he begins, stopping just short of expression.
"Two can play your game."
Inhaling deeply, I shut my eyes and feel him out.
The sensation of his pleasure fans the heat of my fire.
Kindling.
A spark.
The fire grows ferociously with unbridled desire.
But I refuse to slow down, the tight grip of his hand mussing
up my hair.
Power fills me.
His face fades away, Kyle replaces it.

I am in control. I decide how I make him feel.
I decide what happens to me and my body.
Me.
I have a voice, at least in the confines of this truck.
The moment may be finite, but it will live forever in my mind,
and for that I am grateful.

"Laurel," he begins to protest.
His need for me is so absolute, and I am relentless in my quest
to take full advantage of our moment.
"Laurel... I..."
He tries gently to pull my hair up, his hands incoherently
grasping as he is deafened by a wave of satisfaction.
Those baby blues widen in a mixture of pride, lust, and
horror.
"You didn't have to do that," he pants, "I- I mean, you didn't
owe me that."
I roll my eyes, "Maybe I wanted to," I wink.

"I don't think I'm going to sleep tonight," Kyle rasps down at me, taking my chin between his fingers.
"Well, I'm going to sleep like a baby thanks to you," I wink shyly.
"So coy, I love it."

I brush my hair back from its distressed state and scan my face in his mirror.
"Just in time for curfew, too," I comment, looking at the green light.
"Damn, we are good! But seriously, tomorrow. I'm going to bring you flowers because you deserve to smile and what woman can frown with a bouquet in her hands?"
Pulling him tight against me I hugged him, and he obliged, holding me tight for a long while, "I wish we had time to just lay down here for a bit."
"I know, but I should go."
Prying the door open takes up all my strength, and I have to remind myself that tomorrow is not far off.
"Tomorrow night," he calls out as I stalk off, trying to get the satisfied smile off my face.
I wouldn't miss it for the world.

As I pace away, I can't help but hope that he is awake.
That he dares to kiss me goodnight tonight.
To plunge his tongue into the mouth that Kyle had just inhabited.
I hope he can taste him.
Swallow down my victory.
What I know for a fact is that daddy will be getting a goodnight kiss from his little girl, even if it's just on the cheek.

Mikey

If Laurel wants me to protect her, then I will.
I don't care what it takes.
I walk in hot. Door swinging behind me.
I feel motivated, and slightly drunk still.

For a while I sat waiting for the booze to flood my system, but not fully dissipate, lest it weakens my resolve.
I will be the hero of this story.

"Dad," I call out, glancing at Rachel who is busy washing a sink of dishes, clunky trashcan headphones burrowed beneath red locks.
She sways, deaf to the sound of my entry.
I have a bone to pick, the one that had been in my sister, and no one was going to stop me.
No more.

...

I find him in his bedroom, stripped down to his briefs, a toothbrush in his mouth, yet I'm the one foaming at the lips.
"Son," he comments, nodding my way, a large bruise circling his right eye.
Pride swells at the memory of my fist meeting his face.
Deep breath.
My finger dances along the waistband of my bands, the clip digging into my hip.
"Dad."
Cautious.
"What do you need?"
What do I need?
Let me tell you, dad.
Love. Acceptance. A normal fucking father.
Why can't he just give me that?

Instead I settle for her, my drunkenness fading to a buzz, one that gives me enough courage.
"I need you to leave Laurel alone."
It's a plea.
One last chance.
Taken by surprise, he stops brushing his teeth, white dripping at the crease, before he sets the brush down on his dresser.
"What are you saying?"

"You know exactly what I'm saying," my courage flaring outside of myself.
A hiss emits from his clenched jaw, "Keep your voice down son."

…

What ensues is shockingly vivid.
His hand pushes me, my back bumping the wall with a thud.

Perfect.
Rile him up. Get him to smack you.
A fight gone wrong.
Motive for whatever might come.

I lose all sense of time.
My hand pushed against him.
I fall over him, straddling him, fists slamming into his chest, rapidly and heavily like an angered gorilla fending its turf.
My claim.
He tries to push me off, hands reaching up, my own hands pulsing to his neck, fingers aching as I squeeze.
The man I call dad's eyes begin to bulge; his nails dig into my hand.
Too much.
Shit!
Get him. Get him now.

Scrambling, he coughs, limping away as if he may pass out at any moment.
I breathe in deep, my heart palpitating, breathless from the rage I had just exerted.
Stumbling to my own feet I charge at him as he scrambles against the wall.
This time I'm ready, shoving him against the wall, frames crashing all around splintering glass falling around us.
Pushing me away, we crash to the ground and I'm left perplexed as to how Rachel has not heard this and run up screaming at us.

Rolling on top of him with a crunch I feel glass catch my knee as I straddle him once more.
The sting is almost unbearable as glass grinds against my skin with a crunch.
He screams like a dying animal.
Exactly what he was about to be.
Eyes roll back in his head as my fist contacts his nose. Once, twice, a crunch, as a vicious spurt of hot blood streams down, saturating his chest hairs as it canvases the landscape of tight coils.
Clawing up this time, he tries to catch my face.

I am going to end this.
Right here. Right now.
Once and for all.

The animal takes over. More beast than man. Iron caking my fingers.
He goes limp, momentarily.
Not long enough.

Violent shaking along my hands, my fingers reaching into the leather strap, peeling danger from its sheath.
I don't hesitate.
Not for a moment, and just like that, I make a decision that I will never be able to take back; I slam the knife down, catching him beneath his armpit a sharp sound emitting as the blade pierces the skin tearing away at life.
I look at the sharp shine, a droplet pebbling and falling onto his chest followed by my knife.
It squelches a wet pop as I drive it between the bones of his chest.
A gasp from below, his eyes shooting wide open as his body rebooted its nerve endings.

Panic. Acceptance. Fear.
Yes, fear, glossing his eyes over.
Satisfaction.
He lays still now groaning madly, trying to thrash at me.

Weakened by the wounds I had inflicted, I easily pin his arm
about his head, staring deeply into the eyes of a fading life.
I would have to wait him out I decide as my strength leaves
me, the knife burrowed in his chest, blood escaping around its
phallic handle.
Can't feel my hands but I know that they are wet with his
blood.
My hearing doesn't slow, not even for a moment, and I know
exactly what's happening.
Screaming in my head.
Blisteringly loud.

Tangible groans fall from his mouth, his body spasming
beneath me, those raspy groans so similar to his love making
sputter.
His face is so close I can almost taste him.
The pain. The euphoria.
"What did you do?"
He cries it out now and I glance down in awe of my work.
It feels so right.
"Son…" he trails off.
Stumbling down the stairs, I leave him in the hall,
bleeding and incapacitated from the pain.
Now it's time to let my prey weaken and bleed out.
A quick death would be too easy for him, and hell if he does
not die it might not get locked up for the rest of my life.
What happens will happen, but I need some time.
At least enough time to show Laurel.
Now it was time for damage control.
A desperate bid for more time.

Rachel is facing the sink, headphones glued to her ears as she
moves her hips against the suds that tower over the tub's
boundaries.
Ava upset in her playpen, a rattle in her fists.
I could leave now, but I know it's not an option, not when I
need time.
Time to let him fade.
She won't be still long enough for that to happen.

Rachel turns, the creaking of the floorboard traveling to her spot.
Eyes widen as she sees the red on my hands.
Stunned.
Frozen, but only for a moment.
Grabbing my hands, she pulls them to her, examining me for the source of the bleeding.
I am not ready to go.
Not yet.
Her eyes widened in horror at the realization that this wasn't my blood.
Bits of jade expand to juicy emeralds.
I know I have to act fast.

Laurel

Air nips at me from all angles as I quicken my pace, blood pumping.
I keep trying to force the smile from my face, but it refuses to settle.
There's joy here that I hope he can see.
Joy, another man brought me.

Mikey

Rick Astley streams from her discarded headphones, the fluff saturated now as they absorb the water from the counters.
Never gonna give you up.
Never gonna let you down.
I will never give her up.
But I had let her down. Miserably.
Not anymore.
She will be free soon, and so proud of me, beaming down.
I will be free even if they toss me into a rusty prison.
Now she will know.
She will really know how much I love her.
A taste of true freedom.
On to Rachel. She is guilty too.

But I don't want to hurt her. I just need her out of the way for a moment so I can finish up.
I wish she could see what that man does.
Taking my sister and playing with her before putting her back in the tallest shelf.
Dusting her off when he sees fit.
Looking down at my fingers throws me into a momentary panic.
What did you do? Oh my God.
Is that his? Oh my God!

Swallowing hard, I allow my heart to return to its normal pattern of beating.
On the surface, I am the picture of calamity, a roaring fire of panic within.
A panic that understands the gravity of my actions.
Rachel trembles with fear latching onto my arm, screams that remind me of the buck dad had injured last summer.
A true attack on my ear drum.
The sound of unfiltered fear.
Fear that leaves her shaking.
It only takes a curl of my hands in her hair and a good smack against the countertop, and she is out.
I let go. Scan my arms.
It stings, little bits of white lined with specks of blood peek through.
Ava is screaming now in her playpen, red faced and angered by the lack of attention.
"It's ok, Ava," I soothe her.
"I'm ok too, you know, "I tell her, picking her up, pressing her to my chest, hyperventilating, my ribs rattling.
Knees threatening to cave in.
I find it wise to set her back down, instantly picking up her angry screaming where she had left them.

My eyes scan over the kitchen, blood reeking into the air, a drop rolling down my arm now.
Red streaks dribbling onto the floors from the sink, the water still hissing out of its faucet.

I walk over, shut it off, completely unwilling to get too close to Rachel who is lying still on the floor, her chest rising and falling with life.
I begin to make my way out in desperate need of fresh air that does not stink of life, hanging in the balance, desperation, and blood.
Blood.
So much less blood than I had expected.
With legs as shaky as a fawn, I stumble out.

…

The glow of Halloween lights and Jack-o'-lanterns streak through the trees and down the sparse driveway giving me hope that something warm will be waiting for me inside.
The small porch up front is lined with flashing glowing bulbs, blinking to announce our excitement for the upcoming holiday, it's of fake cobwebs sticking to the string, bits of crunchy leaves weaving and tangling their way into the fluffy synthetic clouds.
Rachel had been dead set on making Halloween great this year, her desperate grasp for her Norman Rockwell fantasy.
Except here there are no grandmas in little white aprons doting over an obscenely large turkey, and no kids sneaking into ponds for summer dips, and there is certainly no child sitting at a cafe with the local cop, a belly full of ice cream and butterflies.
There was a family that was slowly falling apart and a mother who wanted nothing more than a picture of perfection and she was going to get it no matter what.

Determined to bring the holiday spirit around she cleaned and climbed ladders, pinned lights to deck posts, and carved pumpkins.
Even got Ava a little elephant costume, the trunk long enough to brush her eyes.
Picking up the pace to escape the nip in the air, it turns to a jog, my purse smacking me square in the hip.
It would probably leave a bruise.

One Kyle can kiss away tomorrow.

The thought sends jolts between my thighs and a litany of
wild butterflies swirling in my belly, the blush warm enough
to keep the chill at arm's length.
The flush that horizons my cheeks and nose deepens as my
brain replays what we had just done.
It mushrooms, as I recall our plans.
Eight.
Ava asleep.
Rachel and Dad long gone to the lake for the night, preferably
and probably plastered.
My room.
Dresser to block the door.
Movie playing on my screen.
Popcorn.
A couple of condoms that we probably won't use tucked in the
bible that sits in my desk drawer, dad would never open that
book.

No bra. Sodas.
Bubbly. No panties.
Just skin on skin.
My chest would flush.
Warm body completely accepting of him, nothing between us.
When all is said and done, we would hold each other.
Lips reluctant to separate.

I reach the opening past the large pines, the lights flickering,
the porch swings steadily in the silence of the night.
Everything is so still.
Even Mikey, who is unexplainably sitting by the front door,
swaying ever so slightly as he pushes something to his lips.
Chewing.
"Mikey, what are you doing out here?"
He doesn't reply.
Doesn't even acknowledge me.

Instead, I watched him reach into the black bowl of candy that Rachel had prepared for the few trick-or-treaters, who were willing to drift this far away from the center of town where all the houses sat close together.

He grips a chocolate bar, a shiny golden wrapper falling to the ground next to him in an array of litter.

Blue peanut candies.

Shiny lollipop wrappers.

Chocolate balls with twisted ends.

Foils that once contained sugar balls.

"What are you up to?"

Smiling up at me with a mouth stuffed full of sugar, I can tell something isn't right.

"Just eating some candy. "

Eyes roll, "I see that. It's freezing out here, can we finish this up inside?"

His head shakes no, not hesitating for a moment, "No… not yet."

Behind the door, I can hear Ava screaming.

"What's up with Ava?"

He doesn't answer my question instead he lifts apologetic eyes and aims them right into my own, "I did something. Please don't be mad."

"Mikey, what are you talking about?"

He pats the spot on the wooden plank next to him, "Will you please just sit with me?"

I want to, but something in his mannerisms is concerning, "Mikey can you just tell me what's going on?"

"You know I love you right?"

Nonchalant. Random

Concern fills me, "I love you too, Mikey… let's go in."

I glance down, the bottom of his shirt is wet, stinks of soap and something I can't pinpoint.

Oddly familiar.

"What happened to your arm!"

I cry out now, grabbing his wrist, long, superficial marks running in every direction, his hand shakes uncontrollably now, a tear falls down his cheek.

Animalistic marks.
Painful. Reddening around the edges.
"I did something bad, and I can't take it back… I'm sorry,
Laurel, I'm… I'm so sorry."
Tears dry in an instant.
His face is expressionless. Voice flat. Unaffected.
A joke? He was pulling my leg.

Sitting next to him I pull him to me in a tight embrace, "Haha,
very funny."
Pulling away I poke at his ribs, trying to force a smile.
No response, his expression as flat as a plain.
"I love you, Laurel…I'm not joking."
Gripping my arm he mutters it once again followed by a plea,
"Don't be mad, ok?"
My mouth parts, head bobs, "I'm not mad."
"You will be."
I stroke his cheek, "I'm going to go get Ava, and we can talk
about whatever is going on when I get back."

Stepping inside the heat floods me, my grateful body softens
at the gentle touch of warmth.
My nostrils flare as an unpleasant stream of stink wafts into
my nose.
Rancid.
A sour smell fills the air.
Spoiled milk and soapy water.
Rusty, a metallic stink that makes my stomach churn
painfully.
My ears perk at Ava's pleas for attention, my maternal instinct
on overdrive as a static jolt runs down my spine, hair standing
on edge along my skin.
Something isn't right.
I am filled with fear, my legs begging to contract and flee from
this place.

Reaching into the playpen and scoop her up in one swift
motion right.

Her mouth is wide open in a scream, eyes scrunched up, the trail of old tears stream down to a chin that trembles in punishment.

"It's ok, Ava," I worked hard to comfort her, pulling the Velcro of her bib free and tucking it into my front pocket.

I sniff the air, pulling Ava's bottom to my nose, and taking a whiff.

"Is your diaper dirty?"

Her cries are slow now.

"Where is mamma?"

I tickle her belly, an overwhelming sense of dread in the pit of my guts.

Rachel would never leave Ava alone.

Ava is not dirty, my eyes scan the room, taking in dish soap and dinner.

Blood, that's the smell, hot coppery blood.

Heavy.

I glance over to the kitchen, eyes scanning over something, a heavy form slummed on the floor.

Rachel.

My body jolts as if a shock passes through me hard, almost collapsing flat on my back with Ava soothing herself against my shoulder, the couch keeping my feet on the ground as I press myself against it.

Oh my God! Rachel. Oh my God.

I begin to pray under my breath, a babble of nonsensical words and heavy breathing, "Oh… oh my God… God help me," I pant under my breath.

Rachel is slumped along the bottom cabinet, chest barely rising, legs splayed open provocatively and she groans Ava's name and my own.

I scream a silent scream that won't leave my tongue, my chest rising and falling in a frantic pattern.

What did he do?

Throbbing in my ears.

Instinct telling me to run. Rationality telling me to stay put.

I want to vomit, my stomach begins to clench heat flaring in my mouth, drool running from the corners.

Ava protests as I squeeze her tight against me, as the incoherent prayers begin to dissipate.
I need to act but I can't contract anything but my lips, "It's me, Rachel, everything is going to be ok."
Frozen like a half-sculpted statue, material not yet dry, heavy legs being sucked into the planks of the floor by some invisible vortex.

I snap out of it, a thud upstairs, followed by some shuffling snaps me back to reality.
Moving for the cordless phone I clench it tight, setting Ava down, the flat buzz sitting on the line, my finger flicking over the nine.
Full of fear. At what I might see I take the steps slowly, I push the one, Ava screaming beneath me.
The hall is brightly lit, my mind illuminated to the carnage I had suspected I would find.

A violent streak of red sits smeared across the off-white wall, falling downwards before ending abruptly.
Dad lays just feet away, groaning and shaking, blood puddling beneath him, seeping into the patterned runner rug Rachel had added to brighten up the house.
It was now tarnished, saturated with blood, and the strong scent of urine that had certainly bolted from his bladder as the terror surged into his animalistic cerebral cortex, his limbic system fried.
Lying on his side he desperately nuzzles the dusty baseboard, his fingers curled around the hilt of a blade, plunged deep into his chest.
He clings on to it desperately, aching for help, desperate to keep the blade in place.
Mikey's folding knife.
The one grandma had gifted him on our birthday for he and my father's summer hunting trip they hadn't gone on.

The full blade is not buried in him, but he has been hit deep, just not deep enough for a quick death.

A deep low groaning falls from his mouth like the buzzing of a streetlight.
Warmth inexplicably fills me.
I feel powerful seeing him curled up like a wounded child.
Panic leaves me.
This feels different from seeing Rachel.

The line trills in my hand after my finger lifts from the one, a concerned woman answers.
I relay the address, dad groans louder now as I cup the bottom to not allow her to hear his increasingly erratic struggle.
"I think my brother hurt my dad… he's been stabbed and my stepmom-" I stop my breath catching in my throat, hitching.
"It's ok."
"Sh…she's passed out downstairs, but I think she is ok."
A surprised voice, the clicking of keys, "You said someone's been stabbed? I need their location in the house."
"Upstairs hallway," I reply, a cool numbness washing through my buzzing brain, before shakily relaying, trying not to cry, that we need help and fast.
"How many victims are there?"
"T- two. My dad and my stepmom."

The tears start to fall but I'm not sure if they're tears of fear or tears of relief.
"We have help on the way, Laurel. Just stay put and answer a few questions for me.
"How old are you, Laurel?"
"Sixteen."
"How old are the victims?"
"I uh- I think forty-one and I- I think my stepmom is in her thirties, but I'm not sure."
"Is there anyone else in the house?"
I tell her that Mikey and Ava are also here.
"It's going to be ok," she tries to assure me but all I can do is bob my head, beaming at his pathetic display.

Writhing almost silently, desperation curves its sharp nails around him.

He couldn't even groan loud enough to get help.
Helpless.
My father was in a hopeless state, a place I had always wanted
to see him in.

Pressing my finger over the phone I walk to him, scared to get
too close, delighted to feel myself find the courage to
approach.
He whispers my name, "Laurel," seeing me as his salvation
when I haven't decided if I would be that for him.
I am teetering on the edge of sin and relief, finding pleasure in
his helpless situation, and a deep sadness for his suffering.
Pity.
I pity the man, the one that had made me call him lover.
Not anymore.
I still love him despite everything, and I whisper as much, my
hand clenched over the mouthpiece of the phone.
"Can you tell me if he is still breathing?"
I don't answer.
Temptation.
My desire to end him now takes a grip.
The pot of gold at the end of a perpetually dark rainbow.
The light at the end of a deep dark tunnel.
An opened cage after years of captivity.
My escape.

"Laurel," he groans louder now.
"Ma'am, is he still breathing, and if he isn't, are you able to
perform CPR?"
"I… I- think he is dead," my lips relay, my wicked tongue
thick with lies.
She is persistent, "Are you able to approach the victims and
check for a pulse?"
I tell her I can, knowing full well that they both held on to life.
"If there are any foreign objects in either victim, you cannot
remove them. Just leave them intact."
I hear her fingers clicking away on the other end, tapping on a
keyboard spreading the information.

Staring at the hilt of the knife shaking with each breath he takes I find my heart hardening; blood begins to dry on the handle.
Unwanted penetration. Deep.
Twisting inside of him. Refusing to leave.
Knowing that the emptiness would hurt much more, than the intrusion he holds on tight, the real bleeding happens after the fact.
Ironic.

 "There is nothing in him…not that I can see, but it looks like he was stabbed," I lied about his state, "I think he's dead."
Switching direction, I get to the other end of the hall and set the phone on the top step telling her that I am going to check for a pulse and that I would have to set down the phone.
"Do you know where the weapon is?"
"No, but I think… I think my brother did this."
"Where is he, Laurel?"
With my hand tight around the phone I informed her that Mikey was unarmed on the porch, then I set the phone down.
Out of earshot, I kneel next to Daddy dearest.
Blood oozing from his mouth, from internal hemorrhaging.
Pity.
His bare chest sports a stab mark, blood almost as dark as night seeps, his hands slashed deeply, bits of thin skin ribboning around the base of his fingers.
He had struggled.
Put up a fight.
I admire his resilience, the ability to fight for his life, something he had never instilled in me.
It leaves me green with jealousy.

"Laurel," he tries to pacify me, his voice a mere whisper.
I think he knows exactly what I'm feeling right now.
Finally.
"I called for help dad."
Hope flickers across his face a small streak of blood drying at the corner of his dehydrated lips, "Laurel- pl…please."

"They won't make it in time," I interrupt his groaning abruptly with the need to let him know what is going to happen.
"Cold," he chatters as if to milk some sympathy.
"That's because you're dying, dad."
Ice flows through my veins, my words exiting foggy and cool.
A calm I have never felt before instructs my every word.
I want to make his last moments as miserable as possible.
"What…doing?"
"Choosing myself for once," I tell him coldly, my heart thrashing within.
There is no reality where he makes it out alive and doesn't continue to kill me slowly.
His eyes shoot down at my hands, as I reach into my pocket for Ava's bib.
Legs kicking miserably beneath me as I straddle him, something I had done many times before, and this is the first time he has ever objected, "You used to love this dad."
I don't recognize my voice as anything less than evil, my hands mimicking as I feel for the blade, wrapping the bib around the sleek handle.
With our eyes locked I tinker with the butt of the stuck blade and his emotions.
"Laurel."
Ignoring him, I curl my hand around the handle, just the way he liked to be gripped and slowly tighten.
Eagerly, I smooth my hand down its shaft once before lifting the knife from his body, inch by painful inch, his hand shooting up wrapping around mine in an effort to keep the blade in and when that slips, silver meeting my eyes he tries to grip onto the blade instead.
Desperation at the certain doom, the sharp edge slicing into the inner side of his fingers, mouth wide with pain.
"No."
Eyes bugging, the whiskey on his breath wafts over me pleasurably, it would aid in a precipitous bleed.

I easily overpower him in his weakened state and with one hard pull I yank the remaining length of metal free, blood spurting, flowing to caress my bare knees, and puddle around him.

"It will get better. I promise," I plainly recite the words he had used on me, in a whisper.

His eyes flicker in horror one last time before rolling back with a gurgle.

"I love you," I kiss the proof along his face, my saliva melding with his tears.

It's not a lie. A tear falls with that realization.

The absence of the knife is the true catalyst to my freedom.

He had confused his damnation for his salvation.

Mikey

It didn't feel good, well not as good as I had thought. It felt necessary, like a chore.

I had imagined a tsunami of relief would fill me when I confronted him.

The power of an earthquake shattering my hatred. The flooding of control.

But I was absent of any such feelings.

The ones I had been looking for have fled and left me yearning.

Killing him had just been killing a part of myself.

The bits that I hated.

There is no taking it back. No recovery.

 A shaking Laurel comes out with Ava, she sits next to me, her hand on mine.

It's wet, greedy and sanguine.

She knows what I did, yet she doesn't say anything.

Ava sniffles on her chest, pulled into Laurel's coat, snot lolling between her nose and Laurel.

She knows just what to do and wraps her hands around the back of my head, her featherlike fingers feeling maternal against me, Ava teetering between us and pulls my face to hers, kissing my forehead, holding me.

Embracing me with a fire I have never felt, her hands tangling in my hair, each stroke of her mouth against my cheeks and my face is filled with gratitude, wet with salinity.
"I'm scared," she sadly admits, breaking the seal before grazing my cheek gently as if I may shatter, or perhaps I had already shattered, and she feared injury on any of my jagged edges.

A touch like Novocain filling me with relief before she pulls Ava free, setting her next to us.
Tears fall between us, our bodies cocooning into a hug to morph into one form.
She won't thank me, but I know that her embrace is exactly that.
A token of her gratitude. Affection for her hero.
Iron and salt from our tears that swirl and tangle with such intensity along each other's cheeks as we cry.
 Hands fusing and playing.
I feel love in abundance. A love I can never feel again. Love I will never feel again.
She is the pinnacle of perfection and I no longer ponder his obsession with her.
Perfection.
A specimen of beauty I could keep in a glass case; caging her but never losing sight of such beautiful things and truly it is the beautiful things in life that still bring about a tingle.
The beauty of mornings is revealed.
The way embers twinkle like stars in the pit.
The stars themselves sparkled with mystery.
The twinkle in her eyes as she pulls away, and we sit breathing rapidly, panting, our eyes cemented to one another's.

I want her in a way I can't have her, in my debt, and always in my pocket, and by my side.
Possession.
I need my body to greet hers from the warmth of her interior, the vast depths of her heart belong to me. It always had, as we formed together, side by side.

She is everything, the beating of my heart, the air on my lungs, the mouthpiece through which I speak.
Without her I am nothing, and she is void without me.

Swiftly, I pet her and pull her close breathing with feverous desperation to touch her one last time.
I can't stop and she doesn't stop me.
I need her. The contrast is harsh; she doesn't need me. Not anymore.
The thought fills me with violent shame.
I pull away as her breath takes mine once more, taking me closer to death, plummeting me straight to hell.

"Laurel, it's over now."
Her smile almost killed me then as she whispered to me how wrong I was, "This is just the beginning."
Silence swirls violently in the eye of the storm.
A dead giveaway to the incoming rolling chaos.
The storm had just begun.
I released her.
Lightning was approaching now in streams of red, white, and blue.
"This is just the start Mikey."
Our foreheads press, salinity is shared.

Laurel

I can't explain it.
Why I held him so?
The stupid feminine part of my brain giving him what he's always hungered for, telling me that he deserves every swipe of my lips against his cheeks.
I am nothing less than passion and nothing more than love.
My survival instinct kicks into harbor and adore my protector and in the muddied lukewarm place between hatred and love for my brother.
 I freely give my heart to him.
Kissing him, holding him to me, his head falling between my breasts, showing him proof of the life he has saved.

My still beating heart deceives me and will until I draw my final breath.

Forgive me

About the Author

French born and a first-generation immigrant to the USA, M.Day.Kendall has always found solace in books. In her going years she began writing based on the constant flood of daydreams and worlds she built in her mind. She enjoys her coffee dark and steamy, and her story line even darker. In her free time she and her spouse and three children go to the movies, enjoy reading, hiking and swimming.

Follow on Social Media.

Email: author.day.kendall@gmail.com

Instagram: @authorm.day.kendall

TikTok: @authorm.day.kend

Facebook: @ Author M.Day.Kendall Book Page

Inspiration Board: https://pin.it/2eOsO8L